POWER AND
THE PURSUIT OF
PEACE

POWER AND THE PURSUIT OF PEACE

THEORY AND PRACTICE IN THE HISTORY OF RELATIONS BETWEEN STATES

BY

F. H. HINSLEY

CAMBRIDGE UNIVERSITY PRESS

CAMBRIDGE

LONDON   NEW YORK   NEW ROCHELLE
MELBOURNE   SYDNEY

PUBLISHED BY THE PRESS SYNDICATE OF THE UNIVERSITY OF CAMBRIDGE
The Pitt Building, Trumpington Street, Cambridge, United Kingdom

CAMBRIDGE UNIVERSITY PRESS
The Edinburgh Building, Cambridge CB2 2RU, UK
40 West 20th Street, New York NY 10011- 4211, USA
477 Williamstown Road, Port Melbourne, VIC 3207, Australia
Ruiz de Alarcón 13, 28014 Madrid, Spain
Dock House, The Waterfront, Cape Town 8001, South Africa

http://www.cambridge.org

© Cambridge University Press 1963

First published 1963
Reprinted 1967
First paperback edition 1967
Reprinted 1978, 1980

A catalogue record for this book is available from the British Library

ISBN 0 521 05274 2 hardback
ISBN 0 521 09448 8 paperback

Transferred to digital printing 2004

CONIUGI
DILECTISSIMAE

'*Monboddo*. The history of manners is the most valuable. I never set a high value on any other history.
Johnson. Nor I, and therefore I esteem biography, as
giving us what comes near to ourselves, what we can
turn to use. *Boswell*. But in the course of general
history, we find manners. In wars we see the dispositions of people, their degrees of humanity and
other particulars. *Johnson*. Yes, but then you must
take all the facts to get this, and it is but a little you
get. *Monboddo*. And it is that little which makes
history·valuable.'

JAMES BOSWELL, *Journal of a Tour to the Hebrides,*
entry for 21 August 1773

CONTENTS

INTRODUCTION

WE cannot say who first devised a plan for perpetual peace: the aim cannot be much less old than the practice of war. The interest men have shown in this aim—the concern they have felt at the absence of peace or for the maintenance of peace—has fluctuated throughout history. It has been most intense during and immediately after periods of especially frequent, especially extensive or especially destructive war. Such periods have occurred at all times, in the fifth century B.C. no less than during the past fifty years. Perhaps the first step to sanity in facing this problem is the realisation that it is not a new one. Even so, if only because war has become increasingly more extensive and destructive—though not more frequent—since the sixteenth century, the interest in peace, while continuing to be more than usually acute from time to time, has become more intense, more widespread and more continuous throughout modern times.

In the history of modern Europe it was only rarely before the eighteenth century that proposals for the solution of international problems were devoted primarily to the preservation of peace. Interest in peace for its own sake was more extensive and unbroken during the nineteenth century, a period of comparative peace, than in the eighteenth century with all its wars. It was in the last years of the nineteenth century that for the first time in the history of the present European-based world civilisation—if not in all history—peace proposals were propagated for fear of the danger of war rather than in consequence of its outbreak. Warfare has become even more extensive and destructive since then, and at an even more rapid rate. It is unlikely that the problem will ever again recede from the fore-front of people's minds even if further large-scale war is avoided. So great, indeed, is the potential destructiveness of war in the future that only if war between the major States is not avoided will the need to avoid it cease to be the paramount problem in politics.

During modern history men have sought to solve the problem by various routes. Some have hoped that by the improvement of human nature not only the resort to armed conflict but even the sources of conflict itself might be eliminated. More frequently the inevitability of human rivalry has been accepted and men have hoped to limit it, to stop it short of armed conflict, by different devices—by international organisation, by political domination, by the development of international law, by the resources of international politics and diplomacy. Each of these different methods has a history as old, or almost as old, as the search for peace itself.

Pacifism, one expression of the hope for man's moral regeneration, was recommended by Euripides and Aristophanes to the ancient Greeks and was embraced by the early Christians. The medieval Church preferred moral rearmament, another expression of the same hope. These programmes still have their advocates. When Sully outlined a plan for international organisation in the seventeenth century his models were the amphictyonic leagues of the Greek city states. Rousseau had these leagues as well as Sully in mind when, one hundred and twenty-five years later, he wrote that 'this method may seem new (and as a matter of fact it has really been understood by the moderns only) yet the ancients were not unacquainted with it'. The men who conceived of the League of Nations looked back to Sully and Rousseau, not to speak of even earlier writers. Dante, Leibniz and Napoleon, bent on the perfection of international organisation by another route, by means of political primacy, looked back to the Empires of Charlemagne and ancient Rome; and if men have since then ceased to be inspired by these models it is less certain that they have ceased to dream of domination. It has been said that so long as the Roman and medieval Empires existed there was no room and no need for international law. Even those who hold this view—on the ground that international law, defined as a law between sovereign and equal states, was necessarily a product of the rise of the modern independent state in the fifteenth and sixteenth centuries—go back to the Romans, not to speak of the Jews and the ancient Greeks, for the roots of modern international law. It is certainly necessary to do this in the case of international politics. As a means of avoiding war no less than as an adjunct to winning it the resources of diplomacy and such notions as the balance of power have been recognized since the earliest times and practised in all ages. In the twentieth century, with the development of historiography, anthropology, sociology and psychology, the hope has been expressed that war—if not rivalry itself—might be eliminated if men, instead of trying to regenerate man, could succeed in understanding him. Except in this single direction it is true of the means as of the end that the modern period has produced no novel contribution of its own.

This is not surprising. Men run to simple and radical solutions for basic problems; there are not many simple solutions to so basic a problem as that of peace and war. Given the problem, every age will independently propound these solutions just as, given time, every civilisation will independently discover the wheel. What is surprising is the absence of development and refinement in the approach to the problem *within* the modern age. That a civilisation which has broken through immense barriers in almost every other direction, and which has surpassed all its predecessors on innumerable fronts, should still hold views and pursue programmes in international politics that it held and pursued when it was young—this is the outstanding failure of recent times.

Only one thing is more surprising: we do not yet recognise this failure. We should think it odd if some of us still thought in the way in which the seventeenth century thought of the rights of women or the powers of kings. We all solemnly place our hopes for peace in internationalist theories that are quite as antiquated. Every scheme for the elimination of war that men have advocated since 1917 has been nothing but a copy or an elaboration of some seventeenth-century programme—as the seventeenth-century programmes were copies of still earlier schemes. What is worse, those programmes are far more widely accepted as wisdom now than they were when they were first propagated. Nor is this the full extent of our stupidity.

The seventeenth-century proposals, like earlier ones, were advocated in a world that was quite different from the modern world. We persist in emphasising their relevance to the modern world because we will not try to see them against their own historical background. To this mistake of omission we add a sin of commission. The seventeenth-century proposals were studied by considerable minds in the eighteenth and nineteenth centuries and were subjected by those minds to devastating criticism. In the twentieth century these reconsiderations, like the original schemes, have been reprinted as tracts for the times—and the criticism has been misinterpreted as advocacy. In the long history of the misapplication of scholarly industry, in all the annals of the innocent distortion of evidence, it would be difficult to find a more glaring example of maltreatment than that which modern commentators have accorded, and still accord, to the views of men like Rousseau, Kant and Bentham—unless it is their misinterpretation of the earlier ideas which Rousseau, Kant and Bentham were criticising.

The first part of what follows, a study of modern peace proposals in their historical setting and on the basis of a close analysis of their texts, is an attempt to focus attention on these shortcomings in the contemporary outlook on the international problem. It leads naturally to the second part. We have not been content with ignoring the historical context of theories propounded long ago and with distorting the views of their critics. We have displayed a marked reluctance to test the theories against the actual development and operation of the system of relations between states in modern times. It is against the dangers and deficiencies of this system that these antiquated theories are still invoked. What those dangers and deficiencies are we take on trust, and whether the theories are even applicable to them is a question we never stop to consider.

This is largely due to the fact that in public issues men rarely pay much attention to historians, as historians have the best of reasons for knowing. It is also to be accounted for by a failure on the part of historians themselves. Diplomatic historians long ago raised their standards of scholarship to a highly professional level. In the past fifty years, especially, they have added enormously to our knowledge; and it is safe to say that further progress was impossible until this knowledge had been made available. To this day, however, their valuable labours have done little more than erect an immense scaffolding of facts; in the work of understanding and explaining the facts we have not made much progress since, 130 years ago, von Ranke wrote his essay on 'The Great Powers'. Theories about the nature and development of international relations have, of course, been propounded, and valuable insights have been brought to bear on the subject. But no more than the average account by the diplomatic historian do these—the economic determinism, for example, which Lenin and his followers have applied to this as to every field, or the work of German historians on the permanent elements in men's attitude to international power—constitute a serious attempt to reconstruct and explain the origin, the nature and the development of that continuous phenomenon of modern times, the modern states' system.

Least of all has this attempt been made for the years since von Ranke was writing; for the best analyses since his day—that of Albert Sorel, for example—have been analyses of the eighteenth century, of the period when international relations were being transformed and the modern system was in its infancy. Von Ranke's Great Powers were those which had arisen in that century and which defeated Napoleon. They were also the Powers, it has often been observed, which fought the First World War—with the marginal addition of Italy after 1861. With the marginal deletion of Austria the same Powers fought the Second World War. But changes and complications of a momentous kind had clearly entered by then. As to when those complications arose and as to what they were there is now much controversy, and much premature speculation. Nor is this to be wondered at. There cannot be any agreement about these things until there is some understanding of, and agreement about, the intervening years. If we need this understanding for its own sake we need it, too, for the light which it alone can throw upon international relations in our own generation. Yet when we turn to these intervening years we find there has been little attempt to answer the obvious questions that demand an answer. Did they, from the point of view of international relations, form a single, consistent whole— or did they witness shifts as decisive as those which the eighteenth century experienced? Whether they formed essentially one phase in modern international relations or more than one, through what stages did international relations then evolve, for what reasons, under what pressures, with what decisive changes or mild alterations of assumption, aim and motive? What was the Congress system, to take concrete examples? How and why did it yield to the Concert of Europe? And what was that? When and why did the Concert die if it had ever existed? In what ways and for what reasons did the frame and texture of international relations differ after 1871 from what they had been earlier or from what they became after the 1890's? If we could answer these questions we could perhaps begin to say something valuable about the international unsettlement which began in the 1890's and continued until the end of the Second World War, making these years to 1945 the longest stretch of unrelieved disorder in modern times; and instead of continuing to rely on theories propounded in even deeper ignorance than our own, in a much earlier age, we should perhaps be able to evolve something valuable as an antidote to international unsettlement.

Until we can answer them we should be wise to recognise that the study of international relations is still in the state in which biology was before Darwin, or economics was before Keynes. It may be doomed to remain so. The subject may resist all attempts to raise it to a comparable level of general theory. On the one hand, however, economics has proved valuable even though economists cannot forecast, and may be unable to cure, the next Great Depression; and, on the other hand, progress is made even in the natural, as opposed to the unnatural or social sciences, by painfully testing assumptions and hypotheses against painfully accumulated facts. Neither the conviction that we might not be wholly successful nor the sheer mass of the facts should deter us any longer from attempting to raise the study of international relations—that field in which assumptions and hypotheses have always abounded but in which the effort to test assumptions has rarely as yet been made—to a more scientific level.

The second part of the book is a first effort in this direction; I wish I could say it were more. After years of intense specialisation in historical studies—in the history of ideas, of science, of historiography; in economic history, diplomatic history, social history, legal history; and now in world history, which is fast becoming another specialism —it sets out to amalgamate some of the findings of all these disciplines around the evolution of the modern system of relations between states. It does so in the hope, if not with the conviction, that if we can advance our knowledge and understanding of this evolution we shall be better placed to deal intelligently with present and future international problems—but without the belief that the study of history is the only available guide.

It ends, as does the first part, at a point in time when men were about to concentrate their efforts to solve these problems, and their hopes for peace, on the suppression or the supersession of the state— and when the increase in the power, the competence and the organisation of the individual state was becoming the outstanding political development in international history. If all the schemes for the elimination of war which men have advocated in the twentieth century have been refurbishings of older theories, the schemes which they have elected to try to put into practice in this same period have been those which sought to subject the state to an international organisation. And this was because the coincidence of the rise of the modern state with an increase in international unsettlement and in the intensity of warfare—themselves the product of the developments that were forging the modern state—produced the assumption that the first of these phenomena was the root cause of the others.

It is easy to understand and sympathise with this assumption—even when we know that men in earlier times were convinced that disorder and war were consequences of the weakness of the state or of the lack of it. It is easy to see why men had such high hopes of the solution it led them to try to adopt. The modern state was also emerging at a time when administrative and technological developments were destroying barriers and shrinking distances, making the world more homogeneous on these levels than it had ever been since the end of the Middle Ages. It is not to be expected that modern men would remember that their own political divisions had themselves arisen out of a medieval structure which had been at least as homogeneous—or suspect that a single administrative and technological framework for political action would not necessarily produce a single political system: a successful international organisation or a world state. Nor, if they had entertained such thoughts, would they necessarily have been wise to be deterred by them. But these considerations do nothing to excuse our subsequent failure to subject the failure of our experiments in international organisation to the test of our own experiences. Rousseau and Kant could judge what the results might be only in the light of their political theory. We have not only misinterpreted their conclusions and failed to use the history of international relations to test our own. We have also ignored or misinterpreted the practical results of international experiments which we have accumulated in the past fifty years.

This fact in its turn is not impossible to understand. A scientist would not try to make a weight move itself uphill; he would find out why it moves down. In politics, in contrast to the sciences, wishes and hopes, which always dictate the work men undertake, similarly dominate the *post-mortems* they conduct upon it. There is also this further difference: in politics *every* experiment has *some* effect even if it is not the result that was hoped for or expected. If only because

7

the League of Nations was once established, its demise was bound to be followed by its reconstitution in some form or another. The inevitability of this reconstitution has led men to treat it as a vindication of the rightness of the principles behind the League—and to overlook the fact that, as a means of solving the international problem by international organisation, the United Nations system is in itself even more peripheral than the League was. The effort to bring about the political integration of western Europe may at last succeed. If it does succeed men will be strengthened in their conviction that political integration is the answer to the international problem despite the fact that the success will have taken place in a changed world situation which renders it irrelevant to a solution of the international problem—and will have taken place because of that changed situation. These considerations help to explain the generally low standard that still obtains in our analyses—in our researches into the failure of the League of Nations and the nature and development of the United Nations. They do nothing to justify it. If anything is more overdue than an effort to rationalise our study of the long history of the states' system it is an improvement, an increased rigour, in our approach to this special aspect of that history in its near-contemporary and contemporary phases.

This is attempted in the third section of the book, where chapters on the League and on the United Nations are placed beside others, which are somewhat provisional, on the character of international relations in the recent past and the probable development of international relations in the near future.

The last is not included to impress scientists: they frequently assert that the test of the scientific approach is the power to make accurate prediction, but they may not be right about this. Would Darwin have accepted it? It owes much to a personal predilection for prophesying; but at least I am not prophesying doom. Nor do I overlook George Eliot's dictum that prophecy is 'the most gratuitous of all forms of error'. If this wise remark has not been heeded, while not being forgotten, it is chiefly for two other reasons.

The most casual study of the record is sufficient to show that it is not by our present forms of international organisation that we shall make progress in the field of international politics—that these forms will only be viable and useful, indeed, if progress is made on other fronts. That is the first reason. The second is as follows. Of those other fronts the one where improvement is most needed, and would be most effectual for progress with the problem as a whole, is that which consists of the outlook of governments and their publics upon the international system of which they form a part. The whole of international history shows that the operation of that system has been at all times what these outlooks have made it, even if it has also always been shaped by forces beyond men's control. It also suggests that those outlooks were saner, those other forces more easily absorbed, when governments had some confidence in their ability to work together and some respect for the need to do so. The final chapter is not, essentially, an attempt to predict the developments of the rest of this century. It is an effort, rather, to introduce a little more light and a touch of sanity into international discussions and policies by using what we might learn from international history to suggest the probable lines of future development and to ridicule the improbable hypotheses which now so generally pass for wisdom.

The present situation might be stated in this way. The Great Powers of the world are today restrained—as they were during the nineteenth century, but far more powerfully—by physical deterrents and by public opinion. They will not remain so for ever. In that earlier period they were restrained as well by the notion, the result of long and bitter experience, that they had a common responsibility for an international order to which they all belonged. In these days such a notion exists once again in the world—we may even say that it has been institutionalised in the United Nations experiment—as a result of the even more shattering experiences of the twentieth century. But on the levels where it is strong—in the public mind and among delegations to the United Nations—it is alloyed with so much ignorance and rubbish that it is deprived of much of its efficiency. There exists a gap, moreover, between these levels and the world of intense suspicion in which the Great Powers conduct their rivalries. The problem is to reduce this ignorance and this suspicion, and thus to destroy this gap, while the physical and the political restraints remain effective, so that when power begins to shift again, and the wind begins to blow, there might be enough vitality in this notion to help us to weather through. There will be nothing else to help us.

If the last chapter is tolerably accurate we shall have the time to do this. The question is whether we shall have the common sense.

PART I

A HISTORY OF INTERNATIONALIST THEORIES

'It will not be an idle nor unprofitable thing, seeing
we are at leisure, to put you in mind of the fountain
and original source whence is derived unto us the
good Pantagruel. For I see that all good historio-
graphers have thus handled their chronicles. . . .'

RABELAIS, Book II, Chapter I

CHAPTER I

TO THE END OF THE SEVENTEENTH CENTURY

PEOPLE often study history less for what they might learn than for what they want to prove. This is one reason why so much is known about internationalist theories since the end of the Middle Ages. Vast efforts have been made, innumerable books have flowed, from the wish to cite Dubois or Dante, Crucé or Sully, as forerunners of the League of Nations or United Europe or the United Nations experiment—and from the even more curious supposition that it was necessary to study these early writings for guidance in creating, improving or saving these twentieth-century projects.

There has in truth been some justification for this faith in the value of past experience. In modern history war-prevention theories have increasingly been based on the argument that it is essential to establish some organisation for regulating the relations of sovereign states; the first plans to use this argument naturally made their appearance in the early days of the modern states' system. For even if it was an immense intellectual achievement to conceive of the wheel, as is often asserted but far from being proved, the same cannot be said of the notion of an organisation between states once separate states existed.* But even if these early plans had had any relevance

* The following comments were made by my son, Hugh Hinsley, aged eleven years, on 10 May 1961, at the time I was writing this chapter. He had asked me to tell him about the Second World War. When I had finished he said, 'Why don't all countries agree to an everlasting-peace-treaty?' I explained that this had been tried but that it was difficult to keep the promise. 'Then why don't they have a governor of the world? If I were governor of the world I'd make them keep their promises.' I explained that world government presented some difficulties, that it was not easy to have a single government for, say, England and Italy. 'I can see Italy and England are too far away [from each other]. But if I were governor of the world I'd live in the middle. I'd live in the middle of the countries like Italy, France, Germany and England—in what's that country in the middle—in Switzerland.' I asked what would happen if, say, Germany still disobeyed his government. 'I'd get all the others to set about her.' I said he would then have a war on his hands. 'Oh, yes, it wouldn't do any good; but wouldn't they all want to keep together if the world was attacked by the Martians?'

I recorded this talk, I believe completely faithfully, at once. I had never previously discussed this kind of subject with him. Probably most modern children think in the same way. Charles Hinsley, aged fourteen, assures me that this is so. Clarissa Hinsley, aged seven, has no opinion on this subject; but I put her in lest she feel put out.

to practicability when they were formulated, which was rarely so, they would still have no relevance to modern situations. They were formulated in a world that was wholly different from the modern world. From the end of the thirteenth century to at least the end of the seventeenth—there was continuity thus far if no farther—from Dante at least to Leibniz, plans which seem at first sight to have been aimed at perpetual peace between states were in reality attempts to solve problems that were more immediate than the problem of war. One of these problems was the political organisation of a Europe which was in the course of a slow but vast transition from medieval notions and institutions to modern ones. The other was the problem of Europe's relations with the outside world: first in the shape of the wish to succeed, where the Middle Ages had failed, in the Crusade; later in the form of the Turkish, and to a smaller extent the Russian, threat to Europe.

Dante in *Monarchia*, written about 1310, was concerned with the first of these problems rather than with peace. He sought to solve it by reviving the political organisation of the past. He wrote of universal peace as 'the best of all things' but was essentially concerned to prop up and expand the medieval Empire. He restated the medieval theory of man's need for two guides, temporal and spiritual; denounced the temporal power of the Papacy, which was to him against the form and essence of the Church; urged that in the temporal sphere, since 'in a multitude of rulers there is evil', the Emperor should be the 'one prince', the Empire 'a unique princedom extending over all persons in time'—which is what he meant by monarchy. He did not base this argument on the evils and injustices of war. It followed from the conviction that since all princes are equal, with no jurisdiction over one another, there must logically be a Sovereign set over all. Peace would follow from order. But peace came after justice. In his attempt to prove that the Roman Empire, his model, had won universal power by lawful means he retained the medieval notion that war is just and must lead to a just decision if it is made with a pure heart and when pacific means have been exhausted.[1]

Even while Dante was hoping to perfect the medieval Empire by restoring that of Rome other men were urging the impracticability of the scheme. Pierre Dubois in 1306 asserted that 'no sane man could really believe that at this period . . . one individual could rule the world. . . . If a tendency in this direction did appear there would be wars and revolutions without end. No man could put them down because of the huge populations involved, the distance and diversity of the countries and the natural propensity of human beings to quarrel.' Twenty years later Marsilius of Padua took the same view in his book *Defensor Pacis*. 'Whether it befits all civilised men in the whole world to have one single government supreme over all, or whether it befits men in the different regions of the world, almost necessarily separated by situation, and especially those who have no common language and who are diverse in manners and customs, to have different supreme governments, deserves a rational enquiry.'[2] Because they were interested less in the Empire than in the new political order that should replace it both men illustrate even more clearly than Dante, though in different ways, the contemporary subservience of the concern for peace to this other problem. In Dubois' case peace also ranked far lower as an aim than did the wish to revitalise the Crusades.

The *Defensor Pacis* reflected the progress of separate sovereign states by being the first treatment of the problem of sovereignty within the state in terms of 'Leviathan' and 'the general will'. Despite its title it did not deal with the international problem, except to state that it was deserving of 'rational enquiry'. It was not even incidentally concerned with the problem of war; Marsilius thought of this as being like the plague, a provision of nature to keep down the population so that the earth may be large enough for it. In his treatise *De Recuperatione Terrae Sanctae* Dubois pleaded for the solemn renunciation of war between Christian and Christian and wrote of peace as 'the object we pursue'. As a means to this end he proposed that the sovereigns of Catholic Europe should form themselves into a Common Council, which would appoint arbitrators to settle all disputes between them, and bind themselves to use sanctions and war against those who refused to comply with the Council's decisions. His primary purposes, however, and the main purposes of his Common Council, were the recovery of the Holy Land and the preservation of the unity of Christendom by other means than the perfection of the medieval Empire.

He retained the Pope, his temporal power destroyed, as the moral leader in the reconquest of the Holy Land: his proposals for the reconquest included European colonisation of the Near East, the conversion of the Mediterranean into a European lake, and war against the Turks. The Pope was also to be the court of moral appeal against the Council's awards within Europe. But despite the emphasis on the world leadership of the Pope, Dubois' Common Council would have been under the political control of the King of France. Not only was the Pope under French influence in those days of the Babylonian captivity. Dubois's scheme for a general pacification of Europe included secret clauses for increasing the power of France at the expense of Germany, Italy, Spain and the Papal lands, as well as of the Eastern Empire. His proposals for the resort to sanctions against disobedient rulers in Europe were intended to further French expansion by justifying the banishment of insubordinate royal houses to the East. In another treatise, *On the Way to Shorten Wars*, he justified French leadership and domination with the argument that Frenchmen were of all people the best fitted to govern others.[3] If he did not want the Empire to be restored and improved he was anxious that it should be replaced by a more effective hegemony. It is perhaps an exaggeration to claim that he was unoriginal and unimportant as a political thinker: his emphasis on the primacy of the French king and his ideas for the expansion of French power came at an early stage in the replacement of the Christian commonwealth by the modern states' system. But there is no justification for regarding him as a pioneer of modern peace theories, rather than of the modern state.

It was not peace but Dubois's objects—or modified versions of them—which continued to inspire most of the solutions for the international problem which men devised in increasing numbers for the next four hundred years. One indication to this effect—one of the reasons, indeed, for this fact—is to be found in the prevailing attitude to war. Pacifists like Erasmus in the early sixteenth century and like the Quakers in the seventeenth century were untypical of the age in abandoning the medieval distinction between just and unjust wars on the ground that all war was incompatible with reason and morality.[4] In so far as this distinction was being generally abandoned—it was still being used by the Jesuits in 1583 to persuade Philip II of the lawfulness and morality of a Spanish conquest of China;[5] it was still the basis of Grotius' work on international law, *De Jure Belli ac Pacis*, which appeared in 1625—it was because the doctrine that war was sometimes justifiable morally was giving way to the doctrine that it was always justifiable politically. How far this was so in practice we know from Europe's history and from such evidence as Rabelais's satires on war and imperialism in the first half of the sixteenth century. Not only Machiavelli's *Prince* but less notorious—because less consistent—writings reveal how much this change was also taking place in men's minds.

Sir Thomas More, a contemporary of Erasmus and Machiavelli, was at one with Erasmus in thinking war 'a thing very beastly', but he agreed with Machiavelli that any measures were justified that would help to win it. When reflecting on French expansion in Europe he ridiculed war in words that might have been used a little later by Rabelais. When it was a question of war for colonisation in the New World, on the other hand, his Utopians 'counte this the most juste cause of war, when anye people holdeth a piece of ground voyde and vacant to no good for profitable use . . . whyche notwithstanding by the lawe of nature ought thereof to be nourished and relieved.' He was careful to explain that they used mercenaries to fight the wars that would demoralise them if they conducted them themselves.[6] Giovanni Botero, a sincere but confused opponent of Machiavelli who was writing in the 1580's, insisted in the old tradition that 'defensive warfare has such absolute justification that offensive warfare is only justified by defence.' He could point out, in the same tradition, that there was no lack of opportunity for extending one's state by just war so long as 'we have the Turks at our gates and on our flank: could there be a juster or more honourable argument for war?' But he could also write that 'military enterprises are the most effective means of keeping a people occupied. . . . A wise prince can placate an enraged people by leading it to war against an external enemy.'[7] What these and other writers reveal is not merely that war was now being taken for granted, as has often been emphasised.[8] It always had been. It is more significant that, in theory as in practice, a continuing tradition of just and unjust war was acquiring, under the influence of the growth of the state, a growing admixture of 'reason of state'.

The strength of this continuing but changing tradition was reflected in most of the so-called peace plans of this period; even they took war for granted. It was not the main reason why peace was not their chief object. This is to be found in the fact that their primary concern remained that of reducing the rapidly developing

states' system to some shape or order; and one of the reasons for this
was that the older programmes for reviving the Crusade were being
replaced by the rapidly growing problem of defence against the
Turk.[9] These developments, the two most considerable forces of the
time, combined to convince the planners, for whom the avoidance of
war was in any case not an issue, that Europe's unity, not peace, was
the urgent need. They could not suppress the suspicion that Europe's
internecine struggles were the cause of the Turkish advance, or the
regret that Christians should fight each other while the infidel pros-
pered. And yet another powerful factor was working in the same
direction. Gierke noted that Machiavelli's typical doctrine came with
a shock to an age that remembered a grander dream of European
empire. The first result of the conflict of the rising sovereign states
with the habits and assumptions left over from the earlier political
and religious system was that some of the sovereign states themselves
took over those habits and assumptions and aspired to re-create that
dream under their own control.* It is in any case the simplest, the
least sophisticated, way of escape from the rivalries of separate states
that one state should dominate over the others.

For these reasons the international plans of the fifteenth, sixteenth
and seventeenth centuries generally sought the unity which Dante
had sought even if, because the rise of independent states was making
that unity increasingly impracticable, they generally sought it not
in Dante's way but by the less traditional imperial means which
Dubois had outlined. It was not for nothing that the pacifists and
Quakers, who almost alone denounced war, were also alone in their
indifference to international organisation as a way to peace, or at
least in regarding it as of minor importance. Erasmus, in so far as
he thought at all of international organisation, questioned—as causti-
cally as he challenged the right of conquest and mocked at plans for
a crusade—the purposes of other men in proposing it. 'Most of us',
he wrote in his treatise on war with Turkey, 'dread the name of
World Empire (*universalis Monarchiae vocabulum*), a title at which
others seem to be aiming. . . . A unified empire would be best if we
could have a sovereign made in the image of God, but, men being
what they are, there is more safety in kingdoms of moderate power
united in a Christian League.'[10]

That Erasmus' distrust was justified by the plans of his time is plain

---

* For detailed treatment of this point see below, Ch. 8, pp. 153-5, 167-75.

enough from the briefest account of those of which we have a record or hear the echoes. In 1458, five years after the fall of Constantinople, George Podiebrad, King of Bohemia, presented one to the King of France for a League or Perpetual Union of Christian Princes, other than the Emperor and the Pope. It was to consist of a federal Parliament of princes, a combined army—which would wage war against the disturbers of peace in Europe as well as against the Turk—and a central executive authority. The removal of the Turkish danger to Europe, by the institution of a crusade, and the abolition of war within Europe were its two professed aims. But its real object—this plan sprang from the wish to avoid domination—was to provide George with the protection of Germany, France and Venice against the Emperor and the Pope. Nor did he confine himself to this suggestion for defending himself, a Hussite and a minor monarch, against Pope and Emperor. He also submitted to Louis XI a plan by which the King of France would assume the title of Emperor in the West while he himself would become German Emperor at Frankfurt and Eastern Emperor at Constantinople. The two plans were drawn up by George's adviser, Antonius Marius or Marini, and were entitled *De Unione Christianorum Contra Turcas* and *Traité des Alliances et Confédérations*.[11] Dante's *Monarchia* itself, another attack on the Pope but also an attempt to revitalise the medieval Empire, was not printed until the sixteenth century: it was put on the *Index* in 1554.* Among the many proposals for a European League against the Turk that were still being produced at the end of the sixteenth century were those of François de la Noue, who had been in the service of Henry IV of France (1587), and of a Greek, Minotto (1609).[12] In about 1600 Campanella, in two books which were not published till the 1620's, *Discorsi politici ai principi d'Italia* and *Monarchia hispanica*, urged that it was the will of God that the world dominion of Spain, exercised in part directly and in part through the medium of semi-autonomous states, and in association also with a spiritually reformed but politically powerful Papacy, should bring salvation to the nations. In the 1630's, after he had been persecuted by the Spaniards and during his asylum in France, he wrote another series of books of which the most important was still entitled *Le Monarchie delle Nationi* (1635). They were a recanta-

---

* A. N. L. Munby kindly provided this information.

tion of the former works only to the extent that, paying thanks to the new protector and homage to the rising star of Richelieu's France, they substituted French dominion for Spanish and looked to the day when the Dauphin, the future Louis XIV, would establish a single state in the Christian world.

Unlike other writers with even less claim to be considered, Campanella is not usually listed among the authors of peace plans. But all his books incorporated the notion of a Catholic Union of Nations, with a senate at Rome under the presidency of the Pope, reaching its decisions by majority vote and governing Catholic Europe by means of a single military force.[13] Except in their overtones—Campanella regarded world monarchy as but a step to a Utopian Sun state—and except that they frankly avowed the aim of a single monarchy for Europe they in no way differed in character from the plans that had preceded them.

They differed considerably, on the other hand, from two other schemes which appeared during this period of the Thirty Years' War. Emeric Crucé's *Nouveau Cynée*, of which two editions were published in 1623 and 1624, was, in the records of modern history, the first proposal for an international organisation that was also a proposal for maintaining peace. The 'Grand Design' of the duc de Sully, details of which appeared in the memoirs he published in 1638 (and also in a second instalment published in 1662), was a singular compound of new and traditional ideas.

Like many men before and after, Crucé advocated an association of states. It was to have a standing assembly of ambassadors at Venice; to reach decisions by majority vote; to collaborate in dealing with refractory states, if necessary by pooling the separate armed forces of its members.[14] But he urged that it should comprise not only both monarchs and republics but also all the nations of the known world: Persia, China, Ethiopia, the East and the West Indies and the Turks, as well as all the European states. What is more, he gave the Turks first rank under the purely formal chairmanship of the Pope on account of the historical claims of Constantinople in relation to those of Rome. On the basis of historical traditions again, the Emperor in Europe was accorded third place, as being more than merely the ruler of Germany. For Crucé, though separate states existed, the notion of the equality of sovereign states did not; and in these rankings the traditions of the Middle Ages were still exerting their force. As against this, the geographical extension, and especially to the Turks, was not the only novel feature of the plan, or even the most startling. That constituted a break with the tradition of the crusade in these theories but in practice the Turks had long been an habitual ally of France. The book's real distinction was that its entire tone and language were a conscious disavowal of previous and contemporary thinking on this subject.

'Peace', it begins, 'is . . . only half searched for. Some exhort the Christian Princes to it . . . against their common enemy, and even a famous personage has shown the means to exterminate the Turks in four years or thereabouts. . . . Others think only of themselves, sowing dissension among their neighbours to get peace for themselves. But I am of a very different opinion, and it seems to me that when you see the house of your neighbour burning or falling, you have a cause for fear as much as compassion, since human society is one body. . . .'[15] And if peace was its primary object it also criticised the continuing search for political control of all Europe, despite its appeal to the traditions of Rome and Constantinople and the Empire. 'If you had subjected the whole world . . . finally you will be forced to repose yourselves, since war is waged to obtain peace. What you would do in a monarchy of the universe, do it in that which is in your hands.'[16] 'Nothing can save an empire except a general peace, of which the principal means consists in the limitation of the monarchies, so that each Prince remains within the lands which he possesses at present, and does not pass beyond them for any pretenses.'[17] Finally, though it did not conceive of states as equal, it appealed to the interests and difficulties of the independent sovereign state as well as showing some recognition that a community of such states was emerging. It offered monarchs universal peace as 'the means to secure your states.'[18]

'Peace being established between all Princes . . . all the Sovereigns . . . would not have much difficulty to make themselves obeyed by their people. . . . For what constrains monarchs to bear with their subjects is the fear that these will associate themselves with strangers, or that these latter should profit by the division and quarrels between the subjects and the Prince. Now this fear would be superfluous . . . with the assistance of the other sovereigns, . . . as all having an interest in the punishment of rebels. And thus the Princes would receive the principal fruit of universal peace. . . .'[19] 'It is not enough to prevent dangers from without: that within is more to be feared. After . . . all the Princes shall be in accord, each of them will care for the affairs of his monarchy, to the end that the scandalous behaviour of his subjects shall not endanger the body of this union. . . . And doing so not only will he oblige the public, in working . . . for the maintenance of general peace, but also will assure his state.'[20] 'It must not be supposed that the grandeur of a King consists in the extent of his lordship . . . ; the true grandeur . . . lies in the prompt obedience of his subjects and the firm possession of his state, which cannot happen so long as he engages in a war.'[21] Just as peace, not empire, was the chief object in Crucé's mind, so he saw the means to peace as being not the supersession but the strengthening of the individual state.

Internationalists have gone further and hailed him as the first to propose international arbitration instead of war as the court of last resort for nations,[22] just as other internationalists have urged that arbitration was 'invented' in the twelfth century or by Erasmus or by the ancient Greeks.[23] Perhaps this is the place for insisting that the notion of arbitration escaped modern writers before the eighteenth century—whatever may have been established about its development among the ancient Greeks—in proportion as they felt the importance of creating a European or a wider international association. The principle underlying the idea of an association or a republic of states and the principle underlying arbitration between states are different, indeed inconsistent. The first presupposes such a unity that war between members is civil war, to be suppressed by the sovereign authority of the association. The second is a procedure by which independent sovereign states submit particular disputes of their own free will to the determination of an authority chosen *ad hoc*. Nor is its underlying principle altered if a Permanent Court is established to replace *ad hoc* tribunals. Before the end of the seventeenth century the only minds which approached the notion of arbitration were those of men like Erasmus, with his distrust of the purposes for which international associations were being proposed, and Grotius, with his greater interest in law and procedure between nations than in their organisation into one political system. From the majority of men it was hidden—and not so much by the lack of development of sovereign states as by their advocacy of a single political structure as the solution of the problems which the rapid development of sovereign states was creating.

Crucé was no exception here. He appealed to the sovereign states even if he did not recognize the principle of equality between them; but the function of his world council was to achieve unity as well as peace between the states. Its structure did not differ from that proposed by the most conscious advocates of the restoration of Empire, and the procedure he laid down for it was just as unformulated and imprecise. But if there was nothing new about the structure and procedure of his proposed League except the extent of its membership—they were otherwise identical with those outlined by earlier writers at least as far back as Dubois—he escaped from the previous subjection of the search for peace to political aims—which went back equally far. The principal feature of the *Nouveau Cynée* is that it did not advocate peace solely or primarily as the by-product of the solution to some political problem—the launching of a crusade, the defence of Europe against the Turk, the reconstruction of a medieval European order that was in decline, the creation of a new Empire. It conceived of political advantages as being the consequence of establishing peace. The political advantages it had in mind were the growth of religious toleration, the freedom and expansion of world trade, the abatement of poverty, the reduction of taxation, as well as the consolidation of the power of the prince;[24] and by peace it meant universal peace. 'We seek a peace which is not patched up, not for three days, but which is voluntary, equitable and permanent: a peace which gives to each one what belongs to him . . . and to all indifferently the liberty of travel and trading.'[25]

If Crucé broke through the barriers of earlier thinking he nevertheless reflected sentiments that were increasing in his day. At the time he was writing the Thirty Years' War was provoking new thought and discussion along the lines he took. The idea of universal peace is frequently met with in pamphlets after 1610.[26] Grotius' book was published in 1625. It was not concerned with the project of perpetual peace. Far from seeking to abolish war, it retained the notions that some wars were just and that, while wars should be waged only for just causes, just wars were divinely approved. But it did grasp that progress lay in replacing the theoretical world unity of the Middle Ages by sociability within a community of independent states, envisaging the day when these states would all work within the limits of a Law of Nations based on contract and justice that would regulate war if it did not guarantee peace. Sully was also affected by this climate of opinion even if he did not come to know the work of Crucé and Grotius directly—and it seems probable that he did. The history of the composition of his memoirs, of the evolution of his 'Grand Design', is testimony to this fact.

The first draft of Sully's memoirs, written between 1611 and 1617, soon after he had retired as a minister of the French Crown, contained only six or seven scattered references to Henry IV's aspirations. Although they were supported by documents which were doctored or completely fabricated, these represented fairly enough what may have been the long-term aims or hopes of the King—or at least of Sully and the King's other advisers. They included 'the translation of the Empire from Austria to France', the reduction of the power of Austria, the reduction of Spain in Europe to the Iberian peninsula, and the redistribution of Austrian and Spanish possessions. They referred to 'une association très chrétienne', which meant the states in opposition to Spanish pretensions, and they spoke of the disinterestedness of France. But they included no mention at all of 'une république très chrétienne', an equilibrium of strength between European states, the expulsion of the Turks from Europe, perpetual peace, a sovereign federal council to settle disputes and maintain the peace, or a religious settlement of Europe. All these leading features of the 'Grand Design', as it emerged in the memoirs that were eventually published, were added between 1620 and 1635.

When the memoirs were published (in 1638) these ideas were also fathered, with a still greater wealth of forged evidence, on Henry IV, but they were the work of Sully's own imagination. When they were added to the original draft the aims laid down there, with which they disagreed, were not altered.* The additions abound in detailed contradictions as between themselves.† All references, both old and new, to what was called the 'Grand Design' remained scattered throughout the printed version; it was not until the editions of the eighteenth century, beginning with that of 1745, that they were collected together into one chapter at the end, under the title:

---

* Thus in the draft the Low Countries were to be divided between French and English barons, but in the first printed edition they are also to be added to the United Provinces.

† Thus in one place the King of Hungary was to be elected by 8 princes, in another 6, in another 7; in one place the European Council is to have 66 members, in another 40.

'Wherein is discussed the Political Scheme, commonly called the Grand Design of Henry IV.' It is no wonder that the 'Grand Design' has been a source of endless confusion.[27]

But one thing more has added to the confusion. When he was altering his original draft, producing the version printed in 1638, Sully was working under two influences. The influence of warfare itself and of opinion represented by men like Crucé and Grotius pulled him one way. His own career as a minister and a diplomat, the ideas he had himself expressed in the original draft and the inspiration of the work of Richelieu, which was at its height while he was revising, all pulled him in the opposite direction. This conflict, even more than the contradictions arising from the way in which it was composed, is the key to an understanding of the printed version of the 'Grand Design'.

Essentially, this remains a plan for the weakening of the Habsburgs and the establishment of French hegemony in Europe, with possible additions in the shape of war against the Turks and Russia. Even in the seventeenth and eighteenth centuries a few writers, while not questioning the attribution of the ideas to Henry IV, recognized this—Vittorio Siri,[28] Leibniz, Rousseau. Leibniz wrote of it that 'Henry IV . . . may be suspected of having had in view more the overturning of the House of Austria than the establishment of a Society of Sovereigns. . . .'[29] Rousseau thought the King had been 'prompted by the secret hope of humbling a formidable enemy' and that, 'while engaging so many people in the downfall of the first potentate of Europe, . . . he did not forget to provide on his own account for getting hold of the same position'.[30] It is impossible for a modern reader to reach any other conclusion. Bourbon interests were still scarcely concealed; the destruction of the Habsburg position in Europe remained a prime objective; the inducement offered to members of the proposed European League was additional territory at the expense of the House of Austria.[31] In so far as it was to serve more than French interests, the plan shared the other features of most plans of this period. An important consequence of the defeat of the Habsburgs, it was argued, was that 'the Empire would again . . . become a dignity to which all princes . . . might aspire'. The Emperor, elected from among the princes in such a way that no two successive Emperors came from the same royal house, would have been 'declared the first and chief magistrate of the whole Christian republic'.* After the defeat of the Habsburgs the military resources of the Republic were to be directed to the expulsion of the Turks—and, if necessary, of the Russians—from Europe and to the acquisition by the European Powers of territory beyond Europe. Above all, Henry IV's aim was stated to be that of establishing 'a political system by which Europe might be regulated and governed', 'a reunion of all the different states', 'and this in a manner so solid and durable that nothing should afterwards be able to shake its foundations'.[33] In its search for an organization and a unity for Europe or for Christendom, and this by means of the retention or resurrection of the old Empire if also by the transfer of its powers to other states; in its subordination of the aim of perpetual peace, though this aim is referred to, to the tradition of the crusade as well as to the problem of the European order—Sully's 'Grand Design' places itself firmly within that succession of proposals which men had been producing since the fourteenth century but which Sully had probably never heard of.

Yet mixed uneasily with longer passages in this vein—on 'the humbling of the House of Austria as an absolute necessity'; on the aim of reducing it 'to the sole kingdom of Spain'; on the European army with which the Powers of the European League, 'after they had . . . conquered all those territories in Europe which they would not share with a stranger . . . , would seek to unite with these conquests such parts of Asia as are most commodiously situated, and particularly the whole coast of Africa'; on the need to turn against Muscovy and Russia, as well as against the Turk, and force them, too, out of Europe, if they 'refuse to conform to any of the Christian doctrines of religion [the Catholic, the Lutheran or the Calvinist, and] . . . to enter into the association'—there are remarks which breathe a different spirit and which derive from opinions and writings which Sully had recently heard and read. They include observations on the tragedy and immorality of war—'the happiness of mankind can never arise from war'. They speak of the futility of aggression—of the tendency for the success and happiness of a state to be in inverse proportion to its size and power. There is the recognition that this warning of the folly of conquest should be heard by France as well as by other states. There is a passionate plea that, in

* According to Sully, Henry IV intended that the Elector of Bavaria, at that time France's most consistent ally, should be the first prince to be elected Emperor.[32]

the condition to which Europe had been reduced, the course of wisdom was for the various states and religions to agree to live together without further struggle.[34] One of the fundamental articles of his Commonwealth, as of Crucé's, was complete freedom of trade.[35] Although there was nothing novel about this different spirit, any more than there was about the detailed international organisation and procedure which Sully proposed, we need not doubt that he genuinely shared it. The pains he took to represent these sentiments, like the rest of the Design, as belonging to Henry IV, to give them the prestige of Henry's name, sufficiently indicate the importance he attached to them.

There is also the fact that their conflict with his other ideas led him to make a novel contribution of his own. In the 'Grand Design' the equivalent of Grotius's concern to establish legal and moral restraints upon states and of Crucé's assertion of the priority of peace over political objectives was not merely an echoing of their different pleas for give-and-take. It is to be found in the relative unimportance of international organisation and in the striking prominence of political methods among the proposals which Sully made for reaching the goal. The means he laid down for achieving his plan included a general council representing all the states—the greater Powers having four representatives, the lesser two—with permanent headquarters near the centre of Europe. It should deal with the initial problem of redistributing conquered Habsburg territory. It should then settle the contributions of the various states to the combined army 'which the success of such an enterprise might require'. Thereafter all disputes should be referred to it and its decrees should be irrevocable. But international machinery was far less important for the implementation of the 'Design' than was his proposal for a re-casting of the political map of Europe. The contribution of the old diplomat and statesmen, as opposed to that of the jurist and the moralist, was a plan 'to divide Europe equally among a certain number of Powers in such a manner that none of them might have cause either of envy or of fear from the possessions or power of others'. 'The whole, therefore, of what seems proper to be done is to support them all in a kind of equilibrium'. This was 'the purport of the Design'.[36] The two main functions even of his general Council of the League were to supervise the redistribution of Austrian territory 'with equity', so as to make fifteen roughly equal 'dominations' out of Europe's existing land, and thereafter to prevent 'those innovations often introduced from time to time into the wisest and most useful institutions'.[37] Sully took the principle of balance so far as to insist that the new territory to be conquered by the European League should be granted to new princes and not to established kings. He took it so seriously that, although he planned to divest the house of Austria of the Empire and of all its possessions in Europe save 'the sole kingdom of Spain', he emphasised that it should retain Mediterranean islands and all its possessions beyond Europe, 'that it might, nevertheless, be equally powerful with the other sovereignties in Europe'.[38]

This idea, if not at variance with his other aspiration of establishing 'a political system by which all Europe might be regulated and governed as one great family', 'a reunion of all the different states', did not entirely square with remarks suggesting that there would continue to be greater and lesser Powers[39]—though Sully need not have been thinking of equilibrium in terms of strict equality. It conflicted even more with his retention of the old method of achieving the reunion—the restoration of the Emperor as first magistrate. Most of all did it conflict with Sully's scarcely disguised intention of confirming the primacy of France by placing the powers of the Emperor under French control. But he was writing at an early stage in a slow transformation of thinking and of facts in the international field, and such contradictions were the direct result. Nothing is more revealing of the intellectual difficulties to which this transformation gave rise than the fact that Sully, who could see the establishment of equilibrium between states as 'the means whereby to stabilise Christendom in that position towards which it has . . . been tending for some time',[40] could nevertheless see no contradiction between aiming at equality between independent states and aiming at the reunion of separate states under a single control. The old traditions and the new forces were, indeed, so equally powerful with him that he could even regard the establishment of an equilibrium between different states as the best means of reuniting them in a single body politic. Nor were these difficulties due simply to the fact that Sully could not suppress his sympathy with French imperial aims. Even Crucé had not hesitated to recommend that his international organisation should be forced upon reluctant states by a few of the major Powers.[41] This recommendation conceals a dilemma which is inherent in the problem of international organisation, and which has no more been escaped by the twentieth century than it was avoided by Crucé and Sully.

When all has been said it remains the case that Sully did attempt to reconcile his two positions, the two conflicting interests under which he was at work, and that the principle of 'equilibrium' was the chief result of his effort. If he still thought in terms of Christendom he spoke as frequently of Europe. If he was still attached to an old conception of the European order he also recognized the vitality of the independent state and the extent to which the European order must be based on it: that the domination of Europe was at least having to become indirect, the Empire a delegated power.

The idea of 'equilibrium' was not only 'the purport of the Design'. It was also Sully's ground for believing that his plan, unlike others of which he must have been hearing, was not 'one of those chimeras or idle speculations . . . , specious perhaps in appearance, but which at bottom have not the least degree of possibility'.[42] Whether he here had in mind plans like Crucé's or plans like Campanella's we cannot say. But one thing does seem clear. Until the end of the seventeenth century plans of the latter kind, based on old ideas and traditional ways of thought, continued to battle stoutly for men's minds with the thought of writers like Crucé and Grotius. In so far as the 'Grand Design' was influential it was its older features, its interest in Europe's political order, not its more novel aspects, the concern for peace and the notion of equilibrium, which attracted most attention.

In about 1642 a play written at the instigation of Richelieu by Desmarets de Saint-Sorlin, who is better remembered as the author of an epic poem entitled *Clovis*, was both a peace project of the old kind and a reflection of Richelieu's policies. It illustrates the close connection that continued between the search for peace and the search for power. It was a programme for peace in Europe—*Europe* was its title—but the peace was to be kept by an alert, powerful and beneficent France. It represented 'Europe' as a princess alarmed by the danger from Spain (*Ibère*) to all her children (the nations of Europe) and choosing to be defended by France (*Francion*).[43] In 1666, according to Leibniz, Ernst, Landgrave of Hesse-Rheinfels, urged the establishment of a Society of Sovereigns. Only Catholic princes were to be admitted. Lucerne, equidistant between France and Austria, was to be its headquarters. It was essential to the plan that the Holy Roman Emperor should be restored in power and given the functions of supreme ruler and military commander for all Europe.[44] Leibniz himself was sent to Paris in 1672 by the Elector of Mainz to submit to the French Government his own '*Consilium Aegypticum*'—a plan by which Louis XIV would lead Christianity in the conquest of Egypt and a final Crusade against Islam before giving permanent peace to Europe. There is little doubt that its real purpose in the mind of the Elector was to divert Louis from an attack on Holland—it represented itself as being a more effective way of damaging Dutch commerce.[45] What chiefly influenced Leibniz in drafting it may be judged from his many subsequent writings on the subject.

In 1677 he published another plan under the pseudonym 'Coesarius Furstenarius'. He was still in the service of the Elector of Mainz; the plan was a plea on behalf of the sovereign rights of the German princes. But it called for the restoration of medieval Christendom, under the supreme temporal direction of the Emperor and the spiritual direction of the Pope, in Europe as a whole. His aim was frankly the rational development of the conceptions and the institutions of the Holy Roman Empire in such a way as to give it the hegemony of Europe. 'All the Christian kings and princes are subject to the orders of the Universal Church, of which the Emperor is the director and temporal head. . . . The Sovereigns recognized this jurisdiction of the Emperor, of the Empire and of the Tribunals which represent them when they appealed from the Pope to the General Council [of Constance]. But to execute the sentences of the Christian Assembly against a recalcitrant Prince it would be necessary to declare him a common enemy. The juridical decisions pronounced against one of the members of the Empire could not be executed except by arming the others against him. The right of the universal Church is exercised rarely, but that does not alter the situation, and if the affairs of Christendom were well governed it would not be less invoked than that of the Emperor who is its image.' Nor were these views confined to his early writings. Well after the beginning of the eighteenth century, in his *Securitas Interna et Externa* and his *Observations sur les Écrits de l'Abbé de Saint-Pierre*, he continued to recommend the reorganisation of Christendom under the supreme control of the Emperor as the means by which Europe could 'regain peace, cease to be disturbed within itself and turn its eyes in the direction where it would find great honour and triumph and many advantages which were not contrary to conscience or displeasing to God'. Only then would its rulers cease trying to seize each others' possessions and learn to cooperate against 'the hereditary enemy, the barbarian, the infidel'.[46]

These views were repeated in a letter Leibniz wrote to Saint-Pierre as late as 1715. Perpetual peace, he wrote, would be most difficult to achieve, but 'to help the Emperor to chase the Turk out of Europe would perhaps be the best means of solving the problem'.[47] In the same letter he criticised Saint-Pierre's own peace plan: it was inferior to the medieval Empire as a means of organising unity in Europe.[48] In another letter of about the same time which also criticised Saint-Pierre he again made the suggestion that a Court of Arbitration be set up at Rome under the presidency of the Pope, that the old spiritual authority of the Church be restored and that excommunication be revived as a punishment. 'Such plans are as likely to succeed as that of M. de Saint-Pierre.'[49]

It has been argued that this suggestion was sarcastic, conveying Leibniz's conviction of the utter impracticability of Saint-Pierre's ideas.[50] It was certainly preceded by the remark that Saint-Pierre's project 'reminds me of an inscription outside a churchyard which ran *Pax Perpetua*. For the dead, it is true, fight no more. But the living are of another mind, and the mightiest among them have little regard for tribunals.' Leibniz expressed similar scepticism in his comment on Sully's 'Grand Design': 'I confess the authority of Henry IV is worth more than all the rest . . . and it is undoubted that if the powerful Sovereigns proposed it, the others would receive it willingly. But I do not know that the lesser princes would dare to propose it to the great ones.'[51] But the fact that he thought little of the practicability of perpetual peace and not much more of the 'Grand Design' should not be allowed to hide what is the central characteristic of all his writings. For him no less than for Dante or Dubois peace was a less important goal than justice and right order in Europe and the struggle against the non-Christian world, and all new proposals for achieving those aims seemed inferior to the restoration of the medieval Empire.

He was not alone in holding these views. In 1688 or thereabouts Charles, Duke of Lorraine, expressed identical ideas for securing peace in Europe through Austrian, rather than French, supremacy. He advised Austria to profit from the Revolution in England, to embroil France with the German Princes and to build up her own power meanwhile in Italy, where she could become the centre of a vast network of commerce from which France could be excluded. 'Combining these instructions with those I have given in my Political Testament, there is no probability that Austria will not prosper and that all Europe will not be eager to come under its rule and that it will not supplant by degrees all those who offer it resistance.'[52] As late as 1735 Alberoni advocated a European alliance for 'reducing the Turkish Empire to the obedience of the Christian Princes and for a partition of the conquest', as part of 'a scheme of perpetual dyet for establishing the public tranquillity' in Europe. Its real aim was the restoration of the position of Spain.[53]

Of all these schemes after the middle of the seventeenth century it may be said, indeed, that they were even less concerned with peace and more with power in Europe than had been the plans of the previous hundred years; and that, compared with those earlier schemes, they treated even the call to action against the Turks less as an end in itself and more as a means to that power. Neither of these developments is surprising. The threat from the Turk was beginning to decline; the power and organization of the European states were mounting more rapidly than ever—and especially those of France. But if it was for these reasons, above all, that the new directions opened up by Crucé and Sully during the Thirty Years' War were not much heeded until the end of the century, it was in reaction against the wars produced by France's abuse of her leadership in power that they were then taken up again by Penn, Bellers and Saint-Pierre.

CHAPTER 2

PENN, BELLERS AND SAINT-PIERRE

WILLIAM PENN published his *Essay towards the Present and Future Peace of Europe* in 1693.[1] John Bellers's *Some Reasons for an European State* appeared in 1710.[2] Charles Francois Irénée Castel de Saint-Pierre first gave his *Perpetual Peace* to the world in 1712; he devoted the next twenty-five years to making his plan more elaborate in some books and to attempting to summarize it in others.[3] Crucé apart, these men were the authors of the first proposals of modern times for establishing an international organisation whose primary object was the maintenance of peace.

There was nothing essentially new in their writings. None of them had heard of Crucé; but all were directly influenced by Sully, as is shown by the full titles* and the texts of their books; and they did little more than reproduce that part of the 'Grand Design' which, influenced by ideas like Crucé's, had sprung from a genuine interest in achieving peace. Nevertheless, they neglected—did not notice, indeed—that part of Sully's thought which had been inspired by traditional political aims. And with their reversion to Crucé's attitude after an interval of years the new approach was at last finally established. After the beginning of the eighteenth century it remained possible—if unusual—for men to suggest that international peace might be obtained by other means than international organisation. It was hardly possible for advocates of international organisation to have as their first object any purpose other than the maintenance of peace.

That this was the object of Penn, Bellers and Saint-Pierre—as much as it had been Crucé's and to a greater extent than had been the case with Sully—is clear enough from the titles of their books. Peace has here replaced 'Monarchia' or 'The Grand Design', not to speak of the recovery of the Holy Land. It is clearer still in the text of their books. In their proposals, as in Crucé's, the search for peace was firmly placed above the cause of Christendom against the infidel and above the goal of predominance in Europe. These other objects

---

* These are given below in references 1, 2 and 3 for this chapter.

indeed, found so little place in their thoughts that, unlike Cruce, they hardly troubled to denounce them.

Where the infidel was concerned they did not go as far as Crucé. Like Sully, they advocated an international organisation that would be confined to Europe. Penn still had Sully's hesitation about including Russia, and he still inclined to the exclusion of the Turk. He specified, it is true, that if Russia and Turkey were to be included they should each have ten representatives in the Diet. But it does not seem that he thought Turkey's inclusion worth serious attention: one of the benefits of his plan in his mind was that 'the reputation of Christianity will be to some degree recovered in the sight of the infidels'; another that the league would provide greater security 'to Christians against the inroads of the Turk'.[4] Bellers's plan was partly inspired by his approval of the call of the Council of State in Holland —in its declaration of a state of war with France—for a European league which would not only check the pretensions of France but also imitate the recent union between the Emperor and the Republic of Venice for resistance to the Turk.[5] On the other hand—and in this they advanced beyond Sully—neither Penn nor Bellers mentioned any of the arrangements outlined by Sully for the expulsion of the infidel and the conquest of extra-European territory. If their union excluded the Turks it was given purely defensive functions against them. And with Saint-Pierre there came a considerable advance beyond even the defensive language of Penn and Bellers— an advance to something equivalent to Crucé's views.

Saint-Pierre included Muscovy and the Turks in his League in the first (1712) edition of his project. In subsequent editions (1713 and 1717) he still had no hesitation in retaining Russia—a testimony to the growth of Europe's relations with Russia since Penn's day—and he excluded the Turks solely because he feared that the inclusion of the whole world 'would cast an air of impossibility upon the whole project'. Still more significant, while his league retained in these editions only a defensive force against Turkey, he substituted for the original inclusion of Turkey the argument that 'the European Union shall endeavour to obtain in Asia a permanent society like that of Europe, that peace may be maintained there also, and especially that it may have no cause to fear any Asiatic sovereign'.[6] A greater sense of what might be practicable—perhaps also a greater sense of the distinctiveness of Europe—was making it impossible to follow

Crucé in suggesting a world-wide organisation. Yet the priority which Saint-Pierre, like Crucé, Penn and Bellers, gave to the maintenance of peace even in the external relations of Europe with the outside world is unmistakable in this alternative suggestion for achieving peace on a wider scale. Needless to say, another factor had helped to bring this about. When Saint-Pierre came to publish the summary of his scheme in 1729 and 1737 there was no further reference to the desirability of 'a permanent society' in Asia. Europe no longer had any cause to fear 'any Asiatic sovereign'.

Peace was given priority over the old search for pre-eminence in Europe as well as over the old notion of the Crusade and of the conquest of extra-European land. This is apparent in the complete absence from these proposals of Sully's ill-concealed concern with the struggle of Habsburg and Bourbon. It is still more clearly established by the omission of even Crucé's concessions to tradition in the matter of rank and precedence. In this last respect a progression is again discernible from Penn to Saint-Pierre.

Penn conceded that his plan seemed 'at the first look . . . to carry with it no small difficulty what votes to allow for the inequality of the princes and the states'. He solved the difficulty by allotting members of his league representatives in the Diet in proportion to their wealth, and by adopting precautions against the consequences.* 'To avoid quarrel for precedency, the room [in which the Diet would meet] may be round and have divers doors'; in order to avoid undue influence by larger states on smaller ones, voting by secret ballot would be 'a shrewd stratagem and an experimental remedy against corruption'.[7] Bellers went somewhat further. He suggested that 'Europe should be divided into one hundred equal cantons or provinces' as the basis for settling the representation of the states in the central parliament and for allotting their contributions in the event of the Union having to call on its joint forces; each canton was to provide 1,000 soldiers or the equivalent. Each state was to have one representative at the centre for each of its cantons; but the disparity in the power of states would be offset by the division into cantons. Saint-Pierre went further still. He gave all members, regardless of size and power, one deputy and one vote. In order that

* He suggested that the German Empire should have 12 representatives, France 10, Spain 10, Italy 8, England 6, Portugal 3, Sweden 4, Denmark 3, Poland 4, Venice 3, the Seven Provinces 4, the Thirteen Cantons 2, the dukedoms of Holstein and Courland 1.

no one state should become too powerful he stipulated that 'the territory of the five most powerful sovereigns shall not be increased' and that no sovereign was to possess two sovereignties except the electors of the Holy Roman Empire in the event of their being elected Emperor.[8] Even this exception was offset by the fact that the Empire as such was not represented in Saint-Pierre's Senate, as it was in Penn's.*

We need not doubt that the tendency which culminated in Saint-Pierre's· adoption of equal representation, his omission of the Emperor and his reference to the 'five most powerful sovereigns' reflected a change in the actual political condition of Europe. The nature of this change is indicated by a further fact. These stipulations laid down by Saint-Pierre were as far as any of these writers went towards Sully's idea of recasting the political map of Europe. Bellers was content to accept the states as they stood after the next peace treaty: all the princes and states in his union were to 'have all the strength of Europe to protect them in the possession of what they shall enjoy by the next peace'.[9] Penn and Saint-Pierre, aware that their proposals involved the permanent maintenance of some fixed distribution of territory and power, were similarly prepared—unlike Sully—to accept some recent *status quo*. Penn felt that it had to be decided 'from what time titles shall take their beginning, or how far back we may look to confirm or dispute them', and also that this was a question that must be left to the decision of 'great pretenders and masters'. For himself, however, he thought it would be sufficient 'to take the last general peace of Nimeguen, or . . . the commencing of this war, or . . . the time of the beginning of the [next] treaty of peace'.[10] Saint-Pierre's perpetual alliance was based on 'the preservation for all time to each of the allies of the territory and all the rights which they actually possess under the latest treaties'—the treaties of Utrecht.[11]

When these writers were aware from reading Sully that Henry IV, to quote Penn, had 'been upon obliging . . . Europe to a political balance'[12]—when Sully himself had urged the establishment of a balance based on rough equality as 'the means whereby to stabilise Christendom in that position towards which it has . . . been tending

---

* The 24 states he named for membership in Article IX were France, Spain, England, Holland, Savoy, Portugal, Bavaria, Venice, Genoa, Florence, Switzerland, Lorraine, Sweden, Denmark, Poland, the Pope, Muscovy, Austria, Courland, Prussia, Saxony, Palatine, Hanover, the ecclesiastical electors.

for some time'—their departure from Sully's political programme and their preparedness to base their system, instead, on the existing *status quo* may safely be ascribed to the influence of an actual if slow transition from circumstances which had favoured the predominance of one Power in Europe towards conditions of near-equality between several states. Just as a greater sense of the distinctiveness of Europe, together with the decline of the Turkish menace, was altering the basis on which the Turk continued to be excluded, so this other development was enabling these writers to abandon the interest of most earlier peace schemes in preserving or refashioning a hierarchial system of control for Europe as a whole.*

The wish to establish peace became the overriding object of these writers as a result of these changes of emphasis. In proportion as they were uninterested in their leagues and unions as the means to extra-European aspirations and to political predominance in Europe they were the more concerned with them as the means of avoiding intra-European quarrels. In proportion as they were preoccupied with this, the peace-preserving role of international organisation, on the other hand, they were not only more specific and detailed than all their predecessors as to the procedure to be observed. They were also brought nearer to the dilemma involved in the need to base peace on the ultimate sanction of force.

This dilemma is inherent in the very notion of achieving peace by organisation between separate states. It was bound to arise as soon as peace became the principal purpose of international organisation. For Dante and Dubois, for Sully and other seventeenth-century writers, the problem had not arisen. Empire, justice or order are not —like peace—incompatible with the use of force. Crucé, though peace was his object, had still avoided the problem by not asking the questions. For Penn, Bellers and Saint-Pierre the dilemma could be solved only by assuming that force, though provided for, would not have to be used.

This applied to the institution of the organisation in the first place, no less than to the procedure they advocated for maintaining it once it had been set up. The lack of interest on the part of these writers in recasting the European political map did not arise from any reluctance to contemplate the use of force in instituting their Union.

* For detailed treatment of this development see Ch. 8, pp. 175 ff., below.

They did not ask for a war to bring about the redistribution of territory, as Sully had done, but they agreed with him, and indeed with Crucé, in not shrinking from establishing their Union by force should that be necessary. But would force be needed? Penn's reply to the objection that 'the richest sovereignty will never agree to it' was that 'he is not stronger than all the rest, and . . . you should promote this and compel him into it, especially before he be so, for then it will be too late to deal with such a one'.[13] Bellers's Union was to begin as a league of the states already allied against France, who should invite all the neutrals to join them: this would 'incline' France herself to join in the end.[14] Saint-Pierre argued that 'if several of the Powers signed the five fundamental articles they would be signed by all within 5 or 6 months, since those who refused would fear being treated as enemies of the general alliance'.[15] To all three it seemed essential that all European states should join, and all were prepared to use force to this end; but at bottom they believed that force would not be required.

They were equally emphatic about the need to base the league on force after it had been established. Crucé and Sully had assumed that some procedure was necessary for settling disputes between members of the league; but they had almost assumed that peace would result, that internecine disputes would cease, from establishing the procedure. They had not specified what should be done if this assumption proved wrong—in sharp contrast to Sully's detailed account of what the United League would achieve abroad and to Crucé's account of how princes could help each other to put down internal revolution. Penn, on the other hand, was not only quite clear that 'the Sovereign or Imperial Diet, Parliament or State of Europe' should be the sovereign assembly, to which all differences should be brought 'that cannot be made up by private embassies', and that the assembly should reach its decisions by majorities of at least three-quarters of the whole number of votes. He laid it down that, should any member 'act independently or refuse to accept the verdict of the Diet, all the other sovereignties, united as one strength, shall compel the submission and performance of the sentence, with damages to the suffering party and charges to the sovereignties that obliged their submission'.[16] Bellers arranged that 'each canton should be appointed to raise 1,000 men, or money or ships of equal value or charge, upon any public occasion . . . , by which means the

Princes and states of Europe may settle all the disputes among themselves . . . and prevent the rash from such dismal adventures as are the consequences of war, whilst they must know that every man in the Senate hath one or two or three thousand men to back what he concludes there'.[17] Saint-Pierre was no less specific. The members of his league, having renounced recourse to war, had first to seek a settlement of their disputes through the mediation of other members. If mediation failed they were bound to accept the decisions of the Senate, which would be reached by a plurality of votes in the first instance and subsequently confirmed by majorities of three-quarters of all the votes. If any state refused to submit to any award or to any regulation laid down by the Senate, or prepared for war without adopting this procedure, then the Senate would use force against it —relying on an international army under a specially appointed generalissimo to which member states must furnish contingents.[18]

These provisions hardly bear out the argument that 'Penn does not really face the question what ought to be done if a recalcitrant nation refused to submit to the decision of the assembly'[19] or the view that Saint-Pierre held 'pacifist ideas' and represented 'a radical pacifism'.[20] They are all the more remarkable, indeed, when it is recalled that Penn and Bellers were Quakers. Yet the desertion by these men of the Quaker tradition of standing aloof from all proposals that professed to aim at peace through international organisation, one of the most interesting features of the time, was undoubtedly made easier for them by the fact that they were not free from the assumption made by Cruce and Sully that peace would result from the mere establishment of the union. If they saw no contradiction in maintaining peace if necessary by force—if Penn and Saint-Pierre extended the use of force against any attempt at secession from the Union or at abstention and neutrality in its debates[21]—it was partly for this reason. Each dealt with the hypothetical question of what would happen if the Powers ignored the procedure. Each replied that the threat of force would ensure that it remained hypothetical. 'No sovereignty . . . having the power', wrote Penn, 'and therefore cannot show the will to dispute the conclusion.' Saint-Pierre's answer was that, although lasting peace depended on the exact observation of the fundamental agreement, 'all will always be intimately concerned to maintain this article for their own security . . . so that the most powerful and the least powerful will have a very great and constant interest in preventing any of the associates from abandoning the method of arbitration'.[22] They clearly did not expect that the force they provided for would have to be invoked.

Two of the four objections to his project which Penn discussed at length were that effeminacy would result from 'the disuse of the trade of soldiery' and that this same outcome would be accompanied by unemployment among younger sons and the poor.[23] He thought that the causes of war were the wish 'to keep, to recover and to add'; that 'this last will find no room in the imperial states—they are an impassable limit to that ambition'; and that 'the other two may come as soon as they please and find the justice of the sovereign court'.[24] Saint-Pierre was equally confident that once his Union was set up there would be no further attempts at conquest. There would be 'nothing important in future to regulate between sovereigns, except future or imminent successions to sovereignties'. Other possible sources of dispute would be 'of very little importance', such as '2 or 3 villages more or less' or 'a few personal quarrels, some trifles about frontiers, or commerce'. No one would be tempted to conquest since 'no conquests are possible'.[25]

Their solution has a modern ring. Ever since their day men have not shrunk from advocating the maintenance of peace by resort to force primarily because they were convinced that it would not in practice be necessary to rely on force once an international organisation has been established. Rationalism in the sense of superficial optimism has been the usual reason for this conclusion—or evasion—in more recent times. It would be wrong, however, to assume that superficial optimism was the sole or even the chief reason why Penn, Bellers and Saint-Pierre had this same conviction. It is more to the point that, although peace was for them the object of international organisation, they still did not clearly see their organisation as an organisation between separate states. As has been said, their concern was rather to 'institutionalise' the notion of Europe[26]—which had also asserted itself in the titles of their books—but their notion of Europe was one which they inherited from the past.

Rationalism may explain why even Quakers deserted the pacifist tradition at this time. Perhaps, indeed, it would be truer to say that Quakers were less able than others to resist the conclusion to which it led in this field: the more one felt the importance of peace the less was one able to avoid the tendency to think that war could be eliminated if reason were enthroned in the governments of states. Rationalism does much to explain Saint-Pierre's attitude. He was so deeply convinced of the waywardness of men's unaided efforts as to assert that 'treaties will never be observed and civil wars and foreign wars will not stop until the sovereigns of Europe sign the five fundamental articles'. He was equally convinced that all these problems would be solved if the articles were signed. This has always been the weakness of the rationalist approach: it justifies its solutions with a belief in the unworthiness and unreliability of human nature of such proportions as to create the suspicion that the solutions will never be effective in this world; the optimism arises from an extreme pessimism. But when all this has been said superficial optimism is scarcely enough to account for the outlook of these men.

For one thing, their tracts abound with non-rationalistic sentiments. This is especially true of Penn. He was so far from being superficially optimistic that he began his essay with highly realistic remarks. 'Properly and truly speaking, men seek their wills by war rather than by peace, and . . . as they will violate it to obtain them, so they will hardly be brought to think of peace unless their appetites be some way gratified.' It was 'in the contraries of peace we see the beauties thereof, which under it, such is the unhappiness of mankind, we are apt to nauseate, as the full stomach loathes the honeycomb'. This weakness of human nature was 'not the least reason why God is pleased to chastise us so frequently with the vices of war'.[27] Even Saint-Pierre, if he believed that the urge to conquest would disappear in his Union, believed that this would be because conquest would always be opposed, not because men would cease to be interested in it. And then there is a second state of mind common to these men which, far more than rationalism, explains their confidence that force will not be needed once their unions are established.

If they thought that peace would result from the organisation they proposed—and result without constant resort to the force for which they provided—it was rather because they did not clearly envisage their organisation as an organisation binding separate states. Internationalist proposals had in their writings at last struggled above the old purposes for which such proposals had long been made. They clearly established internal European peace as the supreme, almost the sole, object. But they had not yet escaped entirely from the traditional framework of these proposals in another respect. They had not decided whether the need was for the better organisation of a single community which was losing its ancient bonds or for the imposition of a new organisation upon individual and competing component states.

The ambivalence of their attitude to this question underlies what is the most interesting inconsistency in their books—more interesting, more peculiar to their time, than the inconsistency of advocating force for the maintenance of peace. Like Crucé, they were never tired of urging their proposals upon princes with the argument that the resulting union would provide an increase in each prince's sovereignty and power. Far from seeing any inconsistency in this argument, its inconsistency was hidden from them by their indifference to the problem whether the resulting union would be an alliance or a single state. It was not that they were uncertain as between the merits of a federal and a confederal solution. They appealed to separate sovereignties; they also assumed that these sovereignties coexisted in what was already a single community, or had been until recently. For them there were separate states, but the states were not sufficiently separate for the choice between federal and confederal schemes to arise.

It is true that they dealt with the objection that sovereign princes and states, in Penn's words, 'will hereby become not sovereign: a thing they will never endure'. It was their recognition of this difficulty that led them to appeal to sovereigns with the reply that they would lose none of their sovereignty. Penn's answer was that 'they remain as sovereign at home as they ever were'; as for their relations with each other they would gain in security what they lost in freedom of action.[28] Saint-Pierre's answer was the same but more detailed. It was not true that a state would 'submit to a dependence' in foreign relations if it gave up the right to decide a dispute by war; dependence on arbitration was no more onerous than dependence on force of arms. As for the internal position of princes, they would 'procure to themselves in times of weakness a much greater security . . . of the possession of sovereignty'. This was because 'it is the actual possession of rights of which the European confederation is guarantor, not only between sovereign and sovereign but also between certain semi-republican peoples and their sovereigns. 'In return for joining the Union each prince will be assisted against rebels by the forces of his confederates. So that by this means . . . they will always be reduced to obedience.' Once the Union has been established 'there can never be civil war' for how would rebels 'have the least hope of success, knowing that they must meet the forces of the whole of Europe'?[29]

The argument recalls Sully as well as Crucé. The 'Grand Design' had proposed a perpetual settlement between the religions as well as the states of Europe: one of the three main religions was to be declared official in each state; all states were to cooperate against 'the production of new sects . . . which should carefully be suppressed on their first appearance'.[30] Only for Saint-Pierre the source of sedition has ceased to be religion. In England, one of those 'semi-republican peoples', for example, he would have safeguarded the rights of the King against a seditious parliament, even though the authority of the parliament would similarly 'always be preserved in the state in which it now is'.[31] With Saint-Pierre, indeed, there was no distinction between civil and international war and the emphasis on collaboration between member states in the cause of the internal *status quo* was quite as prominent as the concern with international peace. He carried it so far as to end up with a political system that is incompatible with the notion of separate states even while appealing to the interests of the heads of separate states on its behalf.

This inconsistency was concealed from him by another. Like Penn and Bellers, he never contemplated closely the political nature of the resulting union, and the inconsistency of their language on this point reveals that this was not yet a problem they could envisage. Penn frequently referred to the 'several sovereign countries', even as he reassured sovereigns that they would lose none of their sovereignty. But he called his Diet 'The Sovereign Dyet, Parliament or State of Europe',[32] or 'the imperial estates',[33] and he referred to the union as 'such an empire'.[34] Bellers discussed the separate contingents to be provided by the separate states in a book which was entitled *Some Reasons for an European State*, and which advocated that all the states should be merged into one state under a single government.[35] It was the same with Saint-Pierre. Although he often talked of 'the allies' or 'the confederacy', he also talked of war as being inevitable 'unless Europe changes its constitution'[36] and referred to the union he hoped to create as 'the all-powerful and immortal society'.[37] It is perhaps no less significant that when he arranged that the contributions of

43

members of the union to the international army should be assessed monthly, in proportion to their revenues, he proposed the introduction of a European month after the pattern of the Roman month.[38] If his plan had abandoned 'the venerable phantom of the Holy Empire' it still used it as a model.

The international army provides another pointer in the same direction. A twentieth-century observer, with his greater refinement in these matters, would say that Penn did not advocate an international army—he asked only that all the loyal members of his Diet should collaborate to enforce order on disloyal ones; that if one member attacked another 'a small force in every other sovereignty . . . will certainly prevent that danger'[39]—and that Saint-Pierre, with his proposal for a generalissimo, did. It seems clear that they would not have recognised any difference between themselves on this point, or have given much weight to it if it had been pointed out. Neither stepped aside at this or any other juncture to canvass the relative merits of alternative methods, of federal and confederal arrangements.

If they made no such distinction it was largely because they presupposed an existing unity in Europe or thought of the European community as endangered by forces of recent growth. Saint-Pierre provides the most revealing illustration of this when dealing with the objections that might be advanced against his project. One of these was the argument that 'great institutions are only gradually made' and that 'we must endure more than one hundred years yet of war in Europe, and in consequence more than two hundred years of sovereignty, before all rulers become fully convinced that no league, no alliance, can be lasting without a permanent arbitration'.[40] In this remark we have not only a further illustration of his inconsistency about sovereignty, an admission that that sovereignty which he had assured princes they would not lose was nevertheless in his opinion the cause of war. We have also an explicit statement of the belief which underlies his uncertainty, and Penn's and Bellers's, about the nature of the community that will result when his proposals are implemented: of the belief that the evil of separate sovereignties had been introduced into Europe just a hundred years before he was writing.

Fundamentally, it was Saint-Pierre's object, as it was Penn's and Bellers's object, to root out this evil. Fundamentally, this has been the object of international plans ever since they wrote. Being nearer

44

to the Middle Ages, they perhaps had more justification than their successors for their conviction that it would be practicable to obliterate separate sovereignties. Yet even they had to face the fact of the existence of the evil to the extent of adopting, as the means of rooting it out, the collaboration of sovereignties in guaranteeing for all time the territorial arrangements and the political rights which the evil had established by the time they were writing. This was the source of all their contradictions and uncertainties.

It was also the stand-by of their critics. Saint-Pierre, if not Penn and Bellers, had followers. Alberoni's plan* was partly inspired by his writings; so were an anonymous peace project of 1745, a plan by von Loen in 1747 for a European Congress, a *Project of Universal and Perpetual Peace* written by Pierre-André Gargaz somewhat later, and the various schemes of Sainthard, Goudar, von Palthen and von Lilienfeld.[41] But the almost universal reaction of the eighteenth century was the criticism that he had neglected the realities of the modern states' system. 'You have forgotten, sir,' the Cardinal Fleury is supposed to have told him, 'a preliminary condition on which your five articles must depend. You must begin by sending out a troop of missionaries to prepare the hearts and minds of the contracting sovereigns.'[42] Frederick the Great made the same point in a letter to Voltaire: 'the thing is most practicable; for its success all that is lacking is the consent of Europe and a few similar trifles.'[43] This was Voltaire's reason for dismissing 'l'impracticable paix de l'Abbé de Saint-Pierre'.[44] He recommended, instead, either reliance on the balance of power or, perhaps in an ironical mood, the pursuit of the principles laid down in Pierre Nicole's *On the Way of Preserving Peace* (1671)—an essay which had urged that there was no way to peace except through prayer and through charity in personal relations[45] and which Voltaire, who never adopted it as a guide for himself, praised as a masterpiece unequalled even in ancient literature. It was also the reason why Rousseau, with more regret than Voltaire, and after undertaking the first modern analysis of the international problem, similarly pronounced Saint-Pierre's project 'an absurd dream'.

* Above, p. 32.

CHAPTER 3

ROUSSEAU

Rousseau's political philosophy was for long misunderstood. People believed that he sang the praises of the noble savage, deplored the advent of political society, when the opinion from which he never wavered—except in his juvenile writings—was that political society was the moralising agency as well as the degrading force in men's lives. His 'individualism' is now seen to have been little more than a myth but his views on perpetual peace are still widely misinterpreted. Everybody knows that he wrote two separate treatises on the subject in the same year; not many people have attempted to explain the apparently glaring contradictions they contain, or have remembered that he wrote much else that helps to explain them.

The first of the two treatises, the *Extrait du Projet de Paix Perpétuelle de Monsieur l'Abbé de Saint-Pierre*, written in 1756 and published in 1761, was a work of piety. Except for one other short piece, it was the sole result of his plan to edit and republish all the voluminous writings of Saint-Pierre, whom he had known. The second was the *Jugement sur la Paix Perpétuelle*: also written in 1756 but not published till 1782.[1] Rousseau added to the *Extrait* an historical introduction and comments of his own, and altered other details. (Like Saint-Pierre he retained the Emperor of Russia and the Pope as members of the League and excluded the Turks, but he brought back the Emperor of the Romans.*) But it was essentially a popularisation of Saint-Pierre's plan for the reconstruction of Europe. Rousseau's own opinions were contained in the *Jugement*. They differed markedly from Saint-Pierre's. The two prominent conclusions of the *Extrait* and the *Jugement*, taken together, were that nothing less than the most rigid and unbreakable of confederations could solve the problem which Saint-Pierre had set out to solve; and that it was perfectly utopian to expect such a confederation to be established.

* Rousseau's list of nineteen members, each of whom was to have one vote, were: the Emperor of the Romans; the Emperor of Russia; the Kings of France, Spain and England; the States-General; the Kings of Denmark, Sweden, Poland and Portugal; the Pope; the King of Prussia; the Elector of Bavaria; the Elector Palatine; the Swiss; the ecclesiastical electors; the Republic of Venice; the King of Naples and the King of Sardinia.[2]

46

The first of these conclusions, the one that has captured attention, is quickly demonstrated. After analysing the state of Europe, after noting that its elements of unity—its common history and culture, its closely integrated balance of power—could not withstand the stresses that lead to war, the *Extrait* asserted that there was but one escape. 'Once these sources of evil are recognised they indicate their own remedy, if any such exists. . . . There must be some power with sanctions to regulate and organise the movements of its members in order to give common interests and mutual engagements the degree of solidity which they could not assume by themselves.' 'If there is any means of getting rid of these dangerous contradictions it can only be by a confederative form of government which, uniting nations by bonds similar to those which unite individuals, submits them all equally to the authority of the laws.' 'The confederation must embrace all the important Powers in its membership; it must have a Legislative Body, with powers to pass laws and ordinances binding upon all its members; it must have a coercive force capable of compelling every state to obey its common resolves whether in the way of command or of prohibition; finally it must be strong and firm enough to make it impossible for any member to withdraw at his own pleasure the moment he conceives his private interest to clash with that of the whole body.'³ Nor was this a mere copying of Saint-Pierre. Rousseau meant what he said when he added in the opening words of the *Jugement* that 'if ever a moral truth was demonstrated, it seems to me it is the general and special utility of this project. . . . Realise [Saint-Pierre's] European Commonwealth for a single day, and the experience would be enough to make it last for ever.'⁴

That he did not believe it could be realised is clear even in the *Extrait*. Apart from the qualifications contained in the above quotations there is its dedication: 'Would that we soon might see it [Saint-Pierre's plan] restored among the Powers! Amongst authors it has never been known, and nowadays it is too much to expect'. The same attitude is revealed in several asides. Speaking of Saint-Pierre: 'I incline to think that the illusions of a truly human heart, whose zeal takes all things as possible, are to be preferred to that sour and repellent reason whose indifference to the public good is always the chief obstacle to every endeavour to promote it.'*⁵ If Saint-Pierre's

---

* This recalls, and also contradicts, another (unpublished) comment of his on Saint-

method had been attempted by 'the German Body, the Swiss League and the States General', but in few other cases and never on a wider scale, 'it is because the best schemes never work out exactly as they were supposed, and because, in politics as in morals, the growth of our knowledge reveals only the vast extent of our woes'.[7] After listing all the advantages that would accrue from a federation: 'If in spite of all this, this project is not carried into execution, it is not because it is chimerical, it is because men are crazy and because to be sane in the midst of madmen is a sort of folly.'[8]

These doubts became positive conclusions in the *Jugement*. Rousseau began this by repeating, as he had already repeated in the *Extrait*, Saint-Pierre's distinction between real interests, which would be met in a confederation for perpetual peace, and apparent interests, which supported a continuation of absolute independence for each state.[9] But he at once added that those same Princes who would defend a federation 'with all their might if it existed, would all the same oppose its introduction'.[10] There was 'nothing impossible in the project except that it should be adopted by these men'.[11] Their view of their internal as well as of their external interests made this so. 'Anyone can see that by the establishment of the European Diet the government of each state is fixed as rigidly as its frontiers, and that no prince can be guaranteed against the revolt of his subjects unless at the same time the subjects are guaranteed against the tyranny of the prince.... Is there a single sovereign in the world who ... would bear without indignation the mere idea of seeing himself forced to be just, not only to foreigners, but even to his own subjects?'[12] As for international rivalries, 'although it is certain that the advantages which should result from a general and perpetual peace would be great, yet, being common to all, they would be realized by none, seeing that such advantages are only felt by contrast, and [as] ... exclusive gains'.[13]

So much was this so that Rousseau at last proceeded to an even more sombre judgement. 'We are not to assume with the Abbé ..., even given the goodwill that we shall never find either in the prince or his ministers, that it would be easy to find a favourable moment to put this scheme into operation, for it would be necessary ... that

Pierre: 'C'était un homme très sage, s'il n'eût eu la folie de la raison. Il semblait ignorer que les princes, comme les autres hommes, ne se mènent que par leurs passions, et ne raisonnent que pour justifier les sottises qu'elles leur font faire.'[6]

the sum of private interests should not outweigh the common interest. . . . Now this demands a concurrence of wisdom in so many heads and a fortuitous concurrence of so many interests such as chance can hardly be expected to bring out. But in default of such an agreement the only thing left is force . . . and instead of writing books you will have to raise troops.'[14]

In this last remark we reach at last the true ground for the apparent inconsistency between the *Extrait* and the *Jugement*, and between the *Jugement's* opening words—the assertion of the moral truth of 'the general and special utility' of the proposal—and its final dismissal of the proposal as 'an absurd dream'.[15] It is a serious weakness of the *Jugement* that, putting so much emphasis on the difference between the real and apparent interests of states and enlarging on the wickedness of princes and ministers, it often gives the impression that Rousseau regarded the folly and avarice of governments as the main obstacle to the execution of the federal plan. This was not so. His real opinion was that it would be utopian 'even given the goodwill that we shall never find either in the prince or his ministers', as stated in the *Jugement* itself. If there is any doubt about this, it can be removed by reference to Rousseau's other writings of the same date, some of which easily surpass the *Jugement* in power of analysis.

The most important of these writings for this purpose is *L'État de Guerre* or *Que l'État de Guerre naît de l'État Social* (*c.* 1755). In this he attacked Hobbes for deducing the nature of man in the primitive state from the nature of man in the civil state, and Grotius for basing the origins of the state and the rights of war on the fact that men will sell their freedom to save their lives. His reply was that by nature man is timid, solitary and peaceful, and that the fact that he might sell his freedom to preserve his life has no bearing on the question of his right to do so. These two positions, which much preoccupied Rousseau,[16] were the key to his analysis of the origins and the rights of war. Montesquieu had said that as soon as man enters into a society he loses the sense of his weakness, equality ceases, and then commences the state of war.[17] Rousseau developed Montesquieu's view. There can be no war between man and man, not even between band and band, either in the state of nature or in the civil state, but only violence and murder. War presupposes the existence of organised communities: 'all the horrors of war derive from the very precautions which men take to prevent it'—from creation of the state. Accordingly states fight, or ought to fight, not to destroy life or to seize territory or slaves, but to vindicate their rights against other states. The sole end of war is, or ought to be, to preserve the existence and assert the equality of the state against other states. The state which launches a war for any other object is assailing a right which is the foundation of its being. The state which uses barbaric methods in war is confusing the body politic, the sole legitimate object of hostility, with the individuals who compose it. In either case there is a violation of the first principles on which the state rests—of its autonomy in the one case, of its corporate structure in the other.[18]

It might be objected that this has no bearing on the question of the possibility of eliminating war, that since Rousseau was discussing in *L'État de Guerre* the rights and the waging of war—what, as he said himself, made war legitimate, not what made it an advantage or a disadvantage to those who waged it[19]—he necessarily assumed its existence. But he used the same analysis to discuss this wider problem. He asked the question: 'Since each of these states, these bodies, is equally solidly based, how is it possible that they ever collide? Should not their very constitution maintain them in a condition of perpetual peace?'[20] And what was his answer? That just as war presupposes the existence of the state, so the existence of the state presupposes the existence of a state of war.

He based this argument, for which he was much indebted to Montesquieu,[21] on a brilliant analysis of international relations. 'The state, being an artificial body', he wrote, 'is not limited in any way. . . . It can always increase; it always feels itself weak if there is another that is stronger. Its security and preservation demand that it make itself more powerful than its neighbours. It can increase, nourish and exercise its power only at their expense. . . . While the inequality of man has natural limits that between societies can grow without cease, until one absorbs all the others.' On the other hand, there has always been the counteraction of other states. 'The formation of the first society necessarily led to the formation of all the others. It was necessary to join it or to unite in order to resist it. It was necessary to imitate it or else be engulfed by it.' Similarly there will always be international rivalry. 'Because the grandeur of the state is purely relative it is forced to compare itself with that of the others. . . . It is in vain that it wishes to keep itself to itself; it becomes small or great, weak or strong, according to whether its neighbour expands or contracts, becomes stronger or declines.' 'A thousand writers have dared to say that the body politic is without passion and that there is no reason of state except reason itself. As if one did not see, on the contrary, that the essence of a society consists in the activity of its members and that a state without movement would be nothing but a corpse.'

The conclusion is clear. 'The chief thing I notice is a patent contradiction in the condition of the human race. . . . Between man and man we live in the condition of the civil state, subjected to laws; between people and people we enjoy natural liberty, which makes the situation worse. Living at the same time in the social order and in the state of nature, we suffer from the inconveniences of both without finding security in either. . . .' 'We see men united by artificial bonds, but united to destroy each other; and all the horrors of war take birth from the precautions they have taken in order to prevent them.' 'War is born of peace, or at least of the precautions which men have taken for the purpose of achieving durable peace.' War properly so-called, the legal as opposed to the natural expression of the state's necessary disposition to destroy the enemy state, was legitimate only if it were properly declared and properly waged. But a permanent state of war was the natural expression of this disposition. It did not necessarily show itself in war, ill will being enough to constitute hostility, but a state of war was 'natural between the Powers'.[22] In this at least he adhered to Hobbes's view that 'the state of commonwealths considered in themselves is natural, that is to say hostile'.[23]

In this analysis there is little room for the selfish and misguided machinations of governments: it professes to explain the behaviour of all states, good and bad. Not for nothing did Rousseau admit elsewhere that 'it is not impossible that a Republic, though in itself well-governed, should enter upon an unjust war'; and that the particular will of a state that was perfectly good for itself might nevertheless provoke the resistance of other states.[24] It supposes that the international problem will remain even if all states are good. Rousseau distinguished as much as any man between states as they were and states as they ought to be. He insisted that there was no necessary coincidence between the interests of a state and the actions of its government, and often dilated—as in the *Jugement*—on the extent to which the governments of his day were motivated by vanity and greed. But he still believed that even a world composed of good states would be a world in a state of war. So long as the particular wills of individual states were not sublimated in such a way as to eliminate an international system altogether, it was true but irrelevant that a state of war was the consequence of men's irrationality and imperfection. Capricious acts were the immediate causes of wars but in the international system it was necessary, not accidental, that such acts should occur.[25]

By the same analysis it was true but irrelevant that a federal organisation between states was the means of avoiding these acts and of preserving perpetual peace. It has been said of Rousseau's *Discours sur l'Inégalité* (1755) that it was not so much a call to action as the hopeless voice of a prophet and a moralist, not so much a theory of Political Right as a fatalistic denunciation of the evils inseparable from civil society. Voltaire criticised it on the ground that the only logical deduction to be drawn from it was a return to the state of nature.[26] In the field of international relations almost exactly the same may be said of the theory Rousseau developed in the *État de Guerre* and applied, without adequate explanation, in the *Jugement*. Since it was not possible for the states to return to the state of nature —they were already in it—the only deduction to be drawn was the one he drew. Since the international struggle was the automatic consequence of the international system nothing less than a federation of all states would eliminate war; but nothing less than the international system prevented the conclusion of a federation.

This, not his poor opinion of princes and governments, is the key to Rousseau's inconsistency in both advocating federation and dismissing it. The inconsistency followed from his views on the international problem, and it is not the case, as is often supposed,[27] that Rousseau adhered to the federal solution after studying its implications. Even less may we suppose that he would have adhered to it if he had studied its implications. In Rousseau's writings on perpetual peace there is, indeed, this second inconsistency: his conception of the international state of nature, which led him to assert that the only solution to the problem of the international anarchy was impracticable, also led him to suppose that the only solution was federation when this ran counter to all his thought on the nature of the state. It was for this reason that he laid federation aside without much

regret. 'There is no prospect of federative leagues being established'
—so he concluded the *Jugement*—'otherwise than by revolutiọn, and
on this assumption which of us would venture to say whether this
European League is more to be desired than feared? It might perhaps
do more harm all of a sudden than it could prevent for centuries.'[28]

Within eighteen months of writing the *Discours sur L'Inégalité*, with
its theory of individual rights that could only mean the advocacy of
a return to the state of nature, he was writing the *Économie Politique*
—the negation of individualism and the real beginning of his political
thought on the nature of the state.[29] He never wrote the equivalent
of the *Économie Politique* in international theory, the counterpart to or
the refinement of the view he applied in the *Jugement*. Draft chapters
on confederation or federation were written but mislaid. The *Contrat
Social*, conceived as part of a larger design, concluded with these
words: 'Having thus laid down the true principles of political right,
and striven to establish the State on a durable foundation, I have
now but to strengthen it on the side of its relations with other
powers. . . . But all this forms a new field which is too vast for my
limited vision. It is better that I confine myself to things nearer at
hand.' We can only guess what his conclusions would have been if
he had proceeded. But the Rousseau that is revealed in all his
writings after 1756 could hardly have clung to the most strict federal
solution of the international problem that he had outlined in the
Extrait and dismissed in the *Jugement*.

We have called it a federal solution. Rousseau usually used the
word 'confederation' when discussing it. But for the fact that the
distinction between confederal and federal forms was still not clearly
understood in his day, he would have found some difficulty in doing
so. The organisation which in the *Extrait* he regarded as the minimum safeguard against war was a federation in every respect. Unlike
the subsequent confederal League of Nations—like the United States
of America rather than the Arıerica of the Articles of Confederation
that had preceded it—Rousseau's League, which is merely a summary of Saint-Pierre's proposals, was to permit no right of secession
and was to have the power of intervening in the internal affairs of
member states. It was to guarantee not only the existing territories of
member states, but also the sovereigns themselves 'alike against he
ambition of irresponsible and iniquitous Pretenders and the revolts of
rebellious subjects'. It was not only to force members to be just and

pacific in the relations towards each other but was to have a central military arm for that purpose.[30] It has been suggested, and it is not impossible, that he omitted some of Saint-Pierre's fundamental proposals (those preserving the *status quo*) from this summary because of his lack of sympathy with them, rather than merely from the wish to make Saint-Pierre's project more readable.[31] Whatever the truth on this score, the proposals retained in the summary cannot be squared with a passage of the *Jugement* in which he also followed Saint-Pierre: 'as to the degree of dependence which each one will be under to the Common Tribunal, it is very clear that it will diminish none of the rights of sovereignty, but on the contrary will strengthen them. . . . The princes will accordingly be none the less absolute and their crowns will be all the more secure. . . .'[32]

Still less can they be squared with a passage from *Émile* (1762). In this, after summarising the analysis of the international problem which he had made in *L'Etat de Guerre*, Rousseau outlined what his object would have been if he had developed his views on federation. 'We shall examine the kind of remedy that men have sought against these evils in Leagues and Federations which, leaving each state master in its own home, arm it against all unjust aggression from without. We shall enquire what are the means of establishing a good form of federal association, what can give it permanence, and how far we can extend the rights of the Federation without trenching on those of sovereignty.'[33] And not only these passages but all Rousseau's writings go to show that if he had examined this problem he would have retreated from Saint-Pierre's position.

Much as he would have liked to use federation to do for the community of all the states what the social contract had already done for the individual by creating the state, he would have run up against that passionate conviction of the superiority of the small state and the necessity of preserving and strengthening it—even of multiplying it—which was, by his own account,[34] the inspiration of all his moral and political writings. It was this conviction which made the *Contrat Social* a key document in the transition of European thought from the acceptance of natural law to the idealisation of the national state and which, more than that, made it in the end an idealisation of Plato's *Polis*. 'That, and not a "return to nature" is the real return of Rousseau.'[35] It was the same conviction which led him, when his own Genevan countrymen were faced with the choice of submission or mediation, to recognise that the latter would mean a surrender of the sovereignty which was theirs of right, and to refuse to advise them to accept it.[36] It was this which induced him to regret that in his own day patriotism was being lost in a welter of sub-national and trans-national interests to the extent that 'there are today no longer Frenchmen, Germans, Spaniards, Englishmen . . . ; there are only Europeans'.[37] Rousseau was the apostle not only of the small state but of modern nationalism.[38] There never was an internationalist who was a more fervent nationalist.

If he had examined the problem, defined by himself as that of uniting 'the external strength of a great nation with the free discipline, the healthy order, of a small one', it is doubtful whether he would have found a solution. Well might he say that 'the subject was wholly untouched, and the first principles of it still to ascertain'.[39] If he had found a solution it would have involved, we can be sure from his writings on Poland, not the federal proposal of the *Extrait*, but the breakdown of Europe's existing states into federal sub-states on the basis of local rule before the re-association of the sub-states in a confederation of Europe on the model of Switzerland.[40] In the *Contrat Social* he argued that the ideal state, based on the sovereignty of the generality of the citizens, could only be realised in the large states of his day by the adoption of a movable metropolis and of internal federation.[41]

In the *Extrait* and the *Jugement* he did not attempt to argue this alternative solution. After urging that Saint-Pierre's solution was the only solution, he abandoned it without putting any other proposal in its place. But he also left it there as an ideal laid up in heaven which men could never attain—towards which, indeed, they could never hope to make progress—but towards which men should strive. He did this despite the fact that it was not an ideal to which he would have subscribed on reflection. He did it, also, despite the fact that, even in these early essays, his sense of the progress that men had already made in history was highly developed. His inconclusiveness and defeatism were, indeed, the result of his failure to reconcile his historical arguments with the initial assumptions of his moral and political philosophy.

This was a failure that ran through all his works. In the *Contrat Social* his historical sense brought him close to realising that the society of a nation was the result of historical evolution and not the result of a contract. It did not take him far enough to enable him to distinguish clearly between the state, which may be conceived of as based on a contract, and society which cannot be so conceived. All the confusion in that work accordingly arose, on the basis of the confusion of state and society, from his disposition to argue at some times that society was the result of a contract, of the wilful use of art and contrivance, and at others that it was the product of long historical growth.[42] As the book proceeded his historical sense increasingly led him to substitute slow growth and long subjection to the discipline of law and government for Locke's Natural Law or Reason as the source of the social contract in the state, to leave aside the consideration of right and qualify his abstract arguments with the recognition that considerations of circumstance, expediency, inherited character, racial tradition—of history—shape and control governments. It was this same bent which put him almost wholly under the influence of Montesquieu, rather than of Plato and Locke, in his later works on politics. Despite the strong bias in the opposite direction which this pupil of Plato and Locke had to overcome, despite the general prejudice of his time against Montesquieu and the historical approach, all his political writings after the *Contrat*—the *Lettres écrites de la Montagne*, the *Projet de Constitution pour la Corse*, the *Considérations sur le Gouvernement de Pologne*—were nothing but the application of this approach, a full acceptance of the historical method.

Yet the two influences were never reconciled, were entangled rather than harmonised, because he never ceased to insist that what has been or what is is no test of what ought to be—because he remained a moralist as well as a political thinker. In the *Contrat Social* he hesitated between the contract and historical growth, and used the word 'natural' throughout the book in two different senses, to mark either the early savage state or the final stage when the consummation would be reached. In the later works he could assert equally firmly both the absolute validity of the sovereignty of the people and the absolute impossibility of achieving this ideal in many communities, and could do so without betraying a suspicion that the one argument runs counter to the other.[43]

What was true of the later writings was true of the early works, the *Extrait* and the *Jugement*. His initial assumption that the international state of nature was comparable with the state of nature that preceded the civil state led him to the conclusion that the solution was the same in the one case as in the other. Nothing but international government, the federal bond, could do for states what the social contract had done for the individual. From this conclusion he never wavered. Yet he himself confuted it—and thus ended by asserting that the only solution was utopian—in two most powerful ways. In the first place, as we have seen, he asserted that the behaviour of the state in the state of nature was *not* the same as the behaviour of the individual must be supposed to have been in his: the state was already an artificial creation and international relations differed from the civil state of nature on account of that fact. In the second place, just as he urged in later works that the state was both the artificial product of a contract and the natural result of historical development, so in these early essays he maintained his initial assumption about the solution to the international state of nature even though it conflicted with his feeling that the system of relations between states was a product of history which was not likely to be influenced—still less to be perfected—by artificial, contractual means.

The resulting confusion is revealed in the inconsistent use he made of historical arguments in the two essays. In the *Extrait* a perceptive historical argument informed the introduction with which he prefaced his summary of the details of Saint-Pierre's scheme. This showed an awareness of the evolution of European international relations, a feeling for Europe as a product of history and not merely as a geographical expression, that was not surpassed, if it was equalled, by anything written by Montesquieu, Voltaire or Hume. It recognised that 'all the European Powers form among themselves a sort of system which unites them by the same religion, the same international law, by customs, literature, commerce, and by a kind of balance of power . . . which, without anyone's studying actually to preserve it, would nevertheless not be quite so easy to disturb as many believe', and 'from which none of the peoples who compose it can withdraw without at once causing trouble'.[44] Rousseau knew that 'this society of nations has not always existed in Europe'. He knew that 'the political organisation of this part of the world is to a certain extent the work of nature'. 'Let us not imagine that this boasted balance of power has been achieved by anyone . . . ; it cer-

tainly exists . . . and can well maintain itself without outside interference. If it should be broken on one side for a moment it would
soon establish itself on another, so that, if the princes who are accused
of aspiring to universal monarchy did really aspire to it, they showed
more ambition than wit. . . . The traditions of Europe make such
a policy a vain one . . . and time soon makes good the violent accidents of fortune, if not for each particular prince, at least for the
general balance of power.'[45]

Yet in the remainder of the *Extrait* the sense of history was entirely
subordinated to his moral ideas. The former brought him close to
realizing that an international system already existed, with its own
rules, the product of historical evolution. The latter left him acutely
aware that this system, if it guaranteed some balance, was far from
guaranteeing peace. 'The pretended brotherhood of the nations . . .
seems nothing but a term of derision'; 'if the present system is founded
on a rock, it is all the more on that account exposed to storms . . .
which, without upsetting [its members] altogether, keep them in a
constant state of unrest.'[46] He therefore used the historical introduction to justify Saint-Pierre. He exaggerated the contemporary 'equal
distribution of force' in order to 'deduce a conclusion of importance
to the project of establishing a general league'. He argued, exactly
as Saint-Pierre had argued, that since a successful league must be
based on stability and the recognition that aggression was pointless,
the existing balance of power and Europe's existing 'primitive ties',
which 'make the society harmful, at the same time render it easy to
perfect', to change the state of war into a perpetual peace.[47] So much
did he emphasise this point that he felt it necessary to meet an objection. 'It must not be objected here that I prove too much, in that if
things were as I represent them, everyone having a genuine interest in
not going to war . . ., peace would in the end establish itself and last
for ever without any confederation. This would be extremely bad
reasoning in the present state of things.'[48] Yet it was the reasoning
to which his historical introduction had pointed.

In the second and longer half of the *Jugement*, which was devoted
to an analysis of Sully's 'Grand Design', he was at first inclined to
use the reputation of Henry IV in the same way—as a justification
for the proposals of Saint-Pierre. But in this case he quickly shifted
his ground, advancing an acute historical assessment of the motives
of Henry IV to confirm the dismissal of the federation solution which

he had already made with the theoretical arguments borrowed from *L'État de Guerre*. As is clear from the dedication to the *Extrait*, he accepted Sully's attribution of the Grand Design to Henry IV. In the *Jugement* he first used this acceptance 'to prove that the project ... is not chimerical'. 'Henry IV was not a fool nor Sully a visionary.' 'The death of this good king plunged Europe again into everlasting wars, of which it can no longer hope to see the end.' But 'when another Henry IV and Sully appear Perpetual Peace will come back again as a reasonable project'.[49] On the other hand he went on to argue that their project had attracted supporters because it was 'prompted ... by the secret hope of humbling a formidable enemy'. It had 'acquired ... a momentum which it could hardly have drawn from the incentive of the common good. . . . What was it . . . that was furthering this general movement? Was it Perpetual Peace? . . . Was it the public interest? The Abbé . . . might have supposed so. But in reality they were all working only from the point of view of their own private ... interest in humiliating a proud power which wanted to dominate them all.' His final conclusion was not that the project would become feasible again when another great leader appeared. It was that, 'while we admire so fair a scheme, let us console ourselves for the fact that it was not carried into execution by the reflection that it could only have been done by violent means which would have staggered humanity'.[50]

It was this twist in the historical argument that led him to the note of consolation in which the *Jugement* ended. 'There is no prospect of federative leagues being established otherwise than by revolution, and on this assumption which of us would venture to say whether the European League is more to be desired than feared.' But if he made a better use of his sense of history in this second essay he did not let it go so far as to induce him to retract the ideal.

His position in relation to international relations, as this was developed in the *Extrait* and the *Jugement*, was accordingly similar to his later opinion of the state. In the *Contrat Social*, as a result of the conflict between his views as a moralist and his recognition that society was essentially the product of circumstance and history, the ideal state—the society that would fulfil the fundamental principles he deduced from his version of the social contract—became no more than an ideal laid up in heaven.[51] In the *Jugement* the European commonwealth, the means to perpetual peace, became an ideal laid up in heaven, unattainable, for essentially the same reasons. He urged it because as a moralist he wanted to urge a solution. He dismissed it as utopian not only because his own theory of international relations, unlike Saint-Pierre's solution to the international problem, was based on the difference between the natural individual and the artificial state, but also because he recognized—again unlike Saint-Pierre—that the international system was the product of history and circumstance and not likely to be changed by artificial means. If he had omitted the notion of contract from the *Contrat Social*, and concentrated on the slow historical growth of the state, he could have avoided the inconsistency of basing a collectivist structure for the ideal state upon a foundation of individualism. In the essays on international peace he could have avoided equally glaring inconsistencies—the inconsistency of both advocating and dismissing the federal solution; the inconsistency of advocating the kind of international government against which all his principles rebelled—if he has been prepared to abandon the international equivalent of the contract which he had taken over from Saint-Pierre but which did not even stand up to his own views. But as a moralist he could no more abandon this solution for some other, as opposed to confessing its impracticability in the world as it is, than he could omit the contract from the *Contrat Social*.

It was not his moral position, as such, so much as the conflict between this and his sense of history that closed Rousseau's eyes to all ideas of progress. What had this effect was the fact that he gave such emphasis both to the moral position and to the historical approach that instead of being integrated in his thought they cancelled each other out. It has been said with truth that while the moral position may conflict with a belief in historical growth—the true philosophy of the progressive—and be an obstacle to belief in political progress, those who cling to it may often be encouraged to look for reform and progress, just as those who emphasise the idea of growth may have only too much historical sense and be opposed to new growth.[52] This was not so in Rousseau's case, the conflict was too great. It was true of Kant. He also retained a moral position. But this did not prevent him from emphasising that the behaviour of the individual and the state in their respective states of nature was not the same; from seeing that, if it is natural for the individual to need one artificial state, it is not natural for him to accept two; from questioning, therefore, the assumption that the only solution to the international problem was that which had been applied to the individual's state of nature; from realising that the international system, which was 'the work of nature', would go on evolving by the light of nature—that what was in 'a constant state of unrest' might be tempered and improved, if it could be improved at all, by nothing but further unrest.

CHAPTER 4

KANT

IMMANUEL KANT expounded his views in the *Idea for a Universal History* (1784) and, more elaborately, in *Thoughts on Perpetual Peace* (1795). He took over Rousseau's conception of the international state of nature: it was 'a state of war which constantly threatens if it is not actually in progress' and in which the true honour of the state was assumed to consist in 'the continual increase of power by any and every means'. Like Rousseau and earlier writers he accordingly believed that 'the state of peace must be *founded*'[1]. But he did not suppose that the way out of the predicament was the merger of the separate states. On the contrary, he insisted on the necessary difference between the problems posed by the civil and international states of nature. For him, as for Spinoza[2] a century before, individuals must combine to survive but states, by their very nature, could not. It was no more logical to hope to solve the international problem by the supersession of the states than it would have been logical to try to end the civil state of nature by the abolition of individuals.

This was a dominant theme in *Perpetual Peace*. It was stated explicitly in the second section of the essay where Kant explained 'the second definitive article of perpetual peace'—the article by which 'the law of nations should be based upon a *federalism* of free states'. 'Nations', this began, 'may be considered like individual men which hurt each other in the state of nature. Therefore each . . . may demand and should demand of the others to enter with him into a constitution similar to a civil one. . . . This would be a *Union of Nations* (Völkerbund) which would not necessarily have to be a *state of nations* (Völkerstaat).' Indeed, 'a state of nations contains a contradiction . . . ; many nations would, in a single state, constitute only one nation, which is contradictory since we are here considering the rights of the nations towards each other as long as they constitute different states and are not joined together into one.' We might think that 'civilised peoples (each united in a state) would hasten to get away from' the international state of nature by coalescing. The fact is that they do not: 'each *state* insists upon seeing the essence of its sovereignty in this, that it is not subject to any external coercion.' It might be argued that they should be forced to coalesce; but 'it cannot be maintained that states under the law of nations are subject to the same rule as individual men in the lawless state of nature: that they ought to leave this state. For states have internally a legal constitution conceived in terms of their own legal norms and hence have outgrown the coercion of others who might desire to put them under . . . their own legal norms'.

Then again: 'It is possible to imagine a people saying, "There shall be no war amongst us, for we want to form a state, i.e. to establish for ourselves a supreme legislative, executive and judicial power...." But if this state says, "There shall not be war between myself and other states, although I do not recognize a supreme legislative authority which secures my right for me ...", it is not easy to comprehend upon what ground it should place its confidence in its right unless it be a substitute for the social contract, namely a free federation. And if authority is to be conceived in such terms reason must necessarily connect such a federation with the concept of the law of nations.'[3]

In view of this analysis it is not surprising that this section of the essay concluded with a statement of the impracticability of world government. 'For states in their relation to each other there cannot according to reason be any other way to avoid the lawless condition which contains nothing but war than to give up (just like individual men) their wild and lawless freedom, to accept public and enforceable laws, and thus to form a world state of all nations. . . . But states do not want this, as not in keeping with their idea of a law of nations, and thus they reject in fact what is true in theory. Therefore, unless all is lost, the positive idea of a *world republic* must be replaced by the negative substitute of a union of nations which maintains itself, prevents wars and steadily expands.'[4]

Far from reaching this conclusion in any spirit of regret or despair at the conduct of states, far from merely accepting the continuing independence of states as inescapable, Kant insisted on it as morally right. Just as he derived the right to freedom of the individual from the dictates of a moral law, so he derived the right to freedom of the state—the route to and the guarantee of the freedom of the individual —from the same moral law. This emphasis was clear in the first section of the book, that which laid down 'the preliminary articles of perpetual peace between states'. These articles not only assumed the autonomy of the state but sought to strengthen it. They read as follows: '1. No treaty of peace shall be held to be such, which is made with the secret reservation of the material for a future war. . . . 2. No state having an independent existence, whether it be small or great, may be acquired by another state, through inheritance, exchange, purchase or gift. . . . 3. Standing armies shall gradually disappear. . . . 4. No debts shall be contracted in connection with the foreign affairs of the state . . . either from without or from within the state. . . . 5. No state shall interfere by force in the constitution and government of another state. . . . 6. No state at war with another shall permit such acts of warfare as must make mutual confidence impossible in time of future peace: such as the employment of assassins . . . the instigation of treason . . . etc.'[5]

The same purpose is clearer still in Kant's comments on the preliminary articles. 'A state', reads the explanation of the second preliminary article, 'is not a possession like the soil. . . . It is a society of men which no one but themselves is called on to command or dispose of. Since, like a tree, such a state has its own roots, to incorporate it as a graft into another state is to take away its existence as a moral person and to make of it a thing.' This would be contradictory to 'the idea of the original contract, without which no right over a people can even be conceived'. Kant's comments on preliminary article 5 were in the same vein. No state should interfere by force in the internal affairs of another because such interference was 'trespass on the rights of an independent people' and 'an actual offence which . . . would tend to render the autonomy of all states insecure'. Similarly the explanation of the third preliminary article demanded the abolition of standing armies because they 'threaten other states with war' and were 'the cause of wars of aggression', but argued that 'the case is entirely different where the citizens of a state voluntarily drill themselves and their fatherland against attacks from without'. This did not lead to war and, unlike the hiring of men as machines in the hands of the state, it was not contrary to the rights of humanity.[6]

In a concluding paragraph to the preliminary articles, Kant even demanded that states which had lost their independence should have it restored. This distinguished between those preliminary articles which were 'valid without consideration of circumstances' and should be introduced at once (articles 1, 5 and 6) and those which, 'though not meant to permit exception from the rule of law, yet allow for a good deal of subjective discretion in respect to their application'—'which permit delay in execution without the purpose being lost sight of'. The latter included article 2 ('no state having an independent existence . . . may be acquired by another state . . .') which now received a further gloss. 'The restitution . . . to certain states of the freedom of which they have been deprived, contrary to our second article, must not be indefinitely put off. The delay is not meant to prevent restitution, but to avoid undue haste which might be contrary to the intrinsic purpose. For the prohibition laid down by the article relates only to the mode of acquisition, which is not to be allowed to continue, but it does not relate to the present state of possessions. This present state, though not providing the needed just title, yet was held to be legitimate at the time of the supposed acquisition, according to the then current public opinion.'[7] This can have meant only one thing. In the course of implementing article 2 there would be conflict between actual possession, on which Saint-Pierre was prepared to rest but which Kant could not allow, and justice in terms of the conception of the state which Kant had taken over from Rousseau. But this conception of the state allowed it to be the product of history as well as of rights, and too much haste in implementing the article might be contrary to the intrinsic purpose of achieving peace on the basis of justice.

Even more remarkable for its emphasis on the independence of the state was another of the definitive articles—the third—in which Kant introduced the notion of 'the Cosmopolitan or World law'. It is not for nothing that generations of commentators have been puzzled by the title Kant gave to this article ('The Cosmopolitan or World law shall be limited to conditions of a universal hospitality'). They have had difficulty in reconciling it with their assumption that he advocated the merger of states. It asserted the right of all men to seek their freedom in as many separate states as natural conditions required—and especially in those backward areas where the state had not yet developed. '*Hospitality* (good neighbourliness) means the right of the foreigner not to be treated with hostility when he arrives on the soil of another'—but 'the native may reject the foreigner if it can be done without his perishing'; 'it is not the right of becoming a permanent inhabitant which the foreigner may request'; 'the right of hospitality, of foreign guests, does not extend further than to the

65

conditions which enable them to attempt the developing of intercourse with the old inhabitants.' Abuse of this limit had led the
European countries to claim the right of conquest overseas. Observance of this limit by the World law was, on the other hand, the way
by which 'remote parts of the world can enter into relationships
which eventually become public and legal and thereby may bring
mankind ever nearer to an eventual world constitution'.[8]

It is in the light of these remarks that we must now establish what
was Kant's conception of the 'federalism of free states' or the 'union
of nations' or 'the free federation' or 'federal union'—of these various
phrases he used to describe 'the eventual world constitution' he had
in mind. Everybody knows that he did not advocate world government or the complete but less universal merger of states: he explicitly
rejects this solution. But because of his use of such phrases most
people firmly believe that he advocated international federation in
our modern sense of the term as the only alternative—provided only
that it was entered into voluntarily.[9] This is not the case. He derived
these phrases from the word *foedus* and used that to mean 'treaty',
which is what it still means. Like the Founding Fathers when they
constructed the American Constitution, he was envisaging the replacement of the existing imperfect, customary international law by
a structure of international society based on a treaty between independent states.

Far from regarding voluntary federation as the only alternative to
world government on account of his objection to force—this is the
standard assumption—he was as much opposed to it as to world
government because of his insistence that the state, like the individual,
could not part with its freedom. The individual must impose the state
on himself in order to remain free. In the same way 'free federation'
for Kant was what the state must impose on itself *while remaining free.*
The prospect held out by *Perpetual Peace* was that, whatever league
or international organisation states might come to develop among
themselves, it would not be that which would preserve the peace, but
their voluntary acceptance as continuing independent nations of a
rule of law that was not backed by international organisation or
physical force. Rousseau had got into difficulties by embracing an
international solution which conflicted with his attachment to the
freedom of the state. Kant insisted that some other solution must

exist—that international peace must be based on and obtained through the freedom of the state—because he took the doctrine of state sovereignty and autonomy to its logical conclusion.

This is clearly established in the *Idea for a Universal History* no less than in *Perpetual Peace*. In the earlier work he had certainly deplored the tendency to ridicule Saint-Pierre's ideas. 'Even though this idea may seem utopian, however much it may be now laughed out of court as it was when advocated by the Abbé Saint-Pierre and Rousseau (perhaps because they believed the idea to be too near its realisation), it is the inevitable escape from the destitution to which human beings bring each other. This must force the states to the resolution (hard as it may seem) to which savage man was forced equally unwillingly, namely: to surrender his brutal freedom under a lawful [international] constitution.' He had, however, defined the ideal state as one whose freedom was limited 'so that it can co-exist with the freedom of other societies' and the lawful international constitution as one 'where every state, even the smallest, may expect its security and its right not from its own power or its own legal views, but alone from this great union of nations (*Foedus Amphictyonum*), from a united power and from decisions according to the united will of them all . And of this union of nations and this united power he had written with still greater precision. Because the need was for 'a counter-balance to the intrinsically healthy resistance of many states against each other, resulting from their freedom', the solution must be 'to introduce a united power which will give support to this balance'. This solution would not be 'without all *danger*, for we must see to it that neither the vitality of mankind goes to sleep nor those states destroy each other as they might without a principle of balance of *equality* in their mutual *effects* and *counter-effects*'.[10] Despite his approval of Saint-Pierre and Rousseau, these remarks constitute a complete departure from their organisational proposals, as does his more detailed exposition of these remarks in *Perpetual Peace*.

The section on the second definitive article of *Perpetual Peace*, after distinguishing between the civil and the international states of nature, stated (as already noted) that if an international authority is to be conceived of at all in circumstances in which there can be no inter-state authority then 'reason must necessarily connect such a federation with the concept of the law of nations'. By this Kant can have meant only that federation in the unavoidable absence of international authority could only take the form of an improved law of nations. In an appendix to the book he enlarged upon the second definitive article in words which confirm that he used such phrases as 'federation' or 'union of states' to describe what was essentially a rule of law between states which remained entirely independent. 'The basic condition of a [true] law of nations is that there should exist a *lawful state*. For without such a state there can be no public law. . . . We have seen above that a federative state among the states which has solely the purpose of eliminating war is the only *lawful* state which can be combined with the freedom of these states. Therefore the agreement of politics with morals is possible only within a federative union. . . .'[11] Kant's dilemma here was the same as that which had faced Rousseau. There could be no lawful international order without an international public law; it was not easy to see how there could be an international public law without an international political system; but there could not be an international public order in the normal sense of a political system. But while Rousseau was driven to abandon the problem at that point, Kant, despite his agreement with Rousseau that there could be no international political system, persisted in outlining the body of international public law which ought to exist and which could, in his view, do the work of an international political system.

This is further confirmed by the remainder of his comments under the second definitive article. After distinguishing the international state of nature from the civil state of nature this proceeded to distinguish the international law as it was from the rule of law as it should be. In doing so it recognised that, even under the rule of law as it should be, there would be no effective international authority, no sanctions except self-discipline, 'because we are here considering the right of nations towards each other as long as they constitute different states'. Under the existing law of nations states could seek their rights only by war. 'Reason . . . condemns war as a method of finding what is right.' Thus the law of nations must be altered. It cannot be altered 'without a treaty of the nations among themselves. Therefore there must exist *a union of a particular kind** which we may call the *pacific union*† (*foedus pacificum*) which would be distinguished from a peace treaty (*pactum pacis*) [in the existing situation] by the

* My italics   † Kant's italics

fact that the latter tries to end merely *one* war while the former tries to end *all* wars for ever. This union is not directed towards securing some additional power of the state, but merely towards maintaining and making secure the *freedom* of each state by and for itself and at the same time of the other states thus allied with each other. And yet [even in this union] these states will not subject themselves (as do men in the state of nature) to laws and to the enforcement of such laws.' More important still, Kant added a further qualification. 'Only such a union may under existing conditions stem the tide of the law-evading bellicose propensities in man, but unfortunately subject to the constant danger of their eruption.'[12]

In the light of this we may safely take 'the preliminary articles of perpetual peace between states' to be a statement of the law of nations as it ought to be—and thus of Kant's solution—and not, as has often been assumed, as a statement of the preliminary progress that must be made before the work of establishing peace could be begun. If the articles were called 'preliminary' it was because the whole of the essay was cast in the form of a treaty—with preliminary and definitive articles and a secret article—and for no other reason. If further confirmation were needed for this conclusion we could add that peace would unquestionably be established if the provisions laid down in the preliminary articles were ever accepted by all states. This cannot have escaped Kant's notice and it should not escape ours. Kant himself supplemented his statement of the preliminary articles by nothing except the conception of 'the Cosmopolitan or World law' which we have already discussed. At the end of his discussion of this under the third definitive article he called it 'the necessary completion of the unwritten code of constitutional and international law to make it a public law of mankind'.[13]

Kant's use of such phrases as 'federation' and 'a union of states' for the rule of law between states has confused many commentators about his solution to the international problem. They have assumed that he envisaged much more than he did: a federation or a union of states in the political sense. A few commentators, avoiding this mistake, have still been confused about Kant's statement of the process by which his solution—a perfected international law—might be attained. They have correctly appreciated his argument thus far: at the level of the state a political system permits individuals to behave ethically; a political system is not desirable or attainable internationally; yet peace is still to be expected between states. They have assumed that this argument was inconsistent or that Kant avoided inconsistency only by the feeble device of asserting that the rule of law could not reign until each state had achieved a good civil constitution.[14] By doing so they have missed Kant's point. He contented himself with the rule of law as a solution to the international dilemma because he judged the problem insoluble by other means. But it was because he judged the international problem to be insoluble by other means that he was confident that it would be solved in that way.

Once again the text of *Perpetual Peace* goes some way towards creating this second confusion. In another of its definitive articles—the first—it stated that 'the civil constitution in each state should be republican'. By republican Kant meant what we today mean by constitutional. Like Rousseau he distinguished between the form of rulership and the form of government. A republican constitution was founded on three principles. 'First the principle of the *freedom* of all members of a society as men. Second, the principle of the *dependence* of all upon a single legislation as subjects; and third, the principle of the *equality* of all as citizens. This is the only constitution which is derived from the idea of an original contract upon which all rightful legislation must be based.' 'Republicanism [as opposed to despotism] means the constitutional principle according to which the executive power is separated from the legislative power.' 'It requires the representative system.' It was easier to evolve such a constitution in a monarchy than in an aristocracy; impossible to achieve it in a democracy. These latter terms applied to the form of rulership; and the democratic form of rulership necessarily led to a despotic form of constitution 'because it establishes an executive power where all may decide regarding one and hence against one who does not agree—a contradiction which implies a contradiction of the general will with itself and with freedom.'[15]

Not content with listing this requirement as 'the first definitive article of the perpetual peace', it was in this section that Kant, for the first time in *Perpetual Peace*, raised the question whether perpetual peace was practicable. If the republican constitution was the only rightful one 'the question we are now facing is whether this is also the only one which can lead to perpetual peace'. His answer was that 'a republican constitution does offer the prospect of the desired purpose, and the reason is as follows: If . . . the consent of the citizens is required in order to decide whether there should be war or not, nothing is more natural than that those who would have to decide to undergo all the deprivations of war will very much hesitate to start such an evil game. . . . By contrast, under a constitution where the subject is not a citizen and which is therefore not republican, it is the easiest thing in the world to start a war . . . as a kind of amusement on very insignificant grounds. . . .'[16]

It is impossible to overlook the lameness of this conclusion. It is not merely that it destroys the force of the distinction which Kant had tried to draw between a republican form of constitution and a democratic form of government—since in a democracy if the majority is despotic, it is also the majority that undergoes all the deprivations. Far more serious is another weakness in the argument. By assuming that republican states will always act rightly it appears to overlook the dilemma which led Rousseau to dismiss perpetual peace as an absurd dream (the conclusion that without rigid international organisation, which was impracticable and undesirable, conflict and war will remain endemic even among good states), while repeating Rousseau's other argument that war is the sport of kings. If this were all that Kant had offered by way of solution we should have to conclude that, while achieving a powerful statement of the nature of the international problem, he had done nothing to suggest how it might be solved.

Later in the essay, however, as already noted, Kant did not overlook this dilemma. He insisted that 'the positive idea of world government must be replaced by the negative substitute of a union of nations'. He limited such a union of nations to the voluntary acceptance by separate states of a rule of law (both because of his view of the state and in the belief that 'only such a union may under existing circumstances stem the tide of the law-evading bellicose propensities of man'). But he also recognised that such a union would be 'unfortunately subject to the constant eruption' of those propensities. It was, moreover, at the point of this dilemma, where Rousseau's contribution to a solution ended, that Kant's real contribution began. His analysis of the process by which perpetual peace might be established was not contained in the first definitive article. He analysed what he thought would produce peace in 'the first addition' to the articles of *Perpetual Peace*, entitled 'On the guarantee of perpetual peace'. The republican civil constitution was there treated as a necessary condition of international peace but not as a guarantee or sufficient cause of it.

The central feature of 'the first addition' was this. Whereas Rousseau had abandoned hope when he had concluded that the independent state could not be constrained by international organisation, Kant deduced the feasibility of perpetual peace—and of its necessary condition, the development of constitutional government in each state—from the very fact that the state would not be constrained in this way. He substituted this prospect for Rousseau's despair essentially because he imagined a gradual and historical process in place of the earlier mechanistic and organisational proposals to which Rousseau had remained attached in spite of his sense of history. At the same time his confidence, like his analysis, was of an entirely different order from that which had inspired Rousseau's predecessors. Because he shared all Rousseau's sense of the importance of the moral element in politics he was able to surmount the fatalism to which rationalism had led other men—Hobbes and Spinoza, for example— as effectively as he surmounted Rousseau's defeatism. But partly because of his philosophy of history and partly because he also shared Rousseau's feeling for the irrational element in politics he equally avoided the shallow confidence of men like Penn and Saint-Pierre. His views on perpetual peace sprang, in fact, from a political philosophy which combined the historical sense, the moral element in politics and the irrational element in man in a new and powerful way.

Kant's philosophy—to emphasise only those aspects of it that are essential for his view of international politics—drew a distinction between the mechanical and the teleological processes in history. Nature, the world of phenomena, was a purely mechanical system; in order to understand its operation it was necessary to postulate an end, a purpose. The end could not be derived from the course of history, from empirical data, from nature itself, but only from the existence of reason and morality in man. As for the relationship between the two processes—that of nature on the one hand and, on the other, that in the realm of moral obligations which instructs men to pursue what seems to them right regardless of their reluctance to pursue it—they must converge. The end was not derivable from nature, which had its own mechanical design; but the design of nature, working in history, could work only to that end. On the other hand, it was not because men willingly used their reason to guide it there that it worked to that end. It did so because the very opposition which the mechanical process of nature set up to the dictates of the moral process forced irrational men to use their reason.

The convergence of the design of nature and the dictates of the moral duty in man, that convergence arising from their conflict, was the essence of the novel unilinear concept of history as continuous progress towards an end which was expounded in his *Idea for a Universal History*.[17] Men do not act like animals, merely according to instinct. They do not, on the other hand, act like rational citizens, according to an agreed and a conscious plan. It might thus seem impossible to find any plan or purpose in their history. But just as marriages and births, a matter of free will and apparently subject to no pattern, nevertheless occur according to stable natural laws, so 'what appears to be complicated and accidental in individuals may yet be understood as a steady, progressive, though slow, evolution of the original endowments of the entire species', in accordance with 'an end of nature' which they 'work to promote' but 'would care little for if they knew about it'. And just as Kepler had discovered an unexpected way of subsuming the eccentric orbits of the planets to definite laws, and Newton had explained these laws by a general cause of nature, so we might one day find the laws and the end of nature, which governed the apparently 'senseless march of human events'.

In Kant's opinion they would be found to rest on certain inescapable principles. 'All natural faculties of a creature are destined to unfold themselves completely and according to an end.' 'In man (as the only rational creature on earth) those natural faculties which aim at the use of reason shall be fully developed in the species, not in the individual.' Reason did not develop instinctively. It required trials, experience and information in order to progress gradually from one level to the next. Nature, having set man a short term of life, thus required 'an endless procession of begettings . . . in order finally to push mankind to that level of development which is appropriate to the purpose of nature'. And then again, because nature had given men reason and the freedom of will that rests upon reason, 'nature has intended man to develop everything which transcends the mechanical ordering of his animal existence entirely by him-

73

self . . . by his own reason and free of instinct'. It was nature's plan that 'man alone should have the credit' for what he accomplished. Unless these assumptions were made it would be necessary to adopt the self-contradictory notions of an organ without use, a regulation without purpose, a nature without laws. Nature, which worked to an end in all other natural arrangements, 'would have to be suspected of childish play when it comes to man'—would have to be thought of as purposeful in detail but purposeless as a whole.

Since reason did not develop instinctively, it could further be assumed that nature pitted itself against man in order to force him to develop the reason it had given him—to make his reason produce what it is capable of but would not of itself intend. The means which nature employed for this purpose was 'the antagonism of men in society'. This antagonism, 'the cause of a lawful order of this society', was in its turn based on the 'asocial sociability' or 'unsocial sociableness' of men, that is their 'propensity to enter into a society, which propensity is, however, linked with a constant mutual resistance which threatens to dissolve this society'. The state is the product of man's unlovely qualities—his love of glory, power and possessions—but it is only in the state that his better capacities can develop. It is constantly threatened by those unlovely qualities; but it is this constant threat of nature that forces him to preserve and improve the state as the means of developing his better qualities and his use of reason. 'Thanks are due to nature for his quarrelsomeness, his enviously competitive vanity, his insatiable desire to possess or to rule, for without them all the excellent faculties of mankind would for ever remain undeveloped. Man wants concord but nature knows better . . . ; nature wants discord. Man wants to live . . . pleasurably but nature intends that he should raise himself out of lethargy . . . into work and trouble . . .' in order to achieve, by his own efforts, the highest task she has set him.

This process was at work in the relations between states as well as in the development of the state. In the international field, as in the relations between men in a society, 'nature has again used quarrelsomeness, in this case that of the great societies and states, as a means of discovering a condition of quiet and security through the very antagonism inevitable among them'. 'Wars, the excessive and never-ending preparation for wars, and the want which every state must feel even in the midst of peace—all these are means by which

74

nature instigates attempts . . . which, after many many devastations, reversals and a very general exhaustion of the states' resources, may accomplish what reason could have suggested to them without so much sad experience, namely: to leave the lawless state of savages and to enter into a union of states. . . .' 'All wars are . . . so many attempts (not in the intention of men, but in the intention of nature) to bring about new relations between the states and to form new bodies by the break-up of the old states to the point where they cannot maintain themselves alongside each other and must therefore suffer revolutions until finally, partly through the best possible arrangement of the civic constitution internally and partly through common agreement and legislation externally, there is created a state which, like a civic constitution, can maintain itself automatically . . . ,' 'a cosmo-political state of public security', a 'joining of the states'.

The end which nature forced men to achieve by these means was the establishment of a completely just civic society in which alone the faculties of men could be fully developed. It could be defined as a society possessing 'the greatest freedom and hence a very general antagonism of its members but also . . . the most precise determination and enforcement of the limit of this freedom so that it can co-exist with the freedom of other societies'. Indeed, 'the problem of the establishment of a perfect civic constitution depends upon the problem of a lawful external relationship of the states and cannot be solved without the latter'. So long as the condition of unrestricted freedom existed between states there could be little use in, and little hope of, restricting that freedom by the achievement of the lawful civic constitution within the state. 'The history of mankind could be viewed on the whole as the realisation of a hidden plan of nature to bring about an internally—and for this purpose also externally—perfect constitution. . . .'

By here regarding the solution of the international problem as a pre-condition of the perfect civic constitution—by referring to the former as 'the half-way mark of mankind's development' which could not be completed 'as long as states will use all their resources for their vain and violent designs and will thus hinder the slow efforts towards the inner shaping of the minds of their citizens'; by arguing that mankind would probably remain incapable of completing its development 'until it has struggled out of the chaotic conditions of the relations between states'—Kant revealed in this work what is clear enough in the later *Perpetual Peace* despite its inconsistency on this point. He regarded the internal improvement of states not as a guarantee of international peace but at most as a condition of it and perhaps as a consequence of it. The central argument of *The Idea for a Universal History* with regard to international relations was that if peace were ever to be established it would be in consequence of nature's exploitation of the rivalry between states. It would be the product of the common need and interest of states in consequence of their continuing, indeed perpetual, rivalry.

This was also the central argument of *Perpetual Peace*, where he repeated his view of the historical process. It followed as directly from that conception of history as it did from his view of the state. 'No one less than the great artist nature', reads "the first addition" to the articles of *Perpetual Peace*,[18] 'offers such a guarantee. Nature's mechanical course evidently reveals a teleology: to produce harmony from the very disharmony of men even against their will. . . . A deep wisdom . . . directed towards a higher end . . . predetermines this evolution. We do not really *observe* this providence in the artifices of nature, nor can we *deduce* it from them. But we can and must *add this thought* . . . in order to form any kind of conception of its possibility. . . .'

'Before we ascertain more specifically how the guarantee is worked out it is necessary to explore the situation which nature has created . . . and which in the last analysis necessitates its guarantee of peace. Only after that can we see how nature provided this guarantee. . . .' This situation is nothing less than the disharmony itself and especially the dispersal of men into different areas and states. 'Nature, by providing that men can live everywhere on earth, has at the same time despotically wanted that they *should* live everywhere.'

'What does nature do in relation to the end which men's reason imposes as a duty. . . . In other words: how does nature guarantee that what man ought to do according to the laws of freedom, but does not do, will be made secure regardless of this . . . by a compulsion of nature which forces him to do it?' The answer is that nature has created the disharmony and the dispersal in order to force men to use their better qualities for overcoming its dangers. This can be seen by studying the process 'in all three relations: *constitutional* law, *international* law and cosmopolitan or world law. . . .'

Under the first of these headings, external wars would force a people to make a state even if internal conflicts did not do so. More important, although many have insisted that men with their selfish propensities are incapable of achieving the republican constitution, the only one which is fully adequate to the right of man, nature forces them towards it by opposing the selfish propensities of some men to the selfish propensities of others. In this way 'nature comes to the aid of the revered but practically ineffectual general will which is founded in reason'. 'Thus man, although not a morally good man, is compelled to be a good citizen. . . . For it is not the moral perfection of mankind, but merely the mechanism of nature . . . [that is required] to arrange the conflict of unpacific attitudes in a given people in such a way that they impel each other to submit themselves to compulsory laws and thus bring about the state of peace in which such laws are enforced.' 'The problem of establishing a state is solvable even for a people of devils, if only they have the intelligence. . . .'

Kant next said that 'it is possible to observe this [process at work] in the actually existing, although imperfectly organised, states'; and the evidence he used for this statement took him from the field of constitutional law to that of international law. 'They approach in external conduct closely to what the idea of law prescribes, although an inner morality is certainly not the cause of it (just as we should not expect a good [civil] constitution from such morality, but rather from such a constitution the good moral development of a people). These existing states show that the mechanism of nature, with its selfish propensities which naturally counteract each other, can be employed by reason as a means. Thus reason's real purpose may be realised, namely, to provide a field for the operation of legal rules whereby to make secure internal and external peace, as far as the state is concerned.' In the same way he emphasised in his comments on the second definitive article that 'in view of the evil nature of man, which can be observed in the free relations between nations, it is surprising that the word *law* has not been entirely banned from the politics of war. . . . This homage which every state renders to the concept of law (at least in words) seems to prove that there exists in man a greater moral quality (though at present a dormant one) to try and master the evil element in him. . . .'[19]

But if nature uses the selfish propensities of states as well as of individuals, and uses them to the same end, peace under law, the equivalent in international affairs of the republican constitution in internal development is not the merger of the states. 'The idea of a law of nations presupposes the separate existence of many states which are independent of each other. Such a situation constitutes in and by itself a state of war. . . . Yet such a situation is from the standpoint of reason better than the complete merging of all these states in one . . . because the laws lose more and more of their effectiveness as the government increases in size, and the resulting soulless despotism is plunged into anarchy after having exterminated all the germs of good [in man].' Nature's purpose in the international field is rather to preserve the separate states and to utilise their conflict. 'It is the desire of every state (or of its ruler) to enter into a permanent state of peace by ruling if possible the entire world. But *nature* has decreed otherwise. Nature employs two means to keep peoples from being mixed and to differentiate them, the difference of *language* and of *religion*. These differences occasion the inclination towards mutual hatred and the excuse for war; yet at the same time they lead, as culture increases and men gradually come closer together, towards a greater agreement on principles for peace and understanding. Such peace and understanding is not brought about . . . by a weakening of all other forces (as it would be under the aforementioned despotism and its graveyard of freedom) but by balancing these forces in a lively competition.'

This agreement on principles, this balanced competition, would thus find its ultimate expression in the cosmopolitan or world law. 'Just as nature wisely separates the nations which the will of each state would like to unite under its sway either by cunning or by force, and even in keeping with the reasoning of the law of nations, so also nature unites [them] . . . by mutual self-interest. It is the *spirit of commerce* which cannot exist with war, and which sooner or later takes hold of every nation. . . . States find themselves impelled (though hardly by moral compulsion) to promote the noble peace. . . . It is as if states were constantly leagued for this purpose.' Already, he added at the conclusion of the section on the third definitive article, the 'community of all nations on earth has in fact progressed so far that a violation of law and right in one place is felt in *all* others. Hence the idea of a cosmopolitan or world law is not a fantastic or Utopian way of looking at law, but a necessary completion of the unwritten code of constitutional and international law to make it a public law of mankind.'[20] By a continuation of the process 'the concept of . . . a world law', which by itself 'would not have protected [the nations] from violence and war', will be enabled to develop between them as the corrective to their continuing rivalry. 'In this way nature guarantees perpetual peace by the mechanism of human inclinations.'

When Kant wrote peace he meant peace. He was as convinced that the development of the rule of law between states would eventually produce international peace as he was convinced that it was the only means of producing it and that it would take a long time to develop. It has been argued that for him as much as for Rousseau perpetual peace was only an ideal laid up in heaven—something to which men should strive but which they could not expect to attain.[21] Others have maintained about his theory that its 'prime implication, obscured by metaphysics, is that peace can be kept [only] by arrangements for the waging of war by states upon states'.[22] Neither of these views is an acceptable deduction from what Kant wrote.

The first is derived essentially from Kant's rejection of political federation as impracticable, undesirable and in any case irrelevant to the problem. Those who have maintained it have been those who, believing themselves that political federation was the sole route to international peace and assuming that Kant also advocated it, have nevertheless been unable to ignore the many comments in which he cast doubts upon their ideal. The second has come more naturally to those who have recognized his insistence on the independent state or have argued that 'federation' was only 'implicit in the Kantian formula'.[23] These have generally been 'realists' who, while seizing joyfully on his rejection of federation, have still allowed their own opinions to distort his text. In this case the comments that have been ignored are those in which Kant expressed his confidence in the eventual establishment of peace as much as his conviction that it would be a long time before peace was established.

Concerned as we are with what Kant wrote and not as yet with whether he was right, we may end by letting some of these comments speak for themselves. In the *Idea for a Universal History* he stated that the problem of establishing the just civic constitution and, for that purpose, a 'lawful external relationship' was 'the most difficult and at the same time the one which mankind solves last'. He admitted, indeed, that 'a complete solution is impossible: one cannot fashion something completely straight from wood which is as crooked as that of which man is made'. All he claimed was that 'nature has imposed on us the task of approximating to this idea'. But he stated equally firmly that, vast as the problem was and long as it would take to solve it, there was some indication that progress had already been made towards a solution even in 'the small distance which man has so far traversed'. If one looked at history since the Greeks one discovered 'a regular procession of improvements in constitutional government in that part of the world which will probably give laws to all other states eventually'. Even though the progress towards a lawful system of relations between states was 'at present discernible only in its broadest outline, a feeling for it is rising in all member states. . . .' These were his grounds for believing that 'when one takes into account the general premise that the world is constituted as a system and considers what little has been observed one can say that the indications are sufficiently reliable to enable us to conclude that such a revolution is real'.[24]

This was also the view he upheld in *Perpetual Peace*. There, after urging that 'nature guarantees lasting peace', he added: 'The certainty is not sufficient to *predict* such a future (theoretically); but for practicable purposes the certainty suffices and makes it one's duty to work for this not simply chimerical state.'[25] And then the concluding words of the whole essay: 'If it is a duty, and if at the same time there is a well-founded hope that we may make a real state of public law, even if only in an indefinitely gradual approximation, then the *eternal* peace which will take the place of peace-makings—falsely so called because they are really just truces—is no empty idea, but a task which, gradually solved, steadily approaches its end, since it is to be hoped that the periods in which equal progress is achieved will become shorter and shorter.'[26]

CHAPTER 5

BENTHAM AND JAMES MILL

LIKE Rousseau and Kant, Bentham broke with the traditional internationalist theory that had come to a head in the arguments of Penn and Saint-Pierre. He broke with it even more decisively, indeed, than they did. Rousseau like most writers since Sully's day—since Dante's day if pacifists and religious writers are excepted—had begun by supposing that states would not be able to follow their real interests and avoid war unless some political union was established between them. His perception had contradicted this assumption but had not led him to abandon it. Instead, he had concluded on a note of despair: political union, the one solution, was unattainable, not to say undesirable if ever attained, because of the conflict between even the real interests of states. Kant had not made this assumption or ended in despair; but he had been at pains to demonstrate why the goal of international integration was unattainable and undesirable and ought to be abandoned. For Bentham international integration was not so much unattainable and undesirable as utterly unnecessary, and it was also unnecessary to show why this was so. Perhaps this was why he himself published no plan for perpetual peace. His *Plan for an Universal and Perpetual Peace* was one of four manuscripts written between 1786 and 1789 which were put together after his death to form his *Principles of International Law*. They were not published till his collected works appeared in 1843.[1]

He did not take this view because he was less concerned to avoid war than his predecessors had been, or because he was less aware than they of the nature of the problem. He believed indeed that some circumstances might justify war as a choice of evils; that it might be necessary, in particular, for defence and security against aggression. '*Defence* is a fair ground for war,' he wrote later on. 'The Quaker's objection cannot stand. What a fine thing it would have been for Buonaparte to have had to do with Quaker nations!'[2] But he was as passionately opposed to war on moral grounds as Rousseau was—and more so than earlier writers had been. To war, moreover, as to everything else, he applied the principle of utility, and was thus equally convinced of its stupidity—of its incompatability, for example, with economic prosperity, which would flow only from free trade.[3] He did not invent the notion of international law; but he may be credited with coining the phrase to take the place of the old Law of Nations,[4] and he saw as clearly as anyone before him had seen that the difference between international law and civil law was that the latter had a 'superordinate' authority to enforce it while the former did not. His lack of interest in international political machinery has a more interesting explanation. He believed that genuine causes of war had already virtually disappeared between states. The day had almost dawned to which Kant believed that man might look forward in the distant future. In so far as action was still called for, it was action to reduce the power of government within states, not action to increase government on the international plane.

In holding this belief Bentham was wholly representative of the prevailing attitude to international relations in the second half of the eighteenth century—in the years between Rousseau's work and Kant's. Imitations and copies of Saint-Pierre's project ceased to achieve the dignity of publication after the middle of the century; Rousseau was the last considerable writer seriously to consider it. Beginning with Rousseau, the *philosophes* turned, indeed, against statesmen and their practices. They contrasted 'true policy' or 'economic policy'—its emphasis being on free trade and the community of interests between states—with 'false policy' or 'power politics' which led to frustration and war. They argued that 'the true purpose of the science called politics is to perfect the interior of the state'; that only 'flatterers assure the princes that the interior is there only to serve foreign policy'. They denounced conquests as crimes. They attacked in particular the assumption that the balance of power was a source of international restraint and a guarantee of peace: it was dismissed as 'the favourite idea of . . . coffee-house politicians', the producer 'of disturbance, of shock and of explosions', the cause of war. They castigated all the apparatus of diplomacy, and especially alliances. Alliances were nothing but 'temporary armistices' and 'preparations for treason'; they were 'always of an offensive nature'; and their secrecy proved that they were the product of 'deceit' and 'intrigue', expressions of 'hatred' and instruments for 'the blind passions of princes'.[5] But what the *philosophes* did not do was to show any interest in the internationalist proposals of the kind that had been propounded up to the middle of the eighteenth century. Their central article of faith in international affairs, like Bentham's, was that the enlightened nations of their day already belonged to 'one society' or 'family of nations' and could get on perfectly peaceably together without assistance if only the governments of their day would learn to let them do so—if only relations between governments were exposed to the criticism and correction of enlightened public opinion and replaced as far as possible by relations between individuals.[6] It was from them that Bentham acquired not only his hatred of colonies and alliances and his enthusiasm for free trade but also his underlying assumptions: that, although it had not always been so, it was now the case that 'between the interests of nations there is nowhere any real conflict, if they appear repugnant anywhere it is only in proportion as they are misunderstood';[7] that in so far as a state of peace did not already prevail, and in so far as there might still be legitimate grounds for war once peace had been established, the solution to these problems already lay to hand in the appeal to reason, to law and public opinion, against the machinations of governments.

In another of the four manuscripts of the period 1786–9 he divided the causes of war into three. There were wars arising from passions, such as religious hatreds, and wars arising from ambition or insolence, from the mad desire for power; and wars might also arise from *bona fide* causes: the offences, real or imagined, of the citizens of one state against the citizens of another.[8] In the *Plan* itself he argued that the days of wars of passion and ambition were over—at least in Europe. 'Europe . . . would have had no wars but for the feudal system, religious antipathy, the rage of conquest and the uncertainties of succession. Of these four causes, the first is happily extinct everywhere, the second and third almost everywhere—at any rate in France and England—and the last might, if not already extinguished, be so with great ease.'[9]

He had his misgivings. The qualification—'at any rate in France and England'—occurs more than this once. When arguing that alliances and armaments had ceased to be necessary and that states might give them up, together with their colonies, without fear of invasion—that 'such madness does not belong to our age . . . , no one would dream of conquest'—he was writing in the limited context of Anglo-French relations.[10] Then again: 'Conquests by New Zealanders have some sense in them. . . . The invasions of France in the days of the Edwards and the Henries had a rational object. . . . Conquests made by a modern despot of the Continent have still some sense in them . . . , their substance . . . goes into his purse. [But] Conquests made by the British nation would be violation of common sense. . . .'[11] But if he believed that circumstances might still provide a rational object for war in some areas, as they had once done everywhere, it was essentially his view that Europe was in a fair way to achieving the condition he believed England and France had reached. It was for this reason that he was able to assert that, 'supposing Great Britain and France thoroughly agreed, the principal difficulties would be removed to the establishment of a plan of general and permanent pacification for all Europe' of the kind he proposed.[12] 'Why should not the European fraternity subsist, as well as the German Diet and the Swiss League? Those latter have no ambitious views. Be it so, but is not this equally become the case with the former?'[13]

Two difficulties stood in the way of Anglo-French reconciliation: the possession of and the struggle for colonies, and the ways of Foreign Offices. These obstacles raised further doubts in his mind. If international morality was low, as he believed it to be, he could not help suspecting that this was due to human nature as much as to the shortcomings of governments. 'The moral feelings of men in matters of national morality are still so far short of morality that . . . justice has not yet gained the ascendency over force. . . . I feel it in my own experience, and . . . what can I expect from the general run of men?'[14] As for the abandoning of colonies, 'the most visionary part of this visionary project is without question that for the emancipation of distant dependencies'.[15] But these doubts only serve to emphasise the strength of his conviction that struggles for 'distant dependencies' and 'secrecy in the operation of the Foreign Department' were the only serious causes of war, at least between the civilised nations, and that public opinion could be educated to the truth of this. His *Plan* was not so much a project for perpetual peace as a diatribe against these two evils. His 'proof' of the proposition that an Anglo-French pacification would lead to a general pacification was no proof at all: it merely repeated the original words of the assertion.[16] The attack on colonies dominated the first third of his thirty-page treatise;[17] the attack on secret diplomacy and its products, dangerous alliances, was the longest section of all.[18] It is not misrepresenting Bentham to conclude that in his opinion, while the removal of these obstacles would have led directly to perpetual peace, no other measures could be expected to have that result if these obstacles were not eliminated. Certainly he gave a subsidiary role to the other measures he discussed. Disarmament was one of these. He dealt with it at some length, perceiving some of the difficulties and providing an early anticipation of the campaign for unilateral disarmament—some nation should take the lead 'in the most public manner'; if Great Britain refused to do so, France should give up her colonies and her navy; disarmament would follow.[19] But just as he explicitly regarded disarmament as something that would follow automatically upon the abandonment of colonies, so he regarded disarmament agreements as something that would be useful in helping to maintain the general and permanent pacification once it had been established by political means. Proposition XII of his plan reads: 'For the maintenance of such a pacification, general and perpetual treaties might be formed for limiting the number of troops. . . .'[20]

He conceived of the Common Court of Judicature or Tribunal of Peace—his only other procedural proposal—as filling a similar role. He supposed that it would be set up when the general pacification had been achieved—when conquest, colonies and secrecy had been abandoned. Its function would be to remove those *bona fide* grounds for war which would still remain between separate nations even in the condition of general and permanent pacification. It would do so by providing a legal procedure for the settlement of those real or assumed grievances that will always exist between states. There is no question that he was presupposing that the general pacification was already in force when he wrote: 'While there is no common tribunal something might be said for war. Establish a common tribunal, the necessity for war no longer follows from difference of opinion. Just or unjust, the decision of the arbiter will save the credit of the contending party.'[21]

It was because the existence of the court presupposed that the general pacification had already been achieved—as well as because he felt that Europe had already almost achieved it—that he advocated no international organisation except a court, though he called this also a 'Congress or Diet'.[22] Although he did not himself state this in so many words, he unquestionably felt on this question what his disciples and the interpreters of his thought were later to feel: that 'a community of nations bound to give assistance to each other's political laws would be a most dangerous alliance; it would be too apt to become a combination of monarchs for the support of despotism'.[23] Much later in his life mediation or arbitration—'calling in commissaries from other nations'[24]—remained his most radical procedural recommendation for the avoidance of war. Even in the *Plan* itself the Tribunal was 'not to be armed with any coercive powers'.[25] Its procedures were to consist of reporting its opinions, circulating its opinions in each state and, after a certain time, 'putting the refractory state under the ban of Europe'. Bentham conceded that it might sometimes be necessary to organise force against such a state, just as he believed that war was morally justifiable against aggression. But the force that would then be used would be that of individual states, and his basic opinion was that force would be unnecessary if liberty of the Press were guaranteed in each state. 'There might perhaps be no harm in regulating as a last resource the contingents to be furnished by the several states for enforcing the decrees of the Court. But the necessity for the employment of this resource would in all human probability be superseded for ever by having recourse to the much more simple and less burthensome expedient of . . . liberty of the Press in each state. . . .'[26]

It is, accordingly, a mistake, but one that is often made,[27] to refer to him as 'a pioneer of the League of Nations'. It is an even greater, though rarer, mistake to believe that his plan was a 'simplification' of Saint-Pierre's.[28] He was the first internationalist to rely on public opinion, and solely on public opinion, to make states keep their pledges and to coerce those who did not keep them. He similarly relied on reason and public opinion for removing those few remaining obstacles, such as colonies and secrecy, which prevented the emergence of the general pacification in which his Tribunal could do its work. It was not for nothing that he announced in the first sentence of his *Plan* that 'the object is . . . an universal and perpetual peace; the globe is the field of dominion to which the author aspires; the Press, the engine, and the only one he employs. . . .'[29]

It was against governments that reason and public opinion were needed. 'There are properly no other criminals', he wrote in another of these early pamphlets, 'than the heads of nations; the subjects are always honest'.[30] Distrust of government is not the same thing as distrust of sovereignty. Bentham's views on sovereignty were as uncompromisingly absolutist as his views on government were uncomprisingly distrustful. For him the sovereignty of a state lay in its law, as devised by its wisest citizens in accordance with rational principles, and he was impatient of any restraint on this legal and legislative power; but of government there should be only the minimum that was necessary to secure the artificial identification of interests between the citizens who make up the state. It has been asserted by some commentators that the only logical outcome of these views in terms of a solution of the international problem is a single world government to secure a similar artificial identification of interests between states; and they have supposed that Bentham refrained from making this proposal only because he regarded it as utterly visionary.[31] The first of these assumptions may or may not be correct. The second is without doubt wrong.

If he did not propose international government it was primarily because he did not think it relevant to the international problem; and if he did not think it relevant it was because he would not have agreed—whatever the facts of the case may be—that world government was the logical outcome of his views. For him the logical deduction was that, as there should be as little government as possible so there should be as little international government as possible; that, as sovereignty lay in the law, so international sovereignty could lie only in international law; and that although states might have to be constrained to obey that law, as citizens had to be constrained to obey the law within the state, public opinion should be an adequate restraint on civilised states as it should be within them.

So much did he believe this that, even though he was prepared to regard his own proposals as 'visionary', he did not discuss international government, even to dismiss it as irrelevant. In this he differed from Kant, who was at pains to state that it was irrelevant. But for all that Bentham lacked Kant's sense of the irrational element in men and the historical element in politics—although he believed that a solution was already at hand if only men would be sensible, whereas Kant deferred the solution to a day in the distant future when men would have learned to be sensible as the result of much bitter experience—the two men agreed about the importance of the independence of the state.

This similarity is clearer still in the work of one of Bentham's disciples. James Mill's essay on the *Law of Nations* faithfully reproduced Bentham's main proposals in the form of an article in the supplement to the fifth edition of the *Encyclopaedia Britannica* (1820).[32] Mill's article was not a peace plan. It devoted two chapters to defining the rights of nations, regarded as the basis of international law, and one of these chapters dealt with the rights of nations in war—with 'what should be regarded as necessary to render the commencement of a war just'; with 'what should be regarded as just and unjust in the modes of carrying on a war'.[33] But the article restated with admirable force and clarity—with more force and clarity than Bentham's own *Plan* had achieved—Bentham's central argument that war could be avoided by independent civilised states with the aid of nothing but public opinion and a rational body of international law.

Mill's first point was that such a thing as government, the source of the command and the sanction that lay behind law, had never existed, and could never exist, as between nations. It was an 'extraordinary hypothesis', 'full of impracticabilities', for several reasons.

It is not understood, that one nation has a right to command another. When one nation can be commanded by another, it is dependent upon that other; and the laws of dependence are different from those which we are at present considering. An independent nation would resent . . . a command . . . by another. . . . Neither can it properly be said that nations, taken aggregately, prescribe . . . laws to one another severally; for when did they ever combine in any such prescription? When did they ever combine to vindicate [punish] the violation of them? And how could they ever be expected to do so? The inconveniences . . . , which must be felt from any movement to lend effect to the law of nations, are . . . formidable; the whole train of the evils of war are almost sure to arise from them. . . . [They] will generally be shunned. A nation is often but too easily stimulated to make war in resentment of injuries done to itself. But it looks with too much coldness upon the injuries done to other nations to incur the chance of any great inconvenience for the redress of them. Besides . . . , the combinations of nations are very difficult things. Nations hardly ever combine without quarrelling. . . . For all nations to combine in any one enterprise is impossible.[34]

This being so, 'the only power which can operate to sanction the laws of nations; in other words, to reward or punish any nation, . . . is the approbation or disapprobation of mankind'. If this could be rendered effective 'a strong security' would be 'gained for a good intercourse among nations' since 'there is no nation which does not value highly the favourable sentiments of other nations'. At the same time, democratic rule within states was an important prerequisite here.

The restraining force [of opinion] is . . . determined by the associations which they who govern . . . have formed with the approbation or disapprobation of mankind. If they have formed strong associations of a pleasurable kind with the approbation, strong associations of a painful kind with the disapprobation of mankind, the restraining force will be great; if they have not formed such associations, it will be feeble and insignificant. . . . The rulers of a country of which the government is either monarchial, or aristocratical, can have these associations in very low degree; as those alone, who are placed on a level with the great body of other men, are placed in circumstances calculated to produce them. It is only then in countries, the rulers of which are drawn from the mass of the people, in other words in democratical countries, that the sanction of the laws of nations can be expected to operate with any considerable effect.[35]

Between states, as within communities, two other things were needed to raise the efficiency of this sanction 'to the greatest pitch', to give precision and certainty to the operation of law.

The one is a strict determination of what the law is, the second, a tribunal so constituted as to yield prompt and accurate execution of the law. . . . Two grand practical measures are obviously not only of primary importance to the attainment of this end, but are of indispensable necessity toward the attainment of it in any tolerable degree. These are, first, the construction of a Code; and, secondly, the establishment of a Tribunal. It is perfectly evident, that nations will be much more likely to conform to the principles of intercourse which are best for all, if they have an accurate set of rules to go by. . . . There is less room for mistake; . . . there is less room for plausible pretexts; and last of all, the approbation and disapprobation of the world is sure to act with a ten-fold concentration, where a precise rule is broken, familiar to all the civilised world, and venerated by it all.[36]

It was not difficult to see 'how the nations of the civilised world might concur in the framing of such a code'. They could appoint delegates who would meet at some central place to agree on a draft for presentation to their governments. Before submitting it for government ratification they should publish it extensively in all the principal languages 'for the sake of two important advantages. The first would be, that the intelligence of the whole world being brought to operate on it . . . , it might be made as perfect as possible. The second would be, that the eyes of all the world being fixed upon the decision of every nation with respect to the code, every nation might be deterred by shame from objecting to any important article in it.' After the code had been ratified it should be given 'all possible publicity and solemnity' in every country since 'the sanction of general opinion is that upon which chiefly . . . such a code must rely for its efficiency. . . .'[37]

Despite the importance of public opinion a Tribunal was needed as well as a Code. Even within communities, under governments, 'the laws, however carefully and accurately constructed, would be of little avail . . . if there was not some organ, by means of which it might be determined when individuals had acted in conformity with them, and when they had not'. How much more was it the case that 'the benefit capable of being derived from an international code must be lost, if it is left destitute of a similar organ?' Ideally each nation should have one delegate or judge at the court; but, 'as all nations could not easily, or would not, send, it would suffice if the more civilised and leading nations of the world concurred in the design. . . .' The delegates could hold the chairmanship of the Court in rotation so long as none was judge in a case in which his own nation was involved. It should convene at a place 'chosen for its accessibility, and for the means of publicity it might afford; the last being, beyond comparison, the advantage of greatest importance'. It should be competent to try all breaches of international code whether both parties to a dispute brought the case or only one party or neither party; and the non-appearance before the Court of parties to disputes should be treated as an offence against the law of nations. For even if neither party sought or was disposed to respect its jurisdiction 'a decision solemnly pronounced by such a tribunal would always have a strong effect upon the imaginations of men. It would fix, and concentrate, the disapprobation of mankind.'[38]

Nevertheless—and here Mill was even more emphatic than Bentham had been—'the intention should never be entertained of supporting the decisions of the international court by force of arms',[39] and this for the two reasons already elaborated. On the one hand, the attempt to take such a step in the direction of international government was bound to end in failure or in war, and probably in both. On the other hand, if the necessary steps were taken to educate public opinion—'the book of the law of nations, and selections from the book of the trials before the international tribunal, should form a subject of study in every school, and a knowledge of them a necessary part of every man's education'—then 'a moral sentiment would grow up, which would, in time, act as a powerful restraining force upon the injustice of nations, and give a wonderful efficacy to the international jurisdiction'; and 'all might be done, which is capable of being done, towards securing the benefits of international law'.[40]

CHAPTER 6

THE FIRST HALF OF THE NINETEENTH CENTURY

IT was the attitude of Bentham and Mill—the belief that 'between the interests of nations there is nowhere any real conflict' and that international law could at once be set up and work successfully, not Rousseau's ultimate conviction that international conflict made progress impossible nor Kant's conclusion that only by means of international conflict would progress be achieved—that dominated men's attitude to this problem in the first half of the nineteenth century. The characteristic, not to say the universal, beliefs of these years were those which Bentham had deduced from the argument that the constitutional state, regarded by Kant as a necessary condition of international peace, was, rather, the sufficient guarantee of it: the grounds for war had almost disappeared among the civilised nations; in so far as war still persisted between them it was due to the stupidity and criminality of existing governments; international organisation as a safeguard against war was undesirable because existing governments could not be trusted; it was also unnecessary because the reform of governments would itself ensure peace by releasing reason and establishing the benevolent sway of public opinion and international law.

These opinions were Bible, first, to all who welcomed the French Revolution. Tom Paine was speaking for all such men when he wrote in the *Rights of Man* (1791) that 'Monarchical sovereignty, the enemy of mankind and the source of misery, is abolished, and sovereignty is restored to its natural and original place, the nation. Were this the case throughout Europe the cause of war would be taken away.'[1] In different circumstances and for different reasons— in the Anglo-Saxon world most markedly, but also on the continent of Europe despite appearances to the contrary—they survived the disillusionment produced by the deterioration of the French Revolution and the outbreak of the Napoleonic wars. Not until the failure of the 1848 revolutions and the outbreak of further wars, beginning with the Crimean War, had produced further disillusionment were they finally and reluctantly discarded.

There were two reasons for the dominance of these views in England and America. Most people there, caught up in the nationalist sentiment of the time, preoccupied with the vast material expansion of their two countries—towards an unprecedented degree of material world leadership in the one case, towards Manifest Destiny in the other—and assured of the safety of turning their backs on the problems of the European continent, displayed no interest in the international question. Because of their isolation or their new strength there was no problem that their countries could not solve by the resources of traditional diplomacy. Thus—and this is the first reason —although there was an increased preoccupation with the problem of peace and war as a result of the excesses of the Napoleonic wars, that increased preoccupation was confined to Peace Societies which were Quaker in origin at a time when the Quakers had long since gone back on Penn's advocacy of international organisation and now relied for progress entirely on a religious, moral and pacifist appeal to the goodness of human nature. If all who were interested in peace were connected with the Peace Societies, all who were connected with the Peace Societies were either Quakers or men who were close to pacifism. They all adopted for this reason an outlook that was close to Bentham's and Mill's.

The British 'Society for the Promotion of Permanent and Universal Peace' was founded by Quakers in 1816. It stood resolutely against all forms of war from the outset, as it continued to do throughout its history—though it advised other pacifists who could not accept complete Non-Resistance, the chief article of its faith, to form auxiliary societies which could pursue the same goal of universal peace from a less absolute position. In 1819, in the first number of its official journal, the *Herald of Peace*, the Society was content to announce by way of a programme for achieving its aim that 'a theme of such paramount importance . . . requires only the aid of its natural ally and powerful auxiliary, the Press, to evince its pretensions and ensure its success'.[2] Subsequently, though with no great alacrity, it added more concrete items to this programme under pressure from the 'American Peace Society';[3] but they were items which entirely conformed with this general statement and with the outlook of Bentham. They were, indeed, taken straight from Bentham *via* the essay by James Mill.

The direct influence of Bentham was the second reason for the predominance of his views. The American Peace Society's constitution, drawn up by William Ladd in 1828, was directly inspired by Mill's essay. It expressed the belief that once 'a healthy public opinion' had been created war would cease because national differences would be submitted to 'amicable discussion and arbitration' through 'a Congress of Nations whose decrees shall be enforced by public opinion that rules the world'.⁴ Arbitration between nations under the auspices of a 'Congress of Nations', the programme developed by Ladd and adopted also by the British Society, remained the only planks in the platform of the movement until collaboration developed between the Peace Societies and the Free Trade movements in the 1840's. And what Ladd meant by a Congress of Nations was no more than what Bentham and Mill had had in mind: international meetings to make possible the establishment of an international court for the settlement of such few genuine disputes as remained between civilised nations. His debt to Mill is very clear in his *Dissertation on a Congress of Nations* (1832) and *Essay on a Congress of Nations* (1840).

He argued that all civilised nations should establish a congress of ambassadors as well as a court of arbitration. The Congress's function would be that of 'settling the principles of international law by compact and agreement, of the nature of a mutual treaty, and of devising and promoting plans for the preservation of peace . . .'. The 'Court of Nations', quite separate from the Congress, was to consist of the most able individuals in the world, not of official representatives of the governments. In this division we have Bentham's and Mill's distinction between the political agreements that were needed to bring about a general pacification between independent nations, and to modify international law, in the first place and the international court that would keep the peace between these nations by arbitrating on the disputes that would arise even when peace had been established. With Ladd as with Bentham and Mill there was no more notion of enforcement than there was of political integration; with him, indeed, unlike with them, the Court would arbitrate only in 'such cases as should be brought before it by the mutual consent of two or more contending nations'. If he regarded the Congress of ambassadors as the legislature of his peace system, and the court as the judiciary, he left all executive functions to public opinion, 'the Queen of the World'. Nor was he content to insist that the court should have no power to insist on arbitration or to enforce its decisions, and that public opinion would be effective in ensuring the resort to arbitration, the execution of the decisions and the preservation of peace. It was an important part of his argument that all previous peace plans had failed because they had envisaged the enforcement of order by the power of the sword, instead of by moral power alone, whereas his proposal 'has nothing to do with physical force and leagues offensive and defensive . . . but depends entirely on the influence of moral power for the good it will do the world. . . .'[5]

There is no proposal for a real Congress of Nations here—no ground for the view that Ladd and the American Peace Society 'contemplated the establishment of federal bonds'[6]—even if hostile contemporary opinion may have thought there was. There is only Bentham's belief that the world is so close to peace and to being a community already that, while diplomacy can achieve the pacification, an international court, backed only by public opinion, can easily preserve it. 'If an Alexander, a Caesar, a Napoleon, bowed down to public opinion, what may we not expect of better men, when public opinion becomes more enlightened? Already there is no nation that can withstand the frown of public opinion. It is therefore necessary, only to enlighten public opinion, still farther. . . .' So Ladd wrote in 1840; and in 1825 he had already declared: 'A revolution of public opinion has commenced, and revolutions do not go back. The time will come and that shortly when nations will settle their disputes by amicable adjustment or arbitration. . . .'[7] Another American, William Jay, took the same view in his *War and Peace* (1842), except that he felt that public opinion would take time to develop and that the international court, though it would eventually be an adequate safeguard of peace, would have to be achieved by stages—by means of the accumulation of individual arbitration agreements in future treaties between individual governments.[8]

This was the programme handed down by the first Universal Peace Congress, organised by the British and the American Peace Societies in London in 1843. It had been stated precisely in a manifesto of the American Society before this Congress met, in 1839: 'The object . . . is to procure the abolition of the custom of war . . . between independent nations. . . . The plan for the overthrow of this custom is, not to induce one nation to surrender its rights to another for the purpose of preserving peace, but to induce the various nations to act on the common-sense principle of referring to arbitration such disputes as they cannot amicably adjust between themselves. . . . The Society does *not* propose to have the International Tribunal invested with power to enforce its decisions, but to have the efficacy of those decisions depend solely on their justice and the honour of nations.'[9] Nor was this programme expanded in any essential respect when, during the 1840's, the Peace Movement lost its predominantly pacifist character as a result of the adhesion of internationalists to the Peace Societies in England and America and of the efforts of the societies to recruit members on the continent of Europe. In one respect it contracted. The second Universal Peace Congress held in Brussels in 1848 added the recommendation that England and the United States should give a lead to the world in disarmament.[10] After 1848, while free trade was added to disarmament and the movement's original demands, the need for even Ladd's conception of a Congress of Nations received less and less emphasis as a result of the alliance with other internationalists.

One reason for this was that, in so far as they were not in any case Quakers, the only men in England and America who in these years surmounted the prevailing indifference or nationalism of the age were men who began by holding what were virtually Quaker views. Richard Cobden, William Ellery Channing and Charles Sumner, the most prominent of the internationalists to appear in England and America, were pacifists or close to pacifism before they became Free Traders and internationalists. Channing, a co-founder of the Massachusetts Peace Society which was later merged in the American Peace Society, was a pacifist before everything, and became a Free Trader solely as a means to peace.[11] Sumner championed Free Trade and upheld the American Constitution as proof that war could be outlawed as an international institution; but he began with the conviction that war was 'unwise, unchristian, unjust'.[12] Cobden is an outstanding example of the same situation. All his earliest writings were on international relations. All his economic ideas were subordinated to a theory of foreign relations which sprang from something close to pacifism. He worked for free trade because he wanted peace, not for peace because he wanted free trade. In 1842 when he sought to ally the free trade movement to the Peace Societies it was as a means of converting Free Traders to pacifism, not of converting the Peace Societies to free trade. If free trade conflicted with peace, as in the case of loans for armaments to foreign governments, he opposed free trade. 'No free trade in cutting throats.'[13] It was because of his starting-point that he could come to believe that free trade would be a means to peace: he never secured from businessmen the support for his peace programme that they gave to his proposals for free trade.

It similarly followed from his starting-point that, whatever tactical differences he might have with the Peace Societies, he would share with them and with Bentham and Mill the conviction that peace could be achieved by massing public opinion behind enlightened policies and that more fundamental measures—political integration and international enforcement procedures—need not be attempted. In the 1830's he believed that free trade and political non-intervention —respect by every sovereign state for the complete independence of every other state—were adequate means of preserving peace. Free trade would give men so strong an interest in peace that they would prevent governments from going to war. It would make international relations safe 'by relieving nations of waste and the perils of strife which come from governmental conduct dictated by obsolete, false concepts of the antagonisms of states'. Free trade and non-intervention together would result in 'as little connection as possible between governments and as much connection as possible between the nations of the world'. This was the way, and a certain way, to peace. It was the message of his *Free Trade as the Best Human Means for Securing Universal and Permanent Peace* (1842).[14] In the 1840's, when he became a major force in the Peace Movement, he easily added its main planks, disarmament and arbitration, to this platform.

While Cobden was not in any case disposed to expand the programme of the Peace Societies, the need to secure the alliance of the Free Trade movement induced him to try to contract it. It was this alliance which enabled the Societies to inaugurate after 1843 the series of Peace Congresses. On the other hand, the Movement was deeply suspect for its pacifism, and its programme, though it asked for only the most limited collaboration between states, was still out of tune with the nationalism of the age.

How much this was so is clear from the hostility of the Press. This had existed before the Movement had elaborated its concrete aims. In 1819 the *Northumberland Monthly Magazine* had criticised it for 'inspiring an abhorrence of war from religious motives [when] such motives cannot be expected to influence any except the civilised part of the world', and for thus conspiring to bring about the situation in which 'every Christian community [would be] exterminated [by] Turkish and heathen nations'.[15] The tone of the Press did not improve when the aims—Arbitration and a Congress of Nations—were made precise and when the alliance with the Free Traders provided the Movement with more publicity. By the time of the second Universal Peace Congress in 1848 *The Times* had concluded, not incorrectly, that if the word 'Peace' were deleted from the Movement's programme its aims would amount to 'nothing else than harmony, mutual consideration, and deference to judicious advice', which, far from being a new discovery, had been the creed of governments for centuries; while, as for a Congress of Nations and an International Code, 'we have these things already: the first in our system of embassies . . . , the second in certain books and precedents of universal authority.'[16] It was not the less hostile on this account. Its comment on the first Universal Peace Congress of 1843 represented a view from which it never changed. 'We have often commented on the fanaticism of association as a distinguishing characteristic of modern times; but of all the developments of this disease which it has been our lot to handle, there is not one that can bear an instant's comparison with the vagaries and delusions of those unhappy individuals who . . . profess no less than the total abolition, throughout the terrestrial globe, of war . . . [and] all physical compulsion on the part of any civil power or authority whatsoever. . . .'[17] Nor need it be doubted that the Press faithfully reflected the general opinion. Liberalism joined with nationalism to ensure that this would distrust collaboration with other Christian nations as well as doubting the possibility of collaboration with heathen ones. British and American hatred of the Holy Alliance and Canning's cry of relief when even the Congress system collapsed—'each nation for itself and God for all of us'—were typical of the age.

Even before Cobden joined them the leaders of the Peace Societies were aware of this sentiment. It was for this reason that Ladd always insisted that his Congress of Nations involved no intervention in the domestic affairs of states and no change in the system of relations between independent states—that it would amount only to a general treaty to be entered into by all nations to enable them to settle their differences by arbitration instead of by force.[18] Later, with the greater publicity that came from organising the congresses, the need to mollify public opinion increased. When presenting the plan for a Congress of Nations to the congresses, Elihu Burritt, Ladd's disciple, always emphasised that the ambassadors to the Congress were to be selected by the parliaments of the member states and that their decisions would be ratified by the parliaments in order to safeguard the independence of the states.[19] And Cobden in his effort to enlist Free Traders and Parliament in support of the Movement, went further still. In 1848, under his influence, the Peace Congress Committee set up national committees in England and America expressly to find a common platform which could be accepted not only by the Peace Societies but also by people whose pacifism did not extend to the denunciation of defensive war. In 1849, he dropped the Movement's demands for a Congress of Nations in his famous motion in the House of Commons. This urged only that the time was ripe for the Government to enter into communication with other Governments for the establishment of a universal system of arbitration. He deliberately avoided arguments from pacifism and Christianity when moving the resolution, as he deliberately limited it to urging arbitration. This, he announced, was a practicable goal: 'it does not embrace the idea of a Congress of Nations, does not imply a belief in the millenium and does not demand homage to the principles of non-resistance.'[20]

From that time on, in further congresses and in resolutions to the American and British Governments, the demand for a Congress of Nations was pushed farther into the background as a result of the struggle between the pacifist and the internationalist wings of the Movement. The third Peace Congress at Paris in 1849, heeding the warning of Lamartine and de Tocqueville that it would jeopardise the cause in Europe if it attempted to recruit Free Trade adherents, avoided the subject of Free Trade despite Cobden's wish to discuss it. In return, Cobden and the internationalists defeated the platform's wish to denounce all war, as they did again at the next congress in Frankfurt in 1850. The Paris Congress confined itself to recommending the education of the public to resist loans for wars 'of ambition and aggression' and to accept the eventual establishment of a Congress of Nations. The Frankfurt Congress urged on governments only arbitration and such disarmament as would be 'without prejudice to such measures as may be considered necessary for the maintenance of the security of their citizens'.[21]

These efforts to make the programme more acceptable to general opinion, though they divided the Movement's Anglo-Saxon organisations, had little success in England and the United States. The religious and pacifist side of the Movement was on the wane after 1843, and Free Trade and Internationalism, disarmament and arbitration, were becoming its major themes. But the stigma of religious fanaticism continued to be attached to it. The efforts had even less effect in Europe. The international congresses of 1843 to 1853, instituted as a means of spreading the Movement to the Continent, served only to reveal the size of the gulf that had opened up between Europe and the Anglo-Saxon world on the question of peace and war since the Napoleonic wars. This was all the more noticeable because the Peace Movement was an early illustration of the increase that was taking place in international communications and because its organisation in Societies and Congresses, in place of the earlier limitation of peace propaganda to the writing and discussion of books, was providing an early indication of the change that was taking place in the structure of society and the composition of public opinion.

Even on the Continent, in spite of these developments, the initiative in spreading the Peace Movement remained with the Anglo-Saxons. It was members of Joseph Sturge's society, a Birmingham auxiliary of the Peace Society, who settled in Russia to establish a peace movement there in 1818. Leading members of the British and American Peace Societies were among the founders of the only national Peace Societies to be established in Europe before 1867—the French Peace Society, *La Société des Amis de la Morale Chrétienne*, in 1821 and Sellon's Geneva Society in 1830—as well as of the many branch societies that were established in France in the 1840's.[22] The Congresses were all organised by the Anglo-American Societies; and at the Congresses it was Anglo-American plans—for disarmament, arbitration and a Congress of Nations—that were always tabled. At the first Universal Peace Congress in London in 1843 there were only 6 delegates from Europe when 292 attended from the United Kingdom and 26 from the United States.[23] This position did not much improve in the next decade. At the third Congress, in Paris in 1849, 670 delegates attended from England, 20 from the United States, 130 from France and Belgium, 30 from the rest of Europe; its organisers feared that the preponderance of British delegates would rob it of its universality.[24] Over 1,000 of the 1,200 delegates to the fifth international Congress in London in 1851 came from Great Britain and 60 from the United States—though there were official representatives from 10 other countries and 12 Parisian working men created a deep impression when they solemnly entered the assembly on the third day.[25] In 1852 it proved impossible to organise an international assembly at all and two congresses at Manchester and Edinburgh in 1853—the last to be held till 1871—were purely British affairs.[26] Nor was continental opinion merely indifferent, as was the bulk of opinion in England and America. By most people in Europe the activities of the Movement were greeted with ill-concealed hostility.

Continental opinion diverged from Anglo-Saxon opinion for two different and contrary reasons. From the point of view of their ultimate aspirations, most European thinkers regarded the programme of the Anglo-Saxon Peace Movement as far too limited: they sought the union of Europe as much as, if not more than, they sought peace. On account of the immediate political situation in Europe they generally dismissed it as going too far: they thought that in Europe, if not in the more fortunate world of England and the United States, the time was not yet ripe even for limited collaboration to bring about the establishment of peace.

The difference between the framework of aspirations in the two areas is not difficult to explain. From the beginning of the nineteenth century the problem of peace at last began to involve more than the relations between the states of Europe, and Anglo-Saxon thinking necessarily regarded peace in wider than European terms. What else could have resulted from the prominence of Americans in the Peace Movement, the rapid development of an Atlantic community, the rise of Great Britain to a position of world-wide power? What Cobden said of the European balance of power he would have been equally ready to apply to the federation of Europe: 'the Equilibrium of Europe was a phrase of some significance when the whole world was in Europe. It has lost its meaning now.'[27] In 1844

E. C. Beckwith, the Secretary of the American Peace Society, proposed the establishment in London of a World Peace Society for the whole world.[28] But all the international history and structure of Europe ensured that European thinking would continue to give the problem of the organisation of Europe priority over the problem of war and peace, or would at least continue to assume that the two problems were the same. These factors are again having the same effects today. In Mazzini's day it was not surprising that they should have done so.

This difference registered itself from the moment of Napoleon's collapse. In England and America all the religious and moral reaction to the recent wars was concentrated in the Peace Societies, which had a limited political programme or none at all. In Europe its earliest and perhaps its most impressive monument was Henri de Saint-Simon's *De la Réorganisation de la Société Européenne, ou de la nécessité et des moyens de rassembler les peuples de l'Europe en un seul corps politique en conservant à chacun son indépendance nationale* (1814). This was a more far-reaching proposal for the federal organisation of Europe than anyone had ever proposed. It advocated a single parliament and a single king for the whole of Europe. These would together regulate not only all questions of common interest, including Europe's colonial expansion, but also the economic and social affairs of the component states. The programme was justified by an appeal to the continent's history and to the earlier advocates of its unity.

Europe once formed a confederal society, united by common institutions, subjected to a general government which was to the peoples what national governments are to individuals. A similar arrangement is the only one that can correct everything. . . . We affect a supreme distrust of the centuries we call the middle ages . . . and we do not remember that it was the only time when the political system of Europe was founded on a true basis, on a general organisation. . . . All agree that the [present] political system . . . dates only from the sixteenth century. . . . And yet it is enough to examine history since then to realise that the balance of power is the falsest combination possible, since peace was its aim and it has produced nothing but wars—and what wars! Two men only have seen the evil and approached the remedy, Henry IV and Saint-Pierre. . . . They were not visionary in seeking to bind all the European peoples in a single political organisation since for six centuries such a system existed and in those centuries war was less frequent and terrible. . . .'[29]

Saint-Simon was not alone in making such a proposal and supporting it with these appeals. Even Napoleon, himself sharing in the reaction against Napoleon, looked forward on St. Helena to the day when his son would 'reunite Europe in indissoluble federal bonds'— would introduce 'the American Congress system' into the affairs of 'the great European family'—by peaceful means. This, he insisted, had been his own object: only England's refusal to collaborate had forced him to realise the project of Saint-Pierre and Rousseau by war. 'Since my fall and the disappearance of my system I do not think that any system has been possible in Europe except the agglomeration and confederation of its chief peoples. The first sovereign who will embrace the good cause of the peoples will find himself at the head of all Europe and will be able to attempt all he wishes.'[30] Alexander I's Holy Alliance did not go so far as this. It assumed that a solemn pledge to respect the principles of Christianity by the European monarchs—and by the American Republic, but not by the Sultan —would be a sufficient guarantee of peace. But if it proposed no political integration—how could a Tsar propose anything like that? —it thought of the chosen independent states as being 'members of one and the same Christian nation', and Alexander sponsored it partly because of his familiarity with the writings of Sully, Saint-Pierre and Rousseau.[31]

It was Saint-Simon who inspired most of the peace plans produced in Europe in the next generation: Pierre Leroux's *Organon des vollkommen Friedens* (1837); Gustav d'Eichthal's *De l'Unité Européenne* (1840); Victor Considérant's *De la Politique générale et du rôle de la France en Europe* (1840); Constantin Pecqueur's *De la Paix* (1841).[32] All these proposals involved federation—a single government—for Europe. Mazzini and his followers had the same goal, defined by Mazzini in the statutes he drew up for 'Young Europe' in 1834 as 'a unity that will be free, spontaneous, such as would exist in a regular Federation in which all the peoples sit in complete equality . . . , each remaining master of its own interests, its local affairs, its special faculties'.[33] Nor was this programme confined to Mazzinian, Saint-Simonian and other radical and socialist circles. It is even more significant of the strength of the forces working in this direction in Europe that, although the Geneva Peace Society was founded in 1830 expressly to cooperate with the Peace Societies in England and the United States, its founder, the Comte de Sellon, instituted a prize of a gold medal for the best essay outlining practical suggestions for realising the 'Grand Design' of Henry IV.[34] In the same way, when French economists, led by Bastiat and Vésinet, formed a Free Trade Society under Cobden's inspiration in 1847, their discussions on the international future soon took the same course, advocating and envisaging a United States of Europe as Cobden and the British Free Traders never did.[35] Victor Hugo, welcoming the delegates as president of the *Congrès des Amis de la Paix*, the third Universal Peace Congress, in Paris in 1849, looked forward to the day when 'we shall see those two immense communities, the United States of America and the United States of Europe, holding hands across the sea. . . . A day will come when you, France—you, Russia—you, Italy—you, England—you, Germany—all of you, nations of the Continent, will, without losing your distinctive qualities and your glorious individuality, be blended into a superior unity and constitute a European fraternity . . . by the universal suffrage of the nations, by the venerable arbitration of a great sovereign senate, which will be to Europe what the Parliament is to England, what the Diet is to Germany, what the legislative Assembly is to France.'[36] He was echoing an aspiration which had deep roots in the European consciousness and was widely entertained in his day.

The emphasis on federation necessitated some attempt to define Europe; and not all views were as expansive as Hugo's. The importance attached to democratic régimes as the basis of federation produced an almost universal assumption that Great Britain would belong to the new Europe. Saint-Simon had argued that the universal European Parliament could take its beginning from an Anglo-French union with a common Parliament, even as Bentham had seen an Anglo-French agreement as the way to a general pacification.[37] Czartoryski in his *Essai sur la Diplomatie* (1830) urged Sully's arguments in favour of his plea for a European community and similarly saw an Anglo-French *entente* as the first step to its achievement.[38] The conception of Europe could not be stretched to include the United States of America; but it was widely accepted that, as Hugo expressed it, there would be collaboration and fraternity between the two federations. But the same presumption that European federation must be based on the achievement of liberty within each state led most people to a definition of Europe that excluded Russia.

The 'Congress of Nations' of Ladd and Burritt would have admitted even autocratic states—though with their basis in Christian pacifism they were less sure whether non-Christian states could be included. The free trade and public opinion principles of men like Cobden could tolerate no exclusion at all. But European opinion scarcely considered even the possibility that Russia might cease to be autocratic. In the period before 1848 Mazzini and Pecqueur, a Saint-Simonian, explicitly excluded her from their European Federation. Mazzini even allowed the inclusion of non-Russian slavs as a sub-department of his Young Europe in order to create a barrier between Russia and the Western World. After 1848, Michael Chevalier expressed what was still the prevailing view when he excluded Russia on the grounds that 'the Russian Empire was destined to form indefinitely a unity of its own'. Others excluded her more permanently still by basing their European Federation on historical and ethnical, rather than political, uniformity. Émile Littré for these reasons called only for a federation of 'all the West' which excluded all slavs but admitted the Roman Catholic Poles.[39]

The European tendency to think in federal terms, and yet in a framework limited to western Europe, was not the only indication that the union of Europe was being given precedence over peace. Nor was it the immediate obstacle to European cooperation with the Anglo-American Peace Societies. More significant in the one direction, more serious in the other, was the refusal of most Europeans to work for peace at all, or even for Europe's integration, in the existing state of things. The Saint-Simonians, the socialist economists, the Mazzinians—all held aloof from the Congresses, distrusting the internationalist wing of the Movement as well as spurning its pacifist wing, and misunderstanding especially the intended scope of the proposed Congress of Nations, which they indignantly rejected as a Free Traders' plot to unite Europe before it was reformed and republicanised.[40] Their views directly reflected all those circumstances as a result of which even western Europe lagged behind the Anglo-Saxon world in political and social development. In Great Britain and the United States liberalism and nationalism were increasingly being satisfied. In Europe these were the years of restored absolutism, dissatisfied nationalism and frustrated liberalism. They were so to such an extent that the men in Europe who would otherwise have been in the forefront of the effort for peace, at this time when the effort was almost the monopoly of pacifist and liberal sentiment, abandoned the search for it altogether, at least as an immediate goal. The existing governments must be overthrown before peace could be established.

Auguste Comte had set this note in 1818 in a criticism of Saint-Pierre. 'The idea of the worthy Abbé was in itself good, but it erred by the false combination by means of which he wished to carry it out, for he proposed a coalition of kings—something like what we today call the Holy Alliance—to maintain peace. He might as well have proposed that wolves should guard the sheep. . . . It is only now . . . that it becomes possible to establish a lasting peace because the kings will not exclusively control it . . . and soon, by the power of public opinion, enlightened by the press . . . , the people will actually govern.'[41] Even earlier, in 1814, Saint-Simon's view had been essentially the same. In propounding the closest of European federations he had not supposed that it was immediately practicable.[42] On the contrary, he had asserted that it would never be practicable until it could be a League of peoples rather than of governments.

Assemble congress after congress, multiply treaties, conventions, arrangements and all that you do will still end only in war. . . . In all reunions of peoples . . . you must have common institutions, an organisation; otherwise all will be decided by force. . . . Saint-Pierre [however] proposed only a coalition of sovereigns; and tried to render permanent the imperfectible structure of the eighteenth century. He ignored the excellent principles of the papal organisation [in the middle ages]: 1. all organisation binding peoples together must respect their national independence; 2. the general government must be independent of the . . . national governments; 3. it ought to have its own power and not rely on the external power of the governments, and its own power can only be public opinion. The papal organisation was founded on these principles and it was these which made it work. . . . If everywhere in the old organisation one replaced feudal rulers by parliamentary government one would obtain a new organisation more perfect than the earlier one.[43]

His book was a plea for parliamentary government in each state as much as for a united Europe. Not for nothing was it entitled *De la Réorganisation de la Société Européenne.*

In later years, as liberal hopes died and the struggle between liberalism and autocracy was joined in Europe, the widespread acceptance of these ideas forced men's interest in peace even further into the background. Those who continued to propagate federal views as the means to peace usually pointed to the Germanic Confederation as their model; but they invariably pointed to England and the United

States as an indication of the extent to which Europe must be re-formed before their views would become practicable, and most of them believed that Europe would have to undergo a long series of wars and revolutions before that day would dawn. Nor were they content merely to state this belief. Pecqueur was almost alone in thinking that the development of international government, like the growth of nations, would not 'be achieved as the men of systems, the system makers, imagine: it will not be the result of choice and unanimous decision, nor come in a uniform manner everywhere. . . . In things like this old societies develop like old trees.'[44] More often, the wish to restore Europe to what was thought to have been its ancient unity was accompanied by the argument that one of Europe's states should reform Europe by force, in much the same way as earlier sovereigns and, more recently, the French Revolution and Napoleon had aspired to control and reform it.

Even Saint-Simon, in more hopeful days, had urged this upon his countrymen. 'Now that France can join England in defence of liberal principles it only remains to unite their strength and to use it to help Europe to reorganise itself. This union . . . can change the state of Europe because England and France united are stronger than the rest of Europe. Messieurs! you alone can hasten this revolution in Europe.'[45] Considérant, in his *De la Politique générale et du rôle de la France en Europe* (1840), was more emphatic. He urged that France must lead Europe to integration—if necessary by force.[46] This was one of the objectives of some of the men of 1848 in Paris. France, declared Sarrans, should announce the resumption of her old alliance with the oppressed peoples she had befriended under the old monarchy as well as under the Republic and the Empire. 'Who had defended Christendom against Rome? France. Who had freed the European littoral of Venetian despotism? France. Who had defeated the frightening efforts of the House of Austria? France. Who had defeated Protestantism and the philosophical revolt? Catholic France. Who had helped the young American Republic to triumph? France again; always France.'[47] Louis Blanc thought it one of the saddest proofs of the unsound condition of the world that it was necessary to support war on behalf of the oppressed peoples. He condemned the French middle class for 'being extravagantly desirous of peace' both on this account and because of his own nationalist feeling. The English with their commercial motives sought to domi-

nate other nations; the role of France was to use her strength to help
them to advance to freedom as well as to save herself from English
domination. 'Ten years of peace have broken us more than half a
century of war could have done.'[48] Nor can there be much doubt that
Napoleon III's foreign policy was influenced by these ideas, as well
as by his uncle's achievement and Saint-Simon's writings, in its search
for leadership in Europe. 'My aim', he wrote, 'is to prove that when
Providence throws up men like Caesar, Charlemagne, Napoleon,
it is to show people the way. . . . Happy the people who will follow.'[49]

These opinions were not confined to France; they were shared by
the leaders of the oppressed peoples. Mazzini did not go so far as the
Abbé Gioberti, whose book, *The Moral and Civil Primacy of the Italians*
(1843), argued that Italy alone was worthy to head a federal
Europe.[50] But far from urging any kind of peace plan he called for
war until the millenium should have arrived—as the means, indeed,
of bringing the millenium about. Mazzini held that there could be
no 'Holy Alliance of the Peoples' until the Holy Alliance of old-style
rulers 'against the future', 'the league of governments founded on
privilege', had been destroyed.[51] In order to destroy it, he wrote in
1832, 'war cannot be avoided; it must be waged in such a way as to
render peace or truce impossible until the Italian soil is free'.[52]
Nationality must be established 'if necessary by the sword'—and by
'the war of the masses', not by mere 'guerilla warfare'.[53] 'Is it enough,
he demanded in 1847, 'to preach peace and non-intervention, and
leave Force unchallenged ruler over three-fourths of Europe, to intervene, for its own unhallowed ends, when, where and how it thinks
fit?'[54] It was on this ground that in 1853, in direct opposition to
Cobden, he sought to convince England that her 'present duty is
war . . . war with the scope of solving once for all the ancient problem
whether Man is to remain a passive slave . . . war in the noble intention of restoring Truth and Justice, and of arresting Tyranny . . . ,
of rendering the Nations free and happy . . . , of crowning political
and religious liberty. . . .'[55]

In the same vein Marx maintained in the *Communist Manifesto* that
war was the only road to peace. He urged that the exploitation of
one nation by another would be ended only when the exploitation
of one individual by another within the state had been made impossible. 'With the end of the conflict of classes within the nations
the hostile attitude of nations against each other is removed.' And if

he glorified the class war as the necessary tool of social revolution, he also justified nationalism and international war as another means of bringing it about in his own country and as the means of spreading it to others. He regarded the Danish war of 1848 as a step towards the 'more progressive war', involving Prussia with Great Britain and Russia, 'which the slumbering German movement needs'.[56] For him as for Mazzini, and for them as much as for Hegel and Clausewitz, if only until the political and social order had been reformed, war was 'a mere continuation of policy by other means' and it seemed unquestionable that 'nations are strengthened as a result of war'.

The lack of interest of European writers in immediate peace, like the fact that European thought exhibited a strong drift towards federal ideas, towards an eventual United States of Europe, can be explained by historical traditions and political circumstances, which were so different in Europe from those in which Bentham, Mill and Cobden operated. They must not be allowed to conceal another fact: that in their different circumstances the European and the Anglo-Saxon schools of thought reached different conclusions on the international question on the basis of common assumptions. By political conditions, by historical antecedents, they were driven apart. On the intellectual plane they shared a single outlook.

One illustration of this—one indication that in circumstances similar to those of their European contemporaries the Anglo-Saxons would have taken up similar positions—is to be found in the strong undercurrent of distrust of government which marked even English and American liberal views. Anglo-American liberal opinion hated the Holy Alliance as much as did liberal opinion in Europe, even if it was not disposed to help to overthrow European governments. Its attitude to its own governments could afford to be more tolerant; it was not lacking in distrust. John Bright went further in this distrust than Ladd and Cobden had gone when, from the 1850's, he began to argue that wars were financed by the working class, which stood to lose most by them. The scorn of Ladd and Cobden for all governments had nevertheless extended to their own. It was under Ladd's influence that the Peace Societies began, in the 1830's, the practice of petitioning Parliament and Congress and memorialising other governments. His justification of this approach to other governments was one which he would equally have applied to petitions to Congress: 'Some may ask of what use it is to address crowned heads. We expect little from them; but, as they are so elevated, may it not be wise to use them as a flagstaff on which to hoist our colours?'[57] Cobden's efforts to moderate the programme of the Peace Movement, to make it more acceptable to Parliament and the Foreign Office, were entirely a question of tactics, unimportant beside his conviction that 'the intercourse between communities is nothing more than the intercourse of individuals in the aggregate', to which the intervention of governments was but an obstacle.[58]

A still more significant pointer in the same direction is that the Anglo-Saxon Liberal—and even the pacifist—sometimes adopted the European Liberal's justification of war. Thoreau opposed government wars but, like Marx, he was quite ready to condone war to destroy a class that was exploiting American society—the slaveowners of the South.[59] On this same issue William Lloyd Garrison, a pacifist who had split the American Peace Society in 1838 because it would not commit itself to complete Non-Resistance, declared in 1856 that he would countenance war as a means of eradicating slavery from the United States: 'Peace or war is a secondary consideration in view of our present perils.' The approach of the Civil War was disastrous to the American Peace Society precisely because the chief champions of peace—except for the strict Quakers—were also the chief advocates of forcible Abolition. They remind one of Dickens's list in *Barnaby Rudge* of those who contributed to the campaign funds of Lord George Gordon: 'The Friends of Reason, half-a-guinea. The Friends of Liberty, half-a-guinea. The Friends of Peace, half-a-guinea. The Friends of Charity, half-a-guinea. The Friends of Mercy, half-a-guinea. . . .' They salved their conscience with the argument that the South was threatening not international war but rebellion against the American Union. They justified war to save federation in America in much the same way as it was justified in Europe as a means of bringing federation about.[60]

These extreme views were the product of abnormal circumstances. But they also arose, as did the more normal advocacy of peace in these circles, from the Anglo-Saxon liberal conception of society and the state. This was based on the belief that, though individual behaviour was selfish, there was nevertheless a natural harmony between individuals which would lead to a just and progressive society if only the intervention of government were minimal and correctly inspired. This natural harmony would lead to a progressive society only in proportion as steps were taken to avoid too much government and government of the wrong kind—what J. S. Mill dismissed in *On Liberty* as 'the extravagance of government and . . . the greatest errors of administration'. Where unnatural privilege and other feudal abuses continued to exist it was because they were buttressed by government of the wrong kind which must be attacked and destroyed. These same assumptions were applied to produce the Anglo-Saxon liberal view of the relations between states. What shaped the attitude of England and America to the problem of peace and war from Bentham's day was the rise of the emphasis on material and economic, as opposed to political, ends; the rise of the conceptions of nation and society in antithesis to the conceptions of government and the state; and the rise of the conviction that, whereas there was a natural disharmony between governments and states, there was a natural harmony between nations and societies. These factors produced the belief that progress was destined to replace inter-governmental relations by the free play of enlightened public opinion between societies. And when that day dawned—when international relations became relations between nations or peoples—war, which was materially profitless and absurd and morally wrong, would be replaced by free and peaceful economic competitions, and such sources of dispute as still remained would easily be settled by judicial procedure.

This same distrust of existing governments, this same belief in the international millenium, registered themselves in Europe. They registered themselves more widely and more forcibly there because hated governments seemed more entrenched, the millenium farther away. But they registered themselves there on the basis of the same assumptions. If Europeans felt that peace must be deferred it was with Bentham's conviction that it need be deferred only until these hated governments had been removed, not from Kant's belief that it could only be the product of further international struggle. If they equated the establishment of peace with the federation of Europe it was not solely because of the force of historical traditions. It was also because, in violent contrast to Kant's conclusion that peace could only be the product of an arrangement between separate states, they believed that peace would be the automatic consequence of the replacement of relations between states by relations between nations and societies—once the old-order governments had been destroyed and a just social system had been established in each society. In different political and historical circumstances they could not share the Anglo-Saxon interest in immediate peace and the Anglo-Saxon lack of interest in federal forms; but their different conclusions were made in the same mould as those of the Anglo-Saxons.

Saint-Simon, unlike Bentham, wanted a single European Parliament and a single European state. It was entirely in the Bentham tradition, however, that he believed that an Anglo-French Parliament was the first step to the millenium, and that the single European state would be achieved and would operate 'without difficulty the moment all the peoples of Europe live under a parliamentary régime'. For him and for Comte and for their followers in the first half of the nineteenth century, again in the Bentham tradition, it was the support of public opinion throughout the European structure that alone could give the federal government its power—and that would infallibly give it that power.[61] The opinion of Marx and Mazzini was the same. It has often been noted that Marx said nothing about how perpetual peace was to be obtained once his social conditions had been met. Mazzini never stated precisely what form the European Federation would take once the republican ideal had prevailed in the internal politics of states and the arrangement of the map of Europe, and never outlined the steps by which it would be achieved. No doubt this was partly because their pre-conditions were never achieved. But it was also due to the fact that, on this point at least, they thought like Bentham and Cobden.

Marx was firmly attached to a belief in perpetual peace. If he said little about it it was because he believed that it would follow automatically upon the withering away of the state. It was essential for Mazzini that the Federation should be one in which 'all the peoples sit in complete equality . . . , each remaining master of its own interests, its local affairs, its individual faculties'. But far from seeing in these conditions some hint of possible incompatibility between his insistence on nationality and his hope of a Federation, he had such high hopes of the potentialities of full national development as to believe that federation would naturally follow from it. By 1849, indeed, he was writing of the future organisation of Europe in terms which were almost indistinguishable from the outlook of Bentham and Cobden—in terms which made federation unnecessary and the fraternal spirit sufficient in its place. 'Nationality should be to humanity only what the division of labour is in the workshop.' 'The indisputable tendency of the epoch is towards a reconstruction of Europe, in accordance with different national vocations, into a certain number of states as nearly as possible equal in population and extent. The states . . . become more and more intimately associated through the medium of democracy. . . . They will gradually unite in a common faith and common pact in all that regards their international life. The Europe of the future will be One, avoiding alike the anarchy of absolute independence and the centralisation of conquest.'[62] If unsatisfied nationality rendered international organisation unacceptable to him, satisfied nationality would of itself produce such organisation as would be required—if any were required.

CHAPTER 7

FROM THE CRIMEAN WAR TO THE LEAGUE OF NATIONS

FROM the middle of the nineteenth century these earlier basic beliefs were slowly forced to the side. They did not die; they remained as powerful as ever in some minds. But a complex process altered the total context in which they operated. The avoidance of war became a problem of more widespread concern; the discussion of it ceased to be the monopoly of those drawn to it by moral fervour and pacifist conviction. At the same time the belief in an antithesis between society and the state—in a necessary conflict between a nation and its government—gave way in most men's minds to a different conception of the political community.

The widening of interest in the maintenance of peace was partly due to the influence of the Peace Movement. In 1853 the *Manchester Examiner* could write that 'the principles of the Peace Society, fanatical as they are, have unquestionably gained ground among us; statesmen shrink from war now, not only on account of its risks, its cost, its possible unpopularity, but from a new-born sense of the tremendous moral responsibility which lies on those who . . . bring upon humanity such an awful curse.'[1] None of these considerations prevented the third quarter of the century from being a generation of wars. But all of them were underlined in those years by the prevalence of war itself in a world which had avoided serious conflicts in the previous forty years, which was experiencing vast technological changes towards increased destructiveness in warfare and which was becoming more closely integrated.

It was not only the western world as a whole that was becoming more integrated. Each of its individual states was moving internally in the same direction. As society became more industrialized and more complex, changes in the nature of society forced governments to become more representative more efficient and more just regulators of their communities—even as the increase in knowledge and technology enabled them to become so. The same changes in the nature of society, together with the improvement of government and the extension of the suffrage, reconciled the mass of public opinion to the state. From both of these directions the manifold relations of government and society underwent a distinct alteration towards greater cohesion from about the 1860's in all the more developed countries. This was prominently displayed in the changing character of national sentiment. Nationalism became increasingly concentrated on the organs and symbols of the state after long years in which the sense of community had been either not national sentiment at all or else a sense of nationality that was in conflict with government. Nor was this the only sign of the emergence of the modern state in our modern sense of the phrase. Socialism was the logical as well as the chronological successor to Liberalism for another reason than that it made its appeal to the masses of men. It would itself use all the powers of modern government to achieve its ends, even if it believed that the state would wither away when these ends had been achieved. As for the growing cohesion of society, consider the changes that took place in the organisation of the Peace Movement itself. Up to 1889 it consisted of individual groups of men each seeking international affiliations. In 1889 these international affiliations were further advanced by the establishment of the Inter-Parliamentary Conference and the revival of the earlier Universal Peace Congresses,[2] but the groups still lacked national organisation. After 1902 the various groups in each state inaugurated National Peace Congresses and national executive committees to enable them to work out a common policy in advance of the annual Universal Congresses.[3]

Such changes were necessarily reflected in men's outlook on international relations—in their thinking about the problem of peace and war. Since criticism of and conflict with government became less the order of the day the solutions proposed even by those who remained idealistically inclined ceased to ignore the state's increasing power. As concern with the international problem ceased to be virtually the monopoly of critics of government a new kind of publicist, who was not at loggerheads with government, found an interest in the field. Being a jurist or a political scientist he propounded empirical, down-to-earth blue-prints, and this at a time when to be empirical meant above all to take into account the changing character and increasing power of the state. Eventually, though most slowly and reluctantly, governments themselves began to contemplate the problem and study the blue-prints, for the first time at least in modern history. But even before governments began to take a hand the prevailing attitude was, for these two reasons, already dominated by their existence and reshaped in accordance with their changing nature. This development was the central feature of this phase in the history of peace plans. The key to that history between the time of Dante and the middle of the eighteenth century lies in the struggle of the notion of an international organisation for the maintenance of peace between separate states to free itself from, and rise above, the earlier and tenacious conception of 'a single political system maintained by a single supreme authority in the interests of order. There had emerged from this struggle, first, proposals for the closest federation of the separate states; and then the criticism and dismissal of that solution that we find in Rousseau, Kant and Bentham. The key to the phase which stretches from the middle of the nineteenth century to the First World War will be found to lie in the struggle of the conception of an organisation for purposes strictly limited to the peaceful settlement of international problems, between separate and vastly more powerful and more integrated states, to free itself from, and rise above, both the goal of avoiding war by means of a comprehensive federal merger of separate states and the belief which reached its final development in the generation after Bentham and James Mill—the belief that the maintenance of peace in a world of separate states required no international organisation at all.

This middle-way or confederal approach had, indeed, emerged before: there will be exceptions to all such generalisations. At the time of the defeat of Napoleon not only Alexander I in his Holy Alliance and the leading Powers as a whole in their Congress System, but also the occasional writer in Germany, using the German Confederation as his point of departure, had urged that cooperation between or an alliance of states would be a sufficient guarantee against war. This had been the argument of Karl Krause in his *Entwurf eines europäischen Staatenbundes* (1814). In the first half of the nineteenth century occasional writers in France, Émile de Girardin and Henri Feugueray among them, had similarly recommended only a confederation of states, a diet of government representatives; while one of the more empirical of the Saint-Simonian federalists, Pecqueur, had granted that it would be necessary to move through the stage of a confederal diet between free governments towards the full federal ideal.[4] But these had been isolated voices. In Europe up to the 1850's the prevailing opinion had run direct to the complete suppression of state sovereignties, and had excluded inter-governmental schemes as effectively as in the Anglo-Saxon world it had excluded any form of international organisation whatsoever.

The rise of the new approach was not at all rapid during the rest of the century. In the Anglo-Saxon background men had to reach it by concluding that the improvement of international relations and the avoidance of war required an international organisation with some at least of the attributes of government—even as they had to discover that stronger and more active government was the guarantee of internal progress within the state. In Europe they had to reach it by concluding that, since international organisation would necessarily be shaped by the existence and growing power of separate governments, the hope of an automatic and total federal merger of reformed societies—and even the localised goal of an exclusive European federation—must be abandoned in favour of a more limited arrangement between states. Against these opposite obstacles, in the two different worlds, the shift to the new approach was slow for two reasons. In both areas it was the rise of the modern state that chiefly forced the compromise, as it was the changing character of the state that reconciled men to it; and this was itself a far from obvious process, and one that was but dimly understood at the time. It did not rapidly alter people's views. Then, secondly, the confederal solution presupposed the collaboration of governments. And if these were the years in which governments at last turned their attention to the possibilities of international machinery they were also years in which governments' powers were expanding and in which governments asserted their independence and freedom of action more firmly than ever—until they, too, were driven in the confederal direction by the outbreak of the First World War.

It was not only for these reasons that the process was a slow one. The new approach had constantly to battle with the earlier ideas. These were never wholly abandoned—they have not been abandoned to this day. They represented from one point of view an earlier and more unsophisticated stage in the understanding of international problems. From another point of view they were but the early nineteenth-century version of a basic tendency to over-simplification in some men's thinking about international relations. Not all people have displayed this tendency at any time but some people have displayed it at all times—at least since the seventeenth century—and still display it. Of them we may say what Burke said of the loyalty of eighteenth-century country gentlemen to the House of Hanover: they change the idol but they preserve the idolatry. In the seventeenth and eighteenth centuries such men had believed that the uniform achievement of enlightened despotism would guarantee international peace. Far from being confounded by the French Revolution and Napoleonic wars, the tendency merely took a different course with early nineteenth-century liberals and socialists. They spurned the despot but assumed with no less confidence that enlightened opinion in liberal or democratic communities would guarantee peace. And far from being confounded by the wars of the third quarter of the nineteenth century, men of this basic persuasion either found in them evidence with which to buttress the early nineteenth-century views or—if they were attracted by the Socialist creed which increasingly rivalled Liberalism in these years—used them, with but another shift of detail, with only a different definition of the enlightened community, to prove that war would be as unthinkable between working-men or socialist societies as it was incurable between the old-style governments or liberal *bourgeois* states.

One result of these wars, as of the spread of Socialism, was thus to redouble the activities of those who still clung to the assumptions of the first half of the century. In England the Crimean War produced the foundation (1854), by the combined efforts of Sturge, Cobden, and the Peace Society, of the *Morning Star* newspaper to undertake what the war had revealed to be so regrettably necessary—the moral reform of public opinion in international questions.[5] From the United States in 1853 Burritt, anticipating organised Socialism's appeal to class consciousness as a provision against war, demanded 'an organised strike of the working-men of Christendom against war', an idea which John Bright had already toyed with.[6] There followed with the approach of the Civil War the discomfiture of the American Peace Society; but as soon as that war was over the men in the United States who had been disturbed by the non-pacifist record of the Peace Society founded new organisations. These organisations— the Universal Peace Union, the Peace Organisation of the Friends, the Peace Organisation of the American Bible Society—upheld the old attitudes. So did the new organisations that were being founded in England to recruit support in new sections of the public. The Reform League, founded in 1864, condemned war in the interests of the working class in all countries. The original declaration of the International Working Men's Association, founded in 1865 with a similar programme by the same men, spoke in the old vein to these new sections. 'Despotism', it announced, 'and arbitrary power are detestable in whatever shape they appear. . . . Our interest is one and the same. . . . We can have no interest in injuring one another. . . War is the mad and wicked game played by Emperors and Kings with the lives and wealth of the people; place it under your ban. If you refuse . . . the bloody game must cease. . . . How the power of the tyrant and the despot would be paralysed; how trade and commerce would spring forth with fresh elasticity. . . . All this rests with you.'[7]

This declaration was issued in the form of an 'Address to the Peoples of Europe'. All the new American and English societies resumed the old effort to establish links with kindred spirits on the Continent. They did so with more success than before. The first noticeable effect on European opinion of the increasing efficiency and responsibility of government was to end the days when the favoured means of working for peace had been revolt against governments and war upon them. Nor could it be overlooked that established authority had public opinion on its side: if governments could no longer be ove turned by force, public opinion still stood in need of education. The earlier aloofness of European liberals, radicals and republicans from peace propaganda and from peace congresses accordingly came to an end. It was Edmond Potonié-Pierre, a French republican, who first advocated, in 1858–9, a resumption of the earlier international Peace Congresses and then founded the *Ligue du Bien Public*, the first of many new European organisations to be established in the next few years.

In Europe as in England and America, however, it was the old convictions that received a new lease of life, that were in the first instance propagated by the new method of leagues for publicity and discussion. Democracy—at least in the shape of the extension of the suffrages—and nationalism were producing wars instead of peace. But were they not doing so because they had been taken under the wing of despotic governments—of men like Bismarck and Cavour— or distorted by the possessing classes? Potonié-Pierre's *Ligue* began to issue a polyglot monthly journal, *Le Cosmopolite*, in 1866. Its programme was 'to secure what conquerors have never secured by the force of arms, nor legislators by the force of law, nor the founders of religion by the power of dogma . . . , the inauguration of that universal republic in which all men, all peoples, must one day unite.'[8] In 1867 there followed the foundation of Ferdinand Santallier's *Union de la Paix* at Le Havre and of Frederick Passy's *Ligue International et Permanent de la Paix* at Paris. These laid less emphasis than Potonié-Pierre on republicanism, but their essentially pacifist programmes still involved a distrust of governments. In Santallier's view even the peace organisations of the first half of the century had been too much concerned to obtain the cooperation of governments. The right approach was to agitate in the press and from the pulpit until a strong pacifist sentiment, if not a pacifist majority, had been created in all countries. Only then would it be safe to establish a committee to draw up an international code and create an international governing body to administer it. He resisted all attempts to centralise the efforts of the new peace organisations until every society had, like his own, agreed to eliminate from its programme the appeal to governments. He applied this ban to Passy's *Ligue*, though that specialised in the publication of addresses from the working-men of France to the working-men of other countries.[9]

Even Santallier took exception, as did Passy, to the programme of a third organisation as being too extreme. This was The International League of Peace and Liberty, set up, also in 1867, with yet another journal, *Les États Unis de L'Europe*, by a meeting of 'the friends of peace' in Geneva under the presidency of Garibaldi. Its guiding spirit was the veteran Saint-Simonian, Charles Lemonnier. Its programme—ostensibly to examine the bases of peace, to promote the discussion of international problems and to educate public opinion in all classes in the direction of peace—resolved itself into an attack on 'old systems of government' by these new procedures. The bases of peace were defined as the substitution of democracy for monarchy in all countries; the separation of Church and State in all countries; the formation of the United States of Europe. Passy, with his single pacifist aim of 'war on war', repudiated Lemonnier's 'ulterior motives'. Santallier wrote that whereas Passy's *Ligue* and his *Union* believed liberty to be unattainable without peace, and therefore stood resolutely against war, The International League of Peace and

Liberty preached liberty as a prior condition of peace and would be willing to secure it by means of war.[10]

Despite these criticisms it was Lemonnier's organisation that captured most attention and following in Europe in the next few years, just as in England—where the leaders of the Reform League established a branch of The International League in December 1867—the pace was set not by the older pacifist Peace Society but the Reform League and the International Working Men's Association, which did not subscribe to Lemonnier's federal goal but otherwise pursued similar aims. Thirteen countries were represented at the International League's first annual conference in 1868. It declared war to be 'justifiable only for legitimate defence'; demanded the abolition of standing armies and the establishment of an international 'army of peace' against aggression; but also refused to discuss disarmament as being impracticable until the United States of Europe had become a reality. In 1869 the next annual conference reiterated the demand for the United States of Europe on a republican basis—though in sharp contrast to its earlier demand for an international army it also proclaimed the right of every nation to decide its own questions of peace and war.[11]

It was not only in these organisations that earlier aspirations and the old attitude to governments continued to find expression. One of the responses to the outbreak of the Franco-Prussian War was the foundation of peace societies in European countries where they had not previously existed—in Belgium, the Netherlands and Italy. They conformed to the new methods, seeking to establish peace, in the words of the Netherlands Peace League, by 'persuasion, encouragement and reasoning'. But the Netherlands Peace League—or at least some members of it—sought also the reform of the Netherlands Constitution in such a way as to deprive the Crown of the power of declaring war without consulting the people; while Morelli, a leader of the Italian movement, invited the Italian Parliament to propose to the world the institution of an Amphictyonic League.[12] Nor was the spread of these societies the only result of the war of 1870. Men who otherwise had no connection with any of the peace societies—men like Renan and Pardieu in France and, even in England, the historian Seeley—were induced by this further shock to urge the federation of Europe.[13] By that time, moreover, other developments, as well as the succession of wars in Europe, were beginning to be invoked on behalf of that goal. Michael Chevalier, in the *Revue des Deux Mondes* in 1866, was perhaps the first to urge the unification of Europe as a necessary counter-weight to the American 'political colossus' that was emerging on the other side of the Atlantic.[14] In 1883 an industrialist, J. B. André Godin, in his book, *Le Gouvernement*, proposed a European Federation, with an international army, as well as a permanent international arbitration congress.[15]

The time never came, indeed, when these attitudes and this goal were wholly abandoned. Cobden's insistence that there was no difference between the relations of states and the relations between individuals—or, at least, that there ought not to be—still remained the basis of much peace propaganda in the 1890's. 'The principle of right and morality for nations', declared the Universal Peace Congress at Rome in 1891, 'is identical with that of right and morality for individuals. As no one has the power to exact justice for himself, so no state has the power to declare war on another.'[16] The old peace programmes—the federation of Europe, the public or democratic control of foreign policy, the socialisation of all countries—similarly continued to have their advocates.

The same Peace Congress of 1891 invited the European Peace Societies 'to make the United States of Europe the chief aim of their propaganda'.[17] The Universal Peace Congress of 1892 called for the confederation of Europe on the lines laid down by Lemonnier.[18] In 1891 Engels announced that 'between a Socialist France and a ditto Germany an Alsace-Lorraine problem has no existence at all';[19] and the Congress of International Working Men's Associations resolved that peace could only be secured when the Associations' proletarian aims had been achieved.[20] Two years earlier the second Working Men's International had denounced war as 'an expression of the bourgeois capitalist régime'.[21] In 1903, when the Boer War had redoubled his conviction that peace was safe only with the workers, Cremer, founder and organiser of the International Working Men's Association in Great Britain, endowed the association with the money he had received with the Nobel prize on condition that two-thirds of its council should always be chosen from 'the industrialised classes . . . the future rulers of the world'.[22] From 1885 until his death in 1908 he campaigned each year in the House of Commons for complete parliamentary control of foreign and imperial policy and the removal from the Crown of the power to make treaties and declare war without parliamentary approval—the programme for which the leader of the British Peace Society had established The Anti-Aggression League in 1882, after the annexation of the Transvaal and the occupation of Egypt. The Universal Peace Congress of 1890 voiced the same demand. The American Peace Society began to insist on it in 1898 as a result of the Spanish-American War and the occupation of the Philippines.[23]

And after the 1890's, as will be seen, there came a marked revival of the popularity of these nostrums and an increase in the vigour with which they were pressed.

These facts must not be allowed to conceal the change that came over the tactics, if not always over the assumptions and objectives, of the leaders of the Peace Movement after the 1850's.

The older and strictly pacifist organisations—the British and the American Peace Societies—still concentrated, as before, on the demand for disarmament and an international tribunal, a programme which went back to Bentham and Mill; and there was little change in the methods they adopted. They devoted themselves to the task of moving resolutions on these subjects in the House of Commons and in Congress, and to the work of stimulating European parliamentary deputies to table similar resolutions; but they had already been drawn into this campaign in the first half of the nineteenth century, by the fact of advocating these measures requiring government collaboration no less than by the fact that they were seeking to influence public opinion in states where government depended to some extent on public opinion.[24] Even so, their resolutions now revealed a different attitude to government. In the first half of the century these had not been accompanied by the hope of obtaining government collaboration so much as by the conviction that public and parliamentarian pressure must be used to limit the machinations of government and to enforce a change in government behaviour. This conviction was being replaced by the belief that the best way to progress was to persuade governments of the merits of the peace programme. It was a change that was reinforced by an alteration in the attitude of the Peace Societies to public opinion. In 1864 the British Peace Society denounced nationalism as 'a poor, low, selfish, unchristian idea . . . , fatal not only to peace but to all progress in liberty and good government'. In the controversies aroused by the

Polish insurrection of the 1860's it supported non-intervention—preferred the maintenance of Russian authority to the establishment of Polish independence—on the side of Palmerston against Cobden and Bright.[25]

Such a shift as this could easily have destroyed the possibility of collaboration between these old organisations and the newer peace societies which sprang up in the 1860's. But the new organisations, whose foundation itself represented one step towards compromise—towards the policy of influencing opinion in preference to the policy of overthrowing governments—moved farther in the same direction from the outset. They had been formed to appeal to sections of society which the older groups—as revealed by their comments on nationalism—did not trust. Many of their members retained the militant anti-government beliefs—and, at least in Europe, the federalist hopes—of the first half of the century. In so far as they were pacifist, they represented a secular and anti-clerical pacifism and not the religious pacifism of the original Peace Societies. If they were able to work with the original societies it was because they made the even greater sacrifice of subordinating or deferring these favoured doctrines. Most of them joined the older societies in 1870 in making an appeal to governments in an attempt to avert the Franco-Prussian War.[26] Thereafter, most of them concentrated their efforts on the demand for arbitration and disarmament and their hopes on the conversion of governments to this programme.

In 1870 the British Reform League set up a Workmen's Peace Committee. After being enlarged and re-christened the International Workmen's Peace Association, this produced in 1871 an 'Outline of a Plan for the establishment of High Court of Nations'. Despite the strong connections of the Association with Lemonnier's International League for Peace and Liberty, this programme was in substance as well as in name an exact repetition of James Mill's proposal, fifty years earlier, for an international law code and an international Court—of that proposal on which the older societies were still concentrating all their efforts. Like Mill, moreover, it decided against military sanctions to enforce the decisions of the Court, and so preserved the Association's ability to work with the Peace Society, whose pacifist objection to all use of force ruled out the acceptance of sanctions.[27] By 1880 the Association had gone further still in this direction: it continued to appeal to working class solidarity but it had changed its name again, from The International Workmen's Peace Association to The International Arbitration League.[28]

By the same date the same transformation had gone far on the Continent. The campaign for arbitration was the main plank in the platform of the societies founded in Europe after the Franco-Prussian War. One of these groups, the Spanish Peace Society, instituted in 1872 a prize essay competition on the subject, *The Best Means of Establishing a Representative European Arbitral Assembly*.[29] Pacifist groups which appeared in Berlin in 1874 and Vienna in 1876 went one step further still by suggesting that the best means of advancing this cause would be to form a 'Universal Parliamentary Peace Union' composed of members from every legislature.[30] Even the societies founded in the 1860's gave priority to the same programme. Lemonnier at Geneva associated his International League with it: in 1874 he advocated in his journal a plan by which governments should accept permanent treaties of arbitration.[31] Passy adopted arbitration as his watchword; and his League, which had changed its name to the French Society of the Friends of Peace in 1872, changed it again in 1883, when it became *La Société Française de l'Arbitration entre les Nations*.[32] In 1884 even Santallier, that vigorous opponent of collusion with governments, joined Passy in presenting to the French Chamber a petition calling for government agreement to the establishment of an Arbitration Tribunal.[33]

In Europe this concentration on a limited programme was not so easily effected as in England and the United States. At a conference of all the peace organisations in 1878, assembled in Paris on the invitation of the London Workmen's Peace Association, delegates from 13 countries denounced war as brigandage; attacked the Church and the Press; demanded liberty of conscience in all states; insisted that if the trade unions would speak out against war there would be permanent peace; and urged the establishment of a European Parliament. Nevertheless, the movement's leaders steered the Conference into adopting resolutions advocating the creation of an Arbitration Committee, composed of two representatives from each state, and of an international committee to investigate the armaments situation; into accepting the federation of all the peace organisations behind this programme; into sending a delegation from the Conference to the Congress of Berlin with the proposal that the assembled delegates should follow up the mediation clause in the Treaty of Paris by discussing the establishment of an arbitration procedure. Lemonnier accepted a place on the committee set up to organise the federation.[34]

It is clear, indeed, that they had no choice but to take this course. The difficulties it created for them with their own followings were less than those which would have resulted from not making this adjustment to the growth of government prestige and the alteration in public sentiment. It was those forces which led Lemonnier to confess in 1888 that 'a federation of peoples' was not yet realisable.[35] The same forces had driven Santallier's and Potonié's mixture of pacifism and republicanism out of business after the Franco-Prussian War, and they led Potonié to revive his League in Berlin, not in France.[36] By 1878 they were driving even Passy's unpolitical pacifism out of existence: his society was dying before it changed its name in 1883, and its change of name resulted from its absorption by a new organisation, the *Comité de Paris de la Fédération International de l'Arbitrage et de la Paix*, which was not primarily pacifist.[37] And where these forces continued to be neglected by the Peace Movement it was with serious results. It was because some of the organisers of the Netherlands Peace League persisted in working for the limitation of the control of the Crown over foreign policy, as well as for peace, that the League steadily disintegrated—that by 1891, after 20 years, only 2 of its original branches, nearly 30 in all, survived.[38] When the British Peace Society adopted this same demand after 1880, in addition to its campaign for arbitration and disarmament, it only reared up a powerful rival organisation and reduced its own following.[39]

Despite these adjustments—the change in tactics, the limitation of programme—the peace societies, both the old ones and those founded in the 1860's and 1870's, were still overtaken by another development. From the middle of the century a new kind of man, different from the member of the peace societies, began to concern himself with international relations, and particularly with the avoidance of war, in greater numbers than in Cobden's day—the man with professional training, the jurist, the Member of Parliament, the political scientist. From the 1870's he began to go beyond the peace societies in his preparedness to work with governments and his concentration on limited aims. His response to the new situation was less enforced than theirs, less liable to retraction at times of stress.

At first these men joined the old peace societies and even became founder-members of new peace societies. In 1860 the American lawyer, David Dudley Field, read a paper on disarmament to a meeting of the Peace Society at Manchester.[40] The leadership in founding a peace movement in Italy between 1868 and 1871 was provided by five members of the Italian Parliament, one of whom—Mancini—was also a professor of International Law.[41] A senator, Marcoartu, was the founder of the peace movement in Spain.[42] In 1873 another American lawyer, J. B. Miles, toured Europe with a plan for a permanent system of arbitration, drawn up by himself, Dudley Field and other lawyers in collaboration with Burritt, and presented it to a conference of European peace-movement leaders at Brussels.[43] The collaboration of such men undoubtedly helped the peace movement to adjust to circumstances. But the year 1873 also marked an important stage in their emergence as a separate organised force. The Brussels conference revealed that differences of approach were developing between them and the peace organisations despite the adjustment of the latter. It was followed by their creation of independent associations.

The growing interest of professional men in international problems had already been revealed by the foundation of the Social Science Association in London in 1871—and perhaps by the establishment of two Arbitration Societies, in Yorkshire and Lancashire, in 1872.[44] In 1873 came the establishment of The International Code Committee in the United States and of the *Institut de Droit International* and The Association for the Reform and Codification of International Law, later (1895) restyled The International Law Association, in Europe. These groups shared the Peace Movement's interest in peace: as their names suggest, they had the object of codifying international law so as to make it 'an organ of the world's conscience' and an effective means of settling international disputes without recourse to war. But except in the case of the *Institut* their membership was not confined to lawyers—it was open to all who were interested—and their foundation also represented a growing uneasiness with even the modified attitude of the Peace Movement's leaders.

This uneasiness was openly revealed at the Brussel's conference by the tendency of the lawyers to advocate a programme that was in some respects less pacifist and idealist, and in other respects more restricted, than that of the Peace Movement. The arbitration plan drawn up by Miles and Dudley Field raised the issue of military sanctions when presented to the conference. Field's book, *International Tribunal* (1872), had not proposed sanctions. The plan of 1873 showed him to be veering towards the need for them, and this disturbed pacifist peace leaders. They were still more disturbed by the suggestion made at the conference by Bluntschli, Professor of Law at Heidelberg. He argued that international arbitration would be safer and more practicable if disputes arising from 'the vital interests' of states were excluded from its operation. His argument was vehemently opposed by Richard, of the British Peace Society, and Passy.[45] Another source of dispute was the problem of disarmament. The *Institut* and The Association for the Reform and Codification of International Law both expressly excluded disarmament from their programme—not because it was an issue beyond the scope of international law but because they judged the time not ripe for it. The peace organisations, notably the British Peace Society and the Workmen's Peace Association, continued to campaign for disarmament as ardently as for the establishment of arbitration procedure.[46] Indeed, their demand for it increased in intensity with the growth in the size and cost of armaments programmes and with the publication of such anti-militarist works as Bertha von Suttner's novel *Die Waffen Nieder* (1889).

The Peace Movement was disconcerted by the tendency of the law associations. It could hardly denounce their programme, which had been narrowed down by 1877 to the demand for the insertion of clauses for the obligatory arbitration of some but not—as a result of arguments like Bluntschli's—of all disputes in all future treaties between states.[47] But the programme, indeed the very foundation, of another society was deplored by some of the peace societies. The International Arbitration and Peace Society of Great Britain and Ireland, inaugurated by Hodgson Pratt in 1880, was partly an attempt to publicise the aims of the international law associations by adopting the propaganda devices which had hitherto been left to the peace movement. Dudley Field took an active part, for example, in promoting branches for Hodgson Pratt in the United States.[48] It was also a retaliation against the return of the British Peace Society and

The International Working-Men's Peace Association (lately re-christened the International Arbitration League) to the policy of denouncing British annexations and demanding the establishment of parliamentary control over foreign policy and decisions of peace and war—against the movement which led Richard to set up The Anti-Aggression League in 1882.*

Pratt argued that the peace societies, with their spiritual pacifism and Christian view-point, were out of date. The times called for a purely secular organisation and programme. He argued that these needed to be much wider in appeal and understanding than such secular but equally old-fashioned groups as the International Working-Men's Peace Association. His methods, like theirs, was to work on public opinion by establishing societies in all countries and publishing a new journal, *Concord*. Not unlike theirs, his programme called for arbitration instead of war, for the development of friendly feelings between different nations, for the correction of the false statements made on international affairs in the Press and in Parliaments. But while it was pacifist to the extent that it deplored the use of force except for defence, it did not include disarmament or even the avoidance of all war. It insisted as much as the Peace Movement that progress lay with the spread of information and of democracy. It also insisted, however, that progress depended on the maintenance by each state of adequate armaments as the means of obtaining justice from other states.[49]

The British Peace Society denounced this programme as Palmerstonian. Not all the peace societies were able to take so vigorous a stand. The *Comité* which absorbed Passy's League in France in 1883 was the group which Hodgson Pratt had formed in Paris; and thereafter French pacifists never ceased to affirm, like Pratt, that there must always remain the right of legitimate defence against unprovoked aggression and against a government that refused the pacific settlement of a dispute.[50] The Italian peace movement, chiefly composed of Workmen's Associations up to 1880, and inclined to press for disarmament and the democratic control of foreign policy as well as for arbitration, was in that year almost wholly swept into Pratt's organisation, renamed the National Association for Arbitration and Peace—and revitalised. It had 79 branches at the end of a further 10 years.[51] In Scandinavia, where there had been no peace move-

* Above, p. 123.

ment before 1880, it was chiefly under Pratt's influence that societies were founded in Denmark, Sweden and Norway in 1882–3.[52] Pratt's movement had established itself in 9 European countries by 1889, as well as in England and the United States, while the British Peace Society was able only to attempt—and to fail—to expand into Japan and China.[53] The International Arbitration and Peace Society was the outstanding success of the 1880's, as the pacifist leagues had been in the 1860's and as Lemonnier's International League and the International Working-Men's Association had been in the 1870's. It would be difficult to find a better indication of the character and extent of the change that was taking place in men's attitude to international problems.

A further sign of the times was the formation of an international association of the parliamentary members of the movement for arbitration. The proposal that, pending the eventual formation of an International Court, a series of inter-parliamentary conferences should watch over and assist the gradual development of arbitration had been mooted from time to time since 1874, when it was first advocated by a pacifist group in Berlin. Marcoartu included it in his arbitration plan of 1885, which was notable for advocating the gradual development of arbitration on the basis of existing international law, rather than the immediate establishment of an International Tribunal.[54] It was at last taken up in 1889 when the first Inter-Parliamentary Conference for International Arbitration,* meeting at Paris, was attended by delegates from France, Great Britain, the United States, Italy, Spain, Denmark, Belgium, Hungary and Liberia. There followed in 1892 the organisation of The Inter-Parliamentary Union and The Inter-Parliamentary Bureau, a coordinating body and a secretariat to keep the parliamentary delegations in touch between their annual meetings.

The decision to summon the first conference stimulated the peace societies to revive in the same year, 1889, the Universal Peace Congresses of the 1840's and 1850's, and to set up at last their own single secretariat, The International Peace Bureau, in 1892. But these steps marked the beginning of another retreat by the Peace Movement. Conference and Congress were closely interlocked. A notable Peace Movement leader—Cremer of the International Working-Men's

---

* It was not until 1899 that the words 'for International Arbitration' were deleted from the formal title.

Peace Association—took the initiative in calling the first inter-Parliamentary Conference. The Conference was confined to those Members of Parliament who were interested in organising peace. It was planned that the Congress and the Conference should meet annually in the same city—though in a different city each year—at such times as would enable the Members of Parliament to attend both. But the divisions within the Congress and between the Congress and the Conference soon ensured that the more practicable got the better of the more radical elements in the movement.

At the Congresses four distinct kinds of peace society—four successive historical levels in the growth of the Peace Movement during the nineteenth century—were represented: the British and American Peace Societies with their religious pacifism; the secular pacifist leagues of the 1860's; organisations modelled on Lemonnier's Geneva League and sharing its democratic, if not its federalist, aspirations; the international law associations and the movement inspired by Hodgson Pratt. They were bound to differ. But their agreement to the revival of the Congresses after so long an interval was itself an indication of their wish to agree; and in their efforts to avoid differences they found another compelling reason for limiting their programme to the demand for arbitration between states. Arbitration was the only subject on which they could agree—though even on that subject they had their differences—and arbitration was accordingly the subject to which they devoted most attention. The Congress of 1893 discussed a plan for an International Court drawn up by American lawyers. That of 1894 declared that 'the most practicable and just means of settling international disputes is that of permanent arbitration agreements with definite pacific sanctions'. That of 1896 adopted a draft project for an International Code—for which it invoked the blessing of the Pope.

Even so, the Congresses did not always suppress their more rebellious members or follow the lead of the most vigorous societies—those of Hodgson Pratt. A divergence at once emerged between their idealism and the more practical and prudent standpoint of the Conferences of parliamentary delegates, who invited delegates from governments—not excluding the governments of Russia and other non-parliamentary states—to attend their meetings after 1896. The Congresses burst out from time to time, as has already been noticed, with resolutions demanding the democratic control of foreign policies, asserting the primacy of moral considerations in international affairs and calling for the federation of Europe.* They also remained more radical than the Inter-Parliamentary Conferences on the question of arbitration. The Conferences, easily restraining the more ardent among the parliamentarians, confined themselves to discussing the best tactical means of developing arbitration and to increasing their influence on governments. The Conference of 1889 formally invited governments to conclude arbitration treaties without prejudice to their national independence and advocated the inclusion of an arbitration clause in all future commercial treaties. In contrast to this, the inaugural Congress of 1889 advocated arbitration in uncompromising terms. Arbitration should form a fundamental part of the constitution of every state; it should be embodied in every future treaty. And the Congress of 1897, sweeping aside Hodgson Pratt's insistence that no government could specify in advance the type of dispute it would invariably submit to arbitration, resolved that all governments should modify their constitutions in such a way as to incorporate the acceptance of arbitration in all disputes without exception. It was no doubt partly on account of these differences that except in 1913, despite the original intention, Conference and Congress ceased to meet in the same place after the gatherings of 1896 in Budapest.[55]

This very divergence, combined with the fact that parliamentary peace-workers were now meeting regularly with the aim of bringing influence to bear directly on governments, enabled the peace societies to temper their remaining idealism with a novel argument. Darby, the Secretary of the British Peace Society, declared before the Congress of 1893 that 'our work is to provide principles, not policies for governments. . . . The attempt to furnish policies will surely be resented as an interference with the prerogative of governments, and expose us to the charge of arrogant meddlesomeness.'[56] The aim of enforcing a change of policy on governments, or even of overthrowing them, had earlier given way to the hope of persuading governments to see the light. That hope itself was now giving way to the view that Members of Parliament and governments were themselves the best judges of what was feasible. After 1900 ministers and other representatives of governments were regularly invited to attend both the Parliamentary Conference and the Universal Congress, and regularly

* Above, pp. 122-3.

did so; and the resolutions of the Conference and the Congress were notified to governments each year.[57]

Darby's regard for the prerogative of governments summed up an attitude which, following the lead of its allies among lawyers and parliamentarians, the Peace Movement had been adopting for more than a generation. His reference to principles came at a time when, in the field of theory no less than in those of tactics and organisation, the Movement was being overtaken by these allies. Ever since the middle of the century the peace plans that had poured forth in increasing numbers from the press and the lecture-stand had been the productions of professional men, and especially of the lawyers. And ever since then some of them had taken a significant turn away from the ideas of Bentham and Ladd, and also away from the federal ideas of the Saint-Simonians in Europe, towards what we have called the confederal approach.

As early as 1857 a book published by Gustave de Molinari had provided the first indication of what the new approach would be. Molinari's book, a direct reaction to the Crimean War and especially to the disadvantages it had occasioned to neutral states, revived the ideas of Sully, Saint-Pierre, Rousseau and Kant—its title was *L'Abbé de Saint-Pierre, membre de L'Académie Française: sa vie et ses œuvres, précédees d'une appréciation et d'un précis historique de l'idée de la paix perpétuelle, suivies du jugement de Rousseau . . . ainsi que du projet attribué à Henri IV, et du plan d'Emmanuel Kant pour rendre la paix universelle, etc., etc., avec des notes. . . .*[58] Despite this fact the proposal which Molinari prefixed to his summary of these older views bore little resemblance to those views. It differed from Kant's, as from Bentham's, in proposing some kind of political organisation between states. It differed from all of them except Kant's in accepting the fact of, and reflecting the growth of, the power of the state. Against all the trend of thought—if not of the practice of states—in the past half century, Molinari neither urged a federation of states nor was content with the resources of international law. He advocated a *concert universel*, even a *Sainte Alliance universelle*, between governments. He did so because he thought that the destinies of Europe had in fact been controlled since 1815 by five Great Powers. This led him to argue that if the Great Power system could be extended to include all the states, though this would take time, peace would no longer be seriously endangered. Peace might still break down occasionally, but this did not disconcert him. It also led him to limit the machinery of the concert to an international tribunal and an international police force, and the functions of the concert to the settlement by one or the other of these means of strictly inter-state disputes. He was perhaps the first writer to contemplate an international government that would be so limited in machinery and function and yet still be an international government. Earlier writers had either demanded an international organisation with far more comprehensive powers and functions or else, like Bentham and Ladd, they had supposed that no international organisation was needed once international law had been codified, but only a court. Molinari advocated an international organisation solely in order that an international tribunal should have at its disposal the force neces-sary to make it a real court, and not a mere channel for voluntary arbitration, in disputes between states—and solely in such disputes.[59]

This early attempt to seek a midway solution was followed ten years later by similar proposals by James Lorimer, Professor of Law at Edinburgh, in a paper entitled *The Application of the Prin-ciple of Relative or Proportional Equality to International Organisation.* This attacked earlier plans for an international organisation for assuming that the existing international *status quo* could be made permanent and for seeking federation on the basis of politically equal states. It dismissed the words used by Sully of his 'Grand Design'—*irrévocable, irréformable*—as being 'as meaningless in the mouths of princes as of other people'. It accordingly advocated not only the need for proportional and changing representation of the states in an international body but also the principle that a successful international organisation must be based on the loosest possible bonds. Even a confederation of states would be too rigid to avert the danger of rupture as circumstances changed. What was required was an organisation in which the jurisdiction of an inter-national Parliament and its Court should be strictly limited to inter-national disputes, but in which the awards of the Court should be enforced, if necessary, by an international army.[60]

Bluntschli's ideas, developed during the 1870's, were an elabora-tion of the views of Molinari and Lorimer in some respects and a watering down of them in others. They are of interest here for being much more conscious of, and more explicit about, the forces which were taking peace plans in this direction. He, too, thought that all previous plans for an international organisation had been impracticable because they had sought the establishment of either a universal monarchy or a universal republic. In Europe, not to speak of the world, huge differences of history, culture and race made these goals unattainable. And not only unattainable: 'the fundamental condition of the problem of European organisations is the preservation of the independence and freedom of the confederated states.' It was for this reason, primarily, that he confined himself to proposing that an international legislature of government delegates, heavily weighted in favour of the six Great Powers, should draw up a code of international law; that the declaration of the law in disputed questions should be carried out by majority vote of the legislature; and that, in the event of a majority decision being required to be executed by force, the force should be that of the Great Powers acting as a college of the legislature.[61] We are getting close here to the notions which later underlay the League of Nations and the original constitution of the United Nations. Bluntschli was no more able to say then than men are able to say now what steps should be taken if the Great Powers themselves disagreed. But at least he was frank enough to admit that his proposals would not do away with all wars and that disarmament and the abandonment of national armies would not naturally follow. On the contrary, unlike Molinari, he was opposed to an international army and favoured the retention of national armed forces.

Bluntschli's concessions to the Great Powers stimulated Lorimer to develop his own earlier ideas. Bluntschli's involved, said Lorimer, the abandonment of the 'international factor'. 'It is to go back to the "European Concert" which is held together by no permanent bond of union and acts, if it acts at all, only after the event.'[62] Of Lorimer's own new plan, published in 1877, it has been said that it was 'the first attempt seriously to define the juridical form of a European federation';[63] and that it 'caught at the vision of an international government with its own officials to serve it'.[64] Certainly, though Ladd had already preceded him in propounding the establishment not only of an international legislature and an international judicature but also of an international exchequer, Lorimer's plan was an advance on Ladd's in proposing an international executive with its own international civil servants and its own standing army; while the separate national governments were to agree by treaty to reduce their armies to the scale required for internal police purposes. But the plan was scarcely a federal plan. On the contrary, it made impressive concessions to those developments which had induced Molinari and Bluntschli to adopt a confederal way out.

Lorimer, defining more elaborately than Molinari or Bluntschli the distinction between national and international questions, interpreted international questions more broadly than they had done. Civil wars, claims for territorial changes within Europe and international debts were placed within the jurisdiction of his international government. But he was as concerned as they had been to limit that jurisdiction to international questions. All national questions were explicitly excluded from it—as were, indeed, all colonial and extra-European international disputes that did not involve peace and war between European states. He prided himself on being the first to suggest that the national and the international fields should be rigidly separated and that the sphere of the international government should be rigidly confined to the latter.

Then, again, his international government was to be closely dependent on the member states. The executive was to be a ministry of fifteen members elected by the two houses of the international legislature, but it was to include at least one representative from each of the Great Powers. The houses of the legislature were themselves to consist of representatives appointed by the separate governments, and once again representation was to be heavily weighted in favour of the Great Powers—although it was proposed that the members of the upper house should also become hereditary international peers so as to reduce in due course their character as national delegates. In the judiciary at least 6 of the 15 judges were to be chosen from nationals of the Great Powers—though they again were to become hereditary international peers. National armies were to be reduced to the level required for police purposes but also in such a way as 'to preserve the *relative* power of each state unchanged'. The small international army was to be made up of contingents supplied by the separate member states. If it needed to be enlarged for emergencies it would be enlarged by calling on those states to supply additional contingents. There was yet another concession to the importance of the member nations. The legislature, at least, was to meet only once a year—in the autumn, between the sessions of the national legislatures.[65] It is not for nothing that this plan, like Bluntschli's, reminds one of the later League of Nations and the present-day United Nations more than it reminds one of a federal state.

These ideas represented not only the views of some academic lawyers but also the aspirations of some men in government circles. In the 1870's the earlier conception of the Concert of Europe was not yet dead. Even *The Times* hailed the Congress of Berlin as 'the first instance of a real Parliament of the Great Powers'.[66] Gladstone undoubtedly thought on similar lines in his effort to revive the Concert of Europe. He could still argue in 1893 that the erection of a 'Council of the Great Powers' in Europe was a more practicable aim than a treaty of permanent arbitration between Great Britain and the United States.[67] But the impact of the growing power of the sovereign state on international relations was such as to destroy the concert idea completely in the 1880's and 1890's.* Confederal ideas—even the adoption of arbitration for the settlement of disputes—became anathema to governments. And this process produced a further, if temporary, reduction in the scope of international proposals. The makers of these, and especially the lawyers, now concentrated on producing plans for codifying international law and on elaborating an arbitration procedure working without sanctions—on the programme which Ladd had advocated, which the Peace Movement in Great Britain and the United States had supported ever since.

John Noble's project for a supreme Court of Nations (1865);[68] the *Draft Project of a Council and High Court of Arbitration* which Leone Levi, Professor of International Law in London, first outlined to the Social Science Association in 1871 and then elaborated in 1886;[69] Dudley Field's book, *International Tribunal* (1872); the *Rules of Procedure for a Court of Arbitration* drawn up by the International Law Association in 1875;[70] the Hon. Philip Stanhope's report on a Permanent International Court of Arbitration, which was considered by the Inter-Parliamentary Conference in 1894 and 1895;[71] the plan for an Arbitration Tribunal drawn up by a Committee of the International Law Association in 1893[72]—these and many other schemes of the time all shared one feature in common with Ladd's. As Levi put it, they did not seek 'to provide for the exercise of physical force or to compel compliance' with the awards of the arbitration court: 'the

---

* For an account of this process see below, Chapter 11.

authority of the Council and the Court is moral not physical.' Stanhope expressed the same thing in a different way. The execution of an award was to lie 'with the honour of both parties' concerned.

The Peace Societies and their lawyer allies could both accept this principle. Many of the lawyers insisted on it from tenderness for the independence of the state, or from regard for practicability in the light of the problems created by that independence. The Peace Societies insisted on it because of their pacifism. Because of this difference of emphasis, however, some of these arbitration plans acquired another characteristic under the influence of their lawyer advocates which the Peace Movement could not swallow. Stanhope's insisted that the adhesion of governments to the International Court must be optional. The International Law Association's plan of 1893 distinguished between disputes which could be settled by arbitration and disputes involving the honour and national independence of the states. This was the point that Bluntschli had raised in 1873; and this difference between the lawyers and the Peace Societies was still the main difference between the Universal Peace Congress and the inter-Parliamentary Conferences in the 1890's in their attitudes to arbitration. The Peace Movement would tolerate no loopholes, as it would tolerate no force. And by the latter date another serious difference was beginning to emerge.

As the nineteenth century drew to its close the increasing tension between the Great Powers began to disturb the complacency of the previous twenty years. Impelled by the worsening international situation and also by their effort to elaborate an effective system of arbitration the lawyers, while not returning to federal schemes, were beginning to desert the principle that there should be no restraint except moral force and the power of public opinion. In his book, *De la Solution des Conflits Internationaux* (1889), C. de Mougins de Roquefort complained that arbitration proposals were still dangerously vague: the acceptance of arbitration, or of mediation in non-justiciable disputes, had not yet been raised to the level of an international obligation. The implication was that governments must reconcile themselves and the principle of national sovereignty to a system of sanctions.[73] In 1892, even the Universal Peace Congress was split by the discussion of sanctions. It finally resolved that no sanctions would be justified which amounted to acts of war—and the older, religious peace societies, still denouncing the use of material force for any purpose, including the holding of governments to their pledges, voted against even this resolution.[74] But the demand for enforcement was being raised in the Peace Societies as well as among international lawyers.

It would not be long before all except strict pacifists in the peace movement were agreeing with the lawyers that military sanctions were essential to a system of obligatory and automatic arbitration. Theory was returning to the confederal solution by the back door; for if governments were able to accept such a system—and abide by it—the result would not be very different from that advocated by Molinari, Lorimer and Bluntschli. *Ce n'est que le premier pas qui coûte.*

It was at this point—when the Peace Movement had changed its tactics and acquired some confidence in governments; when lawyers and parliamentarians had surpassed it in these directions; when peace programmes had come to concentrate on demanding the arbitration of disputes between states; when in the discussion of arbitration schemes, on the other hand, theory was beginning to converge upon a confederal programme from two opposite directions, by a departure from Bentham after an earlier departure from full federal aims—it was then that governments themselves were brought to contemplate joint action for the first time since the collapse of the Concert system; and with sobering results. In the pan-American and the Anglo-American negotiations which preceded the first Hague Conference of 1899 and at that and a second Hague Conference in 1907, though something was achieved, they displayed that they were unable or unwilling to accept an effective system of arbitration.*

This experience could be read in two different ways—it was, indeed, the product of two conflicting actual trends—and men so read it. Some regarded the Hague Conferences as being—what, indeed, they were—'the first truly international assemblies meeting in time of peace for the purpose of preserving peace, not of concluding a war then in progress'; the work, moreover, of governments and diplomats. They judged them to be the beginning of 'an epoch in international relations', proof that peace had at last become 'an integral part of the creed of statesmen', and extracted from them renewed confidence in the possibility of progress by agreement between governments.[75] Others responded either with the despairing conclusion that inter-

* Below, Ch. 11, pp. 266–70.

national progress was impossible or with the conviction that arbitration was not enough. It was perhaps an adequate procedure for legal disputes or for disputes between states which could not in any case engage in war; it could not operate in political conflicts or be 'a substitute for war'. Progress was only possible through a return to more radical, and generally to federal, schemes. One of the chief characteristics of international thinking in the early twentieth century was the marked revival of federal ideas.

More interesting still, the leadership in this revival was provided from Great Britain, where the project for the unification of Europe had not been advanced since the days of Bellers and Penn, and not from Europe, where this project had never quite died. It was a British writer who, in 1903, criticised the Peace Societies for their refusal to accept sanctions, the international lawyers for 'their easy acceptance of abstract phrases about the rights of nations', and both for their attempt to 'do what is impossible by an impossible method': namely, to eliminate war when justice might sometimes have to be fought for and to seek either peace or justice by arbitration agreements between independent states.[76] Another British figure, Sir Max Waechter, took up the idea of the United States of Europe in 1909 and founded a European Unity League in 1913.[77] Even the British Peace Society was pushed in the same direction by its fixed opposition to the use of force. Concluding, reluctantly, that the lesson of the Hague Conferences was that force was essential if contracts were to be upheld between independent states, it decided that only the complete merger of states would remove both the danger to peace and the need to maintain peace by resorting to war. Darby welcomed the establishment of the Central American Court of Justice in 1907 as the 'first step towards the federation of the world'; by 1916 he was quoting Swiss, German and American history as proof that 'federalism was no new or untried or impracticable policy'.[78] The British Quakers took the same course for the same reason. In 1910, again for the first time since Bellers and Penn, they exhibited an interest in international organisation—and embraced the project for a United States of Europe. In 1911, on their initiative, this programme was endorsed by the British National Peace League, the national organisation recently set up by all the British peace groups to coordinate their work.[79]

The same goal was adopted, in 1910, by the Berne Peace Bureau, the permanent secretariat of the Universal Peace Congresses.[80] Now, however, the British and European peace movements were reversing their roles of the nineteenth century. The British societies were embracing the idea of united Europe; European opinion was turning against it. As early as 1900, although the Paris Congress of Political Sciences placed the 'United States of Europe' on its agenda, its committee on the subject explicitly put aside the federal solution: a confederation between states, on lines laid down by Lorimer and including an international army, was the sole feasible solution. Even this proposal was dismissed as too radical by the *rapporteur-général* of the Congress. He insisted that the Union should respect 'the national individuality of all members' and be no more than a 'League of European States'.[81] A. Nowichow's *La Fédération de l'Europe* (1901) conceded that federation must be achieved by stages, beginning with a confederation between the states, and admitted that progress would be slow.[82] It was largely under British pressure that the Berne Bureau reached its conclusion of 1910.

There were two reasons for the European change of front, apart from the deepening of enmities between some of the European nations. In 1900 the same French *rapporteur-général* still concluded that 'Russia could not have a place in a true United States of Europe because of her régime and her lack of common culture with the rest'; on the contrary, if Europe ever federated it would be chiefly to avoid 'the domination of Russia'.[83] In 1903 an English advocate of federation admitted that 'the great obstacle' was that 'we can scarcely picture Russia as a reliable member of such a union'; and argued that 'the best thing for Europe might be that Russia . . . should be regarded as a serious danger to all the civilised Powers of the West. *That* would bring us nearer to the United States of Europe. . . .'[84] How, then, could federation seem practicable to Frenchmen and other Europeans when they now needed the alliance of Russia against a pressing danger? And this was only one facet of a wider problem—the mounting impossibility of regarding Europe as isolated from the rest of the world. If such books as Norman Angell's *The Great Illusion* (1909) and Prince Kropotkin's *Mutual Aid* (1902) had any message at all, beyond the argument that war had ceased 'to pay', it was the interdependence of a society of states that was wider than Europe. Twenty-six states, including five beyond Europe, had attended the first Hague Conference in 1899. Forty-four states attended the second in 1907, of which twenty-four were non-European. When a committee of the Inter-Parliamentary Conference was established in 1905 to consider the project of an international Parliament it adopted a world-wide framework for its studies.[85] As early as 1900 the same *rapporteur-général* in Paris had doubted whether Great Britain could ever be entirely and solidly integrated in Europe because of her world empire.[86] In 1912 the German jurist Schücking was perhaps the first to emphasise that the European Powers themselves, and not only Great Britain, had extra-European interests that were too important to permit them to establish a union that was limited to Europe.[87] After the outbreak of war in 1914 the chief internationalist groups, in Europe, Great Britain and the United States, disagreed among themselves about which states should be members of a post-war League. All agreed, as we shall see, that it must include at least the important non-European states.

These developments were not lost on British and American opinion. Although this did turn to the programme of united Europe, it did not confine itself to that programme. As early as 1900, W. T. Stead founded the International Arbitration Union to press for the improvement of world-wide arbitration schemes by the incorporation of a system of sanctions. When the British National Peace League was established in 1904 it leaned in the same direction; and the British Peace Society resisted complete federation with other groups in the League because of its suspicion that this was becoming the League's programme. In 1903 and 1907 the American peace movement memorialised Congress with a plan for a world legislature to make arbitration more effective.[88] In 1904, Andrew Carnegie addressed to the Universal Peace Congress a letter in which he proposed that a union of all the Great Powers should declare that there should be no further war and should announce their determination to enforce this declaration.[89]

Despite the interest shown in a united Europe in 1908, the prime concern of the international movement—of the Inter-Parliamentary Conferences and the Universal Peace Congresses—also remained that of developing an arbitration system of greater efficiency than that which had been produced by the Hague Conferences, and of universal scope. In 1902 the Congress accepted a draft treaty by which all states would renounce war, accept arbitration in all disputes and agree that in the last resort a disobedient state should be constrained by all the others, whose duty it would be to aid the arbitrators 'with the means of enforcing their award'. Only the means were unspecified because of the opposition of the British Peace Society which, at the Congress of 1906, defeated even the proposal that states should agree to uphold arbitration awards by material measures short of war—by economic boycott. In 1905 the Conference advanced as far as advocating a world legislature as well as a world Court: its committee on the establishment of an international Parliament recommended that The Hague Conference should become the world tribunal and that the Inter-Parliamentary Union should itself be converted into a universal legislature. The Congress in 1908 advanced a step further—to Lorimer's position—by adopting a scheme for a complete Society of Nations, with a single executive as well as a legislative Council to supervise an international code and a court to apply it, and for the reduction of national armies to the minimum required for police purposes. The question of sanctions remained unsettled, but in 1913 the Congress set up a committee on that subject.[90]

This trend was further advanced by the outbreak of war in 1914. The outstanding features of the war years were the complete, if not the permanent, defeat of the conception of United Europe before the recognition of the need for a wider organisation and, in relation to that wider organisation, the final victory of confederal ideas—of programmes envisaging an inter-government organisation for restricted purposes—over the ideas of Bentham and Ladd, no less than over federal projects. The second development was partly a necessary consequence of the first: few men could be content to leave unchanged an international system that had resulted in so great a disaster but fewer still could bring themselves to accept the practicability of a federal state for all the world.

It is true that the war provoked at first a renewed demand for a federal solution, especially in Great Britain. There was a revival of interest in the federal proposals of Penn and Saint-Pierre and in what were thought to be the federal ideas of Rousseau.[91] In 1915 J. A. Hobson advocated a super-state with an international executive, an international legislature and the power to use force on the vote of a majority against dissentient states;[92] and G. Lowes Dickinson wanted the reorganisation of Europe 'on the basis of nationality instead of on a basis of states' as the prerequisite of a permanent League which would have a single army and be prepared to use it both for maintaining internal order and for defence against external Powers.[93] Nor were such sentiments confined to Great Britain. Auguste Schvan, a Swede, advocated a World Law, a World Court of Justice and a World State in which the existing states would be "stripped of sovereignty and independence, and transformed into subdivisions of humanity'.[94] But this ardour soon cooled. A. J. Jacobs, in 1918, still proposed a world state in which neutrality would be forbidden and every breach of the peace regarded as a domestic matter against which all members must act; but he took the view that it was premature to set up an international court or an international executive immediately—such organs could only evolve with the passage of time.[95] Even in his early pamphlets Lowes Dickinson admitted that 'I do not imagine a federation of Europe to be possible in an immediate future. What I do believe possible, as soon as the war is over, is a League of the Powers to keep the peace of Europe'; he also noted that the medieval ideal of 'one Church, one Empire' was so dead that 'now there is hardly a philosopher or historian who does not urge that the sovereignty of independent states is the last word of political fact and political wisdom'.[96] In a later work, *The Choice before Us* (1917), it was because 'a European State, and *a fortiori* a World State, even in a form of the loosest federation that could be called a state, is not at present a serious political conception' that he fell back upon a League founded upon a treaty between the Powers.[97]

This had all along been the objective of all the organised groups among the internationalists who had applied themselves to the problem in increased numbers since the beginning of the War. The group led by Viscount Bryce since 1914; the British League of Nations Society, founded in 1915; the American League to Enforce Peace, also founded in 1915; the Fabian Society which published its proposals in 1916; the *Organisation Centrale pour une Paix durable*, founded at The Hague in 1916 and representing the belligerents on both sides as well as the neutrals; the British League of Free Nations Association which joined the British League of Nations Society in 1918 to form the League of Nations Union; the French *Association de la Paix par le Droit*; the International Peace Bureau—all these most active and vociferous organisations agreed in advocating a system between states in which justiciable disputes should go to a Court of Arbitration and political disputes should be referred to a Council of Conciliation or Council of the League; in which states should bind themselves to use these channels in preference to the resort to war; in which there should be some kind of legislature or conference procedure. Even the Union of Democratic Control, founded in England in 1914 with a programme giving priority to the democratic control of British foreign policy, the abolition of secret diplomacy, the renunciation of treaties and alliances, and British leadership in world disarmament —with a programme that might have been drafted by Jeremy Bentham—gave its support to the establishment of a League of Nations.[98] A League, indeed, became all things to all men. But on whatever else they might differ all men envisaged a league of states, not a union of nations; and the central question in war-time discussion was how far sovereign states should accept restrictions on their freedom.

Apart from their differences on the question of the membership of the organisation—some wished to exclude non-democratic nations—the various projects produced by these groups disagreed mainly about the relative weight to be allowed to the Great Powers and about the circumstances in which member states should be obliged to resort to force against other members and external Powers. None went so far as H. N. Brailsford whose book, *A League of Nations* (1917), not only gave the Great Powers larger voting rights than smaller states in the international Court and the League's Legislature, but also restricted membership of the League's Council or Executive to the Great Powers.[99] But many of them favoured the Great Powers.[100] Bryce's group envisaged the Executive and the Legislature as being dominated by the six European Great Powers, the United States and Japan.[101] The Fabian Society gave these same eight states a veto over the proceedings of the Legislature.[102] On the other hand, the Fabians insisted that every member state must ratify any international law before it could become operative, as did the *Organisation Centrale*, which, speaking from The Hague, was mindful of the interests of small states. Eight of the ten war-time plans for a post-war international organisation made alterations of the territorial *status quo* conditional on the holding of plebiscites and the right of self-determination inherent in every national group. The *Organisation Centrale* went further still in recommending that resort to arbitration should not be compulsory, that the Council dealing with non-justiciable disputes should not be empowered to discuss disputes involving the honour or vital interests of states and that the Council should reach its decisions only by majority votes which included the votes of those states against which the decisions were given.[103]

This same concern for the independence of the state was revealed even more clearly by the proposals made on the question of the rights and duties of member states to resort to force in carrying out the League's decisions. Few went farther than Bryce's proposals of 1915 which made no provision for the enforcement of an arbitration decision of either the Council or the Court upon an unwilling member. He allowed individual members the right to go to war in their own cause either twelve months after submitting a dispute to the Court or the Council if a decision had not by then been handed down, or six months after the publication of a decision if it had not been complied with. He thus limited the obligation of member states to use their joint force against another member to those occasions when a member state resorted to war before applying to the Court or the Council or before these time limits had elapsed.[104] But he did lay down this duty, and he did specify in addition that members should have the duty of discussing what collective action, if any, might be practicable in the event of a recalcitrant member ignoring a decision.[105] Other British associations followed him on these points. The Fabian Society, indeed, contemplated a system in which member states would be obliged to use economic sanctions against a member engaging in war in defiance of a decision of the Court, as well as to go to war in the event of a resort to war by another member before application to the Court or Council.[106] The *Association de la Paix par le Droit* similarly urged the resort to economic sanctions and even the use of an international police force to ensure the execution of arbitration decisions.[107] But other groups would not go so far as Bryce. The *Organisation Centrale*[108] and the American League to Enforce Peace refused to accept any duty on member states to use force to uphold awards, as opposed to the obligation of using force against any state which went to war before attempting arbitration; and three other American plans declared, like the British Peace Society, for moral sanctions only.[109] The American League also allowed members of the League to withdraw from membership—a point not discussed by the other organisations. It was not a League to enforce peace that this association advocated but, as was said at the time, a League to enforce consideration before war was resorted to. It was not without justification that its advocates could reassure critics that 'the creation of a League of Nations does not mean the loving of any other country as much as your own; nor complete disarmament of nations; nor making national defence ineffective; nor abandoning the Monroe Doctrine; nor free trade; nor letting Germany off easy'.[110] It also disliked the emphasis put by some war-time plans on the right of self-determination: plebiscites might involve the right of secession which the United States had fought the Civil War to prevent.[111]

At the end of the war the League to Enforce Peace made an advance beyond this position. It adopted a programme which allowed not only that the decisions of the Court were to be enforceable by member states, but also that the League as a whole should have the duty of determining what action should be taken in non-justiciable disputes if the parties to them failed to agree in the Council.[112] The programme of the League of Nations Union, formed in Great Britain in 1918, was almost identical.[113] There was the less difficulty in making this advance in that the governments of the major Powers had by then achieved it. By January 1917 most of the European governments had expressed their agreement with President Wilson's proposal that a League should be established. By the end of the war all had agreed that it should have these functions. But the adhesion of governments to the idea of a League watered down the war-time theories in one respect even while it expanded them in another.

The conviction of governments that they must pass beyond the policies and attitudes they had maintained at the time of The Hague Conferences—a conviction to which they were driven by the war—made it certain that the League established in 1919 would be more extensive in its functions than that which the war-time plans had proposed. These plans, usually the productions of lawyers, had been largely a logical extension of the arbitration discussion of the previous twenty years. They had outlined a League that was primarily a judicial organisation—a means of avoiding war at the point of actual crisis, not an international instrument for the continuous use of governments in operating and improving the international system. Politics, however, are more than legality; governments are not lawyers. This fact, together with the huge public demand for a real departure in international conduct to which governments could not but be responsive, ensured that the League of Nations would advance beyond the war-time proposals in this direction.

When governments and their committees of lawyers and civil servants first turned their attention to the problem at the end of 1916 they, too, conceived of the League as a judicial device for circumventing war in a crisis, not as a regular institution, and of the Council of the League as merely an additional diplomatic safety-valve—an emergency conference of their ambassadors in the capital which was chosen as the League's headquarters. When these ideas expanded, as they quickly did under the pressure of the public demand for a more permanent body with the more positive role of seeking the maintenance of peace and security and progress towards more stable international conditions, they still clung to the conception of a League 'confined'—to quote Colonel House—'to the Great Powers, giving the smaller Powers any benefits that may be derived therefrom'. But Wilson, Smuts and Lord Robert Cecil went further still. In giving greater weight to the Assembly—though it remained an Assembly in which the members would vote as states—they not only emphasised the existing tendency of government blue-prints to emphasise the avoidance of disputes by diplomacy and discussion instead of the settlement of disputes by a court. They replaced the strict rules and procedures of the lawyers and the officials by the politician's reliance on the public opinion of the world.[114] When Wilson introduced the Covenant of the League to the Peace Conference, he declared that 'throughout this instrument we are dependent primarily and chiefly upon one great force, and that is the moral force of the public opinion of the world—the cleansing and clarifying and compelling influences of publicity'. In the Body of Delegates, the eventual Assembly, the sinister actions of nations would be subjected to 'the overwhelming light of the universal expression of the condemnation of the world'.[115] Lord Robert Cecil similarly asserted that 'the great weapon we rely on is public opinion . . . and if we are wrong about it, then the whole thing is wrong'.[116] We are back to Bentham; but Bentham was now enthroned; and the confidence in public opinion which had once encouraged strenuous opposition to an international organisation between states now ensured that governments would establish for the first time in history an organisation that attempted to answer long-standing internationalist aspirations.

Even in the hands of a Bentham, however, governments remain governments. This made it certain that the League of Nations, while expanded in its role, would be rendered even more loosely confederal in its organisation than the war-time groups of internationalists had envisaged. In the hands of governments it acquired a more continuous organisation as well as a more continuous role. But just as the role changed—so that what was set up was an organisation 'to secure agreement not to enforce decisions; to help what is good in the nations to assert itself, not to compel the nations to be good'[117]—so the organisation lost all the logical and clear-cut procedure laid down for it in several of the early drafts. As emphasis on arbitration yielded to reliance on discussion—the Court to the General Assembly; as the Assembly gained also as against the conception of a Great Power Council—the result of the objections of the smaller states no less than of Wilson's regard for world opinion; as the lawyer, the political scientist and even the government official gave way before the politician—the organisation of the League became more flexible and less well-defined; and its chief characteristic became the contrast between its expanded role and its loosened structure.

The first international organisation in modern history was more far-reaching in composition, more general in competence, more fully supplied with special institutions, than any previous confederation between states; but was less solidly built than any confederation. Its aims and functions were more numerous and more ambitious than those of any previous alliance between states, but it involved fewer restrictions on the freedom of action of its members than any traditional alliance. It attempted to place limitations on the exercise of state sovereignty by imposing obligations on member states and by seeking to develop in them a recognition of the interests of the international order as a whole in preference to the interests of the individual state. Yet far from denying the sovereignty of member states, it protected this sovereignty by confining the functions of the League in most matters to advice and recommendation, by permitting withdrawal from membership, and by requiring unanimity for the passage of any important resolution. It was this conflict, between its ambitious functions and its weak structure, which before very long decided its fate. But before we consider the failure of the League of Nations we must undertake some analysis of the previous development in practice of the relations between its member states.

PART II

A HISTORY OF THE MODERN STATES' SYSTEM TO 1900

'The complexity, in many ways praiseworthy, with which the history of an age now has to be composed, naturally causes everyone to worry as to how our later descendants are going to cope with the burden of history which, after some centuries, we are going to leave them. Without doubt they will care for the history of the distant past, for which the documents will long since have perished, only from the standpoint which interests them, namely, what nations and governments have contributed to a world order or how they have damaged it.'

IMMANUEL KANT, *Idea for a Universal History*, 1784

CHAPTER 8

THE BEGINNINGS OF THE SYSTEM

HISTORIANS are liable to ante-date the completion of massive developments because of their preoccupation with origins. They are given to ante-dating the beginnings of massive developments for the same reason and also because such developments are rarely finally completed: when the end of one phase is usually but the preliminary to the onset of the next it is easy to mistake the onset of another phase for the beginning of an entirely new departure. These opposite hazards have affected our assessments of the origin and evolution of the modern states' system. Only when due allowance is made for the first can it be seen that a new European states' system emerged in the eighteenth century, and not at an earlier date. Only when careful regard is paid to the second can it be seen that, for all the twists and phases it has recently undergone, the system which then emerged or finally matured in Europe is the system which still holds the world in its framework. The present-day structure of world international relations is a structure between Great Powers, and it has come down in unbroken descent from the days when such a structure first materialised in Europe. It was during the eighteenth century that the actuality and the conception of a collection of Great Powers in Europe finally replaced an earlier framework of existing fact and inherited thought in which, while more than one state had always existed, it had been natural for one Power to be rated above the rest and impossible for that Power's pretensions—resisted though they had always been by other states—to stop short of the control and protection of Christendom.

This had been Charles V's conception of his position, and Philip II's and Louis XIV's. The ideas, indeed, of the first Napoleon were still made in the same mould. He undertook the domination of the Continent—the refashioning of its kingdoms within a single empire to replace the Holy Roman Empire, which he insisted on suppressing; the subjection to that empire of the papacy, his instrument for the control of 'the Church of the West, if not the Church of Universal Christendom';[1] the creation of Paris as the centre for the archives of all Europe, no less than for its political and cultural life[2]—with the conscious aim of restoring the Empire of Charlemagne. Whether he went further, subsequently taking the Western Roman Augustus as his model and finally aspiring to reunite the Western and the Eastern Roman Empires, may be debated.*[3] It cannot be doubted that French opinion looked to him to do so. Nor need these things surprise us. Until not long before his day there had hardly been a time in Europe when the collective memory had not been stirred by the remembrance of Rome or the medieval Empire as a unified state and when the policies of the leading states had not been shaped by nostalgia for those days, if not by the determination to restore them. It is not to be expected that a new and different structure of thought and practice could finally emerge without resistance from that French state which had most recently attempted to operate the old and come nearest—nearer than any medieval monarch as well as nearer than other states in early modern times—to perfecting it. But Napoleon's conception of his position was not so widely shared as had been that of Charles, Philip and Louis.

He never got so bad a name as Wilhelm II and Hitler were to get for attempting much less after 100 and 130 years more. Despite the lengths to which he had gone, he was able to assume after Waterloo that he would be allowed to spend his declining days as a country gentlemen 'within ten or twelve leagues of London'.[4] Interesting facts which throw much light upon his Europe. Nevertheless, he ran foul of—as he also helped to advance even further—an unprecedented degree of resistance to the idea of a European super-state. He did so because of the slow rise into acceptance and in fact in the previous 100 years of a Europe consisting of several Great Powers. This—and not the nationalist spirit in any modern sense of that phrase—was why he met with resistance that was not only greater than but different from that which had faced his predecessors.

* Driault, a leading French authority, maintained that he did. Koebner, on the other hand, has more recently used the fact that Napoleon rejected the titles 'Augustus' and 'Germanicus' when the *Institut de France* proposed to accord these to him on the Arc de Triomphe in 1809—and did so on the ground that to accept them would be to disavow his predecessors since Clovis as Emperor of the French—as evidence that he gladly accepted the heritage of Charlemagne but repudiated that of the Roman Caesars. But Koebner concedes that the Empire was an elastic concept, growing with the increase of Napoleon's power; and it is not in dispute that the *Institut's* proposal faithfully reflected French sentiment in favour of the revival of the Roman model and of Roman titles. This had been powerful under the Republic and it was increased when what was spoken of as Napoleon's *domination sublime* had revived what were called *de glorieux souvenirs*.

The Beginnings

The most general facts suggest that this was so. Charles, Philip and Louis had been resisted in their time, not to speak of the medieval emperors. Philip and Louis had been resisted by recognisable early versions of the Powers which fought Napoleon. But whereas, when the empire of Charles V and the Spain of Philip II had been brought to a standstill, another Power repeated their pretensions and aspired to their position of primacy, Napoleon was brought low by a coalition of Powers who formally assumed, for the first time, the status of Great Powers and proceeded to govern Europe by a Congress. Nor is this all. Whereas Napoleon's thought ran naturally back to Charlemagne and to Rome, no succeeding would-be conqueror of the Continent has thought in this way—if, indeed, he has had any conscious successor. Napoleon III, of all men, sought not to emulate Napoleon I in this role but to avoid what he thought had been his uncle's mistake in assuming it; and did so because his attachment to what he thought were the lessons of history was more powerful than his attachment to the Napoleonic legend.[5] Later aspirants to the control of Europe, ignoring even the lessons of history, have rationalised their drives by appealing to racial purity or the superiority of their ideology or the world balance of power or the need for *Lebensraum*—by everything but an appeal to Europe's past.

All this suggests that a decisive change in the international structure—a change of kind and not merely of degree—had completed itself by the beginning of the nineteenth century. Another fact on the same level indicates that the change had first registered itself during the eighteenth—that if France in the person of Napoleon was reacting against a whole trend in Europe she was reacting against a comparatively recent trend. When the France of Louis XIV was stopped by a coalition of Powers, early in the eighteenth century, there was no early resumption of the struggle for domination, no immediate successor to the claims of Louis, as there had been on all previous occasions.

A closer enquiry into the intellectual changes of pre-Napoleonic Europe confirms this general impression of the eighteenth century as the period which experienced the final replacement of an older set of circumstances and emphases by a new one. It was then that a wholly new conception of Europe made its appearance.

During the Middle Ages the notion of Europe was confined to

155

strictly geographical contexts, and Europe meant very little even on maps. Though Christendom never appeared on maps—it had difficulty in acquiring a geographical significance because of the tendency to equate it with the body of all Christians everywhere, or else with the vision of a continuing Roman Empire under the headship of the Pope—the notion of Christendom took the place of Europe for all political and polemical purposes. From the thirteenth century, and even more rapidly in the fourteenth and fifteenth centuries, the notion of Europe returned; and the identification of Europe with Christendom, and of both with the geographical area of the European continent, was established despite the continuing universal pretensions of the Pope and the continuing tendency of European theorists to think of the Western Emperor as the emperor of the world.

The geographical restriction of the idea of Christendom to Europe was the inevitable consequence of two developments: the consolidation of Christianity within Europe, and the decline of Christianity's pretensions beyond Europe in face of the advance of the Mamluks and the Ottoman Turks. The reappearance of the idea of Europe as an alternative to Christendom was a natural consequence of the rise of opposition to the pretensions of Pope and Emperor to universal rule within the continent. For even while it was becoming more of a unit culturally and economically, and thus more likely to be equated with Christendom, Europe was losing its political unity. It was becoming more difficult to equate Europe and Christendom for other than geographical purposes even while it was becoming natural to equate them geographically.[6] The stage was being set for the total eviction of the notion of a united Christendom and for the replacement of a purely geographical conception of Europe by a wholly novel conception of Europe itself.

The impressive thing is how long this process was delayed, how long it was before this new conception appeared. 'Christendom' remained a viable term, interchangeable with 'Europe', throughout the sixteenth and seventeenth centuries. Although every development of the time might seem to have been 'inimical to the reality of Christendom', it was not until the end of the seventeenth century that it began slowly to enter 'the limbo of archaic words'. When every development of the time might seem to have contributed to 'the reality of Europe', 'Europe' until the beginning of the eighteenth century either remained the equivalent of a Christendom that was still conceived of as a single structure or else was a purely geographical expression—the name of one among several continents.[7] And what is far more important, it was not until towards the middle of the eighteenth century—despite the blow of the Reformation to the single centralised church, the subjection of churches to governments, the growth in this and other respects of the power of Europe's states, the ever-growing rivalry between those states, the ever-increasing use of the terms 'Europe' and 'European'—that the notion of Europe as interchangeable with Christendom or as a geographical expression finally gave way to the quite new conception of Europe as a system that was the sum of its historical and political parts.

As might be expected, this change took place in stages; and three stages stand out as prominent in retrospect. In the first stage the idea of Europe as a unity was joined by the recognition that Europe was also a collectivity of states; but the emphasis continued to be placed on the single framework, not on the independence of the parts. Except in special circumstances like Machiavelli's, this was essentially an achievement of the seventeenth century. It was from about the 1620's that men began to recognise that Europe contained a multiplicity of states;[8] that, with Grotius, this recognition became part of the professional equipment of writers on international law; that historians began to treat the history of Europe as an aggregate of the histories of the different countries;[9] that writers on politics began to develop as many views of the international situation as there were separate states with independent interests;[10] that, with Crucé and Sully, the makers of peace plans began to desert, or at least to modify, the objective of domination in Europe that had previously coloured such plans.* But the seventeenth century's achievement was essentially limited to this stage. Machiavelli, in his special Italian environment in the sixteenth century, had not only contrasted Europe with Asia and Africa on the strength of its 'multiplicity of states'. He had concluded that it was the very multiplicity that 'encourages the development of *virtù*, that is, the capacity for action in the individual',[11] and this had enabled him to reach an early, if imperfect, formulation of the modern principle of the balance of power. If Christendom and Europe remained interchangeable in the seventeenth century it was largely because, in their view of Europe as a whole, men did not get this far.

* Above, Chapter I.

157

How far attention continued to be focused on the collectivity of Europe, rather than on the independence of its separate states, has already been illustrated by the peace plans of the period. This was the root cause of Sully's contradictions—the reason why he evolved the new notion of equilibrium as a means of achieving the older aim of restoring unity to Europe in new conditions.* Sixty and seventy years later the inability to decide whether the need was for the reorganisation of a single community or the better organisation of competing states was still giving hardly less difficulty to Penn, Bellers, Leibniz and Saint-Pierre.† It may be argued that these writers, preoccupied with the question of war and peace, were more disposed than others to emphasise the unity of Europe. But writers who were more realistically inclined and more concerned with the policies of individual states—the most 'Machiavellian' writers of the time—continued to show the same emphasis. Henri de Rohan's *De l'Interest des Princes et Estates de la Chrestienté*, which appeared in 1638, the year in which Sully's memoirs were published, was full of the same contradictions as Sully, and for the same reasons. The book argued that, since Spain was fighting to establish a universal monarchy, France must form a counterpoise against her. It also regarded the states of Christendom so much as one body, argued so firmly that all conflict between them was reprehensible in view of the need to re-establish the *pax* in Christendom, that it had great difficulty in avoiding the conclusion that peace required the success of the Spanish aim—and equal difficulty in avoiding the argument that the best result of all would be a victory for France of such proportions as would enable her to establish a universal monarchy in the place of Spain.[12] Nor had these contradictions been solved at the end of the century, when such writers were still more imbued than Rohan had been with the importance of *raison d'état*.

Courtilz de Sandras in his *Nouveaux Interets des Princes de l'Europe* (1685) was not much guided by a sense of the unity of Europe as a whole; the notion of Europe as a juxtaposition of independent states, each pursuing its own *raison d'état*, had made some progress. Nevertheless, he not only assumed that Louis XIV's goal was universal monarchy; he still approved of that goal. He thought the effort to attain it should be limited by those Christian obligations to which

* Above, Chapter 1.
† Above, Chapter 2.

all power policy ought to be subjected. He recalls Sully, and was close to Leibniz, his contemporary, with the argument that, if one wanted to have only one religion in the universal monarchy, it should be possible to create a composite religion out of Protestant and Catholic creeds. These concessions existed uneasily alongside his interest in realistic policies. The main problem to result for him from his developed sense of power politics was that he wanted both to recommend to France what steps to take in pursuit of universal monarchy and to advise other states on the right steps to take to prevent it.[13] This advocate of *raison d'état* was no more able to free himself from the old framework of thought than were Penn, Bellers and Saint-Pierre, in the means they proposed for preserving universal peace.

It was this difficulty which forced Leibniz to wish to restore the political system of the Middle Ages and to be sceptical of the efforts of the peace planners to combine the old and the new elements in the situation. Other writers followed the peace planners, but fused the old and the new elements in a different way. Thus Fénelon at the end of the seventeenth century, instead of seeking to perpetuate Christendom in proposals for an international organisation, attempted to reconcile the notion of a single Christian community with the principle of the balance of power. In his effort to do this he came close to the views that were soon to prevail. 'Christendom', he wrote, 'is a kind of general republic, with common interests, common fears and common precautions to be observed. All the members of this great body owe it to themselves to prevent all progress by any one of them which would upset the balance and lead to the inevitable ruin of the other members of the same body.' Yet if his views are studied closely the similarity between them and those which emerged later is seen to be deceptive on account of the extent to which, with him, too, the emphasis is still placed on the general republic of Europe and not on the component states.

This emerges clearly in his *Télémaque* (1690), and most clearly in his insistence on the analogy between the structure of the whole and the structure of a single state. 'If you entered a republic where there were no magistrates or judges, and where every family believed it necessary to seek justice for itself by violence against the claims of its neighbours, you would deplore such a situation. . . . Do you think that the Gods could contemplate this world, which is a single republic, with any less horror if each people, being only part of one great family, believed itself fully entitled to seek justice for itself by violence against other people? . . . Should not justice be still more sacred and inviolable for kings, representing whole countries, than for families . . . ?'[14] It was on this ground that he regarded it as a duty upon governments always to have regard to the balance and always to settle their differences by arbitration.

The same analogy was invoked by Penn and Saint-Pierre in support of their plans for international organisation. Sully had confined his appeal on behalf of the practicability of his scheme to the reputation of Henry IV. Penn and Saint-Pierre relied heavily on that same reputation. But they relied even more on the argument that, 'as government in kingdoms . . . prevents men being judges in their own cause while they have resigned the original claim to the benefit and comfort of society, so . . . it will not be hard to conceive or frame, nor yet to execute, the design I have here proposed';[15] and on the belief that a treaty between states would be 'sufficient to preserve the union in spite of future grounds of difference, in the same way as subjects of the same states are always one body in spite of their law-suits'.[16]

Just as Fénelon's proposals for international collaboration, like these others, were justified by a belief in the prior unity of the states, that belief being even buttressed by the growing concentration of political science on the study of the individual state, so it will be found that until the end of the seventeenth century other advocates of the balance of power, and not only Fénelon, elaborated it within a context in which Europe was still regarded as a single *civitas*. It was similarly as a means of preserving the stability of the whole, not as a means of advancing the interests of each member, that Sir William Temple, F. P. de Lisola[17] and William of Orange[18] developed the balance principle. They no more took it beyond the notion of universal defence than other writers, against whom they were developing it, freed their understanding of *raison d'état* from the old objective of universal monarchy. Nor is it surprising that most French writers, uncritical—unlike Fénelon—of the French state, deplored the advocacy of the balance principle as destructive of the unity of Europe which he professed to want to preserve.

It was not until after the War of Spanish Succession that the second stage of advance was reached. Jean Rousset, a political journalist, has been credited with the invention in the 1730's of the term *droit de convenance* to express the conception of the balance of power in Europe as something that was maintained by the cooperation of several independent Powers for reasons of expediency.[19] But Rousset was one writer in a whole school which now emphasised the doctrine of 'the true interest of states' as the one safe guide, the balance of power as the one stabilising factor, in an international system based on a brutal struggle for advantage between the states. It was a school that included Bolingbroke in England. Bolingbroke was typical not only in his attempt to define the true interests of the state but also in his use of the analogy between the political society and the family to assert that not unity but discord was the natural relationship between states. The personal needs of men were met by the development of society out of the family. Self-love, which originally assisted this development and produced separate societies, then ensured that the development would spread no further. 'The great commonwealth of mankind cannot be brought under one government, nor subsist without any.'[20] As Bolingbroke used these views to make himself an early advocate of a maritime, insular, colonial Great Britain, intervening in European affairs only when her interest in the balance of power required it, so the continental writers of his time completely abandoned the traditional belief in Christendom or Europe as a structure above or at least additional to its component states. By dealing with the interests of each state in isolation they tore Europe into its separate parts; even when studying the interests of its separate parts they failed to recognize any interconnected states' system in which the policy of one state might affect and be affected by the policies of all the others. It is true that they stopped short of considering every state as an autonomous unit, but this was not because they retained any interest in Europe as a whole. It was because they made a sharp distinction between the Great Powers and the smaller states, which could not have an independent policy. With the exception of Rousset himself, who remained uncertain whether the balance of power was a principle to be operated in the interests of Europe as a whole or in the interests of each of the Powers who practised it, they replaced the older conception of Europe with the belief that there existed a limited number of rival political systems, each grouped around a Great Power,[21] and not with a new conception of Europe.

It was by way of reaction to this attitude that men evolved a new conception of Europe after the 1730's; and it was inescapable that the new conception would be one in which the relationship of the parts to the whole was different from what it had been during the seventeenth century. In this third stage in the process by which Christendom was replaced by a new notion of Europe the idea of Europe as a whole was restored, but there was at last a shift of emphasis, from concentration on Europe's unity to concentration on the autonomy of its states. That autonomy was moderated now by a renewed sense of Europe's unity; but the content and significance of that unity were wholly changed. Rousset was close to making this shift. In another ten or fifteen years, in the writings of men like Montesquieu, Voltaire, Hume and Rousseau, we have for the first time abundant evidence that it has been made.

Their significance in this context is not, as has been suggested, that it was they who first viewed Europe as a political and cultural unity.[22] They did so view it; but the term Europe had had this overtone from the time when it began to be interchangeable with Christendom, after the end of the thirteenth century, and the sense of Europe's political and cultural unity had grown markedly throughout the seventeenth century.[23] It is only in contrast to their immediate predecessors, the advocates of 'the true interests of states', that it appears to be the prominent element in their approach that they stressed that Europe was a unity rather than a diversity. In any longer perspective what came in with these writers of the 1740's and 1750's, was the widespread recognition that Europe was a diversity as well as a unity—a unity because of its diversity.

For Montesquieu Europe was a single whole. 'The state of things in Europe is that all the states depend on each other. . . . Europe is a single state composed of several provinces.' But it was because of the multiplicity of its several states that, to him as to Machiavelli, it represented progress as opposed to the stagnation of Asia; and he showed in *De L'Esprit des Lois* (1748) an acute sense of the fundamental nature of the rivalry between its states. Although they belonged to the same collectivity, it was impossible to subject them to a single law like that which governed the individuals in a single state. In some cases offensive war was justified as a form of defence; there was a right of war and of conquest; the most that could be hoped for was that the different provinces would do each other as much good as possible in peace and as little harm as possible in war.[24] Voltaire in 1751 also wrote of 'Christian Europe'. It had long been 'a sort of great republic divided into several states, some monarchial, the others mixed . . . , but all in harmony with each other, all possessing the same religious foundation, even if divided into several confessions, all possessing the same principles of public and political law, unknown in other parts of the world. . . .' But he also wrote that these states were 'above all . . . at one in the wise policy of maintaining among themselves as far as possible an equal balance of power'.[25] The new emphasis comes out most forcibly here in the reference to equal balance among several states. Hume was equally sure in the same year (1751) that the balance of power was founded on common sense, 'the supposition being that enormous monarchies are probably destructive to human nature'; and he felt that for that reason it had been practised throughout Europe's history.[26] Rousseau had the same consciousness of the history of Europe as the development of a system of states within a balance of power. He expressed it all the more vividly because he was less convinced that the balance of power was a wise principle, less confident as to where it might lead,* but even his doubts on this score, in the essays of 1756, reflected the main emphasis of writers since Montesquieu.

This was not 'the acceptance of the European peoples as politically one'.[27] Despite the references to the fact that they were culturally one and politically interrelated, the main emphasis now, in contrast to earlier thinking, is that, though culturally and politically interrelated, the European states were also politically several. And this was the conception of Europe that prevailed after the middle of the eighteenth century, among those who criticised the international system no less than among those who accepted it. With the critics we shall be concerned later. For the moment it is sufficient to quote Burke and Gibbon. In 1760 Burke, like Rousseau, was convinced that the balance of power had long operated to preserve the liberty of Europe's states, if not to keep the peace between them.[28] Writing in the 1770's Gibbon took this new antithesis for granted and placed the emphasis where these earlier writers had been first to place it. 'The division of Europe into a number of independent states, connected, however, with each other by the general resemblance of religion, language and manners, is productive of the most beneficial consequences to the liberty of mankind.' 'The cities of

* Above, pp. 57–9.

ancient Greece were cast in the happy mixture of union and independence, which is repeated on a larger scale, but in a looser form, by the nations of modern Europe: the union of language, religion and manners, which renders them spectators and judges of each other's merit; the independence of government and interest, which asserts their separate freedom, and excites them to strive for pre-eminence in the career of glory.'[29]

We may trace the same change, and see it taking place at the same time, in the specialised field of writings on international law.

The very notion of international law involves the notion of a plurality of states; there cannot properly be a body of such law for men who assume that there is not more than one political system. It might be wondered, therefore, how there could have been any international law in Europe before the eighteenth century if there was not, before that date, a clear understanding that Europe consisted of a plurality of independent states. The answer is that what in any case came to be called international law only at the end of the eighteenth century was a law between laws—and, because municipal laws had been territorially based since early in the Middle Ages, a law between territories—before it became a law between states. It was because these laws and territories were conceived of as belonging politically to a single *civitas*, to the same Christian world, that this law developed as it did in its earlier stages; and it was in the middle of the eighteenth century, and not before, that international lawyers made the transition from emphasising Christendom, with its law between laws, to insisting that international law was the law between Europe's component states.

When Grotius undertook the first systematisation of this body of law early in the seventeenth century the conception of statehood had long existed alongside the notion of a single Christendom that was made up of the fact of different territorially organised laws. It had not yet made serious inroads either into this other notion or into this historical fact. The state—the prince—had evolved from the territory. It—he—was necessarily associated with the possession of a territory. But possession was still personal in the princes; and while some princes could gain territories at the expense of others, the acquisition of fresh territories did not involve their incorporation into the state that was based on the territory the prince ruled. This was partly because the old known world had long ago been zoned out between municipal law systems. The process of struggle was not one by which state frontiers were advanced a few miles here and withdrawn a few miles there; whole provinces changed hands when there were changes of duke or prince, but local law and organisation continued unaltered under new management. But it was also in part because the notion of the state had not yet made sufficient headway against the conviction that, politically, all these territories were part of a single overriding system. If Grotius's book was in one respect, as has been said, a statement of the Roman law of property and contract written especially for princes, it was also a statement written for princes who were seen not as independent rulers but as associated agents in the governing of Christendom. It was a set of rules for the conduct of war and the transfer of provinces within a single *civitas*. It regarded the subjection of peoples and the acquisition of provinces beyond Christendom as not subject to these rules, as beyond the pale.*

So much was this so that Grotius took as the basis for these rules the Roman *Ius Gentium*, a collection of rules and customs common to the tribes and nations of the Empire which had not had the civil law of Rome, and quite overlooked the Roman *Ius inter Gentes* or *Ius Feciale* which had been the Roman approach to a real international law. For the same reason he equated the old *Ius Gentium* with the *Ius Naturale*, a set of ethical rules of divine origin to which the reason of Christian men commanded obedience. And what is still more significant, all so-called international law writings after Grotius went on drawing scarcely any distinction between ethics or Natural Law on the one hand and international law on the other until the eighteenth century. It is true that Pufendorf differentiated between ethics and law in *De Jure Naturale et Gentium* in 1672, by which time states were in practice ceasing to advance claims of right in justification of their wars and beginning to advance the absolute right to make war. But on the assumption that there was a single political society to which all the states belonged, what passed for international law still went on being equated with norms of conduct imposed above the law established in each state.[30] It was in this tradition that Christian Wolff published his *Ius gentium methodo scientifica pertractatum* in 1749. In 1754, to take an example from England, Thomas Ruther-

* I am indebted to Dr Clive Parry of Downing College for clarifying this problem for me.

ford's *Institutes of Natural Law* still repeated the same traditional view of the law of nations.

This tradition was undermined before it was directly attacked. Men like Montesquieu and Voltaire developed their new approach without any conscious intention of rejecting traditional writings on the subject of the law of nations, and probably without any knowledge of them; and among men whose interests lay closer to international law the first new departure was similarly, and at almost the same time, the result of their interest in a new field, rather than of a conscious break with legal tradition. The Abbé de Mably's *Droit Public de l'Europe fondé sur les Traités* of 1747 was not a legal study so much as a historical collection of the important political and commercial treaties made since the treaties of Westphalia. But it was one of the earliest attempts to make such a collection—to look at the international system as it had actually functioned since Westphalia rather than through the miasma of inherited conceptions about the law of nations which had prevented men from seeing that system which was developing before their eyes—and to assert that this was the basis of Europe's public law. It could not be long before the influence of this approach, as of men like Voltaire, produced a direct rejection of the old law of nations itself.

The first direct onslaught on the traditional international law was made by Vattel in 1758. He made it in the course of translating Wolff's book. Like Voltaire or Rousseau, Vattel in his treatise on the law of nations emphasised that the states of Europe were politically and culturally interrelated, that they were more interrelated, indeed, than they had once been. He might have been quoting Voltaire when he wrote:

Europe forms a political system in which the nations inhabiting this part of the world are bound together by their relations and various interests into a single body. It is no longer, as in former times, a confused heap of detached parts, each of which had but little concern for the lot of the others. . . . The constant attention of sovereigns to all that goes on, the custom of resident ministers, the continual negotiations that take place, make modern Europe a sort of republic, whose members—each independent, but all bound together by a common interest—unite for the maintenance of order and the preservation of liberty. This is what has given rise to the well-known principle of the balance of power, by which is meant an arrangement of affairs so that no state shall be in a position to have absolute mastery and dominate over the others.[31]

But despite his insistence that Europe was 'a single body'—and in the introduction to a treatise which he began with the idea of rendering Wolff's abstract Latin into elegant French—he also objected strongly to Wolff's traditional conception of international law.

From the outset, [he wrote] it will be seen that I differ entirely from Mr Wolff in the foundation I lay down for that division of the law of nations which we term *voluntary*. Mr Wolff deduces it from the idea of a sort of great republic (*civitas maxima*) set up by nature herself, of which all the nations of the world are members. To his mind the *voluntary* law of nations acts as the civil law of this great republic. This does not satisfy me, and I find the fiction of such a republic neither reasonable nor well enough founded to deduce therefrom the rules of a Law of Nations at once universal in character and necessarily accepted by sovereign states. I recognise no other natural society among nations than that which nature has set up among men in general. It is essential to every civil society (*civitas*) that each member should yield certain of his rights to the general body, and that there should be some authority capable of giving commands, prescribing laws and compelling those who refuse to obey. Such an idea is not to be thought of as between nations. Each independent state claims to be, and actually is, independent of all the others. . . . It is clear that there is by no means the same necessity for a civil society among Nations as among individuals. It cannot be said that nature recommends it to an equal degree, far less that it prescribes it.[32]

In politics practice often precedes theory, and especially the rationalisation of lawyers. When we turn from the intellectual level to the policies of states we might expect that the comparable change of emphasis, from the collectivity to the independence of the parts, had taken place much earlier. Meinecke has rightly emphasised that every state in 'every epoch and every special spiritual and moral mode of thought has attempted, with its own weapons and on the basis of its own particular aims in life, to struggle with the daemon of *raison d'état*'.[33] Every state in every epoch, it may be added, whatever its weapons, however great its struggle, has also practised *raison d'état*, which is 'nothing else, succinctly expressed, than . . . the discovery of the element of necessity in political conduct'.[34] Hume was undoubtedly right in thinking that the balance of power—as a necessary device in, if not as the objective of, policy—has been practised throughout history. But if we concentrate not on the conscious pursuit by European governments of *raison d'état*, nor on their unconscious and inarticulate resort to the balance of power, but on their recognition of Europe as consisting of several states and of the principle of the balance of power as the necessary object of policy in such a situation, then with them we find what was found with the publicists and lawyers. We find that the Italian experience of earlier modern times was not learned and completely absorbed before the eighteenth century in Europe as a whole.

The struggle of Reformation and counter-Reformation had forced governments to accept by the seventeenth century that states should be either Catholic or Protestant and that Protestant and Catholic states must exist alongside one another. The multi-national treaties of Westphalia (1648) had formally recognised the existence of separate sovereignties in one society of nations and had stipulated that the states were equal as well as independent. These treaties came to be looked upon as the public law of Europe. But just as the acceptance of religious uniformity within the state, on the principle of *cujus regio ejus religio*, itself gave way only very gradually to the further realisation that the attempt to enforce it must lead to internal political disintegration, so men continued to oppose to the anarchical international practice that followed from the growing independence and power of states, not a search for a basis of co-existence between states, but the old effort to restore a traditional unity to the structure of Europe—and failed to see that that effort must lead to international disintegration. States pursued the egotistical precepts of Machiavelli, indeed, in their methods. Have they ever done otherwise? But so far as their aims were concerned they resisted until the end of the seventeenth century the balance principle which Machiavelli had begun to draw from the existence of separate states because they were still working to the rules of an older political framework. Some governments still aimed above all things at the leadership of Christendom. The others still feared this above all else.

This fact is reflected in the history of the word for 'empire'. It was with the Italian humanists after the 1430's that the expression *imperium*—hitherto applied only to the one empire, the Roman Empire—had replaced *principatus* or *regnum* as the term for the lawful independent rule of other kings. Even then the tendency remained strong among theorists to apply the term only to states that were remarkable for territorial extent or determination to expand; and the tendency remained strong in political circles to reserve it solely for the Roman Empire.[35] It is equally clear that it was precisely in those states which most satisfied these new criteria of the theorists that rulers and political writers were most reluctant to adopt the title 'Empire' for their own countries. Henry VIII in a small state, and one that lay outside the Continent, rushed to announce that 'this realm of England is an empire'. Charles V and his successors as the rulers of Spain and Spanish America, and the rulers of France until the death of Louis XIV, resisted this temptation. It was they who persisted in regarding the Holy Roman Empire as unique—or at least in extending the title 'Empire' beyond it only to the great Turkish state which had conquered the empire of the Greeks.[36] The reason is not far to seek. If they did not themselves possess the unique European empire they still wanted to acquire it.

It is sometimes overlooked that this was true of Charles V. His attachment to his many local titles and lordships—which stretched as far east as Patras and Athens—and especially to Burgundy was as prominent as his concern for the Empire; and he made no attempt to coordinate these lordships into a single structure of imperial rule. But any such consolidation would have been incompatible with the contemporary conception of Empire, as any idea of delegating his powers as local lord would have been incompatible with the conception of lordship and territorial law. He must be lord in each of his lordships; other kings were lords in their kingdoms; but he was also the Emperor over them all. Historians have especially doubted whether this was the aim of so late a ruler as Louis XIV. They have done so because they have confused the search for the leadership of Christendom, the headship of Europe, with the search for the actual conquest and direct government of all the Continent. Louis did not seek the latter; his policies, like his resources, were in this direction limited to using force to gain the Rhine and the other natural frontiers of France and to acquiring only such conquests beyond that as could be achieved without striking a blow. This does not alter the fact that total leadership on another level—in terms of the prestige of himself and the deference of others—was just as much an object of his ambition as the more limited advance of French direct rule. There is no justification for the view that the advance of French interests was his 'realistic' policy and that the object of being the sole arbiter of European arrangements was simply a façade behind which his realistic policy developed—something which flattered his vanity without engaging his interest.[37] Empire in Europe had ceased to be equated with the direct rule of Europe long before his day—if the two had ever been equated. Since his day great states have not ceased to be interested in prestige. Yet Louis's utter determination to make all and everything bow before him was different in quality from the interest in prestige that Great Powers have exhibited—that has been the essence of being a Great Power—in more modern times. It was the expression of his will to be the sole arbiter, the leading monarch, in Europe at a time when this position, which was what was meant by universal monarchy, had passed beyond the reach of the Emperor and of Spain.

This was never questioned by Louis's contemporaries. It is indeed impossible to overlook the immense difficulty which contemporaries experienced in judging where Louis's interest in advancing French frontiers stopped and where his interest in advancing the universal monarchy began. In 1685 Courtilz de Sandras believed that the Sun King's real aim was to acquire the dignity of emperor and that he was seeking to conceal it by professing to want nothing but the Rhine frontier.[38] Even if Louis's actual ranking of the priorities was the reverse of this—it is more likely that the different objectives were not clearly separated in his mind, that practicalities, not priorities, determined his conduct—contemporary governments necessarily agreed with Sandras. Until the end of the war of Spanish Succession in the opening years of the eighteenth century the other states of Europe were drawn together by the efforts of the House of Bourbon to dominate the structure—or at least by their fears that it aimed to do so—as some of them had previously been drawn together by the similar efforts of the House of Habsburg, and by similar fears.

Because of the growing reach and power of the state—of the French state even more than of others—more of them were drawn more closely together by their resistance during the seventeenth century than had been the case in the sixteenth. Localised international rivalries, in Italy and Germany, in eastern Europe and on the Channel, were drawn more than before into a single network. Europe acquired for this reason more sense of unity in some respects even while it was moving towards greater diversity in others. And if only for this same reason, in political and diplomatic circles no less than in others, in the states which resisted France no less than in France itself, men went on using the traditional terminology—the 'Christian Republic', the 'Christian world', the 'provinces of Christendom', the 'Christian princes of Europe'—and the conscious acceptance of the alternative conception of a multilateral balance of power operating throughout this network, which had failed to develop during the sixteenth century,[39] similarly failed to develop in the seventeenth. The treaties of Utrecht (1713) still referred to the *Respublica Christiana*, though they were the last treaties to do so.[40]

They were also the first to declare that they were made in order to preserve the European balance of power.[41] But their reference to the *Respublica Christiana* shows that even in 1713, for governments as for writers, the balance of power was still deriving its main impulse from the old conception of Europe. The principle was still being used in the seventeenth-century sense. It still meant what we should expect it to mean when all the trends had run for so long towards the hegemony of a single Power: the need for collaboration against that hegemony. For British policy and opinion, indeed, it continued to have only this meaning for another generation. In the days of William III and Marlborough the British understanding of the balance of power had understandably been associated with defence of 'the Common Cause' against 'the ambitious House of Bourbon'. For a brief period after the peace of Utrecht British governments tried to operate the principle in a more universal form—as a means of controlling and weakening the strongest state in Europe, whatever state that might be—and used it to justify collaboration with France and opposition to Austria.[42] But even if a few men were ceasing to assume that France was the one Power against whom the balance must invariably be maintained, all continued to believe that it was the aim of some Power or other to dominate Europe; that this was still the standing menace; that a Grand Alliance of all Europe was the necessary reply to it. By 1740, moreover, when Cardinal Fleury had Europe at his feet, when the Emperor Charles VI had just died and when a Bourbon possessed the throne of Spain, it was easy to feel that the old aim was still pursued by its old protagonist. The Duke of Newcastle spoke for most people when he suggested in that year that 'some kind of concert might be set on foot with the Dutch, the emperor, the czarina, the king of Prussia, the king of Poland, the landgrave of Hesse, etc., to form a kind of grand alliance to oppose the ambitious views of the House of Bourbon'.[43]

In continuing to believe as late as 1762 that the rest of England and Europe were as frightened by the Bourbons as he was himself Newcastle was less typical.[44] The change which by then had left him somewhat isolated in his views was nevertheless a recent change. It was with justifiable astonishment that in 1745 the Dutch diplomatist Bentinck wondered what earlier English statesmen would have thought 'if they had heard an English nobleman say that it signify as little who is Emperor, as who is Lord Mayor of London'.[45] An English pamphlet of 1755 believed that the advisability of remaining aloof from European politics had 'never entered into any Man's heart till of late years'.[46] The elder Pitt complained in the same year that until that moment 'we have suffered ourselves to be deceived by names and sounds, the balance of power, the liberty of Europe, a common cause . . . , without any other meaning than to exhaust our wealth.'[47] Later in the 1750's he was himself the first British statesman to combine British isolationism and the European balance of power in a new structure of policy, with a new conception of the balance of power.[48] Even then there was the danger that in Pitt's hands the wheel would go full circle—that he would move back from isolationism not only to interventionism but also to the demand that Great Britain should step into the role once played by Habsburg and Bourbon. 'A million more were but a pittance to put you at the head of Europe.' 'Now is the time to humiliate the whole House of Bourbon.' 'Some time before I should have been content to bring that country [France] to her knees, but now I shall not rest content until I have lain her upon her back.' These arguments of Pitt's in favour of extending the Seven Years' War to Spain were no doubt momentary exaggerations of his wishes. In any case they aroused others to complain of 'the madness of the times' and were followed by Pitt's loss of office. They are nevertheless symptomatic of the strength of old ways of thought—or else of the perennial attraction of vistas of dominance.

In Europe during these same years the principle of the balance of power, despite its enunciation in the treaties of Utrecht, suffered from a different limitation. The older fear of the danger of hegemony in Europe was disappearing faster there than in England. But the principle of the balance of power remained utterly ineffective—as ineffective as the declining sense of Europe's unity—in shaping and controlling the practice of states. What Frederick the Great was soon to call 'the political maelstrom of Europe' was checked for some years after the treaties of Utrecht by the fact that most states were exhausted by the recent wars. For this reason and also because some memory of the unity of Christendom still lingered—the Treaty of Aix-la-Chapelle in 1748 still described itself as 'The Definitive Treaty of Christian, Universal and Perpetual Peace and Union'[49]— there was a short-lived approximation, in the practice of the states no less than on the intellectual level with Rousset, to the conscious operation of the balance as a principle of co-existence serving the interests of Europe as a whole as well as the interests of the leading states. By the 1730's Rousset was regretting that this system—which had found expression in the Quadruple Alliance and the Congresses of Cambrai (1724-5) and Soissons (1728) and 'whose glory it had been', in his opinion, 'to restore peace in Europe more than once, and to maintain it'—was passing away.[50] It gave way to a period in which the acquisitiveness and the absolute autonomy of the individual State were to be emphasised as never before. International relations, no longer canalised by the much greater power and reach of one state as against the others and not much restricted by the memory or illusion of an earlier unity in Europe, were not yet bound and regulated by anything else—were bound and regulated by nothing but the limitations and the egotisms of the individual states.

It was only after this period—as a result of this 'maelstrom' which also produced Voltaire's *Candide* (1759), that unsurpassed satire on war—that the states of Europe began to approximate in their practice—as states they could do no more—to the new conception of Europe and the balance of power that was being developed in the writings of men like Voltaire in reaction to these excesses.

Before this transition is studied in greater detail it is necessary to ask why these changes on the intellectual level and in the practice of states were so long deferred.

The delay was no doubt partly due to the continuing menace of the Turkish advance. It was not until 1683, when it came west in great strength and might have reached the Rhine, that this was finally turned. The peace plans of the second half of the seventeenth century reveal the strength of the desire for peace among all Christians as a means of resisting it. But these plans also, perhaps mainly, sought to re-establish in Europe the traditional structural unity that had existed or was believed to have existed long before the Turkish danger; and while they produced no collaboration against the Turk, the practice of states amounting rather to the *de facto* acceptance of the Moslem state, governments still hoped for the leadership of the European structure, or feared it. What we are faced with here is an example of the longevity of notions that are based on all previous history, of the power of such notions to remain alive until countervailing forces become completely dominant—and of the way, too, in which the firm hold of the past upon the public imagination can be buttressed by the firm hold of traditional pretensions upon the aspirations of governments until those countervailing forces compel a change.

The existence of a unified, peaceful Christian Europe in the Middle Ages can scarcely be accepted by modern historians as a reality. It is belied by the practices and policies to which the different parts of medieval Europe in fact subscribed. But this notion was so much the solid substance of all medieval life, so much the major source of the ideas upon which Europe's major institutions were then built, that in the Middle Ages themselves 'the myth stands out and becomes almost reality'.[51] It was subjected to far greater pressures after the fifteenth century than ever before, but it retained a powerful influence as the frame of reference for international ideas long after it had lost its hold in religion and the internal affairs of states. If anyone doubts this let him not only recall how European peace plans —if we may so call them—from the time of Dante to the time of Leibniz all sought to improve on the imperfect, not to say chimerical, unity of the Middle Ages. Let him reflect that the rise of a new conception of, and of new beliefs and practices by, the individual state necessarily preceded the demise of old notions and norms of conduct in international relations. And let him remember, also, what all history reveals—that the old international notions would not be superseded without difficulty and the passage of long years.

Nearly every civilisation of which we have record, and not only medieval and early modern Europe, has developed the myth and the symbols of political unity. Whether they were built on the basis of mere cultural affinity or of earlier actual political conquest, nearly every civilisation has retained this myth and these symbols long after they ceased to conform—if they had ever conformed—with realities.*

* The Mesopotamian civilisation of the fourth millennium B.C. thought of the world as a universal state when it was itself riven with frontier wars. The myth of China's unity, not to say of her dominion of the entire world, has rarely conformed with the facts, but it was based on the widespread belief that greater China had once been ruled by a single monarch, and it has always controlled the minds of the Chinese. Ancient India held fast

The Beginnings

In most civilisations, it is equally clear, the power of such myths has gone on encouraging one or several of the separate states to seek to restore or create an actual unity, under their own supremacy, unless and until such time as circumstances most powerfully restrained them from doing so.* Whenever circumstances do not powerfully restrain them it may do so again in the future, in areas like Africa and the Muslim world. In the light of all history we must accept the fact that men have usually regarded their own political hegemony over their various worlds as the natural and logical solution of the international problem. In comparison with the constantly repeated strivings for this goal, those periods and areas were rare in which, before recent times, they consciously accepted, instead, co-existence or a balance of power between separate states within a single area possessing the memory or the myth of unified rule. And special circumstances, working massively in the opposite direction, have always been needed before these more sophisticated notions could take root.

What were these circumstances in modern Europe? What were the equivalent conditions to those which underlay the success of the *Polis* and the city state in dominating men's international behaviour within the smaller framework of classical Greece or fifteenth-century Italy, to take the obvious among the few periods before modern times when co-existence was practised consciously? What was the equivalent to the circumstances which produced such rare intellectual rationalisations of the balance of power to appear before the

to the mythical ideal of a universal world empire under a virtuous world monarch when its separate states ruthlessly sought power in rivalry. The image of a politically unified Muslim world was always contradicted by its division into many sovereignties, yet it is still experienced as a reality. In Byzantium in the Middle Ages, no less than in Islam and Western Europe, political theory never ceased to uphold the fiction of unity despite the fact that power and territory were actively divided up among a number of princes. The non-literate peoples of West Africa have formed separate tribes throughout recorded time: but according to their legends there was a time when most of them were joined in a greater union.[52]

* The Mesopotamian civilisation became a political system of city states all vying with each other for total supremacy. Ancient Egypt, developing farther into a centralized and politically unified state, thought of itself as the chosen race, of its Pharoah as the rainmaker for all other countries. The Persian kings of the sixth century B.C. regarded themselves as the only kings in the world, the King of Kings. So did Alexander the Great when, two centuries later, he conquered the Greek and Persian worlds and attempted to express the Hellenistic spirit in a single world organisation. Rome achieved the conquest of its own world and assumed itself to be the sole sovereign of the entire world; and when Rome broke up the successor states in Byzantium, Islam and Western Europe limited themselves to claiming mastery in their own spheres only because they checked each other in the claim to the whole heritage.[53]

eighteenth century as the *Arthashastra* of the Indian Kautilya in the fourth century B.C. and the writings of Machiavelli in the sixteenth century A.D.? What forced European practice and thought in the same direction after the 1720's? The answer to these questions, already hinted at in connection with the career of Napoleon, lies mainly in one direction. In the long process of rise and fall in the relative strength of states, Europe was attaining from the beginning of the eighteenth century a condition in which there was a greater degree of near-equality between a larger number of leading states than ever before in its history.

This was the time when Russia at last made her appearance as a constant factor in European politics, when Prussia at last acquired the rank of a European Power, when, with her solution of internal problems and the cumulative effect of her earlier activity overseas, Great Britain's rivalry with France beyond Europe began to replace the old Austro-French struggle within the Continent as the pivot of international relations. On the other hand, the two major results of the Spanish Succession War had been the break-up of the Spanish-Habsburg power complex and the exhaustion of France. The condition of near-equality between several states, replacing a long-standing situation in which Europe had been dominated by two conflicting leading states, each suspecting the other of the goal of universal monarchy and dividing the rest of Europe into their two rival camps, is the key to the development of the states' system in the high eighteenth century—that period which, just because there had ceased to be a preponderance on the Continent, even historians of Europe have been reduced to calling 'the age of English preponderance'.

It was this which drove relations between the European states to greater extremes of egotism, on a wider geographical scale, than had previously been experienced. On the other hand it was this which also steadily imposed limitations on the freedom of action of the states by the very fact that it increased egotism and insecurity. At first the greater emphasis was on increased acquisitiveness. From the 1730's, as states began to realise that a greater number of themselves were more equal than before—that the previous predominance of France was counterbalanced by English power and French internal problems; that English power was counterbalanced by the fact that English interests lay beyond the Continent—and as newer states flexed their muscles, the slightest acquisition abroad, the slightest advance by one state as against the others, the sort of advance that had been of little value or even impossible for most states when relative strengths had been gravely disproportionate, came to matter enormously to all. Since this was happening when the old Habsburg structure had recently been broken up, and when the new rulers of its component parts did not hold them with the firmness of traditional possession, we cannot be surprised that there set in a process that has been described as 'a swift winning and losing and exchanging of territories',[54] or wonder at Frederick the Great's conclusion in 1743 that 'of all the states from the smallest to the biggest one can safely say that the fundamental rule . . . is the principle of extending their territories'.[55]

Yet the same international near-equality also set up in due course a powerful tendency towards restraint. Because more states were more nearly equal in power, the slightest addition to the power of any affected all. The possible retaliations to any acquisition accordingly became more various, the probability of retaliation more pronounced, than had previously been the case. Because the states were all experiencing an increase in centralisation and government control, it became increasingly impossible for them not to calculate and hesitate before these dangers. On both accounts the great characteristic of the international politics of the *ancien régime*, especially after 1750, was the strong contrast between the realistic and limited nature of the objectives of foreign policy and the acute avidity with which these objectives were pursued. The states tended to be 'ceaselessly agitated and yet at the same time to remain in fixed limits'.[56] They exhibited a kind of schizophrenia, the outcome of the conflict between their urge to expand and their need to be careful. Nor should we underestimate the influence of the international situation in bringing about the greater emphasis on the internal power and centralisation of the state. The development of mercantilism and enlightened absolutism was attempted in every society that was not structurally too advanced—like England—or not structurally too backward—like eastern Europe—for these assertions of central authority to be the appropriate means of increasing internal efficiency. This was not only because one state copied another. It was not a simple consequence of the rationalist spirit of the age. Men were realizing more than before that power and efficiency depended on the organisation and exploitation of existing resources as much as on the territorial acquisitions and dynastic windfalls which had been the chief additions to strength before the eighteenth century. But it was the international situation, putting a premium on the slightest advance in internal efficiency as it put a premium on —but also set obstacles to—the slightest acquisition abroad, which did most to produce this realisation. Kant was not wrong when in 1784 he noticed the factor of near-equality and pointed to its close connection with the enlightenment as well as with the centralism of domestic policies. 'The states are now on such artificial terms towards each other that not one of them can relax its efforts at internal development without losing in comparison with the others. . . . Civic freedom cannot now be interfered with without the state feeling the disadvantage . . . in all its trades . . . and as a result a decline of the power of the state in its foreign relations. Therefore this freedom is being gradually extended.'[57]

The state did not become in the eighteenth century the modern state as we understand it. Historians have rightly been impressed by its continuing weaknesses as much as by its growing strength. They have tended to use these weaknesses to explain the increasing subjection of avidity to restraint in foreign relations after the middle of the century. They have argued that this was due to the fact that international rivalry became increasingly the rivalry of dynastic rulers, rather than the clash of religions and principles, or to the fact that state resources remained limited. Neither of these explanations is entirely satisfactory.

The rivalries of the sixteenth and seventeenth centuries had also been rivalries between dynastic rulers, whatever they had been besides. They had not been restrained on that account. It is as frequently argued that dynasticism caused conflict in the eighteenth century as that it limited it. 'The names of the three chief wars of the first half of the eighteenth century . . . suggest that war only occurred when matrimonial arrangements had failed or become inextricably confused.'[58] Both arguments are equally beside the point. The great feature of the eighteenth century in this respect, as Meinecke showed, was the steady abandonment by even personal rulers of dynastic principles and attitudes in favour of the 'pure power' considerations and calculations of *raison d'état*. 'State interest was more sharply and consciously separated from the dynastic interest in the eighteenth century than ever before and was seen as existing for itself.'[59] This development was especially pronounced in the Prussia of Frederick the Great. But he symbolised, in his pride in being the first servant of the people or the state or the nation, a transition from Louis XIV's *l'état c'est moi* that took place in all the leading states. He was not wrong in diagnosing a move by all of them in this direction as one of the main developments of his day.[60]

The other explanation of the increase of restraint as the century proceeded—the undeveloped powers of the eighteenth-century state —has confused the nature of warfare with the objectives of war and policy. The conduct of warfare at this period was unquestionably 'formalised', 'pedantic', 'inflexible', 'defensive'. It was so partly because of the limited development of the powers of the state—though technical considerations also played a part. Bad communications, the inaccuracy of firearms and the social structure of armies—which consisted of men who were expensively trained and dubiously loyal —all made for close combat and immobility in tactics. When all the technical factors pushed warfare in the direction of close combat, the limited administrative and economic techniques of even the leading states—not to speak of their bankruptcy—made them prefer to avoid the pitched battles and heavy casualties which decisive action in close combat conditions necessarily entailed. But once again these technical and financial limitations had existed in the sixteenth and seventeenth centuries, and had had the same effect on the conduct of warfare, yet this had not prevented wars from being 'wars of righteousness and moral purpose' and far from limited in their objectives. If we make the necessary distinction between the conduct of warfare and the aims of policy in war we shall see that now, on the contrary, the latter were also limited, as they had not been formerly. We shall see, too, that this was because of the increase in the range and competence of the state rather than because of its continuing limitations. Policy—the objectives of war and the decisions as between peace and war—were coming increasingly under governmental control, however true it may be that the range and efficiency of that control remained limited by twentieth-century standards. And the very weaknesses of the increasingly competent state—its bankruptcy, for example—exerted a moderating and restraining influence because that competence was expanding at a time when the international situation was becoming more complex in the way that has been described.

This is nowhere so clearly exhibited as in the career and writings of Frederick the Great. Nothing emerges more clearly from these than the fact that the restraint resulted primarily from the increasing recognition of the international near-equality by increasingly competent governments. In his early writings, in 1738 and 1739, while deploring the domestic political principles of Machiavelli—as having been developed for the use of small and unstable rulers and as being irrelevant in the more efficient and competent contemporary state— he still approved of Machiavellianism, of ruthlessness, in foreign affairs. These he regarded as being highly relevant to the contemporary international situation.[61] In 1743 he was still hoping 'that posterity . . . will distinguish the philosopher in me from the ruler'—the respectable man who deplored the need for modern state expansion from the politician who could not resist any opportunity to extend his state in circumstances in which all states were expanding regardless of respectability.[62] By 1752, however, he was admitting that even in foreign affairs the great state, as opposed to the small, could not escape feelings of responsibility and the claims of rational calculation;[63] and was specifying some of the considerations which were leading the calculating state to be more moderate. At that time it was the greater weight of England and France that 'hinders great conquests from being achieved and makes wars fruitless unless they are conducted with great preponderance of strength and great good fortune'.[64] By 1768 he had got as far as emphasising the importance to a state of a good reputation abroad;[65] and the greater weight he now gave to the humanitarian and philanthropic conception of the state, as opposed to the argument that anything was justified which contributed to an increase in the state's power,[66] was closely connected with his increased recognition that power in Europe was more equally spread between several Great Powers than in the first half of the century.

He now rated England, France, Russia and Austria as the great Powers, whereas France and England had been the only first-class Powers for him in 1752. He no longer judged the remainder according to their relative strengths, but only in proportion as they formed part of the alliance systems of the really great states.[67] Nor could it have escaped him that Prussia, though not ranked among the great, was of a different status from others—was hardly a minor Power. It certainly did not escape him that other states were responding in the same way as Prussia to this situation. In 1746 he still regarded the Russians as a race of wild men, their foreign policy as impelled by brute passion and the blind impulse to domination. He classed them with Turkey as belonging as much to Asia as to Europe—as a factor brought into Europe only as and when French and English policy required. As late as 1752 he was still torn between his fear of the animal nature of the Russian government and his alarm at its apparently realistic policy of alliance with Austria against him. From 1764 his own alliance with Russia was the basis of his policy until the 1780's. In 1768, while still fearing Russian expansion into Europe, he had come to realise that Russia was not only a permanent factor in Europe but also a rational factor—that there was 'a definite, rational, easily ascertainable system of Russian interests'.[68] The progress of his opinions about Austria was identical. In 1746 he was convinced of her inner decay. By 1752 he realised that she had begun to reform her army and her finances, and was turning into a rational Power, even if he still suspected that she remained inspired by the traditional aims of the hereditary monarch of the German Empire. After her alliance with France of 1756—a reversal of policy which conflicted with the permanent political principles of traditional Europe and which was not so much a mere reversal of alliances as the symbol that the transition from traditional Europe to a new structure had been completed—he could not fail to recognise that Austria, in foreign policy as in domestic reform, was following in his own footsteps. In 1768 he was full of respect for the wisdom and systematic activity of Maria Theresa. In 1782 Austria seemed to him to be—as indeed she was—a rational, up-to-date power state, conducted on the lines of enlightened despotism and within the framework of a new international system.[69]

His reactions to these changes which he discerned in the policies of other states and in the general situation are as clearly revealed in his policies as in his writings. Until the end of the 1750's, for all his emphasis on the need for calculation, he remained 'utterly savage in his aims and methods'[70] when carrying out those policies—just as in the conduct of warfare he was content with no object short of the destruction of the enemy, and owed his startling victories to that fact.[71] By 1759 he had fallen back in warfare upon the tactics of war of position and the strategy of accumulating small gains by complex manœuvres and the avoidance of decisive battle,[72] and a similar restraint had imposed itself on his political aims. The change took place because he was being forced to realise, as he wrote in 1768, that 'uncertainty, although every time appearing in a different form, holds sway in all the operations of foreign policy, so that in the case of great alliances the result is the very opposite of what was planned'.[73] In 1775 he stated the same conclusion with even greater precision. 'Arms and military discipline being much the same throughout Europe, and alliances as a rule producing an equality of force between the belligerent parties, all that princes can expect from the greatest advantages at present is to acquire, by accumulation of successes, either some small city on the frontier or some territory which will not pay the expenses of war. . . .'[74] In 1776—so acute was his sense of the deadlock by that date—he was prepared to admit that 'a village on the frontier is worth more than a principality 60 miles beyond it'.[75] Can we doubt that his own change of policy had been produced by this deadlock? Or that the deadlock itself was the product of those features in the situation which he himself so ably analysed—the emergence of several leading states that were more integrated, more powerful and more nearly equal than European states had previously been; their adoption of policies that were more calculating, more flexible and more cautious, if not less egotistical, as a direct consequence of their greater equality and power?

These developments certainly underlay the change that had come over the British outlook on Europe—decided the outcome of the great and confused debate that had raged during the middle years of the century between the continental and the American or insular schools of thought concerning British foreign policy. British opinion was slower than European opinion to conclude that resistance to the universal monarchy of the Bourbons was ceasing to be Europe's supreme and general concern: British interests against France still coincided with the maintenance of such a general concern when the interests of individual European states had gone into new channels; it is not to be wondered at that pamphleters and parliamentary orators found it as difficult as Newcastle to get the old danger and the Grand Alliance out of their heads. It was not until the 1750's that the opinion that this outlook was out of date began to be seriously formulated. When it was formulated it was partly on the suspicion that the old attitude was being maintained in the interests of Hanover—that the British course was being shaped by what Lord Chesterfield called 'the Hanover rudder'. It was partly because colonial and trading interests were acquiring greater influence in the state. These considerations contributed heavily to the growing complaints of the insular school.[76] But the complaints also stemmed from the fact that British observers were realising that things had changed in Europe.

Pitt summed up these complaints in 1755 with his argument that the preservation of the balance of power in Europe had become an irrelevant and wasteful object for British policy. When Israel Mauduit attacked Pitt for nevertheless retaining the Prussian alliance after the defeat of France in Canada, in his *Considerations on the German War* (1761), he used Pitt's own earlier argument and expanded the reasoning which lay behind it. During the Spanish Succession War England's European alliances had been justified by the need for her help in defending Protestantism and opposing the establishment of a universal monarchy in Europe. Nowadays England's alliances were not only positively detrimental to England's own main interest, the expansion of her power beyond the seas, but were unnecessary for these other purposes. And why? The European balance of power could safely be left to look after itself. France no longer had the power to dominate Europe. The more she attempted to do so the more certain would be the reaction, the more adequate the retaliation, of other European Powers. French pretensions on the Continent of course remained a danger to England; her help might sometimes be needed against them. But in the new circumstances it was wiser to wait for the other European Powers to appeal for it, rather than to offer it in the old-fashioned belief that it was essential to offer it, and thus be forced to pay a higher price.[77]

Mauduit did not go the further step of urging that England would be justified in provoking quarrels—in exploiting the balance—in Europe when it suited her own interests. From about the middle of the century there was no lack of writers and orators who did so.[78] More significant still, it would be hard to deny that this argument inspired the actual conduct of British relations with Europe during the Seven Years' War. The war was begun by most people with Pitt's aim of expelling France from North America; even for Newcastle its chief purpose had been to force France to limit her American pretensions by pressing her in Europe. Nobody began it as a means of limiting her pretensions in Europe. In 1761–2, at the end of that war, Newcastle wanted peace because the country was tired of war, and he urged the continuation of fighting on all fronts as the best means of enforcing a peace. Bute wanted peace for the same reason and because of his concern for the popularity of the King; and he would accept sacrifices on all fronts as the means of obtaining it. Grenville wanted more conquests but a minimum of unpopularity and so advocated limiting the war to the sea and the colonies, where it could be carried on for ever. Pitt, also wanting more conquests, had been got rid of for insisting both on the continuation of the war in Germany and the extension of the war by an attack on Spain.[79] Nobody wanted to end the war because the French threat to dominate Europe had been destroyed or to continue the war because French domination still threatened. In the previous war that began in 1739 there had already been fanatics for war in America; they had not been more numerous or vociferous than those who had feared the subjection of the continent and the invasion of England.[80] The briefest comparison of the conduct of Pitt with the conduct of ministers like Walpole, Carteret and Newcastle in that earlier war will show that the Seven Years' War was the first war to be waged by Great Britain with the new order of priorities—even if it was also to be the last.

Pitt incurred Mauduit's attack because he had recognised in office the limitations of his earlier extreme isolationist views. He agreed with Mauduit that England's chief interest in the Continent was fundamentally different from what it had been previously. In 1760 another pamphleteer expressed the truth when he said that Pitt was 'no friend to Continental Measures in general' and especially opposed to 'such Continental measures as engaged us during the three last Wars, as Principals. . . . But the Continental measures now adopted by England were necessary, both with Regard to our Honour and Our Interest.' In December 1761 it was Pitt himself who claimed that America had been conquered in Germany.[81] This summed up his conduct of the war, his combination of continental and colonial warfare. What this amounted to was the conscious recognition for the first time by a man in office that the balance of power in Europe was something that existed, not something that that had to be reared up; the use of that balance by Great Britain for the first time as a means of keeping Europe divided, not as a means of inviting Europe to save England and itself by uniting against a predominant Power. His policy was the natural response in British interests to the limitations imposed upon the continental Powers by the growth of deadlock in Europe by which only Great Britain among an increased number of leading states was not contained.

CHAPTER 9

THE FIRST FIFTY YEARS

In the year 1800 in *L'État de la France à la Fin de l'An VIII*, an anonymous publication written for the French government, Hauterive, perhaps the earliest director of a modern Ministry of Information, criticised the international system as it had operated in Europe since 1760.

At the outbreak of the French Revolution, he wrote, an effective law of nations had no longer existed. 'The true principles of Europe's political and federal constitution were neglected or forgotten.' Indeed, they had been destroyed—by the rise of the Russian Empire as a factor in the north of Europe and 'the intervention of this in the intercourse of the rest'; by the development of Prussia to 'a Power of the highest rank', and especially by her resort to war, to a new form of government, to new military tactics, to the policy of accumulating treasure in the interests of power, which steps had forced all the states into an unnatural and enervating concentration on struggle; by 'the rise and progress of the commercial and colonial system' of Great Britain, which had had equally destructive consequences. By 1789 on account of these developments 'there had long ceased to exist any maxims of government, any federal union, any fixed political principles in Europe. . . . An imaginary principle of aggrandisement . . . had fascinated all governments. . . . The law of nations no longer existed except in appearance. . . . The Revolution was only a loud and formal announcement of its long-determined dissolution.'

Hauterive did not stop there. The war waged against the Revolution had been the logical consequence of the prevailing anarchy. It had been 'a wanton attempt to . . . build a new political system, and establish a new division of power, upon the ruins of the French monarchy'. The attempt had failed and the result of the war had been to re-establish the law of nations. France's victories had restored her 'to the place she ought always to occupy, not only for the sake of her own security, but for the security of all Europe'. In the future, as in the past, Europe would be dependent for the main-

tenance of peace—'for the preservation of its social and political co¬
stitution'—on France. France's political and military greatness and
reformed constitution fitted her to protect and regulate the nations
around her; to establish and preserve the equilibrium among them;
to be, in short, 'the common centre of a system composed of all the
states of Europe'. France would especially be the bulwark of
Europe against Great Britain, 'that single nation which, animated
by private interests, is hostile throughout to the interests of the rest,
which is . . . the mover of the dissensions and wars of Europe' and
which must be 'at length confined within narrower limits'.[1] It would
be difficult to find a better statement of the amalgam of ideas which
inspired the French attitude to international affairs under the first
Napoleon.

This was not the first attack to be delive ed on the international
system of the second half of the eighteenth century. The misfortune
of that system was that if it aroused French resentment at the decline
of empire—of universal monarchy—it also produced, in practice, but
a poor approximation to the conception of Europe which had
replaced that older framework of thought in the years between the
writings of Montesquieu and those of Vattel. These had emphasised
that Europe was divided into independent states. They had also
assumed that the relations between those states were moderat ed by
the recognition that they were members of a common civilisation, no
less than by expediency and 'the wise policy of maintaining among
themselves . . . an equal balance of power'. In practice in those years
international relations were certainly moderated by expediency. But
the growth of near-equality between several leading states—that
development which had destroyed the practicability of the aim of
universal rule and imposed the need for calculation and restraint
upon all the individual states except Great Britain, in her special circumstances—also quite destroyed those notions and attitudes which
had treated Europe as a whole, as a single community, and accentuated the egotism of the individual state, its insistence upon its complete autonomy.

'Never was the isolation of the power-state carried so far', 'never
either before or since did universally European ideas and interests
form such a small part in European policies',[2] as in the resulting
system. It was a system in which a set of particularist states were
linked together solely by the fact that the interests of each ffected

all; in which those individual interests were restrained solely by the same fact; in which egotism was limited by nothing but consideration of egotism. If after 1752 Frederick the Great emphasised that it was wise to abide by treaties, whereas previously he had insisted that breach of agreements was always justified as indispensable to statesmen, this was because *raison d'état* itself, though still 'sacred',[3] was now judged to require conformity to promises in an international situation that was potentially fluid and flexible but actually extremely rigid. Treaties and promises were not always confined, moreover, to accepting the existing situation. The partitions of Poland by agreement were a typical product of the conflict between increased egotism and the increased need for restraint.

There was thus a divergence between international practice in the second half of the eighteenth century and the new conception of Europe which had emerged by the middle of the century. Until the French revolution, however, this was a divergence between practice and a theory which all, including rulers, continued to accept. Frederick the Great compared the *Corps politique* of Europe with the human body as early as 1738; its health was founded on an equilibrium between the different states. His subsequent experiences only confirmed him in this opinion. In 1752 he thought it 'necessary to see Christian Europe as a republic of sovereigns'. In 1759–60 he described the balance of power in words that might have been written by Voltaire or Vattel as 'the wise policy to which we owe the existence of the various European governments', which had enabled the smaller European Powers like Prussia to spring up and become important, 'which has always been opposed to the excesses of ambition'.[4] It may well be objected that he entertained these sentiments in his capacity as yet another writer, and that they did not govern his behaviour as the ruler of a state. Beginning with Rousseau, and with growing insistence after the Seven Years' War, writers certainly criticised him and other rulers for this inconsistency. But they, too, continued to share the new conception of Europe, which they believed that governments were betraying.

The earlier *philosophes* had lauded statesmen and approved of the balance of power; their successors after about 1760 turned against both. But if they now emphasised even more than their predecessors that the various nations belonged to one family or a single society, they did not seek a solution to the conflict between practice and theory in another conception of the international society. They did not desert the view of Europe, as consisting of a multiplicity of independent states, that had grown up by the middle of the century. Their criticism, on the contrary, took the form of denouncing governments for proving unworthy of such a view and of insisting that they must be reformed until they were capable of operating such a Europe. Rousseau abandoned earlier federalist ideas after investigating them. He was the last considerable writer before the French Revolution—as he had been the first—even to investigate them. Men now felt, as Hauterive was to feel, that Europe was in the state of complete anarchy which it had experienced after the collapse of the Roman Empire or which Greece had fallen into after the decline of the empires of Athens and Sparta.[5] But they did not yet advocate the restoration of empire. The culmination of all the development in internationalist theory between the middle of the eighteenth century and the outbreak of the French Revolution was contained in Bentham's verdict that, while international relations were the relations between independent communities, those relations would not be conducted on moral principles until governments were reformed and subjected to publicity or—better still—until international relations became relations between individuals and not between governments.* As usual there is an exception to prove the rule. Unlike Bentham, Tom Paine produced no peace plan for Europe. The object of his *Common Sense* (1776), the first public call for American independence, was to convince Americans that it was their duty to break with the old continent as well as with Great Britain. He had many arguments for his case, not least a belief in the rottenness of the British Constitution. But chief among them were the assertion that, as Rousseau had also concluded, Europe was now too corrupt to achieve a peaceful international constitution—an ideal single republic—and the deduction, which had been beyond Rousseau's range, that it was America's duty to mankind to establish in the New World what men had abandoned in the Old.[6]

The success of the American Revolution was the first blow to this structure of European thought and practice. In the struggle produced by the French Revolution both thought and practice underwent a still more severe test. The significance of that Revolution for internationalist theory was that it combined the pent-up resentment

* See above, pp. 82–3, for further details.

of the French nation at the passing-away of French hegemony with the critical disgust of late-eighteenth-century writers—the old ideal of universal monarchy with disappointment at the betrayal by the *ancien régime* of the newer vision of a happy family of independent states —into an attempt to set up in Europe the ideal single state which had held little attraction for Europe since the early eighteenth century, but which had now been achieved in America.

One of the results of this effort was the powerful ideology poured out by Hauterive. Another was the phenomenon of Napoleon. Yet another, however, was the combination of the European governments in the struggle against Napoleon. And in this struggle it was the newer ideas of the eighteenth century that were ultimately strengthened, the older programme of universal European monarchy —and with it the older and closely associated ideal of a single federated Europe—that was destroyed.

The struggle with Napoleon had one other consequence. The states which combined against him in defence of the newer ideas also acquired in the process a determination to bring their future practice into a closer conformity with those ideas than had been achieved in the second half of the eighteenth century. *On the State of Europe Before and After the French Revolution*, the reply made to Hauterive by Frederick Gentz, 'Counsellor at war to His Prussian Majesty, etc. etc.,' in 1802, is eloquent testimony at this point.

Gentz began his book by denying that Europe had ever had the 'political and federal constitution' which the Frenchman claimed had been neglected and forgotten during the eighteenth century. 'An universal and perpetual system of public law . . . , whereby all future revolutions in the internal situation and the external connections of the states should be foreseen . . . and taken into account by the whole political system,' had never existed. Indeed, 'it is only necessary to state these conditions to point out the impossibility of fulfilling them. The difficulty of defining to the satisfaction of all . . . in one and the same treaty the various and intricate relations, wants and pretensions of so great a number of independent nations as Europe alone contains, is evident.' Such a constitution not only always had been impracticable; it always would be. 'Even supposing that all the states of Europe could enter into such a compact as would serve for the basis of a general federative constitution . . . yet there would still be wanting the means of ensuring the everlasting duration of such a compact, or of providing with any degree of certainty for its future existence. . . . Owing to the inequality of their respective progress, to the unexpected growth of new branches of industry and power . . ., it is impossible to establish an eternal system of public law by means of a general treaty.'⁷ Gentz had made the same point in an earlier book, *Über den Ewigen Frieden* (1800)—an attack on Kant, under whom he had studied at Königsberg.

Europe's public law in the eighteenth century, as at any time, had thus been the changing product of changing circumstances. The eighteenth century had certainly been a period of rapid change. This did not mean that the public law had been non-existent or neglected at that time. The rise of Russia—'the greatest event, after the discovery of America, in the history of modern times'; the development which had removed the danger of an irruption of the backward nations into Europe—had complicated the political relations of the states, multiplied wars and threatened the balance of power and the law of nations because of Russian plans for conquest. It had not weakened the public law of Europe if only because it had been balanced by the rise of Prussia. To say that the rise of Prussia had overturned the public law was to overlook this same fact: 'the Powers of Europe . . . must have found it necessary to create such a state if fate or genius had not anticipated them.' It was also to overlook the fact that, except while Prussia was rising, there had been less, not more, war than before—and none after 1763 until the attack by the Revolution. If anybody had caused the unnatural and enervating concentration on international struggle it was Louis XIV, not Frederick the Great; but essentially the increase of armies, the enlargement of administration and the development of far-reaching and expensive political plans were the result of the general development of political society, industry and riches. It was true that Prussia had replaced France as the protector of the weak German states against the strong; but that was an improvement for European stability, not a source of unrest. The same was true of England's commercial and colonial development. This had not subverted the federal constitution of Europe because no such constitution had ever existed. It had not subverted the law of nations and the balance of power because the increase in economic power, although it had led to jealousies and wars, had not been confined to Great Britain. It had 'adapted itself exceedingly well to the former social relations of Europe' since other states, France not least, had also shared in it. It had thus 'provided in the most natural manner against that abuse of power which might have been favoured by the undivided sway of an individual nation'. And in so far as Great Britain had profited most from economic developments, that fact, like the rise of Prussia, had been a source of added stability. It had 'produced a new weight in the general balance, to be occasionally opposed with advantage to the preponderance of any continental nation'.[8]

For these reasons the outbreak and course of the Revolution—less still its ideological arguments—were not justified by the state of international relations in Europe at the time it broke out. On the contrary, it was the Revolution which had interrupted the progress of the international system at a most favourable moment in its development, and which had created chaos in its place.[9] And under Napoleon, far from replacing chaos with a better system than the old, France had acquired 'a superfluity of political and federal strength', 'a monopoly of influence', which—notwithstanding the fact that 'when in our days a nation is said to give laws to Europe it is understood to do it indirectly and not immediately'—amounted to the old universal monarchy, a 'universal dominion'. Napoleon had created a situation in which 'there no longer exist any independent nations, except some of the principal states', and in which even those principal states were doomed to remain together in a perpetual league as the only refuge against France so long as she retained this position.[10]

The first task of political wisdom in the 'search among the ruins of the former edifice for the materials of a new one' was to undo this unhealthy and permanently dangerous situation by reducing the power of France and restoring Europe's previous system of balance or equilibrium. 'The political system cannot but be extremely defective when it contains such a disproportion of power as nothing but a general league can rectify. And when that difficult and dangerous remedy does not promise certain success . . . the existence of anything like an equilibrium must be quite out of the question.' On the other hand, once equilibrium had been restored, the independence and interests of each state could again be 'the principal ground of its conduct'. This would not eliminate wars and disputes altogether— to ask for that was to ask for the impossible. But the international system would be far more healthy than the present one, which was 'repugnant to every principle of freedom, to all equality of power, to the fundamental laws of the social and federal constitution, to the wishes of the majority of nations and individuals'. 'All the dictates of sound policy prescribe the necessity of a natural or an artificial balance of power, not only to prevent the wanton . . . abuse of power by a preponderating state, but even to maintain a due proportion of strength in these ordinary wars which human wisdom is unable to avert, and to preserve the political system from shocks that might prove fatal to its existence.'[11]

Gentz's argument was basically a plea for a return to the international system of the second half of the eighteenth century. He recognised, however, that statesmen were now faced with another task. 'Accidentally', if only accidentally, the Revolution and Napoleon had had a good effect: they had revealed to governments the imperfections of the eighteenth-century system. These imperfections—'plans of ambition and usurpation . . . , the numberless combinations . . . , the celebrated system of partition'—had been the unavoidable 'consequence of the rapid civilisation of Europe by which the former proportions between the leading states were altered and the disproportion between 4 or 5 preponderant states, on the one hand, and a great number of small, dispersed and insignificant states on the other, was considerably augmented'. The European states had been in a fair way to removing them when the Revolution had brought the system down in ruins. 'The principles of government and the law of nations were advancing towards perfection' when the disaster occurred. But imperfections had unquestionably existed, especially 'the want, so often felt, of a more comprehensive code of public law'. Next only in importance to restoring equilibrium, said Gentz, was the task of ensuring that this progress towards the perfection of the system was resumed.[12] It was not for nothing that he had studied under Kant.

In this, no less than in the bulk of his argument, Gentz also spoke for the governments of his day. In 1804 the younger Pitt recommended in a British state paper that the rights and possessions acquired by the Powers should be fixed and recognised in a treaty in which they 'should bind themselves mutually to protect and support each other against any attempt to infringe' them.[13] Alexander I of Russia concluded in the same year that at the end of the war, 'after having attached the nations to their governments by making these incapable of acting except in the greatest interest of their subjects', the governments must 'fix the relations of the states among each other on more precise rules, such as it will be in the interest of the nations to respect'; and the British Government's reply to his memorandum, despite some reservations, welcomed his proposal for the formation of a league of governments to bring this about and give security to Europe.[14] In 1812 he was more concerned for the interests of sovereigns than for those of their subjects, but he still hoped for a pact under which the sovereigns could 'live like brothers'.[15] And such aspirations were uppermost among the conscious motives of all the victorious governments at the Vienna Congress of 1814–15, where Gentz himself was entrusted with the task of drafting the final comprehensive peace treaty. Kant had not only influenced Gentz. In 1784 he had forecast that 'the effect of each impact of a government upon other governments in our continent, where states have become so very much linked by commerce, will become so noticeable that the other states, compelled by their own danger, will offer themselves as arbiters even when lacking a legal basis, and thus start a future great government of which there is no previous example in history'.[16] A generation later the slow process he had envisaged was about to begin.

These aspirations found expression at Vienna in the spirit in which the assembled victor states agreed among themselves about the detailed resettlement of Europe. They appeared more prominently still in the measures adopted or advocated for upholding that resettlement. The Final Act of the Congress, of June 1815, a document which determined the frontiers of nearly every European state, was regarded as a single instrument, no part of which could be infringed without invalidating the rest; and it gave every signatory the right—though not, indeed, in the absence of a guarantee clause, the duty—to uphold its terms. The second Treaty of Paris of November 1815 between Russia, Great Britain, Austria and Prussia, fixed the frontiers of France and the conditions of peace with her, and bound the four Great Powers to maintain them. In another treaty of Alliance between the four Great Powers—the Treaty of Chaumont, now renewed—the Great Powers not only bound themselves to unite against aggression by France and against the return of the Bonaparte family to the throne of France, and to 'concert together' in the event of further revolutionary disturbance in that country; they also took a distinctly novel step. In Article VI of the Treaty, 'in order to consolidate the intimate tie which unites the four Sovereigns for the happiness of the World, the High Contracting Parties . . . agreed to renew at fixed intervals, either under the immediate auspices of the Sovereigns themselves, or by their respective Ministers, meetings for the purpose of consulting upon their common interests, and for the examination of the measures which at each of these epochs shall be considered most salutary for the repose and prosperity of the Nations and for the maintenance of the peace of Europe'. And then there was the Holy Alliance, negotiated in the autumn of 1815 and published in 1816. Influenced by the religious fanaticism of Baroness Krüdener as well as by the ideas of Sully, Saint-Pierre and Rousseau, Alexander spoke of this as 'the work of Providence, not of any Cabinet', and he hoped it would be the means by which the 'Christian Sovereigns of Europe'—from whom he excluded the Pope as well as the Sultan—would regard each other as brothers and conduct the international affairs of all Europe 'as members of one and the same Christian nation' and in the spirit of 'our Lord and Saviour'.[17]

Many books have been written on the motives of the governments in all these proceedings. Some have argued that their policies were dominated by the search for a balance of power. Others have attempted to show that they were dominated, rather, by something else: by common defence against internal revolution and a repetition of 1789; by legitimism; by pure self-interest. There is, indeed, much detailed evidence for either view. But the conflict of evidence is dispelled when the problem is considered in its proper context.

The balance of power had acquired two meanings by 1815. In early modern times, when all the political and intellectual trends had continued to run towards the hegemony of a single Power, it had signified the need to combine against that hegemony. During the eighteenth century it had come to be equivalent with something else: expediency and egotism in a collectivity of roughly equal and intensely acquisitive states which were bound and regulated by nothing but expediency and egotism. In the struggle against Napoleon it had reacquired the earlier meaning. Gentz in 1802 could still think of it in both contexts, as the opposite of the 'abuse of power by a preponderating state' but also as the system in which, on the basis of an 'equality of power', the interests of each state could be 'the principal ground of its conduct'. A few years later Metternich spoke for everybody when, thinking exclusively of the balance in the earlier sense, he declared that '*le repos sans l'équilibre est une chimère*'. The key to the Congress settlement is that the governments who made it, who were all reeling under the impact of Napoleon, were obsessed by the need for a balance in the earlier sense but revolted by the thought of returning to balance of power politics as between themselves. The Congress system was essentially the first attempt in history—as its almost exact repetition in the shape of the United Nations' experiment has so far been the last—consciously to find an alternative both to the old aim of domination by one Power, of which the latest practitioner had just been laid low, and to the balance of power as it had operated in the eighteenth century, from which all felt it imperative to escape. If, as Sorel wrote, a coalition of states founded on public law for the defence of that law would have been an historical paradox in the eighteenth century, unattainable if not unthinkable, this is precisely what the Congress system was and what all statesmen agreed to be the essential solution to both these dangers.

The Holy Alliance was not the brain-child of an eccentric Tsar but only the most extreme of several versions of the international system demanded by this consensus of opinion—a consensus which was shared by Castlereagh, the British Foreign Secretary, who criticised the Holy Alliance as 'sublime mysticism and nonsense', and Metternich in Austria, for whom it was a 'loud sounding nothing'. Legitimism and the defence of the social order and the determination to stamp out dissidence were parts of that consensus: the states were reeling under the impact of the French Revolution as well as of Napoleon. But the general religious and moral revival included a specific reaction against international politics of force and materialism, as practised in the eighteenth century, that was as intense and widespread as the reaction against alliances and power-politics which followed the outbreak of the First World War. It was under the influence of this reaction that, as well as seeking equilibrium against a recrudescence of French aggression, the Great Powers, in their anxiety to avoid a return to reliance on the operation of a balance among themselves, came in the Congress system as close to adopting the federalist ideas of the peace plans of the early eighteenth century as was consistent with their existence—and with their recent growth—as Great Powers.

It is not inconsistent with this that they pursued their separate interests even while embarking on the Congress system. In the very existence of separate states we have a structure of power in which each state pursues its interests at all times. The historian of international relations is not concerned to show that they do this, still less to wish that they did not. His task is to show why they do it in different ways at different times—how and why interests themselves change. The impressive thing about the behaviour of the Powers in 1815 is that they were prepared, as they had never previously been prepared, to waive their individual interests in the pursuit of an international system. This fact is not rendered any less impressive by the recognition that they were prepared to waive their individual interests because it was in their individual interests to do so. They had recognized for the first time that it was in their interests to do so. Gentz, who was critical of the detailed proceedings at the Congress of Vienna, was rightly impressed with that Congress as 'a preliminary effort' by the Powers 'to work for a political system to consolidate and uphold the public order in Europe'.[18] The political system it established in Europe, he added in 1818, was 'phenomenon unheard of in the history of the world. The principle of equilibrium or, rather, of counterweights formed by particular alliances—the principle which has governed, and too often troubled and engulfed, Europe for 3 centuries—has been succeeded by a principle of general union, uniting all the states by a federative bond under the direction of the 5 principal Powers. . . . The states of the second, third and fourth rank have placed themselves, tacitly and without any stipulation on this point, under the decisions taken jointly by the preponderant Powers; and Europe at last forms a single great political family, reunited under an areopagus of its own creation, in which the members guarantee to each other and to each interested party the tranquil enjoyment of their respective rights.'[19] The first resort to the system after the Vienna settlement, the Congress of Aix-la-Chapelle of 1818, was the first conference ever held between states to regulate international affairs in time of peace.

Gentz was even then speculating on how long the system could endure against the separate interests and rivalries of the Powers. 'The strongest objection to it today', he wrote in an essay on *Le système politique actuellement établi en Europe* in 1818,[20] 'is the evident difficulty of preserving for long the amalgam of heterogeneous

elements of which it is composed. . . . Special circumstances were
necessary to bring such a league into existence; it would be contrary
to the nature of man and of things that it should replace for a
long time the condition of opposition and struggle . . . [between]
a mass of independent Powers, each possessing its own character and
system. . . . The question of the probable duration of this European
league, which has temporarily overcome the gulf of competing
political pretensions but which cannot overcome it for ever, or even
for very long, is thus the most important question facing statesmen
today. . . .' And because of those same competing pretensions 'the
opinion of contemporaries is generally little favourable to the
solidity of the existing state of things. People do not believe that an
edifice which owes its existence to quite extraordinary events and
which rests on a single common interest—though that is the greatest
interest of all—can last. . . .'

He himself did not 'share the conjecture and fears which most
people entertain. I am persuaded that the European federation—
for that is the term that best describes the present system—is not
threatened with early destruction. I won't answer for half a century; but I do not hesitate to say that it will persist for 10 or even
20 years. . . .' He based this forecast—an accurate forecast for the
Congress system as such—on the operation of the balance of power
between the Great Powers, but also on the fact that the prevailing
interest among them would be to preserve the new system. 'My
opinion is based not on the structure of the system, which I recognise
to be extremely fragile, but on the situation in which none can leave
the circle of existing relations with impunity, and without exposing
itself to imminent ruin.' 'The five Powers at the head of the federation are the only ones who could destroy the system by a change of
policy. The twists and turns of the others could never have tr is
effect. . . . [Thus] if the Porte decided to attack Russia the result
would be only a local war which would not upset the general
system. The case would be quite different if Russia were the aggressor; in that eventuality the system in Europe would be faced with
a catastrophe. . . .' But the balance of power and the prevailing
interests between the major Powers were such that there was no
imminent danger of catastrophe.

Austria, Prussia and Great Britain had a powerful interest in
peace and thus in preserving the system. Of Russia and France this

could not be said with the same certainty. Each of these had motives for wishing to change the situation, even before 10 or 20 years were out. But the probability was that they, too, would be restrained. France was the defeated Power for whom the new system was a symbol of defeat; and except for Russia she would be the first Power to recover her strength after the recent wars. But she would not be easily able to reform the system to her liking because she would long remain the object of general distrust. 'A war against France will for a long time be the only popular war in Europe.' Russia was the Power who could most easily ignore the system, and who least needed its support, on account of her strength and her possession of the only formidable army; the one Power who could renounce it with ease if a different system attracted her. She was also the sole Power governed by a complete autocrat. But she was financially weak; and aggression by her would meet the joint resistance of Austria and Prussia and, probably, England. And not less important, Alexander could be trusted to uphold a system of which he thought himself the founder and creator, and of which he wished to be the head. He regarded it as 'the glory of the century and the salvation of the world'.

Gentz was accurate in his forecast—and accurate also in basing it on these grounds. If the Congress System lasted for over ten years it was because the common interest of the Powers in preserving it assisted the balance between them to restrain their rivalries. If it was so short-lived, moreover, this was not simply because their separate interests and rivalries returned as the wars receded, though this fact played its part in destroying it. It was because the return of these rivalries widened original differences of opinion as to how the system should be used. If all the Powers began by agreeing that a new international system was needed in Europe they brought different conceptions of international organisation—and, even, different conceptions of Europe—to the task of reconstruction. It was on the rocks of these differences as to the aims and limits of an international system that the Congress foundered.

These differences were especially marked as between Great Britain and Russia. Their rivalry in the Near East was the issue over which they first emerged. The Vienna settlement did not extend to the Ottoman Empire. It was in the attempt to include the Near East that Castlereagh tried, during the Congress of Vienna, to incorporate in the Vienna Final Act both a guarantee of the integrity of the Ottoman Empire and a clause by which the Final Act, thus extended, would be reinforced by a public declaration by the Powers of 'their determination to unite their influence, and if necessary their arms, against the Power that should attempt to disturb it'. The Tsar liked the proposal for a guarantee of the Final Act—he had long been thinking on similar lines—but he attached impossible conditions to the inclusion in it of a clause upholding Turkish integrity. It is tempting to assume that he did so solely for the obvious reasons. Certainly the British Government reached this conclusion: it would not proceed with a guarantee which would have committed Great Britain to underwrite Russia's recent acquisitions in Poland while leaving Russia unrestrained in the Turkish direction. [21] Certainly Alexander wished to avoid this restraint. Yet power-politics were not his only motive. One of his conditions for accepting the extension of the guarantee to Turkey was that the Powers should first stop, and prevent for the future, Turkish massacres of the Serbs.[22] Whereas Castlereagh's abortive proposal for a guarantee of the Vienna settlement sprang mainly from the wish to protect Turkey against Russia, the Holy Alliance which Alexander produced in its place was so worded that only 'the Christian Sovereigns of Europe' could sign it. Subsequently the Tsar maintained towards Greek revolts against Turkish rule an attitude that was fundamentally different from that which he adopted to revolt against monarchies in Europe. Castlereagh argued that to be logical the Russian government should help to put the Greek revolutionaries down: they were part of the general movement of revolt in Europe against which the governments should collaborate. The Tsar urged, equally logically on his premises, that the European Alliance should support him in bringing order to the Ottoman Empire and in establishing a separate kingdom for the Greeks.[23] It was not for nothing that 'the great object of alarm to the Porte'—as Castlereagh was then informed—'is the Holy Alliance; that the Sultan and his ministers are firmly persuaded of a secret league against the Mohammedan Powers'.[24] Even if the interests of Russia as a Near Eastern Power contributed to strengthen his attachment to it, Alexander had a traditional conception of Europe in relation to the Turks that derived from the outlook of Sully, Saint-Pierre and Rousseau. There was only this difference: unlike some of those writers, he was certain that Russia formed part of Europe.

The Holy Alliance involved a traditional view of the needs of Europe as well as of its relations with the Turk. At the time, to quote C. K. Webster, it was a 'much misunderstood document'. It still is: even C. K. Webster concluded that it 'was simply the expression of Alexander's mystical religious beliefs' or of the fact that the Tsar was 'half mad, at any rate mad on some subjects'.[25] But if it is remembered that it was distrusted by Metternich as well as by Castlereagh; if it is recalled that Alexander and his ministers were alone among the governments of the day in wishing to advance the idea of self-government,[26] as opposed to the ideas of liberalism and nationalism which all governments equated with jacobinism; if it is emphasised that the Tsar, for all his subsequent irresolution on this issue, originally conceived of it as a guarantee system in defence of constitutionalism against monarchs no less than of monarchs against dissidence—then the similarity of the Holy Alliance to the federal ideas of the first half of the eighteenth century, to the plans of Saint-Pierre and his several successors for a league of European sovereigns as the means of avoiding war and promoting good government, may begin to emerge. Nor were these ideas easily abandoned by Alexander. At the end of 1820, after much opposition, he was still determined 'to secure to the other Great Powers of the Continent the same advantages that France enjoyed, viz. that in an especial case of military revolt or revolution by illegitimate means, the European Alliance was to be united against such a nation, and concert together as to the means of coping with it by conciliation or force of arms'. 'To such a reasonable and wise principle' it was not 'natural to suppose that any government would object', especially as the conciliation he envisaged was the restoration of tranquillity on the basis of a well-regulated understanding between the ruler and his government.[27] Castlereagh was not far wrong when he protested in 1821 that the governments could not assume 'such extraordinary powers . . . without either attributing to themselves a supremacy incompatible with the rights of other states or, if to be acquired through the special accession of such states, without introducing a federative system in Europe. . . .'[28]

It was Castlereagh who provided the most serious opposition to, and the only reasoned rebuttal of, the Tsar's ideas for reorganising

Europe. In his resistance to Russia's conception of Europe's relations with Turkey he had the support of the other Holy Alliance Powers, and especially of Austria; their interests, no less than Great Britain's, were opposed to Russian expansion in the Near East. For this material reason, as well as because the Tsar was reluctant to act alone, without the moral support of his League, the Holy Alliance was frustrated in this direction. It was otherwise, at first, with its operations in Europe, where the other European Powers quickly adapted Alexander's notions to a different end of their own. If they were reeling from the impact of Napoleon, they were also reeling under the impact of 1789. Historians sometimes complain that the makers of the Congress system ignored the claims of nationalism and liberalism; they might as well ask that the statesmen in 1945 should have reconstituted the world on the basis of the tenets of Nazism. In the years after 1815 liberalism and nationalism were the forces which governments were determined to stamp out. From the outset the other European governments differed from the Tsar in making no distinction between these forces and constitutionalism; before very long the Tsar himself found it difficult to draw this distinction except in Turkish lands. The main purpose of the Congress system for all the continental states became the suppression of all and every disturbance in Europe; and Castlereagh found himself ranged against all his allies in his attempt to resist the use of the Congress system for the purposes of the Holy Alliance.

His resistance was based on a totally different approach to the international problem from that which inspired the Tsar, and it went back to 1815 itself. When the Powers failed to agree on the inclusion of a guarantee clause in the Final Act of the Vienna Congress, Castlereagh fell back on the proposal contained in Article VI of the Treaty of November 1815—on the article whereby there would be periodic meetings of the Great Powers 'to secure the execution of the present treaty . . . and for the consideration of those measures which . . . shall be considered the most salutary for the repose and prosperity of the nations and for the maintenance of the peace of Europe'. The Tsar welcomed this proposal as a step towards the Holy Alliance which he had already negotiated with Prussia and Austria. But whereas in his mind it was the Holy Alliance, not Article VI, which constituted the new system which Europe needed, it was always Castlereagh's main purpose to keep the Holy Alliance and the Congress system distinct—and, while limiting the former to the expression of a general sentiment, to restrict the Congresses themselves to being a diplomatic device to assist the Powers in the settlement of strictly diplomatic problems. In 1818, in a memorandum to the other Powers at the Congress of Aix-la-Chapelle, he stated this object in so many words. 'The benign principles [of the Holy Alliance] . . . may be considered as constituting the European system in matter of political conscience. It would, however, be derogatory to this solemn act of the Sovereigns to mix its discussion with the ordinary diplomatic obligations which bind State to State, and which are alone to be looked for in the treaties that have been concluded in the accustomed form.'[29]

In 1817, on this account, he opposed Metternich's proposal that the Paris Conference of Ambassadors should become the organ of the Great Powers against the intrigues of revolutionaries all over Europe, insisting that 'the Allied ministers must be kept within the bounds of the original institution and not be suffered to present themselves as an European Council for the management of the affairs of the world'.[30] At the Congress of Aix-la-Chapelle in 1818 he similarly opposed Russia's wish that the Holy Alliance should be buttressed by a universal treaty under which the states of Europe would all guarantee all existing forms of government as well as all frontiers and possessions. Against this conception of '*all the Powers of Europe being bound together in a common league guaranteeing to each other the existing order of things in thrones as well as territories,** all being bound to march, if requisite, against the first Power that offended either by her ambitions or by her revolutionary transgressions'—which was how he described it to the Cabinet—he wrote the memorandum already quoted, which stated his position in great detail.

Some of the treaties concluded on the defeat of France bound all the European states collectively; they were 'the "Great Charte" by which the territorial system of Europe . . . has again been restored to order'. But they were almost wholly territorial in their scope; and they contained no express guarantee for their enforcement (as he himself had hoped they might) because those who framed them 'did not probably see how the whole Confederacy could, without the utmost inconvenience, be made collectively to enforce the observance of these treaties . . .'. They could not therefore be said to form an

* Castlereagh's italics

203

alliance in the strict sense of the word; and certainly, added Castlereagh, with Turkey in mind, they did not give 'any special or superior security to those parts of the European system thus regulated, as compared with those parts which were not affected . . . and which rest for their title upon anterior treaties or public acts of equal and recognised authority'. In addition to these collective treaties there were also treaties peculiar to particular States, notably the Treaty of Alliance of November 1815 between the 'four Great Allied Powers'. This was a treaty in the strictest sense of the word; it had a professed object, 'the conservation of Europe against the power of France', and it declared the forces by which that object was to be secured. It stipulated that further revolutionary disturbance in France might justify the Allies in intervening there. But this stipulation could operate only if the disturbance endangered other states: 'the only safe principle is that of the law of nations'. This was especially the case now that France was being admitted to the circle of the Great Powers. Essentially, therefore, this treaty was also limited to maintaining the new territorial *status quo*. Its purpose had been to place the restored territorial system in Europe, which could not be guaranteed collectively, 'under the protection of the Quadruple Alliance'.

The British Government would loyally observe this treaty. It was prepared to join in periodical Congresses with its allies to ensure its observation. It would not accept the extension of the treaty in directions which involved it in 'transgressing any of the principles of the law of nations or failing in that delicacy which they owe to the rights of other States'. Least of all would it accept its extension into a system of administering Europe on the basis of a general and unqualified guarantee against all internal changes. 'Nothing would be more prejudicial to the character of government generally' than such a system, which could be 'prostituted to the support of established power without any consideration of the extent to which it was abused'.[31]

Castlereagh maintained this position during the rest of his life— in his opposition to the Russian wish to use the Congress against disturbances in Spain in 1820 and in his protests against the proceedings of the Congress of Troppau in 1820 and of Laibach in 1821 for the suppression of revolts in Italy, no less than in his efforts during 1821 to dissuade the Tsar from intervening in support of revolution in Greece.[32] It was a position which he adopted and maintained for a

variety of motives. Neither sympathy with revolution nor the knowledge that British public opinion sympathised with revolution, and
was certainly opposed to its suppression by the Holy Alliance, were
prominent among them. Castlereagh never hesitated to encourage
the other Powers to suppress revolts in areas in which, as Powers, they
were 'legitimately' interested. In 1819 he told Metternich with
regard to disturbances in Germany that, although he had no 'power
to give our approbation openly', 'we are always pleased to see evil
germs destroyed'.[33] In 1820 he was anxious that Austria and the
Italian states should suppress the revolts in Naples.[34] He could not
say these things openly because British public opinion was opposed
to the policy of suppression; but what he called 'the present temper
of this country' neither deterred him from publicly defending, in
1816, the Tsar's motives in instituting the Holy Alliance[35] nor played
much part in shaping his resistance to the Tsar's ideas.

His concern for Great Britain's interests as a Great Power played
a larger part, and produced some inconsistency in his arguments. The
suppression of disturbances in Germany by Austria, in Italy by
Austria or the Italian states, in Poland by Russia, in Spain, even, by
France—this was acceptable. Collective suppression, on the other
hand, would involve the despatch of Russian troops to Spain and
Italy, and this was not acceptable. The Austrians were free to act
separately in Germany or Italy—these areas were within their sphere
of influence under Europe's territorial arrangements—'provided only,
that they were ready to give every reasonable assurance, and their
views were not . . . subversive of the territorial system of Europe',
'His Majesty deeming it his undoubted right and bounden duty to
satisfy himself that the particular measures which any independent
state or states may . . . adopt . . . shall not be so pursued as to endanger or alter the general balance of power as established in
Europe'.[36] It was otherwise with separate Russian intervention in
Turkey—'that would be a new Partition, a repetition of Poland!'[37]
It would be so because he could not recognise that Turkey lay within
Russia's sphere. Against the Tsar's claim to this—and against the
facts—he argued that 'the existing system of Europe, including that
of Turkey, was placed under the provident care and anxious pro-
tection of the general Alliance'.[38] Even this did not prevent separate
Russian action in Turkey if it did not rule out Austrian action in
Italy: he had also to argue that, while the general Alliance must

take no collective action in Europe, there must be nothing except collective action in Turkey. Nor could his inconsistency stop even there. It was collective action in Turkey that Alexander wanted: he demanded that his allies should support him in obtaining independence for the Greeks, in the interests of order in that area, in the same way as he was ready to support them by suppressing revolts in Europe in the interests of order in Europe.[39] Against this demand Castlereagh sometimes urged that the Greek rebels formed a branch —not to say the core—'of that organised spirit of insurrection which is systematically propagating itself throughout Europe' and which, logically, the Tsar should be anxious to suppress.[40] But he was no more prepared to approve Russian intervention for this purpose than for the other; and he knew that Russia would never intervene for this purpose. His ultimate position was thus to confess that 'it will naturally occur to every virtuous and generous mind [to ask]. . . . Ought the Turkish yoke to be for ever on the necks of their suffering and Christian subjects?'—but to argue that any intervention to help them would 'have consequences infinitely worse than the disease'. The claims of the Greeks must be left to 'the hand of time and of Providence'.[41]

Neither these inconsistent arguments, however, nor the concern for British interests from which they sprang, can conceal the fact that Castlereagh's opposition to the conception of the Holy Alliance was fundamentally consistent and arose primarily from another source. His sense of the limits of the practicable in international collaboration was even more influential than his regard for his country's interests. It was because of his conviction that the Congress system must be differently operated if it were to be preserved —and from his anxiety to preserve it—that he argued as he did. He knew that Great Britain as a parliamentary state, her own institutions based on internal revolution, would oppose interference by the Congress in the internal affairs of states; that her commercial and financial interests reinforced this ideology in shaping her attitude to revolutions in Greece, in Italy, in Latin America, in any area lapped by the sea and open to her trade and loans; that if she would not participate in working the Congress for the purpose of suppression neither could she allow the continental states to work such a system harmoniously without her participation. He knew also that even the French danger, against which she had been prepared to institute a treaty system, was quickly receding from most British minds; that Canning was saying as early as 1818 that the 'new and very questionable' Congress system 'necessarily involved us . . . deeply in all the politics of the Continent, whereas our true policy has always been not to interfere except in great emergencies and then with commanding force';[42] that the Cabinet itself, under all these influences, was opposed to the establishment of a 'permanent system' of Congresses on the basis of Article VI, let alone to the conversion of the Congress system into the league or confederation which Alexander desired.[43] But over and above these considerations he felt that such a league was inherently impracticable, and bound to fail, even if Great Britain's attitude and interests had been otherwise—given even a unanimous effort to operate it. And he was determined to oppose it because of his conviction that the attempt to operate it—to extend the Congress system in the direction of the Holy Alliance—would end in the destruction of the system of collaboration that had been so painfully achieved.

All his heartfelt statements were addressed to these points. 'The problem of an universal Alliance for the peace and happiness of the world'—this was how he concluded the memorandum he drew up at Aix-la-Chapelle—'has always been one of speculation and of hope, but it has never yet been reduced to practice, and if an opinion may be hazarded from its difficulty, it never can; but you may in practice approach towards it, and perhaps the design has never been so far realised as in the last four years.'[44] The outcome of the Tsar's proposals would not be to advance the design but to wipe out the progress that had been achieved. 'The more Russia wishes to transport us to the heights', he added in 1820, before the Troppau Congress, 'the further we must descend into the plain.' 'The system of the Emperor does him honour as a monarch and a man. Nothing could be more pure than the ends which he has set before himself . . . ; but this system aims at a perfection, which we do not believe applicable to this century or to mankind. . . . It is a vain hope . . . which England above all cannot pursue. All speculative policy is outside her powers.'[45] In the circular of 1821 in which he protested against the proceedings of the Laibach Congress he maintained the same language. The Tsar's 'federative system' was one which was 'not only unwieldy and ineffectual as to its object, but leading to many most serious inconveniences'.[46]

It was ineffectual because the 'notion of revising, limiting or regulating the course of [internal change in states] . . . either by foreign council or by foreign force'—a notion which in any case Castlereagh found 'objectionable' and 'dangerous to avow'—was 'impossible to execute', 'utterly impracticable'.[47] These phrases, used in the state paper of May 1820 which he wrote in opposition to Russia's wish to send troops to put down revolution in Spain, constantly recur in his arguments. In 1818 he insisted that Spain's hope that the other Powers would provide armed intervention to crush revolt in her American colonies, and thus 'do for her what England refused', was 'delusive'—as delusive as the hope that England 'should be made by their intervention to alter her deliberate course'.[48] In October 1820, after the outbreak of revolts in Naples, he would not let the British Government 'take the field in fruitlessly denouncing [them] by a sweeping joint declaration [because] . . . they do not regard mere declarations as of any real or solid value independent of some practical measure . . . , and what that measure is which can be generally and universally adopted against bad principles overturning feeble governments, they have never yet been able to divine'.[49] In the next month he warned the King of Portugal 'not to build upon what is called the Holy Alliance any expectation that [he] . . . can by force reconquer Portugal. . . . I have always endeavoured to awaken his ministers to the illusory nature of that League as a resource.'[50]

In December 1820, in his protest against the protocol of the Congress of Troppau, he went farther still. He insisted not only that 'the extreme right of interference between nation and nation can never be properly made a matter of stipulation or be assumed as the attribute of any Alliance'—as being against international law and against treaties—and not only that it was impossible to put it into practice. A further difficulty was that its public announcement, far from discouraging revolution, was just as likely to encourage 'that spirit of military energy which was the distinctive and most formidable character of the French Revolution, but of which the late revolutions have as yet exhibited no symptom. . . . What hope in such a case of a better order of things to result . . . among a people agitated by the apprehension of foreign force, and how hopeless on the other hand the attempt to settle by foreign arms or foreign influence alone any stable or national system of government!' Such an attempt could not 'fail to excite public feelings and public discussion throughout Europe, the effects of which . . . no human foresight can estimate and no combination of its Powers may be able to control'.[51]

It was at this point that his first argument led naturally to the second ground of his appeal to the other Powers against their determination to operate the Holy Alliance. If the attempt to operate it was likely to produce effects which 'no combination of Powers may be able to control'—if it was bound not only to be ineffectual but also to lead to 'many most serious consequences'—the most disturbing of these consequences and effects was, in his mind, the probable destruction of the new system of collaboration among the Powers. He stated this as part of his resistance to the policy of suppression in the state paper of May 1820. The partners of the Quadruple Alliance could not expect 'to feel alike on all subjects'. Their interests were not the same; they had not the same means of, or freedom of, action; there was even 'a difference of outlook and method between the autocratic, or eastern, Powers and the constitutional, or western, Powers'. It was not this that would destroy their collaboration, however, but the insistence of one Power, in defiance of these differences, on collective action on such matters as 'the principle of one state intervening in the affairs of another' in which the other Powers could not follow it.[52] Nor was this the only context in which he used this argument. In 1821 he resisted Russia's wish to intervene on behalf of the Greeks partly because he was 'by no means convinced that, were the Turks even miraculously to be withdrawn . . . , the Greek population, as it now subsists or is likely to subsist for a course of years, could frame . . . a system of government less defective. . . .' But the chief ground of his opposition was his fear of 'all the destructive confusion and discussion which such an attempt may lead to, not only in Turkey but in Europe', where it 'must . . . hazard . . . the fortune and destiny of that system [of international relations] to the conservation of which our latest solemn transactions with our allies have bound to us'.[53] In 1816 he had used similar language in reply to Alexander's proposal for the simultaneous reduction of the armed forces of the Powers. 'The settlement of a scale of force for so many Powers, under such different circumstances as to their relative means, frontiers, positions and faculties for rearming, presents a very complicated question for negotiation . . . ; the means of preserving such a system if once created, are not without their difficulties, liable

as all states are to partial necessities for an increase of force; and . . .
on this, as on many subjects of a jealous character, in attempting to
do too much, difficulties are rather brought into view than made to
disappear. . . . The best course might be . . . for each State to carry
its disarmament as far as it could possibly reconcile [it] to its own
view of local expediency'; and the best way of enabling states to
adopt this attitude was by relying on 'a frank and conciliatory
system of diplomacy' and 'holding fast to the principle of the Alliance
which now happily exists. . . .'[54]

What Castlereagh combatted, indeed, was not merely the policy
of suppression but—as he said in the state paper of 1820—'the notion,
but too perceptibly prevalent, that whenever any great political
event shall occur . . . it is to be regarded almost as a matter of course
that it belongs to the Allies to charge themselves collectively with
the responsibility of exercising some jurisdiction. . . .'[55] And what he
combatted it with was no narrow concern for British interests but a
general principle of his own—the principle that the Allies should act
jointly whenever their interests permitted and act circumspectly,
with a regard for the maintenance of their alliance and thus with
tolerance toward each other, whenever, as would often be the case,
their interests did not permit joint action. It was only if they adopted
this principle—only if, as he told the Tsar in 1821, 'each state avow-
ing conscientiously in the face of all the world its own principles, and
at the same time adhering to its peculiar habits of action, will nevertheless remain unalterably true to the fundamental obligations of
the Alliance'—that the Powers could hope that 'the present European
system, thus temperately and prudently administered, will long continue to exist for the safety and repose of Europe'.[56] For only in this
way, in his opinion, could they preserve their Alliance, described by
him in December 1815 as 'the great machine of European safety
which, if it does not consist of the four Powers, is shaken to its foundation'.[57] And only if the Alliance was preserved could they expect to
develop upon its basis the 'frank and conciliatory system of diplomacy' which in October 1820 he called 'this Concert'—and then
defined as a system 'which can often be useful and even necessary in
dealing even with subjects *outside* the scope of the Alliance', and as
one in which Great Britain 'will never refuse to take part'.[58]*

---

* Castlereagh had previously referred to the 'concert', and had similarly contrasted it
with Alexander's demand for an *Alliance Solidaire*, in the memorandum presented to the

The gap between Castlereagh and the Continental states was thus a gap between two interpretations of the Congress system—between the Holy Alliance and his Concert. This gap Castlereagh failed to bridge in his lifetime. It was because he failed to bridge it that, after he had been succeeded as Foreign Secretary by Canning in 1822, the aim of British policy became the destruction of the Holy Alliance system. At the Verona Congress, and again in 1823, Canning refused to be a party to intervention against disturbances in Spain; he equally refused to attend a Conference to discuss the disturbances. In 1824, while refusing to attend a conference on the Eastern Question, he accorded belligerent status to the Greek rebels without consulting the other Powers. In the same year, again without consulting the other Powers, he recognised the independence of Spain's revolted colonies in Latin America; and in 1825 the independence of Portuguese Brazil. By these last actions, he declared in 1826, he had 'called the New World into existence to redress the balance of the Old'. 'The Holy Alliance', he announced in the same year, 'no longer marches *en corps.* I have dissolved them into individuality.'[60] But Canning's policy was not the sole cause of the collapse of the Holy Alliance; and it is not true to say, as it is often said, that 'the conference system was doomed', that Castlereagh's hopes of diplomacy by conference were also destroyed,[61] when it collapsed.

In claiming to have dissolved the Holy Alliance, Canning took the credit for achieving what was in any case taking place. The briefest look at the history of its operation is sufficient to show that Castlereagh was right to put his finger on its impracticability. Such a project, involving as it did constant discussion of proposals for intervention in the internal affairs of European states, had quickly cracked the unity of even the Continental Powers. Austria had flinched at rumours of Russian intrigue in Italy and at the prospect of Russian troops in the Balkans; Prussia and Russia at Austrian activity in Germany; all three at the invasion of Spain by France, the conqueror whom all were committed to restrain. France had been

Congress of Aix-la-Chapelle in October 1818. The last paragraph of this reads: 'The beneficial effects which may be expected to be produced by the four Allied Powers consulting together, and interposing from time to time their good offices . . . for the preservation of peace and order, is considered as equally true with respect to five Powers, the introduction of France into such a system not rendering it too numerous for convenient concert, whilst it must add immensely to the moral right and influence of such a mediating Power.'[59]

disturbed by news of Russian negotiations with the Spanish Court and by her offers of military intervention in Spain. These differences were destroying the system even before Canning sought an open breach with it; his policy only hastened its collapse. If the Congresses of these years were the first meetings ever held to regulate international problems in time of peace, the collapse of the Congress system was the first demonstration of a truth that has subsequently been reinforced more than once—as by the history of the United Nations experiment in the past fifteen years or by the evolution of the British Commonwealth over the past fifty. As many as four or five independent Powers cannot for long collaborate as closely as the Holy Alliance required them to do.

The argument that Castlereagh's notions were equally impracticable is no better established. It is said that in the best of circumstances they could have been applied only spasmodically at a time when Europe's communications were too undeveloped for the establishment of international institutions; that they sought to maintain the *status quo* and were bound to fail in a world of change; that they lacked the backing of public opinion, especially in England; that they could not surmount the differences of interest between the Powers, and particularly the rift between East and West.[62] To say this is to misunderstand Castlereagh's attitude. He did not seek the establishment of international institutions. He did not attach enormous importance to the *status quo*. His ideas were distinguished by their readiness to adjust to the existence of differences of interest between the Powers—and so much so that, unlike Canning, for whom England was the protector of liberalism in what he regarded as an ideological struggle and who also shared the widespread British view of Europe as a system of states which England should exploit for the advance of her own concerns, he did not subordinate his interest in international collaboration to an appeal to public opinion. But it is even more to the point that, far from being as impracticable as the ideas underlying the Holy Alliance, Castlereagh's principles survived when the Holy Alliance collapsed. It is one of the ironies of international history—and perhaps it is also one of the lessons—that the failure of the Congress system marked not the end but the beginning of an age of collaboration between the Great Powers because they then fell back on the Congress system as it had been interpreted by Castlereagh.

CHAPTER 10

THE CONCERT OF EUROPE

WHEN the Congress system proved unworkable the notion of a coalition of leading states, founded on a public law for the defence of that law, was not abandoned. It was set free from its earlier association with the determination to govern the world—from the form the Congress idea at first assumed when it at last replaced, at the beginning of the nineteenth century, the aspiration to universal monarchy. A looser association of the Great Powers continued in existence—an attenuated Congress system limited to dealing with problems as they arose, not seeking to anticipate them or to iron them out of existence. The public law which was applied to these problems was enriched and reinforced by the passage of time and the growth of precedent but was restricted to what the looser association could agree on, and thus to strictly international questions. These were the two outstanding features of what came to be called the Concert of Europe.

This shift to a looser organisation among the Great Powers was reflected in the terminology of the time. Contemporaries did not define the words Congress and Conference precisely. Because of their inconsistencies it remains impossible to state exactly how they distinguished between the functions of these two forms of international proceeding.* But one thing is clear. As Sir Charles Webster noticed,[2] the one consistent difference between a Congress of the Great Powers and a Conference of the Great Powers in the nineteenth century was that a Congress was a meeting attended by the heads of governments or their Foreign Ministers while a Conference was confined (except for the Foreign Minister of the state on whose territory the meeting took place) to the ambassadors accredited to the state where it was

* It has been suggested that a Congress was a meeting attended by the smaller states as well as by the Great Powers and that a Conference was a meeting limited to the Great Powers, or that the name Congress was adopted only when a meeting was held to make a peace treaty. Neither of these distinctions can be made compatible with the evidence. A further suggestion[1] is that Conferences were 'limited to specific subjects' whereas a Congress was a 'European' meeting discussing 'the affairs of all Europe'. This ignores two facts: Conferences after 1822 were also 'European' meetings; and the Congresses held up to 1822 were all held to discuss specific subjects.

held.* It is this which gives significance to a further fact which Sir Charles Webster did not sufficiently emphasise. While holding by and large to this distinction, and while taking part in international meetings as frequently as before, the Powers avoided Congresses after 1822. Between 1830 and 1856 there were eight Conferences attended by all the Great Powers; between 1830 and 1884 no less than seventeen. Of Congresses as opposed to Conferences only two were held in the nineteenth century after the Congress of Verona—that of Paris in 1856 and the Congress of Berlin in 1878.†³

This transition was resisted. Attempts were often made to summon other Congresses; these sometimes reflected the wish to restore the earlier Congress system—the conviction that the system of *ad hoc* Conferences, to which the Powers were being reduced, was inade-

* The two words were never precisely distinguished even in this way. Thus the Conference of London of 1830–2 was reinforced by special envoys and the British and French Foreign Secretaries were sent out to reinforce the Conference of Vienna of 1855. On the other hand the Congress of Paris was to begin with called a Conference in the official papers. But this difference was clearly one that governments tried to maintain.

† The following list omits ambassadorial and other conferences which were not conferences of all the Great Powers, and technical meetings on subjects like armaments or the tolls of the Scheldt:

Congresses

Vienna/Paris	1814–15	(Peace Treaty and Quadruple Alliance)
Aix-la-Chapelle	1818	(France)
Troppau	1820	(Revolutions; the Naples Revolution)
Laibach	1821	(Naples Revolution)
Verona	1822	(Italy; Spain; En. Question)
Paris	1856	(Peace Treaty)
Berlin	1878	(En. Question)

Conferences

London	1830–2	(Belgium)
Rome	1831–2	(Reform of Papal states)
London	1838–9	(Belgium)
Vienna	1839	(En. Question)
London	1840–1	(En. Question)
London	1850–2	(Schleswig-Holstein)
Vienna	1853	(En. Question)
Vienna	1855	(En. Question)
Paris	1858	(Principalities)
Paris	1860–1	(Syria)
London	1864	(Schleswig-Holstein)
London	1867	(Luxembourg)
Paris	1869	(Crete)
London	1871	(Black Sea)
Constantinople	1876–7	(Eastern Question)
Madrid	1880	(Morocco)
Berlin	1884–5	(Africa)

quate. In 1836 Louis Philippe wanted a Congress to draw up a treaty in accordance with which 'no change, no alienation of territory, would have taken place in future without the concurrence of all the Powers—and I would then have realised the idea I have continually pursued of an *entente* of the five Powers for the solution of all the great political questions . . . , for settling all those questions with a general and European interest . . . , for guaranteeing the *status quo* of the territorial delimitation of Europe.'[4] In 1840 Metternich proposed a league of the other four Powers against France which might be developed into an organisation to maintain the future peace of Europe by the renunciation of force and the establishment of a permanent Conference system.[5] In 1849 Louis Napoleon, the new President of France, suggested a general Congress for the revision of the 1815 treaties.[6] When the Powers were negotiating for a meeting in 1859 the Russian Foreign Minister wanted it to be composed of Cabinet Ministers, not of diplomatic agents, and thought it should be called a Congress rather than a Conference, 'as more appropriate to the gravity of the times'.[7] By then such aspirations were beginning to conceal a still more radical discontent. Napoleon III's determination to turn the Conference of 1856 into a Congress, like his proposal of 1863 for a general Congress of the European states to revise the Treaty of Vienna,[8] was partly inspired by his dream of remodelling Europe into a federation of free nations in pursuit of his uncle's prophecy that 'the first ruler who calls upon the peoples of Europe will be able to accomplish anything he wishes'.[9] It is perhaps true to say that of all the Great Powers only Great Britain was generally contented with the system which steadily prevailed over these various efforts to go beyond it. Certainly Palmerston was the only statesman in these years to assume Castlereagh's role and oppose these efforts on generalised grounds.

At the first of the nineteenth-century Conferences, in 1830, he was careful to emphasise that 'we, the Conference, have no right to make an arbitrary distribution of Europe upon the principles of the Holy Alliance or the Congress of Vienna'.[10] In 1849, in opposition to Louis Napoleon's wish to hold a Congress to revise the 1815 treaties, he made the same point: France and England were committed to the view that internal questions were not legitimate subjects for the intervention of a Congress; yet it was by such questions, not by international problems, that Europe was being disturbed.[11] Even for international questions he preferred *ad hoc* Conferences to something more formal. In 1841 he opposed Metternich's further suggestion that there should be set up at least a permanent Conference to deal with the Ottoman question, and opposed it with the argument that when the agreements reached at the recent conference on Turkey had been implemented 'perhaps the next thing will be that the five Powers and Turkey should fall back into their usual state of reciprocal relations. Concert between Powers and centres of negotiation are useful and necessary when some Treaty is in operation which not only requires, but at the same time regulates, their common action; but it would be difficult to establish a permanent concert unaccompanied by any recorded and specifick engagement.'[12] But it was not only Palmerston who insisted on normally maintaining 'the usual state of reciprocal relations'; and he was right in regarding this as the usual state of diplomacy. The attempts to restore something like the earlier Congress system were mainly frustrated, as they were mainly inspired, by the multifarious rivalries of all the Powers.

It is sometimes said that the revolutions of 1830 divided the Great Powers into two ideological groups, the three autocratic states and the constitutional states of France and Great Britain. This rift had grown up before 1830—Castlereagh had often spoken of it --but it is true that the 1830 revolutions kept it alive. Great Britain immediately recognised Louis Philippe after the French Revolution of 1830 despite Russia's hostility to the new régime and despite the fact that the other four Great Powers could be said to be bound by the Quadruple Alliance to meet together to discuss internal changes in France. Russia, Austria and Prussia publicly recognised in the Münchengratz agreement of 1833 the right of any sovereign to call on them for aid against any revolution; and Palmerston engineered the Quadruple Alliance of 1834 as 'a powerful counterpoint'—to use his own words—'to the Holy Alliance of the East'.[13] In 1835 he publicly identified the interests of England with the constitutional cause in Europe and asserted that the Eastern Powers had a secret treaty to put constitutionalism down.[14] In 1836 he spoke of 'the three and the two, who think differently and therefore act differently'.[15] For another twenty years these sentiments were never far below the surface on both sides, and were always quick to revive—so that Austria and Prussia could sign another treaty against 'the revolution' in 1851,[16] and in 1854 the French ambassador in Constantinople could congratulate Napoleon III on the Austro-French-British alliance of that year: 'You have inflicted a mortal blow on the Holy Alliance.'[17] At the same time, however, they were increasingly joined after 1830 by other rivalries which made even settled ideological alignments among the Powers impossible.

On the one hand, with the revival of France, Great Britain found herself cooperating with the Eastern Powers against France as frequently as she cooperated with France against them. This was the pattern during the Belgian crisis of 1831–2, against the French attempt to establish a position of special influence over the new Belgian state. In 1836, though she had been quick to recognise Louis Philippe, she frustrated his plans for a Congress as decisively as did the Russian Government: both suspected that it was not unconnected with the wish to rescue France from the tutelage imposed on her in 1815.[18] On the other hand the growing rivalry of Austria and Prussia in Germany and of Austria and Russia in the Near East produced a similar instability in the eastern camp. Metternich's suggestions of 1840–1 for a permanent conference arose less from concern to restore the old Holy Alliance than from the aim of making Vienna the permanent centre of the European diplomatic system and of enlisting Western aid against Austria's neighbouring Powers. The Tsar opposed them as decisively as did Great Britain, and with words that might have been used by Castlereagh. He told the British ambassador that Metternich must be disabused of his belief that he could 'advise upon every subject' and 'from his closet direct and instruct all the world'.[19] By that date—when France, embittered by commercial and Near Eastern rivalry with Great Britain, was seeking an alliance with Austria; when Great Britain had concluded an agreement with the three eastern Powers against French designs in the Near East; when Russia was asking for still closer relations, for an alliance indeed, with Great Britain as a safeguard against Austria as well as against France—the complex pattern of diplomacy had already been laid down which was to prevail until 1871. It was not simplified by the revolutions of 1848 which revealed that even the autocratic governments would only act, if they would act at all, in their own individual interests. Or by the revival of the Empire in France in 1852—the year in which the British government both welcomed a Russian offer to send 60,000 men to defend Belgian independence if France threatened it and also refused to join the eastern

Powers in demanding from Louis Napoleon a guarantee of his peaceful intentions as a condition of recognising the Empire. Or by the first serious result of, among other things, the new Emperor's restless wish to destroy the Vienna settlement and substitute for it a system of weak federal states under the patronage of France—by the Crimean War. The Crimean War only intensified, indeed, those interlocking jealousies and suspicions between all the Great Powers which explain why special factors were needed before they could agree to assemble even in the individual Congress of 1856—they had been at war among themselves—and why the resort to *ad hoc* conferences was as close as they could normally come to collaboration.

Even that looser system was one which proved difficult to operate on account of these rivalries. After the first conference on Belgium Metternich and Palmerston both obstructed the summoning of another to continue its work: each suspected the other of wishing to have it under his control.[20] In 1833 it was impossible to convene a conference on the Eastern Question because each insisted that it should meet in his own capital—that, in Palmerston's words, 'we are on an equal footing . . .'. It was then that Great Britain herself was charged—and by none other than Metternich—with the wish to dominate diplomacy by reviving the Congress system. He accused Palmerston of trying to make the London Conference permanent, 'to raise it to the standing and the influence of an areopagus in which the representatives of the three Continental Powers would be reduced to the role of accomplices in the reformist policies of the two Maritime Courts'.[21] During the next generation, while no conference proved easy to convene and each met only after a fierce struggle concerning its agenda[22] as well as its venue, the assembled Powers were never unanimously contented with the proceedings. Palmerston complained in 1833 that the way in which the Eastern Powers had behaved at the Belgian Conference had made the whole idea of a further Five-Power Conference unpalatable to his Cabinet;[23] but he also noted of the same Conference that 'the three Eastern Courts have been a little jealous of their Plenipotentiaries',[24] and this was an understatement. Their distrust of the proceedings had been so great that they first sought to reduce the Conference's authority and then insisted on its suspension.[25] It was not able to resume until 1839, but then it confirmed the settlement of 1831—delineating the boundaries of Holland and Belgium and making Belgium a neutral member of the European states' system under the permanent guarantee of the Great Powers—which had been a self-denying ordinance for all the signatories. The proceedings of another Conference in 1839, that held in Vienna on the Turkish question, were bluntly disowned by the Tsar, and it was his opposition to Vienna as the place for discussion that secured the transfer of the Conference to London.[26] So great, indeed, were the strains involved in the conference system that, far from being able to go beyond it in the direction of Congresses, statesmen attempted to evolve a procedure that was even looser and less binding than *ad hoc* conferences.

In 1838, when the Belgian Conference had resumed in London, Palmerston hoped to use it as a means of reaching a five-Power decision on Mehemet Ali, but he told the Austrian Government that what he wanted was not a conference on that subject, merely 'a concert', and Austria went so far as to agree to 'a concert' but not to a conference. The proposal still foundered on Russian opposition, but in the next year, at the beginning of his effort to secure agreement to a conference on the same question at Vienna, Metternich followed this precedent. He disclaimed the wish for a conference—the word should not be used—and asked only for a concert or a *point d'appui*. Neither the Vienna Conference of 1839 nor the London Conference of 1840–1 were technically regarded as conferences. Though they received sufficient authority to be able to give instructions to ambassadors and admirals, they were known as *points d'union* or *points centrals*.[27]

The Concert of Europe suffered under a still more serious limitation. Though conferences met on such questions as Belgium, the Papal states and the Eastern Question—on questions on which, once the Powers could agree among themselves, the business was to impose a settlement on other states—no conference attempted before the Crimean War to impose a settlement on one of the Great Powers or in a question in which a Great Power was deeply involved. At the end of the Austro-Sardinian War of 1848–9 France and Great Britain attempted to assemble all the Powers at a peace conference at Brussels to settle the Italian question. It came to nothing because Austria refused to attend unless the Powers declared in advance against territorial changes.[28] There never was a conference on the Italian question. The only conference ever held on the German question was that which assembled to accept in 1852 the settlement between Prussia and Denmark which Palmerston had been left to negotiate alone.

When these strains and difficulties are considered the development of the conference system may seem to have been a far from impressive achievement. But the relevant question is why the Great Powers did not go further still in these last directions and return to the anarchy of the eighteenth century. Their acceptance of the restraints and frustrations of the Concert system was the consequence rather than the cause of their preparedness to be restrained; it was always reluctant and far from complete. But this is true of all international procedure. Though it is often assumed that leagues and conferences are the solution to international conflict, there must be a preparedness to control that conflict before leagues and conferences can be effective; such preparedness is not easy to achieve and is still less easy to maintain. Why were the Powers still prepared to be restrained? Why —and this is a separate question—did their restraint now take the form of permitting the beginnings, if only the beginnings, of formalised international collaboration in the conference system?

The answer to the first question lies partly in the nature of their rivalries. Each was too divided from all the rest, by interest or ideology or both, to permit them to form alliances; yet each was deterred from too much risk alone by the lack of preponderant power. And then to this factor, already at work before 1789, must be added the new fact that the first half of the nineteenth century was a period of continuous internal upheaval in Europe. All the Great Powers were combinations of monarchical and aristocratic institutions. The eighteenth century had shown that monarchs *can* fight each other—as monarchies and republics can collaborate. But now they were all ranged, if in different degrees, against dissidence in their own societies. Before 1830 they had attempted, and failed, to operate the Congress system for the international suppression of disturbances. After 1830 they still found that their rivalries were too great for such cooperation. But from 1830, the year in which revolutions broke out in France, Belgium, Portugal, Spain, Italy, Greece, Poland and the Ottoman Empire, the year in which 'the revolution' stopped halfway, they were at least restrained in their foreign policies by this common peril at home. And so they remained until they realised, after almost continuous unrest, that the revolutions of 1848 had been 'the turning-point at which history failed to turn'. If they would rarely act together against revolution because of their rivalries, they would never act against each other for fear of encouraging revolution. Frederick Williams IV of Prussia wrote in 1854: 'I shall not allow Austria, the inconvenient, intriguing, Austria, *to be attacked by the Revolution, without drawing the sword on her behalf*, and this from pure love of Prussia, from *self-preservation.*'[29] He was perhaps alone at that date in still believing in the revolutionary danger; but his remark fairly sums up the outlook of all the Powers in the previous generation —and of the Western Powers as well as of the three Eastern Courts.

France, the Power especially associated with 'the revolution', was driven in this direction by her rivalry with Great Britain as much as by her need to avoid driving Great Britain to join the Eastern Powers against her. In 1847, when she concluded the *entente* with Austria which she had been seeking since 1833, Guizot told Metternich that France 'is now disposed and suited to a policy of conservatism . . . a policy of *entente* is therefore natural to us and founded on the facts'.[30] His assessment was not belied when, a year later, the French overthrew monarchy for the last time in a further revolution. Lamartine, the new Foreign Minister, announced in a 'Manifesto to Europe' that 'the treaties of 1815 have no legal existence in the eyes of the French Republic'. But one of the aims of the manifesto was to satisfy radical opinion in France—to avert a more radical revolution there—and for the benefit of Europe it added that the treaties were nevertheless 'a fact which the Republic admits as a basis and starting-point in its relations with other nations'.[31] Lamartine's successors at the Foreign Ministry went further still. Bastide, later in 1848, would not support the cause of German nationalism in the dispute with Denmark because 'German unity would make . . . a power very much more redoubtable to its neighbours than Germany is today and therefore I do not think we have any reason to desire this unity, still less to promote it'.[32] Drouyn de Lhuys, after the re-establishment of the Empire, was always hoping to drive a wedge between Napoleon III and the Liberal-minded cause.[33] Napoleon himself presents a problem to historians because, though sincerely attached to that cause and also anxious to revise the treaties of 1815 in the interests of France, he could not free himself from the pressures which, after he had come to power, forced him along with other governments in the direction of restraint. If European diplomacy became even more bewildering after 1852 than it had been before, this was only partly on account of his unreliability. His unreliability was due to the fact he wanted to advance the liberal-national cause without calling on the spirit of revolution, to revise the treaties without causing a war, to challenge Europe and yet be the champion of order and the *status quo*.

He put the dilemma to the British ambassador soon after becoming Emperor: 'I have every intention of observing these Treaties—but you should recollect how galling they are to France.'[34] He gave this reassurance because he needed the friendship of Great Britain and because Great Britain was more firmly attached to the treaties than any Power—and more firmly attached to them than to any ideological cause. Palmerston was fond of calling himself a pupil of Canning. To begin with he was capable of giving the doctrine of non-intervention a Canningite interpretation—as when, under the terms of the Quadruple Alliance of 1834, he agreed to a French expedition to coerce the Portuguese usurper while opposing any interference by the Eastern Powers. Essentially, however, the policy of actively encouraging the liberal cause against the Holy Alliance died with Canning, and Palmerston, in the priority he gave to the maintenance of the existing treaty system over the advance of the liberal and national causes, was a disciple of Castlereagh. During the revolutions of 1830 and 1848 he took his stand on the treaties of 1815 in resisting popular demands for assistance to the cause of Polish, Italian, Hungarian or German liberation—insisting with Russia on the principle that any changes in the existing treaties would be acts of aggression if they were made without the agreement of the signatories, and departing from the principle of non-intervention only where those treaties, —and British interests—were threatened, as they were by the Prussian attack on Denmark. If it was only in this Schleswig-Holstein dispute that he stood out as the leading opponent of nationalism, he easily accepted its suppression by Russia in Poland and Hungary and by Austria in Italy. He did so in the firm conviction that this was necessary in the interests of 'the political independence and liberties of Europe'.[35] In Italy he hoped, it is true, to persuade Austria to yield and set up an independent kingdom of northern Italy. This was not so much in the interests of the liberties of Italy as from anxiety to anticipate French intervention in Italy and from the belief that Austria, an essential element in the European balance of power, would be strengthened by this policy, as she was being saved by Russian support in Hungary.

Palmerston's attitude illustrates how the fear of disorder exerted a powerful effect—as powerful as the material rivalries within the two camps—in bringing about the interpenetration between the Holy Alliance Powers and the Western Powers and the restraint which prevailed among the Great Powers during these years. It was also one reason why, as well as abstaining from reckless policies, the Great Powers developed, however imperfectly, the system of diplomacy by conference. The first new feature of the situation as compared with the second half of the eighteenth century—the fear of revolution—buttressed the effect of a continuing near-equality of power among the leading states in keeping their policies restrained. The second new feature in the situation was that, although the continental Powers remained roughly equal in strength, Great Britain had now moved far ahead of them in power and influence. It is not unreasonable to regard the Concert of Europe as being from one point of view the system which naturally replaced the aim of universal monarchy during the period of British predominance.

Great Britain was now the Power which overtopped all the rest in material strength, occupying in one sense the position previously enjoyed by Austria or Spain or France. Unlike her predecessors she was outside the continent, not in it; and though her primacy was undoubted, it had been built in a period which also saw the rise in absolute strength of several other Great Powers. For these two reasons she was not able and was not tempted, as earlier Powers had been, to associate her power or her security with the submission of Europe to her rule. On the contrary, it was in her interest to keep Europe divided; and this had been sufficient to make her throw her weight against the successful operation of the Congress system. But whereas in the eighteenth century, when she first became powerful, she had become isolationist, profiting from Europe's divisions to advance her position beyond Europe, she now found it possible and desirable both to profit from Europe's divisions and to remain an influence within Europe in order to keep the divisions in check. Canning was tempted to return to the old isolationist policy. Palmerston, the last man to neglect English interests, constantly identified the defence of them with a policy of remaining in Europe in order to preserve the existing international system.

'The interests of England, the preservation of the balance of power and the maintenance of the peace of Europe'[36] was a phrase that was frequently on his lips. Perhaps the chief of those interests for him was 'to guard with care the maintenance of the balance of power', which would be deranged by 'the attempt of any nation to appropriate to itself territory which belongs to another nation'.[37] And not only for him. In 1852 Lord John Russell summed up the attitude of all British governments in these days, and also indicated how conference diplomacy had followed from it. 'We are connected, and have been for more than a century, with the general system of Europe, and any territorial increase of one Power . . . which disturbs the general balance of power in Europe, . . . could not be a matter of indifference to this country, and would no doubt be the subject of a Conference, and might ultimately, if that balance was seriously threatened, lead to war.'[38]

If British interests had been differently interpreted the Concert system could not have developed. But British policy alone could not have developed it if it had not also responded to the needs and outlook of the European Great Powers. After the attempt to organise themselves into a league to suppress revolution had driven them apart, and at a time when a common fear of revolution merely kept them from being driven further asunder, they were driven together by yet another new feature of the times—by the fear of another Napoleon—as well as by the influence of Great Britain. It was a fear which they shared with Great Britain; and so much so that as she never hesitated to identify British interests with the preservation of the existing international system and both with 'the political independence and liberties of Europe', 'the general interests of Europe', 'European objects'—to use more of Palmerston's phrases—so they never questioned that her primacy did not constitute a Napoleonic danger, that her interests coincided in this respect with theirs. If all the Powers limited their ambitions to making London or Vienna or Paris the centre—or to preventing London or Vienna or Paris from being the centre—of the diplomatic structure it was because they all knew that they all accepted a conception of Europe which had first been developed by writers in the eighteenth century, in reaction to acquisitive policies, but never previously practised by governments. They enunciated it in the nineteenth Protocol of the Belgian Conference in April 1831. *'Chaque nation a ses droits par-*

ticuliers; mais l'Europe aussi a son droit. C'est l'ordre social qui le lui a donné.'[39] It was a conception which represented a retreat from the Holy Alliance in its insistence on each nation's rights; by its emphasis on the rights of Europe it invested the balance of power between the nations with a special significance. Palmerston always spoke of the balance of power not as critics of diplomacy had spoken of it in the second half of the eighteenth century—as incompatible with Europe's 'social order'—but as the essential condition of that order. In his mind it performed this function not merely as the safeguard against an hegemony like Napoleon's. It was this; but it was also the true guide to be followed when changes were unavoidable in Europe's *status quo* and the justification for maintaining that *status quo* as far as possible. It was interchangeable with 'the maintenance of European peace' and the pursuit of 'European objects'. And when he spoke in this way he did so with confidence that all the Powers accepted this equivalence. At this time 'only those who rejected *laissez faire* rejected the Balance of Power—religious extremists at one extreme, international socialists at the other'.[40] But those who accepted *laissez faire* in international relations accepted it within the framework of this theory about Europe.

It was from this theory that the states derived the few principles underlying the conference system: that the Great Powers had a common responsibility for maintaining the territorial *status quo* of the treaties of 1815 and for solving the international problems which arose in Europe; that, when the *status quo* had to be modified or a problem had to be settled, changes should not be made unilaterally and gains should not be made without their formal and common consent; that, since the consent of all was needed, decisions were not to be reached by votes. It was because they all shared this theory that, on the one hand, the refusal to enter into a conference was regarded as evidence of an aggressive attitude—so that the suggestion of a conference was not rejected outright but was avoided by the laying down of unacceptable conditions—and that, on the other hand, the assembling of a conference was not regarded as a diplomatic defeat for those Powers who had been reluctant to attend.[41]

At first sight these principles may not seem any more impressive than the extent to which they were applied in the development of the Concert of Europe. It might be suggested that something like them was, whatever the difficulties, bound to exist between sovereign

225

states disposed to avoid war. Changes to the *status quo* are inescapable in a world of separate Powers. What else could such Powers do but adopt such principles and something on the lines of the Concert system if they did not want to fight—and particularly at this time when they lacked the techniques of communication and transport which were subsequently to make constant discussion and contact between them unavoidable, if not always profitable, and yet had been forced into closer contact than had ever existed before? In fact, the principles were more impressive, their application in the Concert system more difficult, than at first appears. To anyone who understands the nature and difficulty of international relations it will not be necessary to emphasise that the Powers could not have adopted and applied them if, over and above the practice of mere restraint, they had not subscribed to some such conception of the international system, and of their place in it, as that which has been described.

There came a time, indeed, when men's attachment to this conception conflicted with, and proved to be stronger than, their restraint. Far from being able to prevent the Crimean War, the notion of Europe that underlay the Concert was largely responsible for the fact that the war broke out.

At one level the Crimean War arose, as at one level all general wars arise, from the clash between the political ambitions and strategic rivalries of the Great Powers. Russia sought to increase her influence over a nominally independent Turkey—or else to bring about its collapse and partition. When Russia provoked Turkish resistance by going too far in her demands, Napoleon III, who had stirred her into making them by his success in a dispute about the Holy Places, went to Turkey's defence partly because of French financial interests in the Ottoman Empire, partly because of French political interest in advancing the collapse of the 1815 settlement in Europe, partly because he needed to strengthen his position in France. When the British Government joined the French it was not uninterested in reducing the Russian danger to Great Britain's growing position in the Near East and India, and not uninfluenced by a combative and violently anti-Russian public opinion. But none of the three Powers fought the war with these motives or for these objects; 'none of the three had conscious plans of aggression'.[42] Because neither side could be certain of the other's motives, the war developed, as wars often do develop, out of mutual fear; and, as Powers often do, the Powers feared for their prestige as well as for their material interests. But it was not these considerations, either, which overcame their reluctance to fight. There was a war in 1854, as opposed to an international crisis, because Russia's demands on Turkey raised the question how far the public law of Europe, the principles underlying the Concert of Europe, should apply to the Ottoman Empire. Russia drifted into war because she refused to accept any further extension of these principles in the Near East without a struggle; Great Britain and France fought her to establish beyond doubt that the days were ended in which Russia could regard the future of Turkey as solely her own concern; and Austria openly swung over to their side for the same reason. In this sense—if only in this sense—the war was 'in essence an invasion of Russia by the west', a war 'fought for the sake of Europe rather than for the Eastern Question . . . , against Russia, not in favour of Turkey'.[43] It was the nineteenth-century precursor of the war which, after the interval of a century, was fought in Korea by Powers determined to uphold and vindicate one conception of the Charter of the United Nations.

This was one reason why the war was begun with great reluctance on both sides. It was a struggle about the extension of the public law of Europe between Powers which all subscribed to its general validity; and there was no question of treating Russia as other than one of the Powers who upheld that law. The first step towards war was Russia's attempt to evade the Vienna Note of the summer of 1853. In this Note the other four Great Powers laid down the concessions which, in their judgement, Turkey could make to Russia without risking her independence. The Note was submitted to Russia at a conference, and accepted by her, in advance of its transmission to Turkey. Russia then evaded it by claiming that in it 'Europe' had conceded her sole right to protect the Orthodox peoples of Turkey, whereas the Note had placed them under a joint Franco-Russian protectorate exercised on behalf of the European Great Powers. She did so because she could not bring herself to believe that the other members of the old Holy Alliance would oppose her insistence on this interpretation. 'The four of you could dictate to me', the Tsar had told the French ambassador; 'but that will never happen. I can count on Vienna and Berlin.'[44] France and Great Britain did not declare war because Turkey rejected the Note—on the ground that all the Great Powers other than Russia, rather than Russia and France, should be the guarantors of the good behaviour to the Orthodox—or when Turkey declared war on Russia in October 1853. They did not do so because Russia had occupied the Danubian principalities—for though their ultimatum of 27 February 1854 demanded the evacuation of the principalities, these had been occupied by Russia as long ago as May 1853. They declared war at the end of March 1854 after Austria and Prussia had joined them in a further conference which issued a further protocol to warn the Tsar that Europe would be against him if he failed in his promises to respect Turkey's integrity and do nothing to weaken the Sultan's authority over his Christian subjects. They did so because, even after Russia's withdrawal from her evasion of the original Note, they felt it necessary to put an end to future uncertainty by insisting on Russia's formal agreement that the Near East was a matter of European concern. Their delay was due to their wish and their hope that this would be obtained without war. Lord Aberdeen, the British Prime Minister, with his conviction that only British public opinion had forced the Cabinet into war, was no doubt ultra-pacific. This is not enough to explain why, when war had been declared, his government suggested, to the indignation of the Queen, that there should be a day of 'humiliation' to intercede for the success of British arms.[45]

The war was not only begun reluctantly but was fought with reluctance. Even during hostilities diplomacy was 'only occasionally interrupted by battles'.[46] Of course, other considerations intervened, as before the outbreak of war, to help to account for this—and especially that perennial and ubiquitous influence upon the conduct of governments, self-interest and reason of state. Some of the indecision of the Western Powers was due to Napoleon III's concern to win Russian friendship against Austria and Prussia and some of it was due to British suspicion of France; and once war had begun the Western Powers, who had counted on Russia giving way without war, found that they could not count on Austria and Prussia to join them in fighting her. But the basic reason for the negative and hesitant conduct of the war and for the continuation of negotiations during hostilities was mutual regret that the Concert, to which both sides belonged, had failed to avert it.

The negotiations revealed that the two sides were not even seriously divided about the extension of the Concert to the Near East. The war aims of the Western Powers—the Four Points—were drawn up in the summer of 1854 in collaboration with non-belligerent Austria; they were conceived of as a European programme. They stated that stable relations between Turkey and Russia could not be established until the Russian protectorate of the principalities had been replaced by a European guarantee; until the navigation of the Danube had been subjected to international control; until the Straits convention of 1841 had been revised 'in the interests of the balance of power in Europe'; and until the Russian claim to a protectorate over the Turkish Christians had been abandoned in favour of a Turkish guarantee of the security of the Christians given to the five European Great Powers. Russia had already abandoned this last claim, if only under pressure, before the war began. She at once conceded the first two demands, in practice if not in principle, by withdrawing from the principalities in August 1854. For the remainder of the war the struggle concerned the formalisation of these three points and the revision of the Straits convention. At the end of November 1854, indeed, Russia accepted the Four Points unconditionally, and the sole issue left was how the convention governing the Straits should be revised. By January 1855 she had even accepted the interpretation put upon revision by the Western Powers—the Convention would be revised in such a way that 'Russian predominance in the Black Sea should be brought to an end'. What was meant by this, how to achieve it, was all that remained to be settled at the peace conference which assembled as early as March 1855.

Whether this condition should be obtained by limiting Russia's Black Sea Fleet, or by neutralising the Black Sea by excluding both Russian and Turkish ships, or by 'counterpoise'—a system by which, while Russia retained her Black Sea Fleet, Great Britain and France should be free to send ships in to counterbalance it—this was the question which destroyed the conference by June 1855. Russia would accept neither limitation nor neutralisation; the western governments would not accept 'counterpoise'. It also prolonged the war for nearly a year. Russia gave way, exhausted and under the threat that Austria would otherwise join the war against her, only at the beginning of February 1856, when—except that Austria added Russia's surrender of a part of Bessarabia—peace preliminaries were signed on the basis of the original Four Points, and neutralisation of the Black Sea was adopted as the means for revising the Straits Convention.

What prolonged the war was thus a struggle for prestige. And what settled the struggle was superior force. But it is easy to underestimate the extent to which, even in the atmosphere of war and despite the struggle for prestige, the principles of the Concert of Europe and the acceptance of Russia's place in it governed these peace terms as they had governed the outbreak and the conduct of the war. It has been questioned whether the peace-terms were compatible with operation of a Concert among the Great Powers, and especially the neutralisation of the Black Sea, the only condition against which Russia had made a strenuous effort. It has been said that no such compulsory disarmament as neutralisation involved for Russia 'had ever been imposed on a Great Power' since the first Napoleon's treatment of Prussia in 1807; that 'the allies would not have presented such terms to any Power whom they regarded as truly European'; and—in answer to Palmerston's assertion that 'Russia has brought this humiliation upon herself'—that 'France did not bring this humiliation on herself by waging war on all Europe for more than twenty years'.[47] There is no doubt that it was a humiliation. Furthermore, the previous Straits Convention, which closed the Straits to warships only in time of peace, was maintained in addition to the neutralisation of the Black Sea, so that there was nothing to prevent Turkey and her allies from passing a fleet into the Black Sea against a defenceless Russia in time of war.[48] There is no doubt that Russia objected to it; the revision of the Black Sea clauses became one of the chief aims of her diplomacy until she succeeded in having them abolished in 1871. It is also true that the Crimean War was the first occasion on which the Concert of Europe had gone to the lengths of war to constrain a Great Power. But it was in the name of Europe that the other Powers went to war and it was in the cause of the Concert of Europe that Russia was constrained. What guided the other Powers was not the conviction that Russia was not part of the Concert but the determination to make the Near East a part of Europe. To argue that their treatment of Russia was unprecedented is to ignore the limitations imposed on France in 1815 and her sense of humiliation on account of them. And to argue that such terms would not have been presented to a Power which was regarded as part of Europe is to overlook the development of Europe and of the Concert idea since that earlier peace settlement.

The Powers extended the principles of the Concert and particularly the device of international neutralisation further than these had previously been applied. But they did so in the belief that they were adapting a tried solution to what had been a vexed problem since the Black Sea had ceased to be entirely enclosed by Turkish territory in the eighteenth century, when Russian expansion had made her a littoral state. In some minds, indeed, this did not go far enough as a check on Russia to hold out the hope that it would solve that problem. Palmerston felt that 'the treaty will leave Russia a most formidable Power able in a few years . . . to place in danger the great Interests of Europe. But the future must look after itself.'[49] With the shortening of European distances and the decline of the Turks the problem had become—as France had earlier become—a problem for all of them, and neutralisation was thus applied in the name and interests of Europe as a whole, as these words of Palmerston's reveal. We may take them seriously; he meant them so. An attempt was made to save Russia's face by the device of laying down the neutralisation only in a separate Russo-Turkish treaty. He insisted that it should form part of the general peace treaty: 'we stick', he said, 'to the great Principles of Settlement which are required for the future security of Europe. . . .'*[50]

If this was true of the neutralisation of the Black Sea it was true, as well, of the remainder of the peace settlement. The Congress of Paris of 1856, the first Congress to assemble since 1822, took the opportunity provided by the end of the war to reinforce the principles of the Concert in two ways. It extended the public law of Europe geographically to embrace the Ottoman Empire; it increased the body of existing law. These were two of the prominent features of the proceedings. They had, however, another. In the aftermath of the war, as the name Congress suggests, there was in some quarters a disposition not merely to buttress the Concert but to advance beyond its limitations; but the limits of possible progress were soon reached in this third direction. There could be no better illustration

---

* But note that although Russia accepted the neutralisation of the Aaland islands in the Baltic this was arranged in the separate Convention of Paris signed only by Great Britain, Russia and France.

of the assumptions underlying the concert idea, as it had developed in the previous generation, than is provided by the arrangements the Congress was able to make on the one hand and, on the other, the contradictions and the frustrations that followed from this wish to go beyond them.

In the Near East, by the Treaty of Paris of March 1856, the Congress, in addition to neutralising the Black Sea and perpetuating the existing provisions governing the passage of the Straits, established Europe, not Russia, as the protector of the Roumanian principalities, Wallachia and Moldavia—Southern Bessarabia being transferred from Russia to Turkey and incorporated in Moldavia—and set up a European commission to reform the government of the principalities. It established Europe, not Russia, as the protector of Turkey's Christian subjects—if only in the indirect sense that it took note of the Sultan's guarantee to them and of his intention to communicate it to the other signatories of the Treaty, who renounced interference, singly or collectively, in Turkish internal affairs. This protection was necessarily indirect: the Treaty also admitted Turkey to the public law of Europe and to the family of European Powers and this involved the recognition of her as a completely sovereign Power. Turkey's admission to the family arose out of the discussion of the relation between the Sultan and his Christian subjects; but in the treaty it prefaced Article 7, which contained Europe's guarantee of Turkish integrity and independence and the agreement that henceforward any Power or Powers in conflict with Turkey would seek the mediation of a third party before resort to arms.[51]

Of the additions to the existing body of public law one was made in the Treaty itself. This (Article 15) stipulated free navigation on the Danube, established a European Danube Commission to supervise its regulation independently of the territorial governments involved and expressly declared for the first time that free navigation for merchantmen of all nations on all international rivers—a principle implied by some of the arrangements made at the Congress of Vienna—was part of the European public law.[52] Another important set of provisions was contained in the separate Declaration of Paris of April 1856. This supplemented the principle of the freedom of the high seas—a principle generally recognised by the 1820's—by laying down four rules governing sea warfare. Privateering was abolished; the neutral flag covered enemy goods other than contraband of war;

neutral goods other than contraband of war could not be confiscated even when sailing under enemy flag; a blockade must be effective to be binding. To be effective these rules required the accession of other states beyond the signatories of the Declaration (the Great Powers, including Turkey, and Sardinia); fourteen other states acceded to them in 1856, Japan in 1886, Spain in 1908, Mexico in 1909.[53] They were, however, the first provisions to enact international law in the field of naval warfare, where practice had previously been governed by custom only.

The Declaration represented a concession on the part of Great Britain, the leading Power at sea who had hitherto resisted the principle that the neutral flag covered enemy goods. It was on her initiative that an attempt was made to advance the public law in a still more significant direction. A proposal for a resolution in favour of free trade in food and raw materials came to nothing, but Lord Clarendon was successful in gaining Protocol 23 to the Treaty, a resolution in favour of the resort to the mediation of a third Power before the recourse to war. 'The Plenipotentiaries', stated this Protocol, 'do not hesitate to express in the name of their governments, the desire that States . . . should, before appealing to arms, have recourse, so far as circumstances allow, to the good offices of a friendly Power. The Plenipotentiaries hope that governments not represented at the Congress will unite in the sentiment which has inspired the desire recorded in the Protocol.'

Gladstone welcomed this declaration as 'the first time that . . . the principal nations of Europe have given an emphatic utterance to sentiments which contain at least a qualified disapproval of the results of war'. *The Times* hoped that it would make 'all Europe one court of appeal'. It was certainly the first clause of its kind to be included in a multilateral treaty. But the delegation sent to Paris by the British Peace Society, which had put pressure on Clarendon and influenced his initiative, had hoped that he would propose 'some system of international arbitration which may bring the greatest interest of nations within the cognisance of certain fixed rules of justice and right'; and apart from speaking of mediation, and not of arbitration, the Protocol did not add to the body of accepted international law but registered only the view that mediation was desirable.[54] Clarendon himself intended no more than this; and if he had sought to go further he would not have been successful, as is shown by the failure of every effort to use the Congress to air and settle political problems, other than those it was able to regulate as a result of the resort to, and the outcome of, the war.

Napoleon III hoped that after the conclusion of the Peace Treaty the assembled Powers would discuss the outstanding issues dividing them, and especially those created by growing Western dislike of foreign rule and autocracy in Poland, Greece and Italy. During the war he had threatened to make the independence of Poland a condition of peace; Clarendon now joined him in seeking at least a public assurance from Russia that she would change her policy in Poland. When Russia resisted this, however, Poland was passed over by the Congress in silence. Great Britain also failed in her attempt to persuade Russia and France, the other protecting Powers, to join her in using the presence of British and French troops in Greece to put pressure on King Otho to improve his government. With regard to Italy, Cavour's hopes came to nothing—the Congress could not agree to give Parma and Modena to Sardinia and transfer their rulers to the government of the Roumanian principalities—and Clarendon's denunciation of Austrian as well as of papal and Neapolitan misrule was not only toned down before inclusion in the formal proceedings, but was at least partly offset by Austria's success in supplementing the European guarantee with an Anglo-French-Austrian tripartite guarantee of Turkey's independence.

In these Anglo-French efforts it is not fanciful to discern the embryo of a Holy Alliance in reverse; they sought to use the Concert system not, indeed, to stamp out unrest but to remove it by means of the liberation and reform of states. Had they been persisted in they would have destroyed the system, as the persistence of the Holy Alliance had earlier threatened to prevent its development. They were not pressed. This was largely because they conflicted with the essential principle on which the Concert was based and from which it had evolved—the sovereignty of the state and especially of the Great Powers. In the Concert system each state had responsibilities as well as rights; but it had them as an independent state. The Great Powers had more responsibilities and more rights than the other states; and they tended to emphasise their rights more than their responsibilities. For both reasons—from their respect for the sovereignty of each state no less than from their wish to restrict their own responsibilities—the Great Powers continued to limit the direct international role of the Concert as far as possible. Faced with the difficulty of Turkey's imperfect control of the principalities and of the position of the principalities as a buffer area between Turkey, Russia and Austria, they adopted the device of bolstering Turkish suzerainty over them by a direct international guarantee and the establishment of an international commission. Faced with the problem of the Black Sea, on the other hand, they preferred the device of incorporating its neutralisation into the public law without directly guaranteeing the neutralisation—which was a way of adding to Russia's responsibilities without adding to the commitments of the other Great Powers. And faced with the problem of Turkey's Christian subjects they refused to treat it as an international problem requiring their direct intervention, but sought to solve it by burdening Turkey with the responsibilities of a European Great Power— with the duty of safeguarding her subjects' rights. They also extended to Turkey the rights of a European Great Power. The treaty expressly declared '*la Sublime Porte admise à participer aux avantages du droit public et du concert européens*'.[55]

In such a structure of thought upon the international problem there was room for confusion and contradiction, as there is in all structures of thought on the subject. For what were these rights and advantages? Of one of them there is no question: from 1856 until the outbreak of the first World War Turkey was invited, with the other Great Powers, to send delegates to every general conference as a result of her admission to the ring. But as against this Great Britain insisted on excluding Prussia from the peace negotiations in 1856, to which Sardinia was admitted as a belligerent but not as a Great Power, in resentment at the neutrality she had maintained during the war; and when Prussia was later admitted to the Congress, as a signatory to the Straits Convention of 1841 who was entitled to participate in its discussion, Great Britain also defeated her attempt to avoid having this qualification recorded in the treaty. This attempt to restrict participation in the peace settlement to those who had taken part in the war cut across the rights of a Great Power in the Concert; but it arose in part from one interpretation of the responsibilities of a Great Power to the Concert—from the view that in a war fought to uphold the public law strict neutrality amounted to evasion. Then again, Turkey also received a European guarantee of her integrity and independence in the article of the treaty which admitted her to the ring of Great Powers; and the other Powers assumed the duty of seeking the mediation of a third party before resorting to war with her. But it was not assumed that the existing Great Powers had the same protection from the public law or the same duty towards each other as were laid down by treaty in connection with Turkey; and not even in regard to Turkey was the public law regarded as adequate in itself. When the Congress turned to the question of mediation in general, it confined itself to expressing the desire that mediation should be resorted to. Austria, France and Great Britain found it desirable to guarantee the integrity and independence of Turkey in a separate tripartite Treaty.

The truth is that Turkey was recognised to be a special case—a synthetic Great Power—as well as a new recruit. What could be specified by Treaty in her case could not be applied to the other Powers. Their rights were not solely treaty rights—they had grown up with the public law and were the basis of it—whereas in regard to Turkey what could be specified by treaty could be specified only after a war had been fought on the question. And what was true of her rights was also true of her responsibilities. It was laid down by treaty that she was responsible to Europe for the welfare of her Christian subjects. But it was another question how and whether Europe would bring her to task for failure in this charge, for it was also laid down by treaty that the other Powers renounced single or collective intervention in her domestic affairs. Not even such a formal responsibility could be placed upon other Powers. France and Great Britain might wish to assert that Russia had a similar responsibility to the Poles and Austria to the Italians; to have insisted on the assertion would have been to contradict the principle of state sovereignty which was applied even to Turkey—which is why they did not insist on it.

The whole development of the Concert and its law was subject to the sovereign rights and discretion of its established member Powers. The most it could aim for—it was no mean aim—was that these rights would be exercised with restraint and within a framework of law and responsibility that would deepen and expand by consensus and general agreement. In some directions—in developing the laws of war or of international navigation—it was less difficult to extend the law and the responsibility at the expense of rights than it was in others—in restricting, for example, the right to war without mediation. Even in those directions it was less difficult to proceed in the aftermath of war than it was against the inertia and the complications of peace-time relations. With profound political problems like the settlement of Belgium or the rivalries of the Powers in the Near East, it was impossible to proceed at all except when resort to the right of war was threatened or when war itself was resorted to. When Prussia suggested the revision of the Black Sea clauses in 1860, Palmerston replied that he would never be a party to it 'unless it had become inevitable as the consequence of a war, the Results of which enabled Russia to dictate her own Terms to the Rest of Europe...'.[56]. The structure being what it was, the rights and rivalries of states were indispensable for the development of their responsibilities as well as being an obstacle to it. But these rights, and especially the right to war, could also be destructive of the system itself if exercised without restraint.

The question after 1856 was whether the Concert, which had been preserved and—more than that—consciously developed for thirty years, could survive a revision of the map of Europe that was demanded by a generation of slow change in political outlook and the distribution of power. In October 1857 James Anthony Froude urged that the best way of averting such conflicts as the Crimean War, to which he had been violently opposed, would be for the four Empires—Great Britain, France, Austria and Russia—to enter into an alliance and thereafter discuss amicably together and settle fairly all territorial disputes. He forgot Prussia. He admitted that such 'a Concert of the Four Powers would be a conspiracy ... ; it would be a conspiracy in the sense in which all society is a conspiracy —a conspiracy in which the better sort of persons lay their strength together to oblige the rest at their peril to submit to order'.[57] He did not foresee the extent to which order was about to be challenged by nationalist sympathies and aspirations no less than by the rivalries between states.

CHAPTER II

INTERNATIONAL RELATIONS IN THE SECOND HALF OF THE NINETEENTH CENTURY

THERE was a marked contrast between the opening years of this period and the years between 1815 and 1854. After forty years of almost unbroken peace the fourteen years from the end of the Crimean War to 1870 witnessed four more wars involving one or more of the major Powers. In the course of these wars—the Austro-French War in Italy of 1859, the German war with Denmark of 1864, the Austro-Prussian War of 1866, the Franco-Prussian War of 1870–1—the territorial arrangements of 1815 were forcibly revised and the settlement of 1856 did not come through unscathed.

As well as embarking on this succession of wars the European states returned, for the first time since the eighteenth century, to policies and objectives reminiscent of the *ancien régime*. Since 1815 agreements between the Powers had with rare exceptions been either universal agreements, the outcome of conferences and amounting almost to international legislation, or—if not universal—imprecise and temporary associations, understandings rather than alliances. In the same period changes and revisions of territory had received the sanction, and often the guarantee, of all the Great Powers. There was now a return to precise and offensive military alliances, whose primary purpose was to secure the neutrality or the assistance of another Power in a projected war; and demands for unilateral territorial exchanges in return for this assistance, or in compensation for the gains which other Powers had derived from these wars, became the order of the day.

The Pact of Plombières which Cavour concluded with Napoleon III in 1858 has been called 'the first deliberate war plot of the nineteenth century'. Cavour himself described how it involved a search of the map of Italy for a 'non-revolutionary cause of war [against Austria] . . . which was so difficult to find'.[1] It gave Savoy to France in return for a French promise to aid Piedmont in defeating Austria and setting up a kingdom of Northern Italy. The Pact was confirmed by a treaty of January 1859, in which France added Nice to Savoy as her share of the bargain. It was followed by the secret treaty of March 1859 between France and Russia: this provided for Russian neutrality in a French war on Austria in return for French assistance in Russia's efforts to revise the Treaty of Paris. In 1863 Bismarck concluded the Alvensleben Convention with Russia, promising her Prussian help in the suppression of the Polish rising, partly in the hope of securing her neutrality in any war arising out of the struggle in Germany. He also talked openly of ignoring European interest in Poland's independence by occupying Poland should Russia withdraw from it. In 1864 he manœuvred Austria into an alliance with Prussia for the purpose of upholding the Treaty of 1852 in a war against Denmark—and also with the hope that once Denmark had been despoiled of Schleswig-Holstein the future of the Duchies might provide the occasion for a war on Austria. As war approached between Austria and Prussia Napoleon was not proof against Bismarck's suggestion of 1865 that he could interpose as arbiter and obtain Venetia if he remained neutral; he had previously suggested to Bismarck that he would help to secure the incorporation of the Danish duchies into Prussia in return for a *quid pro quo*. Nor did this understanding with Prussia prevent him from negotiating with Austria in June 1866 an agreement whereby, in return for his promise of neutrality, she rewarded him with the promise of a voice in the peace settlement and of the gift of Venetia. The Italo-Prussian Alliance of April 1866 went farther still: it was not only concluded on the assumption that the war would break out but also contained a provision by which it was invalidated if war had not begun within three months of the exchange of signatures. During the Luxemburg crisis of 1867, the outcome of the French demand for the Grand Duchy in compensation for Prussia's defeat of Austria, Napoleon more than once offered Austria an alliance envisaging a war on Prussia. Although she refused, he continued to hope and to negotiate for some such arrangement until the outbreak of his own struggle with Prussia in 1870. In August 1866 and more definitively in March 1868, in preparation for this struggle, Prussia obtained a Russian promise to attack Austria if Austria intervened against Prussia in a Franco-Prussian war—in return for assurance from Bismarck of Prussian support for Russia's denunciation of the Black Sea clauses.

If these were the characteristics of diplomacy in these years the other side of the coin was the eclipse of the conference method. When conferences did meet they were more ineffective than before the Crimean War, at least in face of problems in Europe. Conferences at Paris in 1858, 1860–1 and—on Bismarck's initiative—in 1869 dealt tolerably successfully with disputes concerning the government of the Roumanian principalities, the British and French intervention in Syria to protect the Christians, and the Cretan rebellion of 1866 against Turkish rule. But the two Conferences held on European questions ran into difficulties—and into other difficulties in addition to those created by the lack of trust between the Powers.[3]

The London Conference of 1864 assembled in the attempt to settle the war between Denmark and the German Powers. It was the first international gathering to break away from the principle of treaty rights and to try to apply, instead, the doctrine of self-determination as the basis of a settlement. Despite the British effort to settle the quarrel by a mere revision of the 1852 treaty—despite the protest of Lord John Russell, the ardent supporter of nationalism in Italy, that the idea of self-determination was 'too new in Europe' and that 'the Great Powers had not the habit of consulting populations when questions affecting the Balance of Power had to be settled'[2]— the other Powers backed Napoleon's proposal that the Schleswig-Holstein duchies should be divided on national lines. They found it more difficult to agree on how to determine the nationality division. Treaty rights, as subsequent international conferences have discovered, are less ambiguous and more easily handled by Great Powers than is the application of the nationality principle. On this account and also because the Danes were determined that it should fail, the Conference broke up after burying the 1852 treaty, and war was resumed. In 1867 another Conference in London settled the crisis caused by the French attempt to annex Luxemburg by arranging the withdrawal both of the French plan and of the Prussian garrison and by placing the neutrality of the Grand Duchy, which was now disarmed, under the collective guarantee of the Great Powers. But Great Britain—a further sign of the times—at once put a new interpretation on the meaning of collective guarantee by announcing that if one of the guaranteeing Powers invaded the territory none of the others could be called upon to fulfil its obligations.

The eclipse of the Concert system was revealed in another direction. Conferences were proposed more frequently than before, in proportion as times were more troubled, but statesmen displayed an even greater inability and reluctance to meet in concert than before the Crimean War. An international conference was suggested more than once in an attempt to avoid the outbreak of the Italian war of 1859. Great Britain proposed that the Concert should 'neutralise' Piedmont, as it had previously neutralised the Black Sea, in return for Austria's renunciation of her rights of interference in the central Italian states. Neither Austria nor Piedmont was disposed to accept this plan for insulating the Italian question from the rivalries between the Powers.* A Russian proposal for a congress on the affairs of Italy also came to nothing: Austria refused to participate in a meeting attended by Piedmont—at least before Piedmont had accepted inferiority by agreeing to disarm in advance—and Great Britain refused to cooperate from suspicion that Russia and France would seek to use a conference to revise the treaty of 1856. In 1860 Great Britain suggested a disarmament conference as part of her efforts to settle the Schleswig-Holstein question; but to no avail. After the outbreak of the Polish revolt at the beginning of 1863 France, Great Britain and Austria sent joint notes of protest in which they demanded an armistice in Poland and the summoning of a conference to provide for an autonomous Polish state; but Russia met the first note with the argument that she would accept a conference provided every other European question, and not only Poland, was discussed; and when this proposal was rejected she ignored the second note.

Later, in 1863, Napoleon proposed a conference to discuss disarmament and the revision of the map of Europe. Great Britain would have welcomed a conference if it had been possible by that method to advance some national causes without advancing the interests of Russia and France—which gave, in Palmerston's words, 'Moldo-Wallachia to Austria, and Venetia and Rome to Italy, incorporated Schleswig with Denmark and separated Poland of 1815 from Russia and made it an independent state, [without] . . . touching the question of the Rhine as a French frontier or the relieving Russia from what was imposed upon her by the Treaty of Paris. . . .'[4]

* After the war had begun the British Government sought to use the principle of neutralisation as a means of protecting Austria's most vulnerable flank, and as an alternative to entering the war on Austria's side, by proposing that France should keep Great Britain out of the war by consenting to neutralise the Adriatic.

Because these two programmes were inseparable it was Russell, the champion of national liberties, who denounced Napoleon's proposal in the name of treaty rights and the *status quo*; and he spoke for all the governments addressed when he added that a discussion of every European question would increase tension in Europe rather than lessen it.

With the approach of the Austro-Prussian War in 1866 Napoleon again suggested an international conference to discuss every European question. Austria made her consent conditional on the exclusion of territorial changes from the agenda. Great Britain announced that neither 'English honour nor English interests' were sufficiently involved to enable her to undertake to uphold the decisions of a conference; and even if Great Britain had been willing it is unlikely that Prussia would have been. In 1867 Prussia and Great Britain rejected a proposal by Napoleon for a conference to prop up the temporal power of the Pope after the French defeat of Garibaldi's attempt to take the papal states.* In 1869 Great Britain, at the suggestion of France, repeated her earlier attempt to get agreement to a conference for the discussion of disarmament—this time in an attempt to avert a war between Prussia and France. Bismarck easily evaded it.

Conferences had easily been evaded before the Crimean War. A still more noticeable departure from the practices of the first half of the nineteenth century is to be found in the fact that the Concert of Europe, as well as failing to avert the wars of 1859, 1864, 1866 and 1870, was not invoked to legitimise the territorial changes which the wars effected. When negotiating the preliminary peace of Villafranca in July 1859, Napoleon talked of 'European mediation'; the preliminary peace terms provided for the summoning of a European Congress to confirm the new order in Italy—the Austrian surrender of Lombardy and the establishment of an Italian federation after the princes of Central Italy had returned to their thrones. Great Britain refused to attend when the French Government made it clear that the Congress would be limited to confirming these peace terms; she had originally hoped to use it to get them changed. Austria withdrew her assent to the conference when Napoleon refused

---

* In its anxiety to pack the Conference with Catholic states the French Government invited the lesser German states as well as the Great Powers, thereby breaking an unwritten rule of the Concert system and offending Prussia.

her request that he should disavow a pamphlet, *The Pope and the Congress*, in which French interests had advocated that the Congress should undertake the virtual destruction of the Pope's temporal power. In July 1866, after the Austro-Prussian War, Russia formally proposed a European Congress to settle the future of Germany—partly in the hope of creating an opportunity for the revision of the Treaty of Paris but partly, also, from monarchical and traditional concern for the Concert of Europe. Bismarck retaliated successfully with the bribe that Prussia had 'no interest in continuing the limitations on Russia in the Black Sea' and with the warning that if he was not allowed to reorganise Germany without outside interference he would 'unleash the full national strength of Germany and of neighbouring countries'.[5] Russia dropped her conference proposal, tacitly accepting instead Bismarck's suggestion that she should agree to keep Austria neutral in a war between Prussia and France, and no other Power was inclined to take it up. In August 1870 it was Russia who again asserted, during the Franco-Prussian War, the principle by which, in the words of her Foreign Minister, 'it is impossible that the other Powers be excluded from the future negotiation for peace, even if they did not take part in the war'.[6] Bismarck had no more difficulty in avoiding this—in making the Treaty of Frankfurt a purely Franco-German settlement—than he had in avoiding the mediation of other Powers in an attempt to end the war.

The French efforts to secure mediation were fruitless in Austria, where the Foreign Minister contented himself with the complaint that 'I do not see Europe any more'[7]; in Russia, who would not go beyond her statement of principle; in England, where only Gladstone objected to a policy of complete abstention. Even Gladstone objected to abstention because he regarded the transfer of Alsace and Lorraine from France to Germany as a crime, not because of concern for the Concert system or the balance of power. But even before the Franco-Prussian War had ended there were signs that it would be the last of the series of disturbances which had racked Europe since 1854—that it would mark the end, not the beginning, of unrest. Before the year 1870 was out Gladstone was upholding that principle which was so closely associated with the balance of power and the Concert but which conflicted with the principle of nationality—the sanctity of treaties—and upholding it against Russia's denunciation of those Black Sea clauses which he had opposed in 1856. In September Russia at last freed herself from the humiliation of recent years by denouncing the Black Sea clauses of 1856; and justified her action with the argument that 'it would be difficult to affirm that the written law founded on respect for treaties as the basis of public right and of rule for inter-state relations has preserved the same moral sanction as in former times'.[8] By January 1871 she had withdrawn the denunciation on the understanding that the clauses would be abolished in return for her assent to the British demand that the Powers should declare that international treaties could not be changed by unilateral action. A conference was convened in London—and convened on the initiative of Bismarck—to formalise this bargain. In these confusions and ironies at the conclusion of fifteen years of wars and forcible changes —in Bismarck's avoidance of a European peace conference to end the war and in his initiative in arranging a conference to avoid another; in Gladstone's oscillation between the principle of nationality and the sanctity of treaties; in the expressions of the regret that Europe had collapsed and international morality had declined and in the step taken in 1871 to do something to restore it—we may find the explanation of the eclipse of the Concert since 1856, as of the wars and the changes themselves; and we may also discover a clue to the scope and character of the Concert during the remainder of the nineteenth century.

The main sources of unrest in the years since 1856 had been, on one level, the fact that years of slow change in the distribution of power in Europe had set up pressures making for a change in the *status quo*; on another, the alliance which governments now concluded with the popular force of nationalism; on yet another the withdrawal of Russia and England from European affairs. At first the first of these developments had appeared to represent itself in the recovery of France. Fundamentally, as can now be seen, the central process at work was rather a relative decline in the power of Austria and Russia at the expense of those states of Western Europe which were responding earlier than they were to the spread of industrialism to the Continent. It was a process which in these years spelled the reduction of Austria in Germany by Prussia and in Italy to the advantage of Piedmont; and if France seemed to become more powerful than every European state, instead of merely more powerful than Austria, it was because Napoleon III concentrated his first efforts on the easy target of hastening Austria's reduction in Italy—and because his government was the first of the European governments to embrace the nationalist cause.

Even before the Crimean War Napoleon had made no secret of his wish to destroy the 1815 settlement in the cause of nationalism. After the Congress of Paris—when he regretted that 'what should have been a great political revolution had been reduced to a simple tournament'9—he rapidly exploited Russia's discomfiture, England's sympathy with nationalism, the new enmity of Russia and England and the growing relative weakness of Austria to advance French interests and the Italian national cause. His mistake was to assume that in Italy at first and later on a wider scale, with Poland rendered independent of Russia and a South Germany set up separately from Austria and Prussia, the success of the nationality principle must accord with the interests of France by producing a European system of weak states which could be federated under her patronage. For while this assumption was encouraging him to hammer away at Austria's position he overlooked the danger that the same nationality principle would be embraced by other governments than his own—and that this would produce, in conjunction with the forces of economic growth and Austrian decline, powerful unitary states in Germany and Italy whose emergence would transform the European balance of power to France's detriment as well as to Austria's. Within a decade of the failure of the 1848 revolutions this other powerful impetus towards unrest and forcible change in Europe was at work.

Up to the Crimean War all the governments had been restrained and kept together behind the *status quo* by their common fear of revolution. After 1856 other governments in addition to the French began to ally with the dynamic force of the national principle in their own societies as a means of advancing their interests against other governments. It was in 1856 itself that Cavour, who had previously striven to isolate the aspirations of Piedmont from any association with democracy and nationalism, began secretly encouraging Manin's National Society on condition that it would abandon republicanism—and on condition that he could himself abandon the Society when necessary.10 Bismarck embarked on an even more ruthless exploitation of German nationalism and liberalism, as may be illustrated from his every political move. And not only from his conduct of policy. In 1857 he was reflecting on the revolutionary origins of most of the world's dynasties and dismissing as obsolete the outlook which, in the first half of the century, had induced a 'statesman . . . to direct his whole political endeavour, his domestic and foreign policy alike, by the principle of opposition to revolution, and to use this as the sole touchstone of his relations with other countries'.[11] It was not for nothing that Napoleon slowly abandoned his grandiose dreams of a reconstructed Europe after 1860 and became increasingly the conservative defender of treaty rights against revisionism and of compensation against nationalism—that in 1866 he was regretting that he had 'let the revolution triumph in Italy'[12] and demanding compensation on the Rhine for Prussia's advance in Germany; that in 1867 he was asking for a conference to prop up the papal states, whereas in 1859 he had thought of a conference to reduce the papal temporal power; that from the same year he was constantly seeking an alliance with the Habsburg Empire, on which he had earlier inflicted so many humiliations, for the defence of existing treaties and the *status quo*; and that by 1870 he judged the security of France to depend on friendship with, and reconciliation between, Russia and England.

Russia and England had not been reconciled during the previous fifteen years. At a time when they could have resisted the changes of these years only by adopting a more determined policy of collaboration and intervention than they had pursued after 1815, they were divided by the Crimean War and embittered by mutual suspicion in the Near East. This was one reason why these two Powers, hitherto the staunchest defenders of the settlement of 1815, became less disposed to defend it: its defence called for more collaboration at a time when they were less prepared to collaborate. There were other reasons, however, why each of them had withdrawn from the affairs of Europe—and particularly the contradictions created for their policies by the nationalist movement in Europe.

Russia remained fundamentally opposed to revision and especially —from general conservatism, from fears for Poland—to nationalist revision. 'This disturbs', protested the Tsar in 1856 against French activity in Italy, 'the principles which all governments have in common and outside which there is no stability.'[13] It was because of her continuing concern for these principles—no less than from the hope of thereby obtaining a revision of the Black Sea clauses—that

Russia issued many of the proposals made for international conferences between 1856 and 1870. But this attitude conflicted with her
opportunism in looking to Napoleon and Bismarck to assuage her
desire for revenge on Austria and for assistance in revising the settlement of 1856. And it was because of her opportunism that her intervention on behalf of the *status quo* was confined to making these
usually abortive proposals. Her immediate interest in seeing Austria
reduced and in profiting in the Near East from disturbances in
Europe ruled out an active policy of defending it against Napoleon
to begin with and then against Prussia.

Just as Russian policy was frustrated by the clash between her
interests and her aversion from nationalism, so British policy was
neutralised by the nationalist movement—but by growing British
sympathy with the nationalist cause. This made it impossible for
Br:tish governments to oppose changes which seemed to advance
that cause and especially impossible to collaborate with Russia
against such changes. Beginning with Clarendon's denunciation of
Austria in Italy at the Congress of Paris it even induced them to
encourage them. 'Certainly,' elaborated Clarendon when Cavour
suggested in 1856 that Great Britain would be forced to help Piedmont, 'and it would be gladly and with great energy'; and Palmerston said at the same time that 'for every step the Emperor might be
ready to take in Italian affairs he would probably find us r ady to
take one and a Half'.[14] In 1860 Russell's dispatch to other governments not only approved of Italian unification b··t justified it by
appeal to the will of the people. It constituted a denunciation of any
treaty settlement which conflicted with popular senti ent.[15] But
British support for nationalism, like Russia's attachment to legitimism, was limited to such moral gestures if only because it conflicted
with the concern of British governments for the European balance
of power; and it need not be doubted that the abstention of both
Powers from active intervention during these years was due in the
last resort to their ability to accept the changes that were taking
place as compatible with the balance of power.

British governments, indeed, which were not inhibited by the
material weakness and loss of prestige that forced inactivity on
Russia after the Crimean War, and which were nearer to Western
Europe, were slow to make this assessment. The years which saw the
increase in British sympathy with the national cause saw also an

outburst of suspicion of Napoleon III. The word 'imperialism' made its appearance in the English language in about 1858. It meant at first 'the rule of an emperor, especially when despotic'—as it was to continue to mean for some years—and the dislike of such rule incorporated the fear that France might again seek the domination of the Continent. When Lord Derby's government, in its anxiety to safeguard Austria from defeat, came close to war with France on the outbreak of the Italian war of 1859, it was because the traditional attachment to the European *status quo* was heightened by this new fear. Even the pacific Aberdeen, who had striven to keep England out of the Crimean War, was now anxious to enter this one, from the conviction that the obligations of the Treaty of Vienna were more binding than any commitment to uphold the independence of Turkey. His comment on the argument that England could not be persuaded to fight Napoleon over Italy was that 'if that be so we have fallen from our high state and must rank with Monaco in the scale of European power'.[16] Lord Derby's government was overthrown by pro-Italian sentiment; but this conflict between the claims of the *status quo* and the claims of nationalism was not so easily dispelled. 'The whole drift of our policy', wrote Palmerston in 1861, 'is to prevent France from realising her vast schemes of expansion and aggression in a great number of Quarters.'[17] If he continued up to his death in 1865 to intervene in Europe with advice and threats in defence of the *status quo* it was largely for this reason; and even his professions of sympathy for Italian nationalism were the consequence of a policy that was anti-French rather than pro-nationalism.[18] But it was beginning to emerge before his death that interventionism, which had hitherto been rendered ineffectual by the country's sympathy with the national cause, was being rendered unnecessary by the fact that the expansion of that cause in Europe was turning against the expansion of France.

This recognition joined with the ineffectiveness of Palmerston's policy, with sympathy for nationalism and with a growing preoccupation with extra-European problems—the result of the Indian mutiny in 1857 and of the outbreak of the American Civil War in 1861—to produce in the House of Commons' debate of 1864 a unanimity of opposition to the principles he had pursued in foreign policy since the 1830's. Radicals and liberals urged non-intervention from belief in nationalism and as a principle deduced from the doctrine of *laissez-faire*. Conservatives argued—as Pitt had argued a century before—that Great Britain's national interests lay overseas rather than in Europe and that, in Disraeli's words, the balance of power was 'founded on the obsolete traditions of an antiquated system'.[19] In 1868 the House of Commons deleted from the annual Mutiny Bill the traditional phrase which had declared for so long that the maintenance of the balance of power in Europe was one of the reasons for the existence of the British Army. The action was symbolic of the collapse, with Palmerston's death, of Whig rule—of the victory of Liberalism. It also reflected, however, the conviction that the balance of power was in no danger from the defeat which Prussia had recently inflicted on Austria and the rising threat of Prussia to France, but was rather improved by these developments which Russia also welcomed to the extent that they checked Austria and France.

This assessment was correct for the immediate future: a fact which sometimes escapes attention. Because it is remembered that a balance of power was not to remain established after 1900, and because it is forgotten that the international system may be radically altered without the balance being destroyed, it is often assumed that the balance of power was destroyed in 1870. The developments which culminated in the Prussian defeat of France in 1870 certainly altered the system. 'The myth of *la grande nation*, dominating Europe, was shattered for ever';[20] a structure which had rested for many years on a weak centre surrounded by strong Powers in Austria, France and Russia was replaced by one which incorporated a powerful Germany and at least a united Italy. But it is equally true that 'the Balance of Power survived Bismarck's three wars'.[21] Although the structure was transformed, the near-equality of its component states and the balance between them still remained—as well established as at any time since these features of the international system had emerged in the eighteenth century. Berlin had replaced Vienna and Paris as the centre of the system. The new Germany was sufficiently powerful to ensure that neither Austria nor France could change the situation unaided and that neither could get support in changing it. But these two Powers, despite their defeat by Germany, like Russia despite her humiliation in the Crimean War, remained Great Powers at a time when the gulf between Great Powers and lesser states had become enormous.* There was no obvious obstacle to their recupera-

---

* One has only to list the states to see how great this gap was. In 1871 in Europe

tion, their potentiality was not short of Germany's, in the eyes of most contemporaries—who long expected a French war of revenge against Germany. If a few contemporaries recognised or feared their relative decline they also accepted or insisted that Germany could not extend such lead as she had obtained without great risk—that an attack on any one of the weakened Powers would bring others to its aid. In 1875 Russia and Great Britain, who had been disinterested spectators of the earlier defeat of Austria and France, indicated that they would no more tolerate a repetition of the Franco-Prussian War than they would help to reverse its outcome. Nor was this the only evidence that the recent changes, far from establishing a dangerous degree of German preponderance, had freed Europe from the threat of French domination, which had reappeared with Napoleon III, without putting German predominance in its place. It was not for nothing that Bismarck, for all his threats, insisted that Germany was a satiated state, suffered from nightmares about coalitions and sought the placation of Russia and Austria and the isolation of France; and not for nothing that no Power, not excluding France who most resented them, seriously regarded Bismarck's manœuvres, and the shift from Paris to Berlin that made them possible, as being dangerous to the system or to peace.

A balance of power was preserved in part because the distribution of power remained steady. For all that is said of the force of nationalism which partly inspired them, the wars of 1859 and 1866 stopped short at modifying the system and did not seek to destroy the balance for fear that the neutral Powers would otherwise intervene; and even after the defeat of Austria Bismarck did not at first believe that he could annex the German states north of the Main without giving compensation to France. But if they were Cabinet wars, made by

alongside Germany, Great Britain, France, Austria–Hungary, Russia and Italy there were eleven lesser Powers: Turkey, Spain, Sweden–Norway, Denmark, Portugal, the Netherlands, Switzerland, Belgium, Greece, Serbia and Montenegro. Of these, only Turkey, Spain, Sweden–Norway and Denmark were fully sovereign. Serbia and Montenegro, though autonomous, still belonged legally to the Turkish Empire. Greece was pledged to follow the advice of three protecting Powers, Russia, Great Britain and France. Belgium was bound by the treaty of neutrality imposed on her by the Great Powers in 1839. Switzerland and the Netherlands were similarly bound by the Congress of Vienna. Portugal was allied to Great Britain by long tradition. Only Roumania (1879) and Bulgaria (1878–86) were added to these states before the end of the century. Outside Europe only the United States could be regarded as of Great Power rank in 1871, and neither she nor Japan, after her meteoric rise, can be said to have been incorporated in the international system before 1902.

diplomacy for limited ends, and if this was also true of the Franco-Prussian War in which public excitement and national fervour played a greater role, this was for other reasons as well. All three were conducted by governments which deliberately restricted their aims and deliberately controlled the force of nationalism from a continuing respect for the international system and a concern to preserve order.

Their regard for the international system and its growing body of rules and precedents underlay their technical difficulties in getting the wars started. Prussia in 1866 and 1870—like Napoleon in 1859, when he sought a *casus belli* that was not only 'non-revolutionary', but could also 'be justified in the eyes of diplomacy'[22]—was pursuing a programme which could not be justified by international law. For France, Piedmont and Prussia to have placed their demands on paper and to have declared war would have been to declare themselves aggressors. They avoided these steps: in all three cases war was begun by the conservative Power, by Austria in 1859 and 1866, by France in 1870, which had had to be baited till it 'broke out on its tormentors'.[23] Nor was it only upon the outbreak of war that this consideration played a part. The principles underlying the Concert of Europe were inevitably suspended during this period of wars, when conferences were avoided and it was not practicable to maintain that gains should not be made by individual Powers without general agreement or that the Great Powers had a common responsibility for the problems of Europe and the European *status quo*. But these principles still limited the objects of the wars while they were in suspense. The expanding states regarded themselves as—in Bismarck's phrase—'historical states' entitled to a place in a historical states system. It was constantly the concern of the new Italian Government to be accepted as one of the Great Powers. Bismarck sometimes spoke contemptuously of this system. 'Who is Europe?' he demanded when the British Minister protested in 1863 that Europe would not allow Prussia to occupy Poland. His every action makes it clear that he respected it and subscribed to it as defined by Buchanan in his reply: 'several great nations'.[24]

He used the revolutionary national movement to bring about the reordering of Germany, but he still brought about the revolution from above and without wishing seriously to disturb the European equilibrium; and he recoiled altogether from the thought of applying the national principle in Eastern Europe. In each case, but especially in the East, he acted from the conviction that the national principle would be dangerous to state authority if it got out of control. 'Only historical states are possible.' 'What could be put in that part of Europe now occupied by the Austrian state. . . ? New creations in this territory could only be such as bear a permanently revolutionary character.'[25] He acted, moreover, in the knowledge that the other European governments shared this conviction—that even Napoleon III was becoming conservative on this issue. In May 1866 Napoleon advocated a congress in an attempt to avoid the Austro-Prussian War—and it was mooted that he might propose that Silesia should go to Austria. Bismarck warned the French government that against such a proposal Prussia would appeal to German national feeling, proclaim the Frankfurt Constitution of 1849 and fight for unification on a revolutionary basis.[26] In July of the same year he used the same threat to counter Russia's suggestion that a congress should meet to settle the future of Germany: if Russia interfered in Germany he would 'unleash the full national strength of Germany and of neighbouring countries'.[27] The threats were effective.

It may be doubted whether Bismarck would ever have put them into effect. If his wars were conducted for reasons of state, not on nationalist grounds, they were conducted at a time when the power and the cult of the state were beginning to impose themselves upon society and opinion—and to transform society and opinion. The process was noticeable in the way in which self-determination was given progressively less attention in the post-war settlements and in which the emphasis behind nationalism itself was changing. All the redistributions of territory in the unification of Italy up to 1866, including the transfer of Savoy and Nice to France, were sanctioned by a plebiscite if not by an international conference; and Bismarck was pledged to hold a plebiscite in north Schleswig after acquiring it in the war of 1864. This was due in part to the new strength of national sentiment in Europe after 1848, in part to older traditions. As a result of the origin of the state in a territorialised population as well as in a territorialised law, self-determination was of far more ancient date than the nineteenth century; it had been only temporarily superseded between 1815 and 1850 by the notion that the alteration of the *status quo* was the joint responsibility of the Great Powers in the interests of Europe. But Bismarck's pledge was never carried out in north Schleswig. None of the annexations made by Prussia in subsequent years, neither in Alsace and Lorraine nor in the German area, was accompanied by a plebiscite or sanctioned by a conference. By the treaty of Frankfurt of 1871, on the other hand, the town of Belfort was excluded from the annexation of Alsace-Lorraine on condition that the German army be allowed to parade in Paris. The same process was also seen at work in the arrangements made for the internal reorganisation of the new states that were coming into existence. It was not for nothing that republicans in 1870, regarding the achievements of the first effective phase in the history of European nationalism, spoke of the need 'to start ... a popular revolution as a substitute for the governmental and diplomatic revolutions realised in Piedmont and Prussia'.[28]

The Franco-Prussian War, completing this period of unrest and revision, finally dispelled mid-nineteenth-century dreams of a voluntary federation of Europe's nations, to be realised by the withering away of old-style European governments. The reality which persisted was the old-style system of sovereign Great Powers, each controlled by increasingly powerful governments, but all restrained by traditions and principles as well as by physical checks. The problem for the future was whether this system, shaken in these years but preserved in its essentials, could survive this growth of government power and also adjust to new strains to which it had not yet been subjected.

It survived for another generation. There was an even longer period of peace between the Great Powers after 1871—it was to last till 1914—than there had been between 1815 and 1854. For thirty of these years—until 1900—the new *status quo* in Europe was as unchallenged and as widely accepted as the pre-1854 situation it had replaced. Only in the Balkans were frontiers altered or sovereignty shifted during these years; even these alterations were forced on the reluctant Powers rather than engineered by them. Not even this Eastern Question seriously endangered the peace, though it dominated European relations because the Powers could not escape the complications thrown up by Turkey's collapse but could not solve them by agreeing to Turkey's partition. Beyond Europe, on the contrary, enormous changes, both of frontiers and of sovereignty, were made, changes more rapid and extensive than in any previous age. These, too, were effected without war or serious risk of war between the major Powers. In these circumstances of great fluidity and uncharted courses diplomacy proved no less effective, governments no less cautious, than in the congested and well-trodden paths of the old continent.

Beyond Europe, as within it, this was basically due to the operation of the new balance of power between the major European states. New extra-European Powers were arising; they could go to the lengths of formally declaring war upon another state in the pursuit of their interests, as did Japan against China in 1894, the United States against Spain in 1898. But Japan had to be more cautious after her defeat of China, the United States more cautious in the Far East than in the New World, because of the reach of the European states. Until the 1900's—until the Spanish-American War, from which the United States, with the seizure of the Philippines and the annexation of Hawaii, emerged as a Pacific Power, and until Russia's defeat in the Russo-Japanese War of 1904–5—most problems beyond Europe, except in special areas like North America, which was sealed off by the Monroe doctrine and the British Fleet on which that doctrine rested, and Latin America, where local balances of power developed between the central and the southern states, were dominated by the European Powers. Of those it was only Great Britain, from her special position, who formally declared war even upon a smaller state—as against the Boers—or who—as in the Fashoda crisis—could go to the lengths of openly threatening it against another Great Power or who—as by the occupation of Egypt in 1882—could undertake to make a serious alteration to the existing balance of power. Russia declared war against Turkey in the Near Eastern crisis of the 1870's, though professedly with Christian and European and not with selfish objects; neither she nor the other continental Powers subsequently avoided activity and even fighting beyond Europe. But even in extra-European contexts, still more so in Europe itself, all were restrained from rash activity— from fighting each other, from formal war with other states, from gains for themselves which could not be counterbalanced by gains for the others—by the system of relations which prevailed between them.

It was not solely because of the balance of power, however, that the Powers now reverted to the greater self-restraint of the first half of the nineteenth century. They continued to subscribe to the principles on which a sense of the collectivity of the Powers, of the Concert of Europe, had been based in that earlier period. These principles had survived the recent wars: the continuing tacit acceptance of them was as much the basis of the wide acceptance of the new *status quo* and the common determination to keep the peace after 1871 as was the self-restraint induced by practical considerations arising from the balance of power, though the two factors buttressed each other. While the balance between the Powers checked dangerous activity this other source of self-restraint was what enabled the balance to work. For some years, indeed, it did more than this. It encouraged a return to the forms of collaboration in which the Concert had earlier found expression.

Meetings and conferences of the Great Powers had proved increasingly unworkable during the period of the wars after 1854. The device had not been resorted to for sanctioning the changes which brought that period to an end. Between 1871 and the mid-1880's the conference method was revived in response to the anxieties released by the wars. The London Conference of 1871 endorsed the Russian denunciation of the Black Sea clauses. It did, however, endorse it in accordance with the principle that no changes should be made without the general agreement of the Great Powers; and the Conference also issued a reaffirmation of 'the sanctity of treaties'. In the next crisis engendered by the Eastern Question, between 1875 and 1878, Russia profited so long as she conformed to the agreed decisions of the Powers. After the Constantinople Conference of 1876–7, when Turkey failed to reform in accordance with its recommendations, no Power would move to protect her against Russia's attack. When Russia departed from a programme that was upholding the recommendations of the Concert of Europe, imposing the Treaty of San Stefano on Turkey, she forfeited the forbearance of the other Powers and it was Great Britain, appealing in her turn to the principle that the Eastern Question was the concern of all the Powers, who obtained the outstanding success at the Congress of Berlin of 1878–9. This Congress harked back to the Congress of Vienna in more ways than merely in name. The *London Times* was not alone in hailing it as 'the first instance of a real Parliament of the Great Powers'.[29] It was followed by the Conference of Madrid in 1880, summoned on Great Britain's initiative to deal with the problem of growing disorder in Morocco by introducing reforms there under the supervision of the Powers. The same aspiration underlay Gladstone's insistence on placing the affairs of Egypt under the supervision of the Great Powers after the British occupation of 1882. In 1884–5 the Berlin Conference on Africa recognised the International Association of the Congo as a neutral free-trade zone and also attempted to lay down rules of international law that would define the effective occupation of uncivilised areas. But these conferences which assembled after the Congress of Berlin were not markedly successful and the attempt to work by conference was not sustained.

The Madrid Conference broke down over Anglo-French rivalry concerning the future of Morocco and from the fact that except for Spain, present as an interested lesser state, none of the Powers was prepared to support Great Britain's reform proposals; and it is perhaps significant that except for that of Rome (1831–2)—convened to investigate maladministration by the Pope in the papal states—it was the first conference of the European Great Powers to take place outside the capital of one of these Powers.* Egypt was the subject of technical international committees and of much diplomacy, but never of a conference. Whereas in the first half of the century, moreover, the Powers had not treated the assembling of a conference as a defeat for one of the Powers, the summoning of the Berlin Conference on Africa of 1884 was widely regarded as a diplomatic setback for Great Britain.[30] It is still more significant that, except for the abortive Hague Conference of 1899, that conference was the last international gathering on a political subject—the last visible sign of the operation of the Concert—until 1906, when again the meeting-place was Algeciras instead of one of the European capitals.

This further eclipse of the conference method was one of the ways in which international relations differed after 1878 from those of the earlier period of peace after 1815. It also indicates one of the reasons for the difference. The practice of meeting in conference was giving way before an almost universal feeling that each Great Power must stand on its own feet and reserve its efforts for its own immediate interests. After 1878 Gladstone was almost alone among statesmen in continuing to advocate concerted instead of individual action. Even Gladstone continued to believe that the restoration of a 'Council of the Great Powers' in Europe was more practicable than the

* The Constantinople Conference of 1876–7 is sometimes quoted as a further exception before 1880, but Turkey was technically a member of the Great Power circle after 1856.

newer programme which sought to substitute for the dying Concert, which had been based on the collective discretion of the leading governments, a system of obligatory arbitration based on international legislation.[31] Bismarck and Lord Salisbury, with their intellectual contempt for Gladstone's ideas, were more representative of the age. And if these were its representative statesmen, alliances were its typical diplomatic means.

Beginning with the Three Emperors' League of 1873, and still more decisively with the Austro-German alliance of 1879, there grew up in Europe a network of meticulous written undertakings of the kind that—except during the years of war from 1858 to 1870—had gone out with the *ancien régime*. Every major continental Power came to give and regularly to renew formal pledges to some other. Not even Great Britain, despite her special position, escaped the practice for some years after 1887 when, in the Mediterranean Agreements, she accepted a more binding undertaking than was contained in her agreements with France and Russia twenty years later. These alliances were limited to European contingencies, though they often restrained, sometimes stimulated and always influenced the European rivalries beyond Europe. The extra-European Powers were not yet involved. In both respects the Anglo-Japanese alliance of 1902 was the beginning of a new phase in international relations, an intimation that the search for power and equilibrium was becoming world-wide and extending beyond the narrow circle of the European Powers.

It was also the first of all the alliances contracted since 1873 which, if only on the Japanese side, was as much concerned with war as with peace, with changing the *status quo* as well as with maintaining it. Until then, if international relations differed from those of the first half of the nineteenth century, they were also different from those of the eighteenth century and of the years from 1858 to 1870. Unlike those of those earlier periods, the alliances were without exception defensive. Most of them were explicitly aimed at preserving the *status quo*; the remainder equally lacked the intention of changing it.* Not one of them was an aggressive pact of the kind

---

* The *Three Emperors' League of 1873* began as a Russo–German agreement for mutual aid if one or the other was attacked, and was completed by an Austro–Russian agreement to consult together if an aggression threatened.

The *Austro–German Alliance of 1879* was purely defensive, essentially a promise by the

which had characterised those other periods and whose primary purpose had been to secure the assistance or neutrality of another Power in a projected war. There remained an ironical, if perhaps an unavoidable, contradiction between the contracting of even defensive alliances and the insistence of the Powers on their autonomy, but of this they were acutely aware. Until the 1890's—when the Triple Alliance was renewed in 1891 for 12 years, and prematurely, and the Franco-Russian military convention of 1892, the basis of the Franco-Russian Alliance, was concluded 'to last as long as the 'Triple Alliance'—the alliances were all made for brief periods, usually 3 or 5 years,* for the same reason that they dealt meticulously with precise contingencies: the reluctance of every Power to give up its

two Powers to join together against a Russian attack and to provide benevolent neutrality in the event of an attack by any other Power unaided by Russia.

The *Three Emperors' Alliance of 1881* was a defensive alliance. In any war other than with Turkey, Germany, Russia and Austria promised each other benevolent neutrality, while in any war with Turkey they agreed to consult together beforehand and to make no changes in S.E. Europe without agreement. In this last respect it was essentially a self-denying ordinance imposed by Germany on reluctant Austria and Russia. Also behind it was the anxiety of all three Powers to safeguard existing conquests—Alsace and Lorraine, Bessarabia and Bulgaria, Bosnia and Herzegovina.

The *Triple Alliance of 1882*, an extension of the Austro–German Alliance as a result of the adhesion of Italy, was essentially defensive. If Italy were attacked by France, Germany and Austria would assist her. If Germany were attacked by France, Italy would assist her. If one of the Powers were attacked by two or more other Powers all would join together. Italy promised to stay neutral in a war between Russia and Austria. Behind this alliance was the anxiety to safeguard existing conquests—Italy's, now joined to those of Germany and Austria, being lest those other two Powers would support the Pope over the Papal State.

The *Reinsurance Treaty of 1887* between Germany and Russia was a promise of neutrality by the two Powers except in the event of a Russian attack on Austria or a German attack on France, reservations which had always existed and which were now merely formalised.

The *Franco–Russian Alliance of 1892–4* arranged that Russia would employ all her forces against Germany if France were attacked by Germany or by Italy with German support, and that France would attack Germany if Russia were attacked by Germany or by Austria with German support. It was entirely defensive.

* Whereas no term had been set to the Three Emperors' League of 1873, which was an understanding of the old style, a revival of the Holy Alliance or, rather, of the understandings of pre-1854, all alliances after 1879 were deliberately short-term—3 or 5 years and occasionally 10, as in the Austro–Serbian alliance of 1881—but were renewable.

The *Austro–German Alliance of 1879* was concluded in the first place for 5 years and renewed at 5-year intervals.

The *Three Emperors' Alliance of 1881* was for 3 years and was renewed in 1884 and expired in 1887.

The *Triple Alliance of 1882* was for 5 years, and was renewed for 5 years in 1887, but in 1891, and prematurely, it was renewed for 12 years.

The *Austro–German–Rumanian Alliance of 1883* was for 5 years and renewed at frequent intervals.

The *Reinsurance Treaty of 1887* was for 3 years. It expired in 1890.

freedom of action. After 1890, no less than before, reluctance was the keynote of the negotiation of each of them.*

Partly for this reason, though they were all technically secret alliances, their existence and often their contents were generally known to all the Foreign Offices.† Being precise, short-term and technically secret they left the Powers free, as they were intended to do, in all but the stated and narrow contingencies they envisaged. The Powers used this freedom. It would be an exaggeration to assert that the system of alliances was a façade, ignored except on ceremonial occasions and by gullible persons. It is certain that its nature cannot be understood unless it is emphasised that it was no barrier either to understandings between members of opposed alliances—between Austria and Russia, France and Germany, Germany and Russia, Italy and France—or to disagreements between allies—between Italy and Austria, France and Russia, Austria and Germany. Any Power tempted to adventure was restrained by its allies as much as by its opponents. Bismarck went far towards contracting incompatible alliances with Austria and Russia, with Italy and Austria. There were times when the British government did not remember that it had signed the Mediterranean Agreements or could not decide whether or not the Agreements had lapsed. All the Powers sought to be as isolationist in fact as Great Britain was normally able to be. Their alliances testified to their wish for independence as much as to the difficulty of achieving it.

This difficulty was perhaps inherent in the existence of several states. It was increased by the stupendous development which now took place in the weapons and techniques of war. Bismarck's alliances took their rise from Bismarck's determination to preserve

---

* The reluctance of the Powers in concluding the first of the alliances, that between Austria and Germany, is indicated by the fact that, although it was 'secret', the German Emperor insisted on sending a copy to Russia to prove its defensive character and Austria notified the British Government of its existence. The reluctance of Austria, Italy and Germany to conclude and renew the Triple Alliance varied from time to time and as between the three parties, but it was always a factor in the negotiations. The Franco–Russian Alliance was notoriously an unwelcome bargain between Russia and France—whose reluctance has often been mistakenly attributed by historians merely to the mutual distrust of Tsardom and the French Republic. Great Britain at least was most reluctant to conclude the Anglo–Japanese Alliance in 1902, and this would have been an Anglo–German–Japanese Alliance had not Germany been determined to stay free.

† Parts of the Anglo–Japanese Alliance were published—but it had its secret clauses. Until then the alliances had been secret. Insufficient research has as yet been done on the extent to which, despite this fact, their contents were known. It is clear that on the whole they were.

the advantageous *status quo* of 1871, from his fear that another European war could not be localised and might end in the weakening or dismemberment of Germany. Against this danger he relied on Germany's military preparedness as well as on diplomacy; and if the first alliance inexorably led to others it was because military preparedness increasingly involved the need of an ally. The application of science, technology and industry to the means of war, and of the increasing efficiency and bureaucracy of the state to military organisation, was making continuous readiness, rapid mobilisation, large forces and universal conscription essential for success in resisting an attack with modern transport and modern weapons. All the leading continental states, following Germany's example in these directions, became for the first time nations in arms in time of peace. On the other hand, the greatest single consequence of these developments was that weapon development—which had moved in advance of improvements in locomotion, and made tactics increasingly static, since the sixteenth century—now moved farther ahead of them. Weapon ranges, which were ten times greater in 1870 than in the days of the first Napoleon, were forty times greater by 1898. Weapon efficiency similarly shot forward, especially with the development of machine-guns in the 1860's and of Maxim's truly automatic machine-gun in 1889. But mobility and flexibility on the battlefield—as opposed to the increased strategic mobility resulting from the growth of railways—was reduced by the introduction of larger weapons until the subsequent application of the petrol engine to warfare, which did not come before 1914.* To a greater extent than ever before, battlefield mobility and weapon power had become incompatible. Success in attack against a prepared enemy, if not rendered quite impossible, accordingly required an ever-increasing ratio of superiority by the attack over the defence. When all the Powers were prepared, when technical developments were constantly increasing the expense and the rate of obsolescence of weapons, when increasingly complex and efficient General Staffs planned—as was their habit and, in view of the lack of tactical mobility, to some extent a continuing need—for frontal assaults and—as was their

---

* This was the great difference between naval and military developments at this time. Navies gained in speed and mobility, as well as in weapon power, because of the much earlier development of propulsion at sea compared with that of automotive power on land —and so much so that the difficulty with them, as was shown in the war of 1914, was becoming that of bringing an enemy fleet to battle at all.

function—for victory and not merely for successful defence, and at a time when governments were also spending increasing amounts on education, welfare and other social measures, the burden became so great, both financially* and psychologically, that the Powers felt forced to contract alliances. If these all dealt with precise contingencies it was in the details of mutual military aid that they reached the greatest precision. By 1892 this fact had become so pronounced that what in due course became the Franco-Russian Alliance originated in a strictly military convention, made to balance the military forces of the Triple Alliance of Germany, Austria and Italy, between two Powers who had no intention of concerting their policies and who entered into no commitment to concert them.

If only because they were so directly necessitated by the armaments situation, the resulting alliances accentuated the defensive character of the age by presenting the Great Powers with the choice of only a general war or a general peace. For the same reason they did nothing, on the other hand, to offset the central characteristic of its international dealings—the political and diplomatic self-reliance of each Power. Nor was this reduced by another notable development of the time. It was when the advanced parts of the world were experiencing the first huge proliferation of international legislation and committees on administrative and technical matters that were increasingly of common concern to states, like postage, telegraphs, armaments and public health, that the Great Powers insisted as never before on autonomy in international politics. The Geneva Red Cross organisation was established in 1864; 17 governments signed at St. Petersburg in 1868 a convention governing the use of explosives in war; the Postal Union, which all civilised states had joined in 1897, was founded in 1874 by 22 states who pledged themselves to submit to arbitration all disputes arising in this field. The number of intergovernmental unions and conventions to deal with such questions increased thereafter, by 12 between 1875 and 1899, by 21 between 1900 and 1919. The number of private international organisations grew still more rapidly: 130 were founded between 1875 and 1899

---

* Expenditure on defence between 1874 and 1896 increased by 79% in Germany, 75% in Russia, 47% in Great Britain, 43% in France, 21% in Austria. But this was a much smaller rate of increase than that which took place after 1900 and revenue was growing fast. Only Russia found it crippling in this period. Turkey, however, had succumbed earlier. The main cause of her economic difficulties after 1870 was the attempt she had made earlier in the nineteenth century to create professional fighting forces on the European model without a corresponding development of her economic resources.

and no less than 355 between 1900 and 1919.[32] But by governments, at least, this development was rigidly restricted to the administrative and technical fields by the insistence of the states on their complete independence and total discretion in the political field. Just as the force of nationalism in the late nineteenth century was helping both to disrupt large political units and to produce the concentration of small political units into great states—to break up the historical structures of Turkey, Austria and Russia, as well as to construct the new states of Germany and Italy—so the processes of administrative, economic and technological integration were revealing for the first time that political harmony, let alone political integration, was not their necessary result; that 'the world as a . . . homogeneous scene . . . does not mean . . . the same thing as the world as one state'; that it is an error 'to expect a uniformly constituted world to result from considerations of a technical or economic nature. . . .'[33]

On the contrary, the growing administrative integration between states and the growing insistence of the Powers on political self-reliance—on their ability to work without international political machinery—were equally reflections of the most significant developments of the time. If states began to insist as never before that in foreign affairs, as in such matters as tariffs, the maximum liberty for each would produce the best results for all, it was because those developments which were producing the growth of international administration—the extension of the functions and competence of government and the alteration in the relations of each government to its society—were also accentuating the organisation of the individual state. They were bringing the states into closer and more continuous contact—even as they were making them more like each other in organisation—but they were simultaneously emphasising their political individuality and placing a strain on their political solidarity. The decline of monarchical solidarity in Europe was one symptom of this change. Up to the 1870's this factor, however attenuated, had persisted as a general sentiment on which the arch of the Concert could rest among governments which were all on guard, if in different degrees, against internal dissidence. It now declined even among the Eastern Powers: so that the Three Emperors' League, which was still at least nominally a declaration of monarchical cooperation when set up in 1873, had become simply an alliance when revived in 1881; and the last personal meeting of the Emperors took place in 1884. And what took its place was not a new loyalty uniting governments but a new conception of the state in accordance with which each government was ranged with its own society rather than with other governments against it.

The heightening everywhere of the emotional attachment towards the armed forces as symbols of the national state was another indication of this process in which the character of nationalism itself underwent a change. Except in Central and Eastern Europe, which for the time at least became the only considerable area where nationalist feeling was both strong and unsatisfied, loyalty to the nation gave way to loyalty to the state among the general populations. It was with popular support that governments themselves, and not least the governments of Germany and Italy which had previously profited from the national principle, became intensely nationalist in their policies within their existing borders and anti-nationalist beyond them. Beyond them the principle of nationality, which had previously succeeded only when embraced by a strong government, was ignored by the Congress of Berlin even more than it had been ignored by the Congress of Vienna. Turkey was deprived of half her European territory, but for the purpose of rounding off the territories of the Powers and in the interests of the balance between them, and not in the cause of freeing national minorities. How could there be sympathy, let alone support, for Czechs or Poles or Serbs or Balts when—all other considerations apart—governments within their own states were, with wide popular support, favouring national majorities and making intense efforts to create homogeneous populations by absorbing minorities? When the German government was Germanising Poles and Danes, when centralism in Italy no less than in Austria was ignoring minorities and provincialism, when Russification was as ruthless as Magyarisation and more extensive, when even in England Gladstone was discovering that public sentiment was stubbornly opposed to his plan for Home Rule for Ireland? When even in small states—in Belgium, for example, where the ascendancy of the French over the Flemish element was steadily developed—the governments equally pursued a policy of administrative centralisation and state integration?

This shift, with the accompanying increase in alliances and armaments, added to the normal concern of governments to limit the responsibilities and to guard the security of their own states, and made them reluctant to invoke the conference method even in political disputes which were of interest to them all. It was not only in the Eastern Question and not only by Bismarck that, increasingly after the 1870's, such trouble and risk were regarded as unworthy of the bones of a grenadier. In such an atmosphere it was the more certain that the efforts of men like Gladstone not merely to revive the Concert but to extend it—to convert it back to a Congress system by saddling it with such problems as the internal administration of Egypt, the reform or dissolution of the Ottoman Empire, the opening-up of Africa—would only contribute to its collapse. But these problems which Gladstone tried to submit to it illustrate the importance of another development that was working in the same direction. If governments were more reluctant than before to collaborate in the settlement of even common problems it was also true that an increasing number of international political problems were not of common, or at least of equal, concern to a structure of European Powers. At the same time, for all the continuing primacy of those Powers, some problems were arising which were not the concern of European Powers alone. The political problems of this period arose, to a larger extent than ever before, in areas beyond Europe in which, for both of these reasons, the conditions did not exist for the application of the European Concert machinery or even—despite the effort to apply them there in the 1884 Conference on Africa and the international guarantee of the neutral status of the Congo Free State—of those general notions of a European public law on which such machinery had been based.

This development was the direct consequence of two others. The discrepancy between the developed and the undeveloped parts of the world was becoming acute. It was becoming acute at a time when the world beyond Europe was shrinking with the enormous development of communications, and at a time when the possibilities of exploiting undeveloped areas were being vastly enlarged by this and other technical and organisational developments. On account of the different circumstances and different previous histories of the different parts of the world the industrial and technical revolutions and the rise of the modern state, such prominent features of this period wherever they did occur, did not take place everywhere—any more than, where they did take place, they took place to the same degree and at the same speed. The effects on international relations were momentous. Not only were new Powers emerging for the first time beyond Europe. Though not for the first time, for there had been a growing disparity between Western Europe and other areas since the eighteenth century, yet more rapidly, more extensively and more directly than before—in Turkey's European provinces and in Central Asia from about 1870; in Turkey's North African possessions, in the Near East and Persia, in undeveloped Africa and the undeveloped Pacific from about 1880; in China and Korea from about 1885; in the New World, even, from about 1890 as the United States expanded from her continent into the Caribbean, undertook the Panama Canal and asserted her right under the Monroe Doctrine to be the directing Power in South as well as in North America—the more developed states extended, were perhaps unable to avoid extending, their intervention and their control in areas where society and government were still as they had been in the European Middle Ages. And when none of the problems of this wider world of politics involved all the European Powers, when few of them affected in equal degree even those Powers which were involved, when some of them were more directly the concern of new Powers beyond Europe than they were of some European states, it is not to be wondered at that an older and purely European habit and system of collaboration proved increasingly impossible to uphold.

Whatever further elaboration may be needed for its complete analysis, these developments were the sufficient cause of the increase in imperialist activity and sentiment which marked the last fifteen or twenty years of the century. This imperialism derived much of its character, and no doubt further impetus, from the special economic conditions of the Great Depression and from increased humanitarianism and missionary activity. The age saw a powerful expansion of such activity by the Christian Churches. The expansion was facilitated by material developments—the growth of transport, the improving control over diseases, the development of cheap printing, the mounting wealth of Western countries—no less than by growing concern to spread the Gospel and undertake humanitarian work. In return it stimulated imperialist sentiment if only by stimulating public support for overseas expansion. Increased overseas expansion was also a response to the growing international deadlock in Europe, which encouraged the Powers to search for compensation and leverage effect beyond the Continent. But if imperialism now exceeded in scope and intensity the overseas activity of earlier periods this was ultimately because the disparity between the efficient and the under-developed areas was becoming more pronounced at a time when expansion and exploitation by the efficient areas were becoming more practicable than they had ever been.

These developments within and beyond the old European system —producing imperialism, armaments preparations, alliances and tariff wars—spelled the decline of conference diplomacy by the 1880's. Thereafter they added to the suspicion and strain of inter-national relations between the Powers. But they did not rapidly destroy the attachment of the Powers to moderation and to the general principles—if not to the mechanism—underlying their earlier cooperation. It was now, indeed, that governments made their first attempts to adapt those principles to the changing situation by replacing the older mechanism of international collaboration with one more suited to a wider world of more disparate, more powerful and more highly integrated states.

These attempts took the form of an effort to replace the imperfect customary international law of the Concert by strictly legal pro-cedures and by treaties. They did so in part because the need was arising to regularise international contacts within and with areas where they had never yet been regularised and where they rested on little or no historical or customary basis. If there was a steady in-crease after 1870 in the number of bilateral arbitration treaties, by which states agreed in advance to submit specified categories of disputes to arbitration, most of them were concluded between or with states which had but recently joined 'the comity of nations'. The increase in the resort to *ad hoc* arbitration by states which did not conclude such treaties was most noticeable as between Great Britain and the United States—a Power which was conflicting with British interests in the New World but which as yet remained isolated from, and critical of, the system of relations between the Great Powers. It was not simply because of the predominance of lawyers in the government circles of the United States that the first attempt by governments to go in this direction beyond the *ad hoc* arbitration of individual disputes and the signing of arbitration treaties between individual states—the pan-American Conference of 17 out of the 19 American states which assembled in Washington in

1889 to establish a Tribunal of Arbitration for all inter-American disputes—was made in the Americas.

But this departure was also a response to the other major development of these years—the rise of the modern state. Even earlier, in the years after 1815, the supplementation of customary international procedure by treaty law had been a consequence of an earlier phase of this development—of the phase in which the state was first acquiring its modern bureaucracy and its legal advisers, in foreign as well as in other affairs, but in which its growth had not yet begun to transform the relations between government and society. After the 1860's, as already noted,* the decay of federalist and pacifist programmes and the concentration of international thinking upon the demand for universal and compulsory arbitration, on the basis of treaties between sovereign states, reflected men's growing acceptance of the sovereign state. And after the 1880's the slow and partial acceptance of this programme by governments reflected their growing anxiety about the strains and stresses which were arising from the modern state's development and which had already helped to destroy the conference system. It was in 1898 that the pan-American precedent was first followed up by a European government; and if the Tsar then astounded the world by denouncing war and inviting other governments to meet to discuss its supersession by a procedure for the pacific arbitration of disputes, it was largely because Russia was the first of the Great Powers to find that she was being crippled by the growing armaments burden.

At the end of the nineteenth century the suspicions and strains arising from the growth of the state proved stronger than the anxieties —and not only in old Europe. The treaty which resulted from the pan-American Conference of 1889, aside from providing for only *ad hoc* tribunals for individual disputes, and thus failing to establish a Permanent Court, exempted from arbitration all questions which in the judgement of a signatory state involved its national independence. Even then it was signed only by 11 of the 17 states— and ratified only by 1, Brazil.[34] There followed in 1897 the first attempt to conclude a permanent arbitration treaty between a Great Power in the Old World and a Great Power in the New. The Anglo-American Arbitration Treaty which was the subject of negotiations in that year would, subject to qualifications, have submitted to

* Above, pp. 114–17, 123–39.

arbitration 'all questions of difference between them which they may fail to adjust by diplomatic negotiations'. The qualifications were formidable. Lord Salisbury reserved all questions involving 'the national honour or integrity' and proved reluctant to agree in advance to arbitration in matters of territory and jurisdiction. The United States Government, after protesting against such restrictions, recalled that, since the American Constitution gave the Senate a share in the control of foreign policy and would require Senate approval of all arbitration awards, it could not easily accept an advance obligation to arbitrate on any subject. When this difficulty had been circumvented the Senate first went beyond the British reservations by amending the text so that 'no difference shall be submitted which in the judgement of either Power materially affects its honour, the integrity of its territory or its foreign and domestic policy', and finally refused in May 1897 to ratify the amended treaty.[35]

Its argument on that occasion—'we will be purblind if we put a paper guarantee of peace in place of the moral and military forces that are the supreme elements of strength in our splendid republic' —was soon to be embraced by all the Powers. All the invited governments accepted the Tsar's invitation of August 1898—they included the United States, China, Japan, Siam and Mexico, as well as the European states—and the hopes of peace movements throughout the world now reached new heights. Nor were they wholly belied when the Conference began its work at The Hague in May 1899. The greatest measure of agreement was achieved in conventions which humanised and codified the rules of warfare; in the sphere of disarmament it could do no more than resolve that 'the restriction of military budgets is . . . extremely desirable'. The Conference did also establish for the future a Court of International Arbitration at The Hague. On the other hand, what was set up was neither permanent nor, strictly speaking, a Court. The panel of arbitrators was to be formed anew for each dispute; in each dispute it would have a strong national character, since each party would appoint two judges and the four would select a fifth. Far more serious limitations on its efficiency and scope were the fact that no state bound itself to resort to the Court; that no state could get assistance in bringing an unwilling state to resort to arbitration; and that disputes involving the honour or vital interests of a state were expressly exempted from the

Court's jurisdiction. All the major governments, indeed, shared Salisbury's view that the Conference should not be taken 'too seriously' and the Kaiser's verdict that, beyond regulating the rules of war, its objectives were 'Utopian'. 'Not a single Power', wrote the United States delegate, 'was willing to bring itself to submit all questions to arbitration, and least of all the United States. A few nations were willing to accept it in regard to minor matters—as, for example, postal or monetary difficulties and the like.'[36]

If the first Hague Conference thus provided further proof that the development of arbitration would be rigidly circumscribed by the insistence of states on their complete independence and discretion in international politics, it also revealed the preference of governments for older and looser diplomatic forms of collaboration over rigid legal procedures. It established the right of every government to offer mediation in a dispute without its action being open to interpretation as an unfriendly act. It recommended that a commission of enquiry, composed partly of neutrals, would be 'useful' in moments of acute difference between two Powers. This second step was originally tabled as a provision of the Convention but was watered down to a recommendation because of the strenuous opposition by several states to any step that might prejudice their sovereignty: the insistence on sovereignty was hampering the development of the older, looser, discretionary, political forms of collaboration no less than it was preventing the acceptance of the newer programme of automatic resort to the legal procedure of arbitration.

It should be emphasised, however, that the Hague Conference, in registering this preference of governments for the former over the latter, provided another illustration—the failure of arbitration programmes in the New World was the first—of the fact that the insistence on sovereignty was not the sole obstacle that governments would meet in the new direction in which they were being driven. The sovereignty of the state has always hampered the development of international political procedures, and it always will. It is not incompatible with that development. At the end of the nineteenth century, in consequence of the rise of the modern state, the emphasis on sovereignty was perhaps hampering this development more powerfully than ever before; and after combining with other factors, and notably with the rise of problems and Powers beyond Europe, to destroy conference diplomacy it was slowly destroying, also, the principles and the habits of the Concert system on which conference diplomacy had been based. But the alternative which now developed, to the Concert and to the Conference system, the programme for the acceptance in advance of the automatic arbitration of international disputes, was not only to be hampered by sovereignty in its turn. It was a legal procedure that was by its nature inappropriate for the solution of political disputes and inapplicable to them; and the attempt to adopt it was one day even to prove destructive of the recovery and further development of international political procedures.

The world would learn this only from making the attempt; and in 1900 it was beginning to be driven to make it. At about that date that degree of trust and collaboration between the Great Powers which had still survived despite the final collapse of the Conference system after 1880 was itself at last disappearing. It was disappearing because, on top of the other developments of these years, the balance of power between the Great Powers was itself beginning to change —and with it the objects of their rivalry. As this period ended, a period which had been distinguished by an obvious and ever-growing disparity between the developed and the undeveloped states, another disparity was becoming acute—a disparity between the more developed states, the Powers, themselves. It had been emerging since the 1860's and 1870's. The unification of Germany, the end of the American Civil War, the abolition of serfdom in Russia, the Meiji revolution and, in 1877, the defeat of the last feudal rebellion in Japan, had already laid at that time the foundations of a structure of international power which would be different in significant respects from that which had prevailed since the eighteenth century. Until the end of the nineteenth century—though work was proceeding fast on these foundations, and faster in Germany than elsewhere; though other states, Great Britain and France, who had developed most before 1870, were losing their earlier lead; though others yet, like Austria and Italy, found themselves limited in opportunities and the resources of modern power—the shift in relative strengths had not been rapid or obvious, and it had been overlaid by the checks and balances of the older international order. The older order had still persisted alongside the new. But from about 1900 the old order was at last being destroyed.

In the ensuing struggle and in a new phase of international history —a phase which was to last till 1945 and in which a grave and shifting inequality in the distribution of effective power between the leading states of the world replaced the previous stable balance between the leading states in Europe—Germany sought the mastery of Europe as no Power had sought it for a century and all the Powers at last set aside those principles and that sense of their collectivity which, despite the breakdown of the Concert itself, had helped to restrain them since the 1870's.

Despite subsequent experiments with international organisations, these principles and that sense of collectivity have not yet been revived. Nor will they be until men have assimilated the lessons of the past fifty years of international struggle on a world scale, as the Powers assimilated in the nineteenth century the lessons of the struggles which accompanied the emergence of the modern states' system in the narrower framework of Europe.

PART III

INTERNATIONAL RELATIONS AND INTERNATIONAL ORGANIZATIONS IN THE TWENTIETH CENTURY

'The mind of man pursues whatever it fancies great or beautiful with so much complacency, nay, even with so much ardour, that it is sorry to realise that those objects have frequently nothing real or solid in them. . . .'

MAXIMILIEN DE BÉTHUNE, DUC DE SULLY, *Mémoires* (1635),
Book XXX

CHAPTER 12

INTERNATIONAL RELATIONS IN THE FIRST HALF OF THE TWENTIETH CENTURY

IF you ask people to characterise the politics of the first half of the twentieth century, and especially the international politics of the period, nine out of ten will reply that it had been an age of unparalleled violence. Many of them would add that the world is still faced with a crisis the like of which it has never previously experienced. Nor is it only laymen who take this view. The final volume of the new Cambridge Modern History, published in 1960, has *The Age of Violence* for its title.

In some ways this widespread belief is quite unfounded. The first half of the twentieth century was not the age of violence in the sense that every previous age had been a period of benevolence and peace. Recorded history is not an entirely unbroken saga of violence, but the historian knows that he must look much earlier than the twentieth century for the first examples of all the paraphernalia of violence with which the twentieth century has been familiar. International aggression, continuous, calculated, pathologically inspired? Thucydides is still the author of the best book on that subject; and there is no reason to be more disturbed by Hitler than by Louis XIV or Napoleon. Tireless ideological struggle on the scale of the known world? The contemporary cold war contains no elements that were not present in the battle between the religions in the sixteenth and seventeenth centuries. Bitter class warfare? No one can understand those wars of religion unless he first realises the intensity of the conflicts that raged between the classes in those days. The ruthless suppression of the individual and of minorities by the state? Stalin and Hitler were frightening for their very affinities with Ivan the Terrible or the Inquisition, and the Albigensians in France and the Moors in Spain, to take but two examples, were exterminated centuries before the attempt to exterminate the German Jews. Then take the carving-out of new political communities by the resort to violence. How can we be impressed or dismayed by at any rate the novelty of recent achievements in Ireland or Indonesia or Israel when force has nearly always been the midwife at the birth of new political societies since the beginning of time?

It is not only historical ignorance, moreover, the overlooking of these and other precedents, that distorts the outlook upon recent times. If the pages of history are strewn with examples of violence they are strewn as well, until very recently, with incontestible evidence of men's matter-of-fact acceptance of violence as a part of the order of nature or a manifestation of the will of God. Not many minds before the eighteenth century thought war regrettable. Until well into the eighteenth century, even in western countries, men thought nothing of hanging other men for stealing turnips—any more than they saw anything wrong in owning slaves. But beginning in the eighteenth century, and advancing with a rush in the nineteenth century, there developed a new morality. What had once seemed normal and inescapable began to seem gross; what began to seem gross was less frequently resorted to. Because such a shift of values occurred we have the paradox about the twentieth century that if it has been much more violent than any previous period in some respects it has been much less violent than any previous period in many others. And then, because violence was receding in some fields it began to seem the more alarming that it was not receding in others. This is the explanation behind another apparent paradox of recent times—that as well as seeing more destructive and widespread wars than any previous age they have witnessed the widest and most determined efforts in all history to organise the end of war by one means or another. We tend, in fact, to regard the first half of the twentieth century as having been more violent than any previous age when what we are really thinking is that it was more violent than we, with our modern moral standards, would like it to have been.

Nor is the shift of moral standards the only change that has operated in this direction. It is one of the ironies of the modern world—another paradox, and one more genuine than those others just referred to—that in the past hundred years there have simultaneously developed both an increased moral aversion from violence in most men's minds and a news service of unparalleled efficiency in bringing violence to men's attention. Until a century ago few men heard or read of violence on any wide scale; what they knew of it was what they experienced in their own lives. Most men in the first half of this century—even more today—heard and read every day of violence in train or of violence impending which touched them directly not at all. Even the present-day world can seem peaceful if one is cut off from the pages of the London *Times*. Perhaps it cannot but seem the opposite when it is regarded—as it is almost universally regarded—through the medium of the popular newspapers and television.

For these kinds of reason people not only think that violence increased after 1900 when it did not do so in fact. They think it increased when in fact, in some directions, it most markedly declined. It is not enough merely to hint at this last development, as I have done so far. It needs to be emphasised that the first half of this century, in some fields if not in all, was not 'the age of violence' but the very opposite. Primarily as a result of the development of the modern state, a degree of order and security that was previously undreamed of was introduced into millions and millions of lives. Partly for the same reason and partly because of the change in moral standards and the growth of knowledge and education, many fields —public health, for example, and personal relations: the relations of man to man, of man to woman, of master to man, of adult to child, —witnessed a greater rise of tolerance and regulation, a greater decline in violence and chaos, than had been registered in all previous history, at least in the more fortunate countries. It is no coincidence that people have become obsessed with the dangers to their security. So much security had never before been enjoyed by as many people as have, in general, enjoyed it since this century began.

When all this has been said it remains the case that if the modern state and modern knowledge brought order and tolerance into ordinary lives they also increased men's potentiality and men's resources for creating disorder and destruction when order and tolerance break down. When all allowances have been made, it is still impossible to overlook the evidence for an absolute increase in violence in the first half of the twentieth century in some directions, if only in a few. Such an increase took place in some though not in all aspects of the relations between states.

There were fewer wars in the first half of the twentieth century than in any previous period of the same duration in modern times, and, except for the interval of the nineteenth century, fewer major wars involving leading Powers. An analysis of 278 wars between 1550 and 1945 which includes all wars between members of the modern states' system that were legally recognised, all other wars (e.g. civil wars and wars for colonial expansion) that involved more than 50,000 troops, and a few wars that were on a smaller scale but of some significance, yields the following result:

1550–1600	(when there were	19	effective states)				31 wars
1600–1650	(	,,	,,	34	,,	,,	) 34 wars
1650–1700	(	,,	,,	22	,,	,,	) 30 wars
1700–1750	(	,,	,,	20	,,	,,	) 18 wars
1750–1800	(	,,	,,	32	,,	,,	) 19 wars
1800–1850	(	,,	,,	43	,,	,,	) 41 wars
1850–1900	(	,,	,,	45	,,	,,	) 47 wars
1900–1945	(	,,	,,	57	,,	,,	) 24 wars

Allowing for the increasing number of states and for the geographical spread of the European states' system, the decline after 1900 is very noticeable. Taking major wars to be those wars among the above in which a Great Power participated on each side, and which lasted as long as two years, the figures are as follows:

1550–1600	0
1600–1648	1
1648–1700	3
1700–1750	4
1750–1800	3
1800–1850	1
1850–1900	1
1900–1945	2

But the major wars of the twentieth century have been both more extensive and more intensive, and vastly more destructive, than any the world had previously known.

This is indicated by the noticeable increase in the number of participating countries and by the startling increase in the number of battles per war, compared with earlier periods, no less than by the increase in the expense and casualties of warfare despite a noticeable decline in the duration of wars. The average length of major wars declined from 14 years in the seventeenth century to 8 years in the eighteenth century, to 6 years in the nineteenth century, to 4½ years in the twentieth century. The number of participants in the Thirty Years' War in the first half of the seventeenth century was 25, the number of battles fought was 86. In the Seven Years' War in the second half of the eighteenth century there were 17 belligerents and 111 battles; in Napoleon's war between 1802 and 1815 there were 17 participants and 332 battles. The numbers in the first World War were 38 and 615. In the second World War even these figures were surpassed.[1]

It has been the same with the resort to force in internal politics. The helpless had many times before been deported, dragooned and destroyed by those with power, but never in such numbers as suffered at the hands of Hitler and Stalin. It is the extent and the enormity of these tyrannies which, together with the character of the two World Wars, are the main reasons for the widespread belief that the years since 1914 have been the age of violence *par excellence*.

Neither they nor the wars are facts that can be ignored, nor are the terrible consequences of both. But they can be misunderstood, and there are other considerations—in addition to the violence of earlier ages and the higher moral standards of our own—that should be borne in mind when contemplating them. These most glaring examples of increased violence do not, in the first place, constitute any evidence for an increase in men's readiness to resort to violence or in the range and number of issues on which men have resorted to it. For all that we are told of the monstrous and sadistic purposes of Communism, and for all we have learned of the monstrous character of Nazism, they reveal only an increase in the scale and amount of violence of which men are capable when violence is resorted to. And this increase has an obvious explanation. If wars became more vast and destructive in the first half of this century it was because, with the growth of scientific knowledge and technical power, the world was greatly and rapidly shrinking in size at the same time as men's potentiality for destruction was greatly and rapidly expanding. If governments used force on an unparalleled scale against internal opposition or for internal policies it was because twentieth century governments had at their disposal unparalleled reserves of power on which to draw. But the increased knowledge and power continued to be put—and not more frequently than in earlier days—to age-old uses for age-old purposes. They were not used for new and more diabolical ends but for ends, and with motives, that were as old as the hills, and by men who were no worse, if no better, than men have always been.

This fact that it is men's power that has grown rather than men's nature and political behaviour that has worsened—that it is only the scale of violence that has increased—is widely recognised. In recent years there is no lament that has been more widespread than the complaint that men's wisdom has not kept pace with their increased knowledge and power. It is otherwise with the second point that needs to be made, which is as follows. When one realises the great rapidity and the enormous extent of the increase in men's knowledge and organisation of power during the first fifty years of this century, and when one realises also the complications and opportunities thrown up by the circumstances in which those things grew, then the surprising thing is not that there were such violent wars and tyrannies in that period. It is that the wars and tyrannies were not more frequent and more violent even than they were. The surprising thing is not that men's uses of power were so unrestrained, but that men did not become much worse and much less wise than they had previously been.

Historians can trace the origins of the modern state to the Middle Ages and see its continuous development since the fifteenth century. They sometimes overlook the fact that in some essential respects its rise was virtually a twentieth-century—and a phenomenally rapid—development. As a tolerably integrated, comprehensive and efficient organisation of power the state existed hardly anywhere before 1890, but wherever it did develop to and beyond this level, it then developed with formidable speed, especially after 1914. In the same way, for all the earlier scientific revolutions, the increase in scientific and technical knowledge in all the history of the world before 1900 had been a trickle compared with the stupendous growth that took place in it from about that date—a growth that has amounted to the greatest revolution in its conditions that the world has ever experienced. These two developments, the first appearance of the modern state in the shape of all that is now central to our understanding of the phrase and a growth of scientific knowledge and power that differed in kind and not merely in degree from all earlier expansion, were unquestionably two of the outstanding features of the history of the world in the first fifty years of this century.

There was another feature, even more central to an understanding of that period—and especially to an understanding of its international relations—but even less widely appreciated. Because of the different previous histories and present circumstances of the different parts of the world, the modern state and the modern scientific revolution did not emerge throughout the world, but only in some parts of it. So much was this so that there are many areas today where they have still not made their appearance. Even where they did emerge, moreover, they came at different times and grew at different speeds. While Europe, the United States, Europe's white dependencies and Japan rushed into the twentieth century the rest of the world remained in the Middle Ages. As between the developed areas disparities appeared that were more disturbing even if they were less acute. Great Britain, Germany, the United States—they rushed with few delays into the twentieth century while France and Italy continued to struggle in some limbo between the nineteenth and twentieth centuries, Austria-Hungary to exist between the eighteenth century and the twentieth century, and Russia to wallow between the extremes of the fourteenth century on the one hand and the twentieth century on the other.

The main consequences of the growth of the state and of modern science for international relations were that the basis and the criteria of power were changed—the emphasis shifting from manpower and size of territory to industrial and scientific ability—and that the possibilities of using power and making power effective were greatly enlarged for those states which possessed these abilities. The main consequence of the fact that different parts of the world were affected disproportionately by these changes was even more disturbing for international relations. This created first, from as early as the 1880's, at a time when the world was in any case shrinking on account of technical developments, a greater disparity of strength and efficiency between the developed and the undeveloped parts of the world than had ever existed in history, and secondly, from the 1900's, a more unequal and more rapidly changing distribution of power as between even the most developed states than had ever existed in modern times. As a result of the combination of these two developments there existed during the first half of the twentieth century a greater inequality of effective power between all the world's different areas and states, a greater political disequilibrium on a wider scale, than men had perhaps ever had to contend with.

After 1918 these basic sources of inequality and instability were supplemented by the consequences of the war and of the peace settlement. For all her vast wealth and power the United States, encased in an isolationism that had profound political and historical roots, remained obstinately remote from the system of international relations throughout the period—except for a brief but decisive intervention between 1916 and 1919. For much of the period, as a result of the shattering effect of the first World War on political systems that were tottering even before they underwent that strain, most of the world's old empires were in a state of prostration. In Europe the Russian, the Austro-Hungarian and the Turkish Empires, as well as the German, collapsed as a result of the war, and while the Russian needed time to recover, the Austrian and the Turkish, gone never to return, were replaced in the peace treaties, in accordance with the principle of self-determination, by small, unstable caricatures of modern states whose existence accentuated the enormous disparity of power that resulted when Germany made a more rapid recovery than Russia, among those states that had previously contained her, could achieve. A similar unbalance and disproportion emerged throughout the Far East. There Japan, in consequence of the development of her own naval and air power, the weakness of Russia, the isolationalism of the United States, the collapse of the Chinese Empire and the increased preoccupation with less distant problems of those other previous regulators of the area—of France, Great Britain and Germany—acquired an even more rapid and complete preponderance than that which fell to Germany in Europe.

It was perhaps even more important that the Powers, in the new temper and tempo of the times, became more acutely sensitive than before to such discrepancies as were emerging, and yet became less able than previously to measure them. Because the criteria of power were changing and because, as is indicated by the speed of German recovery, the political situation had also acquired an incalculable quality, the unsettlement was accentuated by an uncertainty of vision that acquired almost psychological proportions. If one outstanding feature of the history of international relations between the two world wars was that the distribution of effective power was more unstable and more rapidly changing than has usually been the case, another was that the states involved became both more preoccupied with relative power and less confident in their ability to assess it. All the main developments in international relations—and not only there—after 1918 were due to the combination of these two features. They underlay the policies of Hitler and the Japanese which led to the second World War, as they had already underlain the tensions between the Great Powers which led to the first. They explain the excesses of tyranny in Russia and Germany and the special appeal of Marxism to backward countries—to Russia after the first War and to China after the second. Not only the dynamism of the Russian revolution of fifty years ago and of the Chinese revolution of today, but also the special character of contemporary nationalism in India, the Middle East and Africa—the aspirations of areas that have never yet been great modern states as well as of those which were once Great Powers—are attributable to them. All these developments have sprung from the temptation to make use of the special opportunities thrown up by the uneven distribution of power; or from the fear that these opportunities would not last long; or from the determination to bring the greater opportunities and the overwhelming strength of others to an end by desperate measures to increase one's own power as rapidly as all the modern means permit. Nothing is so conducive to international violence as the fears and appetites that breed on inequality and instability and on the knowledge that these things exist. There never were such fears and appetites, because there never was such instability between states, as prevailed between 1918 and 1945.

When this is realised, then, as has been suggested, the question that is relevant for the history of those years is not why it witnessed so much violence but why it did not witness so much more. With so much increase in absolute potential power, in inequality in the growth and distribution of power, in consciousness of this increase and maldistribution, the misuse of power did not greatly increase or the frequency of resort to violent uses of it, but only the scale on which power was used when violence was resorted to. We need to understand why this was so.

There is no evidence for believing that it was because men with power became wiser or better than their predecessors—that dictators were more cautious than kings had been, modern mass democracies more upright and intelligent than oligarchies. The explanation lies in another direction. Even while they were being faced with unusual temptations and dangers in conditions of unusual instability, men with power were being subjected to quite unprecedented restraints. The growth of the modern state, the revolution in scientific and technical knowledge and the instability that resulted from the uneven advance of these things were developments which each produced, by what was virtually a dialectical process, its own deterrents. The growth of these deterrents is almost as important, as a key to an understanding of recent times, as the processes which produced them —as significant a characteristic of the years since 1918 as the growth of the modern state, the scientific revolution and the prevailing inequality of power.

The greatest political restraint was the emergence of public opinion as a serious check on government action. Public opinion has always existed. Even tyrants have always been restricted in their power, if only by the limits of what is practicable and of what populations can be forced to bear. But it was a singular development of the first half of the twentieth century that, even for tyrants, these limits rapidly closed—more rapidly than ever before. They were closed by what is called the march of democracy even when, as was the case in most of the areas of the world, it was totalitarian democracy that was on the march. It is a characteristic of forces like democracy that their progress anywhere will register itself everywhere in due course, even if their original conceptions are distorted in the process. 'Is it credible', asked de Tocqueville, 'that the democracy that has annihilated the feudal system and vanquished kings will respect the citizen and the capitalist? Will it stop now that it has grown so strong?' Is it credible that it would respect external boundaries any more than social ones in a world that was rapidly shrinking and becoming more integrated? It did not stop. The first half of the twentieth century was the era of the masses and the common man much more emphatically than it was the age of violence. And for totalitarian and democratic states alike the consequences included not only the growth of state power but the formation of serious limits to its use.

Totalitarian democracy is another name for popular or plebiscitary dictatorship, but even dictatorship, which had been becoming slowly more popular and plebiscitary ever since the French revolution, became so most rapidly after 1914. Stalin and Hitler were tyrants if any man was ever a tyrant. One has but to compare the nature of their power and the structure of their position with that of Louis XIV to realise what limitations this new development imposed on them. It may be an exaggeration to say that their tyrannies were tyrannies that were self-imposed by the peoples whom they ruled. It is unquestionable that the support of their peoples and the justifying and popularising of the actions they took and the policies they pursued had become as necessary for them as in the most constitutional of states. They could undertake and justify enormities that were unthinkable in more advanced and less disturbed countries. The checks on their uses of power were still immensely greater than those which all earlier despots had faced, and they were not much less than those on representative governments.

These latter also greatly increased. In each of these countries immense social changes, brought about almost wholly by mass pressures, have proceeded rapidly and continuously since the 1900's; before that date the pressure hardly existed and these changes had hardly begun. Before 1914 it is almost impossible to find evidence that French or British or American public opinion ever acted as a deterrent to decisions in foreign policy, as opposed to being an incitement to the men who took them. It is almost equally impossible to show that French and British and American foreign policy have ever been free from the hampering effect of public opinion—if only from the hampering effect—since that date. And this has been because for these populations, as for those in constitutionally more backward countries, where it grew but a little more slowly and to almost the same extent, the notion at last developed that government exists for men, not men for governments, and because the concern for security and well-being, necessarily an obstacle to irresponsibility and boldness in politics, must always be prominent whenever the masses of society have to be taken into account.

The growth of technical deterrents to the irresponsible use of power was an equally marked characteristic of these years. It was just before, during and after the first World War that the increase in scientific knowledge and technological advance first seriously affected the age-old battle between weapon and counter-weapon, intensifying it in one generation to a greater extent than had been accumulated in the previous four hundred years. Contrary to widespread popular belief, the result of this intensification was vastly to enlarge the cost of weapons. More serious than the increased cost was the fact that the intensification greatly slowed down the production of effective weapons: their greater complexity, the more rapid rate of obsolescence, the incalculable factor of new technological discovery all contributed to keep weapon development in a fluid state and to hamper weapon production. Even after allowing for changes in money values, a ship of the line built in 1750 cost twenty times less than the equivalent ship of 1920 and remained an effective fighting unit for four times as long—for sixty or seventy years instead of for fifteen or twenty. Nothing is more startling as an illustration of these facts than the almost incredible paucity of the latest weapons with which Germany launched the second World War—except, perhaps, the extent to which Germany was militarily formidable, though only for a brief period, because the other Powers of the world were even less well provided with these weapons than she was herself. Her successes in the *blitzkrieg* were the result of local superiorities that could be measured in tens of aircraft. France was defeated by negligible German local superiorities in tanks. The great Battle of the Atlantic was launched with two or three battleships, with twenty ocean-going U-boats. And what is still more relevant, statesmen between the two world wars—not excluding Hitler—lived on such tenterhooks as never before on account of this situation, and were more circumscribed by it when contemplating action than they ever had been in earlier times.

There had been earlier periods, it is true, when political and technical change had been rapid, when international unbalance had been acute. But the rate of change and the extent of the unbalance had not only been less rapid and less acute than they were in the twentieth century; their consequences had escaped the control of the state and overflowed its limits to a degree which twentieth-century Western minds find it difficult to comprehend. It has been well said that war in the sixteenth century was part of 'a general mêlée'. War against the infidel, civil war, war between Christian states, in spite of all efforts to distinguish between them and judge them differently, merged into each other, as did the condition of war and the condition of peace, in a continuously rhythmic movement in which predominantly internal alternated with predominantly external struggle. In spite of all the efforts of some theorists to assert that defence against external enemies and the maintenance of internal order were equally the prerogative of the state, civil war was in practice not an aberration but a part of the regular institution of war, of the regular structure of politics, and there were other theorists who asserted the right to wage it. Wars beyond Europe were as often as not the business of trading companies and private interests, unrecognised by the state and sometimes in conflict with its dispositions nearer home. War 'was not under the control of statesmen'. It was 'an activity which states controlled, so far as they were able . . . , but it was much more than an activity of states'.[2] By the second half of the eighteenth century the states had extended their competence and power. They had in some cases assumed an absolutist form in their control of the armed forces and in their relationship both to the old forces of society and to the new forces of commerce and industry, and they had in many cases reduced internal disorder to small proportions. But their control of the activities of their nationals beyond their borders, and especially beyond Europe, was still far from complete, and if the days of private armies were over, some of the most efficient navies were still pirate-owned. It will not escape the attention of anyone who works in the official archives that even during the nineteenth century, especially before the 1880's, government supervision and regulation—of overseas activities especially, but also of domestic affairs—retained a good deal of the amateur and casual nature they had had in earlier days. From the end of the nineteenth century, on the contrary, governments proceeded to acquire the professional character and the degree of competence to which we in the twentieth century have become accustomed. This process was one of the aspects of the growth of the modern state, as it is one of the reasons for dating a major advance in this development from that date. It was also the source of yet another set of restraints —of administrative as opposed to political and technical restraints— upon the resort to violence in international matters.

The change in the basis of government and in its relations to society—its increasingly necessary regard for the needs of the masses of men and for public opinion—made governments more cautious, even while it helped them to become more stable and more centralised. The increasing rapidity of technological change and the resulting cost and uncertainty of military preparedness had the same effect, even if they also contributed to the prevailing instability by accentuating the nervousness of the public, the politicians and the statesmen. The new centralisation and the vastly greater power of the state and its approach to a monopoly of the control of force and of the decisions concerning its use—this process that was occurring simultaneously with the others and that was greatly accelerated by them after the first World War—was working in the same direction. Contrary to a cherished belief of internationalists—in the twentieth century itself no less than in earlier days—states as organisations, as cabinets, as civil services with civil service committees, as comprehensively competent but also immensely complicated structures of power, were less and less the causes or the instigators of violence and war, if ever they had been, and were becoming more and more disposed to shift to avoid these things, even as they were becoming more and more capable of doing so. The main trouble afflicting British foreign policy between the wars was not that the government reached wrong decisions but that the Cabinet could often not bring itself to reach a decision at all. Even Hitler had to short-circuit his own civil and diplomatic services.

In the end, in the struggle between the instability and the restraints of the inter-war years, between the unbalance and the deterrents, the restraints and the deterrents proved inadequate. Against the will to power and the urge to expansion of a man like Hitler, and against the temptations that will always arise from an unbalance as acute as that which prevailed during those years, they needed to be stronger than they had as yet become. When peace broke down, moreover, it was the impulsive not the restraining aspects of these twentieth-century developments—the increased solidity of the masses of men, the increased staunchness of public opinion in war conditions, the technological perfection attained in warfare, the vast improvement of the state as a fighting machine—that necessarily came to the fore. But it would be a mistake to ignore the restraining aspects. They are necessary to a proper understanding of this century up to the second World War. And since they were to reappear after that war, and in a position of greater prominence, they are not without importance for an understanding of the contemporary international situation.

CHAPTER 13

THE FIRST WORLD WAR

IF we make a distinction, as we must, between what caused the first World War and what occasioned it we shall find that most people are content to agree that the immediate occasion was the Sarajevo assassination. Although there can be disagreement even on this issue —perhaps the immediate occasion was the Austrian ultimatum to Serbia, the German rejection of negotiations or the Russian mobilisation?—most people are content not to argue about it. They recognise that the immediate occasion of the war can tell us little of value about the causes of it.

The same is true of the Balkan entanglement which underlay the assassination. Most people accept that this in its turn was only the occasion, though a less immediate occasion, of the general war that followed between the Great Powers—that some crisis, and perhaps some war, was so likely to be generated by the Balkan problem that if the Sarajevo assassination had not sparked off a crisis in July 1914 then some other disturbance in the Balkans would have done so at no distant date. There is general agreement that there was a general war in 1914 because the local strains and pressures set up by a problem with which Europe had lived for nearly a century at last interlocked with a wider condition of tension between the Great Powers of which the origin was much more recent; and that if we are to understand the outbreak of that war, if we seek to know what caused it as opposed to what occasioned it, we must explain this interlocking and the growth of that wider tension.

When we turn to this problem of the causes of the general war we find, on the other hand, that the disposition to argue remains as acute as ever it was. Until very recently it arose from the national and other prejudices which always colour and confuse the discussion of events while they retain their obvious relevance to contemporary politics. Not even now is this source of controversy quite dead in relation to 1914. Since 1945, however, when another world war was brought to a close and the Versailles settlement had been buried, the main reason for controversy has been the failure to do some preliminary thinking about the causes of war—and especially about the causes of the war of 1914—in general terms.

Most people recognise that the forces which lead to war, as to other movements and convulsions in history, are of two kinds. Let us call them the impersonal and the man-made. The first arise from the conditions which men are 'given', from the world in which they live. The second are the consequences of human decisions or human indecision—men's own contributions to affairs. And the most elementary source of continuing argument and confusion about 1914 is to be found in the fact that, while both levels of causation are widely recognised to exist, there is an equally widespread disposition to confine the explanation of the outbreak of war to either the one or the other of these two levels of causation.

The mistake of assuming that the given conditions preceding the war of 1914 were the sole causes of the war has always led some people not, indeed, to initiate such theories as that the war was the result of the capitalist system or of rival imperialisms, conflicting colonial ambitions, trade competitions and the intrigues of high finance—for these theories have earlier emotional and doctrinal origins—but to accept them as being confirmed. This mistake is still having this effect—as if the conditions of international rivalry are any less likely to exist between non-capitalist than between capitalist states. Another belief—older, this one, even than Karl Marx—has similarly obtained unwarranted support from the mistake of confusing the conditions preceding the war of 1914 with the basic causes of it. This is the belief that the war was the inescapable consequence of the existence of independent states; and this belief in its turn is still prevalent among us. As if civil wars had not been as frequent in history as international wars. As if the search for power and the resort to force would be removed by the establishment of a single world state, supposing that to be possible.

That the sovereign state, like capitalism or trade competition, was merely one of the given conditions before 1914, even though research into the antecedents of the war will be sure to reveal its existence and its influence—this is perhaps at the root of the opposite views which argue that the general war was caused by the Kaiser or the German General Staff, or by the existence of war-like parties in the Austro-Hungarian or the German or the Russian capital. But it is not chiefly from recognising the truth—from realising that, although the war was a war between states because states existed, as it was a war between capitalist states because the states were capitalist states, it was not because states or capitalism existed that there was a war—that the advocates of these other views have adopted them. They have done so because they go to the opposite extreme of concentrating exclusively upon the human contribution in their search for the causes of the war. And it is difficult to say which is the more unsatisfactory, the more unhistorical—this search for human scapegoats with no regard for men's circumstances or that other search for impersonal, inexorable causes of the war which does not remember that these causes were the conditions in which men and governments evolved their decisions, the problems with which men and governments were presented.

But historians, it will now be protested, surely avoid these alternative elementary errors? Whatever may be said of publicists or of other students working in other fields than the history of their kind —surely historians recognise that both levels of causation are simultaneously at work behind most developments and decisions? That to ignore entirely the existence of the human contribution is to fly in the face of facts, if only because, as Dr Johnson said, 'no man believes himself to be impelled irresistibly; . . . he who says he believes it, lies?' That the assumption that men are not deflected and limited in their decisions by the given conditions is as unrealistic as the determinist position? They do recognise these things, on the whole. They do know that in taking the steps which culminated in the first World War men were restricted by the given conditions without being utterly controlled by them—so that no reputable historian now maintains that the war was caused either by capitalism or by the Kaiser. They even recognise that the relationship between the two levels of causation is not a fixed relationship—that they are faced with the task of assessing an interplay between the two levels which varies from time to time, from issue to issue, from contingency to contingency. But even among historians there is still confusion and controversy about the causes of the first World War because they have been diverted by historiographical factors—by history itself—from bringing these insights—the historical approach—to their study of the problem.

Their work reveals two major weaknesses. The first is this. They have expended oceans of ink on books which have studied the Sarajevo crisis itself with a determination to find the culprit individual or the culprit government but which have approached the antecedents of 1914 in a spirit of rigid determinism. And they still approach the problem in this fashion, as is witnessed by the most recent summary of the findings of historians on the outbreak of war in 1914, a pamphlet by Professor Schmitt which is itself the fruit of a prolonged analysis of the evidence.

This isolates the final Sarajevo crisis by beginning a new section after analysing the pre-1914 tension, and by beginning it with these words: 'All the governments were responsible, in a greater or lesser degree, for the . . . tension which came to a head in July 1914. But they were not equally responsible for the fatal turn of events, the course of which can be followed in microscopic detail.'[1] And it then proceeds to separate the crisis from earlier developments the more completely by following the course of events after Sarajevo solely with the aim of distributing responsibility for every act and every piece of indecision after having previously analysed the causes of the pre-war tension solely in terms of the given conditions, to the exclusion of the human contribution. For despite the statement that 'all the governments were responsible, in a greater or lesser degree', for the pre-1914 tension, this is Professor Schmitt's conclusion on the causes of that tension: 'The primary cause of the war was the conflict between political frontiers and the distribution of peoples, the denial of what is commonly called the right of self-determination. . . . In 1914, from the Rhine eastwards, political frontiers, as determined by the Congress of Vienna a century before and by the wars of the nineteenth century, everywhere cut across well-recognised lines of nationality. . . . More than any other circumstance, this conflict between existing governments and their unhappy minorities was responsible for the catastrophe of 1914. . . .'[2]

If these quotations illustrate what is still the current method of approach they also illustrate one of the reasons which have led historians to adopt it. There is loose thinking here—even among historians—about responsibility and our two levels of causation. How else could Professor Schmitt contrast, in the first of these passages, the statement that before 1914 all the governments were 'responsible in greater or lesser degree' with the statement that they were 'not equally responsible' in 1914 itself? How else could he in the second passage describe nationalist dissatisfaction as being both 'the primary cause of the war' and the chief 'circumstance' responsible for the catastrophe? But the main reasons for this first weakness lie in what we have called historiographical factors of which this pamphlet, coming at the end of a long series of studies, retains little obvious trace.

The Treaty of Versailles, which blamed Germany for the war, first set historians working to uphold or to discredit the 'war-guilt' clauses. It did this at a time when, with the same motives, governments were releasing far more evidence about the events and the decisions that followed Sarajevo than about the policies which preceded it. These considerations explain the concentration of historians on the study of the crisis and their preoccupation with responsibility which went with that concentration; for once a vein of historical enquiry has been opened up it is not easy to persuade people to stop working it in the fashion of their predecessors. This is illustrated by the perpetuation of the tradition among historians who have lost interest in defending or attacking the Versailles settlement. They are led to perpetuate it by their very desire for impartiality. So many charges and counter-charges have been made, they argue, about the Sarajevo crisis that we must investigate them; and since so much more is known about the crisis than about what went before it we must study the evidence on the crisis once again, by itself and on its merits: it is so complete that it can speak to us with an unequivocal voice.

This same desire for impartiality has also been partly responsible for the very different preoccupation with which historians have approached the problem of international developments before the crisis broke out. So much less was known about this, so many strident claims were advanced in connection with it which could easily be dismissed, that it seemed more scholarly to assume that the governments were not responsible—the more so as the growth of tension was clearly a complex development with complex causes. But this disposition was further encouraged by the spirit of the age. The generation between the two world wars was a period of tremendous progress in the study of and the knowledge of the material world. Among historians, as in politics, this progress had contradictory results. It encouraged the belief that men were free to do everything; and the belief that they were free in nothing they did.

It produced that curious frame of mind in which men even entertained both beliefs at the same time. In politics men asserted both that the war of 1914 had been generated by capitalism or by alliances, over which governments had had no control, and that war could easily be avoided in future if governments would only set up a League of Nations. Among historians it was not thought to be odd to believe that impersonal forces had produced the pre-Sarajevo tension while continuing to search the record of the crisis, for the reasons we have discussed, in the hope of finding the culprit who had caused the war.

The second weakness has followed from the first, and its consequences have been far more serious. The first, indeed, might have had no serious consequences, despite the inconsistency and the lack of logic it contains, if it had not led to the second. Confusion and unnecessary controversy would not have followed from approaching the Sarajevo crisis and its antecedents in the different ways we have discussed if the preoccupations underlying these different approaches had not been so strong as also make historians insensitive to evidence. For this second weakness is the fact that they have clung to these different approaches, to the crisis itself on the one hand and to its antecedents on the other, in the face of all the evidence, including the evidence of their common-sense. For if one thing is clear from an impartial view of the problem it is that men and governments lost control of the situation from the time of the Sarajevo assassination after always retaining room for manœuvre up to that point. There is this justification for insulating the study of the final crisis from all that went before. There is no justification whatever for insulating it in the way in which it has been insulated.

So far as the Sarajevo crisis itself is concerned, this would have been recognised long ago if it had not been for the historiographical considerations underlying the first weakness we have discussed, and if that first weakness had not produced the second. For every historian who has concluded since the 1920's that the German government was the most culpable, after the crisis began, another has concluded on the basis of the same evidence that it was not the most culpable—that Austria or Russia or France or Great Britain, or even Serbia, must be accorded that unenviable distinction; or that it must be accorded to some one or other combination of these

Powers; or that the Powers were all equally responsible. Nor have these divisions of opinion fallen along the lines of political allegiance. German historians have opted for Germany's chief responsibility; British historians for Sir Edward Grey's. American and presumably, therefore, impartial verdicts have been divided equally between those which have censured the Triple Alliance and those which have censured the Triple Entente. What must we think, when the evidence is so complete and when it has all been sifted so carefully, of these varying conclusions? No one who has both studied the evidence and, at the same time, tried to cast aside the historiographical blinkers through which it has hitherto been viewed, can doubt what the answer is.

It is not the answer provided by Professor Schmitt in his pamphlet. He concluded in an earlier book that in this final crisis it was primarily the decisions of the German government that led to a general war; he sees no reason for changing this opinion in his latest statement—which emphasises the German government's approval on 5 July 1914 of Austria's plan for the 'isolation and diminution' or 'elimination' of Serbia; its pressure on Austria on 28–29 July, after Serbia's acceptance of the Austrian ultimatum, for immediate military action against Serbia; its rejection on 30 July of British proposals for the opening of negotiations; its insistence on Austrian general mobilisation, which was ordered on the same day as the Russian mobilisation but before the news of Russia's mobilisation had been received; its declaration of war on France on 3 August. He is not alone in reaching this conclusion and in emphasising these grounds for it. Most studies published since the second World War take the same view.[3] But he is quick to add that, if Germany was primarily to blame, there were weighty mitigating circumstances which explain her conduct. The German government had legitimate fears for the future of Austria-Hungary. The Russian government's decision to order general mobilisation, taken on 30 July, was taken with the knowledge that it would lead to German mobilisation (so that in one sense Russia 'willed' the war). Germany was faced with the Franco-Russian alliance and tied by it to the Schlieffen plan, which aimed at the rapid defeat of France.

By emphasising these mitigating circumstances he comes close to cancelling out his own conclusion—so close, indeed, that, after first singling out the German government as being mainly responsible for the general war, he then regrets that the Russian mobilisation was premature and finally says that 'as soon as one Power, in order to reinforce its diplomacy, began to mobilise, its action made military men everywhere jittery, for no general staff was willing to allow a rival to get a start. "Once the dice were set rolling", as the German Chancellor said, "nothing could stop them."[4] Nor is he alone in making this kind of attempt to straddle all the evidence. If most historians since 1945 have concluded that Germany was mainly responsible for the turn of the crisis, most of them have similarly dwelt on these mitigating circumstances. What a pity that they have not gone further still—as far as the evidence was trying to force them to go.

If they had done so they would have recognised that the dice had been set rolling for all the Powers well before Russia mobilised —and not by decisions by any of the Powers but by a Balkan assassination. They would have seen that what makes some governments appear more responsible than others, or some governments more responsible at some stages and other governments more responsible at others, is not the fact that some governments were more instrumental than others in affecting the course of events. It is the fact that the positions of the different governments varied with the course of events over which they had lost control. They would have recognised that, although it is theoretically possible to say that war would have been avoided if this or that government had acted otherwise, it was not practicably possible for them to have acted otherwise. All the evidence goes to show that the beginning of this crisis, which has been studied so largely with a view to discovering and distributing human responsibility, was one of those moments in history when events passed beyond men's control. And this is why studies of the crisis have increasingly concluded that no one government was primarily responsible for the turn of events; and why, with historians increasingly aware of the truth to this extent, their attempts to arrange degrees of responsibility among the various governments in a precise order of merit and demerit will always be arid and inconclusive.

It is all the more surprising that historians have resisted this conclusion on the crisis of July 1914 when one considers their attempts to explain the increasing international tension which preceded it.

Their work on the antecedents of the Sarajevo crisis is almost as much in need of revision as their work on the crisis itself, though in an opposite direction. In this field they have over-emphasised the importance of impersonal forces and underrated the importance of the element of human responsibility.

If it is clear that events at last escaped the control of the governments in July 1914 it is also clear that well before that date the governments were being faced by growing problems as a result of changes that were by no means of their making. No analysis of the antecedents of the Sarajevo crisis would be convincing which ignored this fact. But it is equally clear that until the state of tension between the Great Powers interlocked with the Balkan situation, creating a drift of events which none could control, the influence of deliberate government policies and actions was no less instrumental in causing the increasing tension. The task of studying the interplay between these growing problems and these deliberate policies is no doubt immensely difficult. It is still the case that it has not been successfully undertaken.

Historians have not generally adopted in relation to this task the unrealistic attitude which has governed their approach to the Sarajevo crisis. They have not been wholly concerned to demonstrate that it was primarily the Kaiser or some other person, or primarily this or that government, which caused the growth of tension, but have recognised that impersonal forces must be allowed some weight. In allowing for impersonal forces they have not generally reached the kind of elementary conclusion that we discussed to begin with. Realising that such things were merely the given conditions in which war broke out and by which it was at the most made possible—and that these given conditions are compatible with peace as well as with war—they have not decided that the war was caused by capitalism or by the existence of sovereign states. But they have failed on the whole to provide interpretations which convincingly amalgamate the two factors, the impersonal forces and the human contribution; and they have usually failed from allowing too small a role to that human contribution which, in their study of the final crisis, they have been only too ready to regard as crucial.

The failure is reflected in the choice they have made when deciding which of the impersonal forces that were at work must be regarded as having been most powerful and influential. If they have distinguished between impersonal forces and static given conditions—and refused to take account of static given conditions: the existence of the state and of capitalism—the dynamic impersonal forces which they have chosen to emphasise have sometimes revealed a misunderstanding of the nature of the growing tension between states between 1900 and 1914 which forms the heart of the pre-Sarajevo situation and constitutes one of the basic causes of the war. This tension was the result of increasing suspicion and rivalry between the Great Powers. It can be satisfactorily accounted for in terms of impersonal forces only by emphasising such impersonal forces as directly contributed to increase that suspicion and rivalry. But such developments as dissatisfied nationalism, 'the conflict between existing governments and their unhappy minorities' which Professor Schmitt has selected as the primary cause of the tension, were of little significance by this test. What is true of nationalism is also true of the hastening of the collapse of Turkish power, which was in part another manifestation of that same dissatisfaction and which has also often been urged as crucial; of the increasing hatred of the German for the Slav; of the French determination to regain Alsace-Lorraine—other forces which have not been without their advocates. These factors not only did not contribute directly to the growing rivalry; they acquired increasing importance after the end of the nineteenth century, and thus contributed indirectly to the atmosphere of growing suspicion, solely because the rivalry of the Powers was mounting—and mounting for other reasons.

How else shall we explain why dissatisfied nationalism of equal intensity and on a wider scale did not produce a general war in the generation which ended in 1871, but was on the contrary most deliberately restrained by governments? And if this dissatisfaction was so acute and so destructive of the freedom of governments after 1900, as Professor Schmitt believes, how does he account for the conflict between that fact and other facts to which he draws our attention—that the war broke out 'suddenly and unexpectedly'; that 'the possibility of a general war seemed increasingly remote, at least to the man in the street'; that 'only a few people in any country were psychologically prepared for the catastrophe'?[5] We cannot explain these things—or the fact that Europe had previously lived through a generation of Turkish decline, and through a still longer period of distrust of the Slav, without catastrophe; or the fact that the Powers had in the twenty years before 1900 accomplished such things as the partition of Africa without a war; or the fact that the French demand for revenge and for Alsace-Lorraine had steadily declined, without being extinguished, in the years up to 1900—unless we suppose that if impersonal forces of this kind became important after 1900 it was as a result of other developments and changes which were more directly affecting the structure of relations between the Powers and which were more directly instrumental in increasing the international tension.

Of those developments some were certainly of the nature of impersonal forces; and most certainly was this the case with those which are the most relevant. After a further generation of slow change the redistribution of relative power as between the world's leading states, which had produced forcible but limited adjustments in the middle years of the nineteenth century, was from about the end of that century still more decisively—and at last obviously—shifting these states away from the rough equality of strength which had prevailed among them since the days of the first Napoleon. Those earlier, limited adjustments had been confined to Europe—even to Western Europe. In the further redistribution of power that was becoming obvious from about the 1890's another new factor was equally obviously involved: the emergence of new Great Powers beyond Europe as a result of the spread of industrialisation, the development of modern armies and navies and the increase of wealth and population in the United States and Japan—factors which had expressed themselves in the territorial expansion of those states since the 1860's. The rise and expansion of these new Powers was one aspect of the reduction that was taking place in world distances, which was also reflected in the greater involvement of the European Powers in developments beyond Europe. But it was also the expression of another vast development from the influence of which the European Powers themselves were not immune.

The growth of centralised, highly competent state machines, with greatly increased efficiency in tapping and regulating the resources of their societies and with more cohesive bonds between themselves and their populations, had been taking place for a generation wherever industrial and technological advance had rendered it possible. It was a development which now began to accentuate the emerging disparity of international power. Taking place, as it did, at different speeds according to the different stages of industrial development in different societies, its different extent in the different states in one sense merely registered the discrepancy in power that was establishing itself between them. But in proportion as it went to greater lengths in some states than in others it also exercised its own autonomous influence in driving some of the Powers to a still greater degree of primacy over the others—if only temporarily.

It was on these foundations, at a time when the older European structure of power was being incorporated in a wider world structure but had not yet been wholly incorporated, when more modern criteria of state power were establishing themselves but establishing themselves unevenly and to different degrees even among the leading states, that Germany, especially, after 1900 moved into a new and difficult position. She at last approached a degree of material primacy in Europe which no Power had possessed since 1815—and did so at a time when her power beyond Europe was negligible and when the prospects of enlarging it there were rapidly diminishing. She also acquired a superiority in technical organisation over all other states—but did so at a time when some other states were beginning to move rapidly towards the degree of organisation she had achieved. Already in 1870 Germany was stronger than France (with 37 million tons of coal per annum compared with 16 million tons in France; 2 million tons of pig iron compared with 1½ million tons) and stronger still compared with Austria, Italy or Russia. Her victory over France increased her lead, especially in the coal and the metallurgical industries with the transfer of Lorraine. After 1871 she had forged steadily ahead of France and the other continental Powers but had not passed beyond the resources of a combination of some of those Powers. After the end of depression conditions in 1895–6, however, she was rapidly increasing her lead in industrial production over every other European state except Great Britain, with whom she was rapidly drawing level. In some important respects she also had a lead over Great Britain by 1900. In steel production, for example, while the United States replaced Great Britain as the world's greatest producer by the mid-1880's, Germany had taken second place by 1900, when the United States had one quarter of the world's production, Germany a fifth and Great Britain less than a sixth. Germany produced 7·4 million tons, Great Britain 6 million. France, by contrast, produced 1·9 million tons. At the same time Germany's population surpassed that of every European state except Russia. On the other hand, while her population stood at 56 millions and her birth-rate, like that of most of Western Europe, was beginning to fall, the most significant changes in population since the 1870's were those which had raised Russia from 72 to 116 millions and brought the United States to nearly 80 millions. More significant still, it was from the end of the 1890's that Russia, although still underdeveloped in this direction, and the United States, after relatively slow advance hitherto, began to experience—and to be known to be experiencing—that rate of industrial and technological growth which Great Britain had undergone earlier in the nineteenth century and which Germany had experienced for the past forty years. It was from the same date, moreover, that these facts, and the somewhat less prominent development of Japan, began to express themselves more noticeably than hitherto in the territorial and strategic assertion of these Powers beyond their borders, especially in the Far East.

It requires no great stretch of the imagination to realise that these signs of the displacement of an older structure of power by a new one between the leading states exerted a powerful effect upon the policies of all those states. The displacement would have had this effect if the signs had gone unnoticed. It had it the more decisively because it was taking place at a time when, under the influence of the scientific and industrial revolutions, men were beginning to apply Darwinism to politics and to contemplate power, and particularly international power, in geo-political terms. The twenty years before the outbreak of the first World War witnessed the first great blossoming of geo-political studies, especially in Germany but also, under German influence, elsewhere. If only for this reason, the signs were noticed—not to say exaggerated—at the time. And ever since, if only for the same reason, there has been no lack of commentators who have recognised that in this displacement is to be found the clue to those impersonal forces which most directly underlay the growing instability and tension between the Great Powers in the years between 1900 and 1914. But if the fault of some historians is that they have not recognised this, the fault of those who have recognised it lies in the fact that, being geo-politically inclined, they have generally regarded it as being in itself the sufficient cause of the war.

They have argued that since, to quote Sir Halford MacKinder, an early British geo-politician, 'there is in nature no such thing as equality of opportunity for the nations',[6] the displacement of the old structure of power was but the inevitable result of the unequal distribution of changing resources and opportunities over the face of the globe—and that the war was the inevitable result of the displacement. It was inevitable that some states would attack the *status quo* and that others would defend the *status quo* against those to whose advantage it was changing. The war was the result of the rise of a powerful, unified Germany, whose history and geographical position invited her to contemplate the domination of Europe—and especially, at a time when the Turkish Empire was collapsing and the Habsburg Empire was threatened with disintegration by Balkan nationalism, of Eastern Europe; of the fact that the new German momentum necessarily generated a Russo-German struggle for the Turkish and Habsburg lands and cut across the traditional interests and positions of Great Britain and France; of the fact that these other states necessarily retaliated against the German drive. It is an attractive theory, not least because no shift in international relative power comparable to that which was coming to a head in the years before 1914 has ever yet been completed without generating international suspicion and ending in the resort to international war.

Yet it is incomplete and unsatisfactory because it takes no account of the element of design—of deliberate policy and human responsibility. If international unbalance on this scale has always ended in international war, that is because this element of will and of deliberate policy had always also been present. The impersonal forces which produced the unbalance were on every occasion not the cause of the resulting war, any more than static given conditions like the sovereign state or capitalism were the causes of the resulting war. They constituted, rather, a challenge to statesmanship—a challenge that was greater and more difficult to meet than the challenge set up by static conditions but a challenge nevertheless; and a challenge that statesmen failed to meet. This is as true of the period before 1914 as it is of every comparable period in history. It may even be said that historians recognise it to be true of most of the occasions which confront them with the problem of the interplay on this scale of the impersonal forces and the human element, and that it is only for special reasons that they have been slow to recognise its truth for the years preceding the first World War.

The First World War

Students of Napoleon's wars, or of Louis XIV's or Bismarck's, must battle against an accumulation of contemporary opinion and of earlier research which did not commit this mistake before they can commit it themselves. Those who study the origins of the second World War are brought up against the formidable obstacle, salutary in this context, of Adolf Hitler. The origins of the first World War were considered in a deterministic frame of mind from the outset and were even seen in this way by some contemporaries—and although the mistaken approach is now being adopted in the study of earlier conflicts, the first World War was the first war, and the last, of which this has been so. To this situation there were soon added the special circumstances of the inter-war years. Other contemporaries would have liked to hang the Kaiser, and their crude conclusions were easy to dismiss. The 'war-guilt' clauses quickly earned for the Treaty of Versailles a reputation for injustice. By way of reaction against the political verdict that Germany was responsible for causing the war, these circumstances reinforced the other in producing the widespread consensus that nobody was responsible for causing it. It was not with the Sarajevo crisis in mind, to which it could with justice have been applied, but with reference to the pre-Sarajevo tension that one historian summed up this consensus in 1946 with the statement that 'all historians who have examined the evidence in detail are agreed that the responsibility for the outbreak of war in 1914 cannot be placed exclusively on the shoulders of any one government: there was none that was not willing at that stage to use war in the last resort as an instrument of national policy'.[7] And it is not insignificant—and it is also heartening—that the pioneer efforts made since then to move beyond this stage to a more realistic interpretation of the origins of the war have been made by German historians.

It has not been the object of these German writers to show that any one government was exclusively responsible for the growth of tension before 1914. They recognise that they are dealing with a structure of Great Powers, not with a choir of recording angels. They have not been deflected by the fact that all the Great Powers in the years before 1914 were prepared to use war as an instrument of national policy; they know that in the last resort all Great Powers always are so prepared—and also that in 1914 all the Powers were reluctant to go to war. What they have realised is that, while responsibility cannot be ignored, degrees of responsibility are the most that we can reasonably hope to establish; and that the relevant test is not to be found in readiness or reluctance to go to war but in the aims of the various national policies which the various Powers were prepared to pursue to the lengths of war if that was necessary. And what they have concluded is what must be concluded by anyone who approaches the evidence with these considerations in mind. The German government was primarily responsible for the pre-war tension—and was far more responsible for the war because of the decisions it took between 1904 and 1913 than on account of anything it did after the Sarajevo murder—in consequence of the aims of its policy.

Most historians recognised long ago that German policy after about 1900 was clumsy and erratic in its nature. Some have long realised that it was not clumsy and erratic simply because Germany was a late-comer on the stage of Great Power politics—for they have recalled that Germany as a Great Power was but Prussia writ large and that under Bismarck she had displayed at least as much competence and finesse as any other state—or simply in consequence of the growing instability of the international scene in the years after Bismarck's retirement—for they have noticed that it was more clumsy and erratic than the policy of other states which were faced by the same instability. They have noticed, indeed, that it was inspired by a wilfulness and desperation which were not exhibited elsewhere, except possibly by Austria-Hungary at a later stage and on a much more localised scale, and which slowly destroyed the German government's ability to distinguish between the search for security and the search for domination.[8] Professor Ludwig Dehio has simply taken the evidence to its correct and logical conclusion by showing that the key to the clumsiness is that the German government, conscious now of German superior power, had, like Philip II or Louis XIV or Napoleon I before it, determined to exercise and to extend it as a domination.

After 1900, his argument runs, 'Germany was essentially different from her fellows in the family of nations' and different in the sense that 'many of the characteristics which . . . impress us as specifically German, have appeared . . . among earlier supreme Powers'—indeed, are 'typical of all supreme Powers'. If its policy differed in character from those of other Powers after 1900 it was for the reason that 'the period during which German history was purely continental ended abruptly at the beginning of the present century'. 'Just as Prussia had once broken into the ranks of the great European Powers, so did we Germans hope to break out of the narrow confines of Europe and join the ranks of the World Powers, and we tried to do so by typically Prussian methods: that is by systematic arming— in this case naval arming. But this was impossible without, as it were, forcing the European system into retirement. Nor was it possible without forcing Britain into retirement—without forcing her out of her role of guarantor of the existing balance of power in Europe and out of her position of maritime supremacy in the world beyond. What was the inevitable result of our efforts? We found ourselves embarked on the road to World War.'[9]

It is an argument which takes on some of the overtones of the geo-political and determinist interpretations which we have been discussing. 'The central factor in all the struggles for European hegemony . . . is the conflict which develops each time between the strongest Pqwer on the old continent . . . and the reigning maritime Power.' 'Since the supreme Power stands in the solitude of its supremacy it must face daemonic temptations of a special kind.'[10] Professor Dehio uses not only the pressure of impersonal factors but also the policies of other Powers to explain German policy and perhaps to excuse Germany's behaviour. 'The fact that the war assumed the classic form of a struggle for European hegemony was due to the reaction of Great Britain.' 'The traditional European balance of power . . . we regarded as almost obsolete because of the position of semi-supremacy occupied on the continent by Bismarck's Reich. By her policy of encirclement England gradually forced us into the isolated position of a potential aspirant for European hegemony in the full sense of the term. At the same time the aim of German imperialism was still to become one of the circle of World Powers, without necessarily destroying English maritime supremacy. Thus each of the rivals was fighting against the position of hegemony occupied by the other and appealing for a balance of power; but each attached a totally different sense to the terms hegemony and balance of power.'[11] No one seeking a rounded and satisfying reconstruction of the history of the pre-war years would wish, however, to exclude these elements; and Professor Dehio's reconstruction is convincing because it includes them—and also, with less justification, Germany's youthful exuberance—without obscuring the crucial importance of Germany's conscious and deliberate aims.

He is reluctant to conclude that these caused the war: 'let us ask ourselves not what caused the first World War, but what made it possible.' But his answer to this question is that 'as a World War it was undoubtedly the expansionist pressure of the rejuvenated German nation that made it possible'—and that the pressure was deliberately applied in the shape of policy. 'We turned our uncertain gaze on the wide world but instead of keeping our eyes firmly on the acquisition of particular territories, we gambled on general changes in the entire *status quo* at the expense of our rival.' 'Even before 1914 the pressure of encirclement made us doubt whether the optimistic calculations we had made at the turn of the century would prove right. . . . But the decisive fact is that, in our youthful exuberance, we failed to draw the logical conclusions. . . . In 1913 Plehn could write: "It is an almost universal belief throughout the country that we shall only win our freedom to participate in world politics through a major European war." '[12] What he says about the opinions of German historians between 1900 and 1914 reinforces the point. On Dehio's evidence the mistake they made in assuming that the European balance was becoming a world balance, in which Germany would automatically achieve a world position, was not, as has been claimed, that they failed to see that 'the focus was moving away from Europe and that what happened in Europe was no longer decisive'.[13] It was that they all argued—if they did not all believe—that while 'it must be Germany's task in history to transform the balance of power in Europe into a balance embracing the whole world', Germany would accomplish the task without force and without attempting to conquer Europe—which still remained decisive.[14] The German government saw things differently; and if the focus has since moved away from Europe that is due to its attempt to conquer Europe as much as it is due to anything else.

Any doubts that may remain about the attitude of the government have been removed by Professor Fritz Fischer's still more recent study of the war aims of Imperial Germany. In a comprehensive and dispassionate survey of all the evidence, this has established, in a way that is unlikely to be seriously challenged, that it was the aim of the German government to break through to the position of a World Power by setting up an empire based on Europe to equal the developing world empires of Russia and the United States. It has shown that this aim received its detailed elaboration only during the war itself, when, in addition to envisaging Belgium, Poland, Finland, Roumania, the Ukraine and the Baltic region as far as Esthonia as German buffer states, it encompassed in the west the annexation of parts of Belgium, sections of French frontier territory and Luxembourg; in the east the incorporation of a strip of Poland and of Lithuania and Courland; in central Europe the union of Austria-Hungary to Germany; and the annexation of considerable areas of south-eastern Europe. In a few quarters the significance of these facts about the war-time programme, and of the fact that the German government recognised the programme to be incompatible with the continued acceptance of the British position in the world and sought domination in Europe as a means of destroying that position, has been appreciated for a very long time.[15] But preoccupation with guilt and recrimination has hitherto led historians to argue either that the facts are so monstrous as to be fictitious or so monstrous as to be explicable only as the outcome of war-time fever and excess. Professor Fischer avoids this preoccupation. Like Professor Dehio, he recognises that they were the logical historical outcome of Germany's pre-war aims, as those aims were at least an understandable outcome of Germany's position and power within the pre-war international system.[16]

Since 1871, despite her lead over some of the Powers in some directions, she had been concerned with retaining the new position she had recently acquired, and with the dangers to it. Beginning in the late 1890's her policy acquired an unstable quality because she began both to reflect on her existing degree of primacy and to fear that, in the light of the rise of the United States and Russia, the time might be limited in which she could use it. Her growing relative power would itself have provoked the fears and the retaliation of the other Powers in due course; but what in fact provoked those fears and that retaliation from the early 1900's was the policy she pursued. The other Powers would have feared that policy even if they had been wrong in their suspicions of the aims which underlay it; but war would not necessarily have resulted. In fact they suspected those aims with good cause. It is time that we became prepared to face this explanation of the first World War and to recognise that, in so far as we still need to allot responsibility as well as to explain, the best defence of Germany is not to deny or to overlook that she had these aims, but to ask in what respect her conduct differed from that which it has been customary for Great Powers to pursue in circumstances comparable to those which existed when she entertained them.

To this question the voice of history answers with less certainty— and somewhat less unequivocally than Professor Dehio would have us believe. Germany's policy did indeed exhibit the characteristics which had been typical of all her predecessors in the role of supreme Powers. Modern history has indeed recorded Spanish, Habsburg, French and English eras of aggression, as well as a German era of aggression, against the existing system of relations between states, as it has recorded almost continuous expansion, Russian and American as well as Western European, into no-man's-lands where no such system prevailed. But it also reveals that the system of relations between states has been continuously evolving and expanding; that the standards of international behaviour have been evolving and hardening with it; that what is understandable to historians and was also acceptable to contemporaries in the conduct of Louis XIV or even of Napoleon may still be understandable to historians but was not acceptable to contemporaries in the case of Germany in the years before 1914. It is arguable that the German conduct, however understandable in view of the increasing difficulties of the times, should be regarded even by historians as constituting a regrettable departure from the standards of international behaviour which men had developed over a century. This, at any rate, seems the probable reason why the German historians of the days before the outbreak of the war of 1914 would not frankly face up to the logic of their own arguments or frankly contemplate where Germany was going—and with her the international system.

CHAPTER 14

THE FAILURE OF THE LEAGUE OF NATIONS

IT was a misfortune for the League of Nations that it was brought into existence in these conditions of unusual international instability. But this fact has also had an unfortunate effect on our investigations into the League's failure. Everything we know about the history and the nature of international relations goes to show that the League, as it was constructed, was bound to fail; and that it was bound to be constructed as it was constructed. But those who seek to explain its failure usually argue that the League was based on sound principles and failed only because it was unlucky or premature. Or because, though sound in conception, the principles behind it were faultily applied or inadequately applied.

The argument that it failed because it was ill-timed or unfortunate takes two forms. Some people argue that the founders of the League imagined that it would be working in a normal world. The world in which it had to work was abnormal and unstable. The drafters of the Covenant overlooked the rise of aggressor nations and failed to take into account that there would be so much war-weariness among the peaceful and progressive populations of the world. If only the world had been normal, this school of thought asserts, if only it had been less beset with problems, the League would have pulled through. It failed because of bad luck. Very similar is a variation on this theme: in spite of this instability, in spite of everything, the League nearly succeeded. If only France had been a little less unreasonable, if only Great Britain had been willing to give slightly firmer assurances of support to it, if only it had not treated the Weimar Republic so ungenerously to begin with, if only the United States had not deserted it, if only Russia had become a member earlier—if only Lord Cecil had been British Foreign Secretary instead of Lord Curzon—the League would have been a success.

The other attitude also maintains that the general conception of the League was sound enough but argues that errors were made in implementing it, from which errors the League was never able to shake itself free and on account of which it came to grief. Those who hold this view argue that the Covenant should never have been incorporated in the Treaty of Versailles: this associated the League with defeat and disillusionment in the minds of some peoples and with the maintenance of an unstable *status quo* in the minds of others. Or that it was a grave tactical error not to admit the defeated states at once and on an equal footing with the victor Powers. Alternatively, they attribute its failure to the fact that the principles underlying it were not sufficiently radically applied at the outset. It compromised too much with national sovereignties and other unpleasant facts of life. For example, its proceedings were subjected to the unanimity rule: this stultified all action by the League by ensuring that always, on every issue, there were some members who could block action against their interests. It failed only because, as a result of such compromises, the Covenant was not carried out by its members. The principles were not given a fair trial.

It may be objected that these explanations represent the untutored opinions of the ordinary public, not the considered verdict of students of international politics. In fact, the chief result of scholarship on the subject has been to produce not alternatives to these explanations but an amalgamation of them. Confidence in the League was shaken by unusual developments, 'by depression and aggression', after the Locarno period. Beginning with the Manchurian dispute it failed to handle really grave crises involving violence or threats of violence: these 'were the immediate causes of the League's collapse'. 'The failure of the League was due to many factors, of which the early loss of faith of the United States and the opposition of Germany and Russia, because of the conditions of the League's origin and its close relationship to the peace treaties, were of great importance. Without these influences the League's effort to solve the basic problems might have been successful.' Even so it could have done better if it had been provided with a better structure and better procedures—if, particularly, its Secretariat had been given the right of direct access to the public in all countries in the world; if it had made sanctions automatic or had in some other way been able to ensure that member states would fulfil their obligations towards collective security; if it had had a more certain procedure for dealing with political disputes and for introducing peaceful changes in the *status quo*. It was impossible, however, to improve its structure and procedures once they had been laid down: witness the controversy among member states whenever this was attempted. The League remained as it began, a League of governments and not of peoples. This on the whole is the mixed message of those who have studied the League of Nations.[1] It was not bad luck or bad management or a bad start or bad faith which killed the League, but all those things.

Now whether we take them separately or together, these explanations are inadequate. To argue that the League was unfortunate because the world was unexpectedly unstable when it was launched is wishful thinking. If we must wait for a 'normal' world before there can be a successful international political organisation, for a world in which there is no instability and no aggressor nation, it would never be possible to have one; and if there were no instability it would be unnecessary to have one. This argument overlooks, moreover, the fact that the League had failed in its real purpose before the aggressor nations had become aggressive and the serious problems of the inter-war years had come to a head. As for the accident theory, the argument that the League would have succeeded but for this or the other misfortune, we may confidently reply that, if these particular obstacles to success had not existed, others would have taken their place. The same applies to the structural and procedural criticism. If President Wilson had not resisted all attempts to separate the Covenant of the League from the Peace Treaties the Covenant might never have been accepted at all. The exclusion of the defeated Powers and the unanimity rule may have been unwise and may now be regretted; both of them were central to the ideology on which the League was based, as the exclusion of Russia and the retirement of the United States were central to world conditions at the time the League was launched. But perhaps the least satisfactory of all these explanations is the argument that the League failed because it was not upheld or was not sufficiently far-reaching and radical in conception. This is mere tautology. It tells us that the League failed because it failed when what we want to know is why it was not made more far-reaching than it was to begin with and why, created as it was, it was not upheld.

When we turn to these questions the first thing that becomes suspect is the one thing which these explanations have in common: the assumption that there was nothing impracticable about the ideas and the principles on which the League was based. It becomes doubly suspect when it is realised that these ideas and principles went back almost without change to the seventeenth century. In the second half of the twentieth century it cannot be too soon to insist that they ignore the existence of two sorts of obstacle to the establishment and successful operation of any international political organisation which has the objects which the League was intended to have and faces the problems which the League was bound to face.

The first set of obstacles are those which must be overcome before the organisation can even be established—the obstacles which explain why Europe was so long in giving Sully and Saint-Pierre a trial and why their ideas were inevitably given an incomplete first trial in the shape of the League of Nations. They may conveniently be introduced by a remark of one of the earliest protagonists of these ideas. 'To succeed in the execution of this plan', wrote Sully, 'will not appear difficult if we suppose that all the Christian Princes unanimously concurred in it.' Frederick the Great put his finger on them in a comment on Saint-Pierre's proposals. 'The thing is most practicable; for its success, all that is lacking is the consent of Europe and a few similar trifles.' The consent of Europe has come to mean more since the eighteenth century than the consent of princes. These obstacles have not in any way diminished on that account. Those who still belittle them usually assert that peoples may be trusted more than princes could ever be. The evidence is all against them. The most serious obstacle to the movement towards European unity in recent years has not been the reluctance of governments to embrace it—they are enthusiastic—but the opposition of interests and sentiments in the general populations. It must also be remembered that international organisation has come to require more than the consent of Christian Europe. If anything, a successful international organisation has become even more difficult to achieve in the twentieth century, in a world that comprises multifarious communities with disparate histories and at violently different stages of growth, than it was when men who had at least some justification for believing in the unity of Christian Europe first propounded the ideas on which the effort continues to be based.

It was because of these initial obstacles that the League could not but be a loose structure when it was established. Clearly, for example, it could not be a federation. Men sometimes argue that the process of welding states together was successfully carried out in the eighteenth century by the founders of the United States, and that what was done by the Founding Fathers could surely have been achieved by Europe or by the whole world in 1918, when the world's technological distances had been reduced to something like eighteenth-century American proportions. What strikes the historian is not the closeness of the parallel but the immensity of the differences. The American colonies were homogeneous in language, descent, traditions, laws, institutions—in everything, not excluding the lack of separate, strong, historical, unified political structures—as the nations of Europe in 1918, let alone many of the different parts of the world, were not. Throughout their history they had been administered as part of a single empire, an experience which most countries of the world have never had and which others have not had since the fall of Rome. Nor is this all. Most internationalists recognise these differences, and we need not disagree when they argue that, nevertheless, the existing divisions of Europe or the world could have been surmounted if the interest and the will to overcome them had been sufficiently strong. The real differences between the American situation—or the German experience—in the past and the twentieth-century situation and experience on a wider scale are to be found in this field of interest and will. Even if the will to federation had existed it would still be doubtful, in actual fact, whether men could have set up a federal organisation in 1918. It is still doubtful whether Europe can federate today when the interest and will have to some extent come to exist. Frustrated by difficulties and delays, integrationists now talk of achieving Europe federation by stages; this is so close to being a contradiction in terms that, whatever will be achieved in Europe, it is unlikely to be political federation. It is not the evidence of history that where there is a will there is always a way. But with regard to the League we need not insist on these points. In 1918 the interest in and the will to federation were absent. Men sought, as a result of the crisis through which they had recently passed, a new departure in international relations. But what they sought was, as a result of all their history, a league of governments and not a merger of peoples—a confederal League.

Now a confederation was less difficult to establish than a federation would have been. The confederal system is that which compromises most with the stubborn initial obstacles to organisation that we are discussing. It is precisely for the same reason, on the other hand, that if any political system is more difficult than a federation to operate and maintain, it is a confederal system. There is no case known to history in which such a system has not been forced either into a unitary framework or, more frequently, into disintegration and collapse. Even in the United States the Founding Fathers did not conceive of themselves as establishing the world's first modern federation. They set up a confederation which was slowly forced to become a centralist federation in order to avoid collapse. Because it compromised with these obstacles in order to get established at all the League could not be so radical and far reaching in its powers and functions as some people now wish it had been. Safeguards had to be accepted in the interests of its sovereign member states; loopholes had to be left by which they could retain their freedom of action.

In arranging for the settlement of disputes the Covenant took over existing ideas on arbitration and judicial settlement. Only disputes which the disputing parties agreed to be susceptible to these processes—only legal disputes—were to be subjected to them (Article 13); and states covenanted only to accept awards handed down (Article 13) and only to refrain from going to war against a non-complying state for three months after the award or the decision had been handed down (Article 12). The Covenant supplemented these processes of settlement by providing that political disputes, disputes not susceptible to these legal processes, might be referred to enquiry by the Council of the League (Article 12). But in such cases it also adopted the qualification that had accompanied the development of arbitration: the Council could not make recommendations in matters that fell within a state's domestic jurisdiction (Article 15). In such cases as still qualified for submission to this procedure of conciliation by the League, moreover, the parties were not bound to accept the League's recommendation: if the recommendation was unanimous, they agreed only not to go to war; failing unanimity, they agreed only to accept the three month's moratorium laid down in Article 12 before attacking a non-complying state. It was the same with a further Article, Article 19. This empowered the Assembly of the League to advise the reconsideration of treaties and conditions which, though legally in force, had come to endanger peace on account of the passage of time, and to make recommendations for revision. But the recommendations had to be unanimous; and they were not binding on the members. Things could have been otherwise only if the League Assembly had been a true legislature superior to the member states.

Even more than the exclusion of disputes involving the domestic jurisdiction of states, the need for unanimity (disputants excepted) was a serious restriction on the efficiency of the League in the settlement of disputes. It was on its account that Article 19 was scarcely ever resorted to—and not once after 1929. It was known in advance that the veto of some member would always block action by this method. For the same reason the League could not successfully deal with most of the disputes that were referred to it. In all its history it was seized of sixty-six international disputes under Articles of the Covenant or of special treaties between member states. It failed to settle eleven of them, and these the most serious. It transferred twenty to the channels of ordinary diplomacy—the good offices of states, councils of ambassadors, special conferences. It dealt successfully with the remaining thirty-five. But only four of these—the Albanian frontier dispute between Albania, Yugoslavia and Greece in 1921–4; the Mosul dispute between Great Britain, Iraq and Turkey in 1924–6; the Demir Kapu incident between Bulgaria and Greece in 1925–6; and the Leticia incident between Columbia and Peru in 1932–5—involved hostilities; and it may be said with complete confidence that these would have been settled in much the same way, with much the same resort to and abstention from hostilities, if the League had never existed.

It has been concluded from this record that 'the League's experience indicates the extreme difficulty of dealing with serious political disputes without more authority than the League possessed'.[2] This is not to be quarrelled with. But the lesson to be learned from the record is not that the League could have avoided these weaknesses by being given more authority. It is that it could not have avoided them because it could not have been given more authority. The League of Nations provided men with their first experience in practice—but not with their last—of one of the real dilemmas facing an international experiment in the field of politics. All thought and effort along this approach must either deny that the merging, even partially, of separate sovereignties presents any serious difficulty, in which case it makes no headway against these stubborn initial obstacles, or it must recognise those obstacles and compromise with them, in which case it necessarily falls short from the outset of achieving the minimum of central authority that is indispensable for success.

Nor is this the sole dilemma. We have so far been concerned with the way in which the founders of the League compromised with the difficulties arising from the existence of separate states. But the Covenant ignored those difficulties in some Articles while necessarily admitting them in others. The collapse of the League, as opposed to the limited effectiveness that followed from the restrictions so far discussed, arose from the further obligations that were incorporated in Articles we have still to consider—from the fact that in them an attempt was made to make the League more radical than the initial obstacles would allow. These bring us to the second kind of obstacle that faced the League.

One of these further Articles (Article 16) provided for the punishment, in the precise form of automatic economic sanctions, of any resort to war by a member state in defiance of Articles 12, 13 or 15. It also laid down that violation of any other part of the Covenant would be punished by expulsion from the League. In Article 10, which contained the other major obligation, members undertook to preserve as against external aggression the territorial integrity and political independence of all member states. If these obligations had been upheld by its members—this is the second kind of obstacle to international organisation—the League would not have eliminated war and struggle in international relations, whatever else it might have achieved. It would have produced, on the contrary, an intensification of struggle and an extension of war. It would have had this result because it would have created a heavily armed world that was always ready and frequently required to crush resistance either against an established order that was unsatisfactory to some states or against changes to an established order that would have been unwelcome to others. And it would have produced such a world as a logical consequence of the central ideas on which these obligations were based.

The basic structure of this part of the Covenant was not that all war was immoral and that all change was to be avoided. Sanctions and force were directed under Article 16 against wars entered into in circumstances where an honourable settlement was deemed to be possible by peaceful means—against a state which made war in defiance of conciliation procedure (Article 12) or which attacked another state that had complied with a League award (Article 13) or with a unaminous Council recommendation (Article 15). The Covenant did not illegalise other wars and it did not visit them with sanctions. In the same spirit it offset Article 10 by Article 19, recognising by the establishment of this procedure for arranging for peaceful changes to the *status quo* that altered circumstances might constitute some justification for war if conditions were not adjusted by agreement. It was based, indeed, on notions that were similar to the medieval distinction between just and unjust wars; and against unjust war—against wars conducted in contravention of Articles 12, 13 and 15, and by states which would not attempt to secure peaceful change or which would not accept it—it took its stand on the arguments that such war was unlawful, the state which started it a law-breaker, and that such states were not to be tolerated in the civilised world of the twentieth century. Neutrality was not to be allowed in such cases. 'Nobody', declared President Wilson, 'can hereafter be neutral as respect the disturbance of the world's peace for an object which the world's opinion cannot sanction.'

Unfortunately this ideology was easier to state than to apply. In the first place it contradicted another deeply held sentiment that found expression in the establishment of the League. From the beginning there were those who supported the League because it was founded to preserve the peace and those who supported it by insisting that it could only be upheld if it was prepared to resort to war against unjust war. For a time, indeed, this issue was confused by the belief that war would not be necessary against the law-breaker—that measures short of war, such as economic sanctions and world opinion, would be sufficient check; and this enabled the League to be supported by the same people on both grounds at the same time. But before very long a yet more serious problem had arisen—a problem that was only briefly obscured by the belief that it would not be difficult to settle political disputes and to introduce changes to the *status quo* by inquiry and debate. When it was discovered that this belief was fallacious and that the need for the resort to force would be frequent and not rare—and when it also emerged that, despite the hope that economic sanctions and public opinion would be adequate deterrents, the force required might be force to the lengths of war—

the League was doomed by the determination of its members to evade these obligations which bound them to resort to war.

There are people who think that this belief was discovered to be merely temporarily inapplicable in the conditions that prevailed after 1918. This would be enough to explain why the League failed. But if we are to understand what the League would have become if it had succeeded we must recognise the permanence of the fallacy. The dilemma confronting all hopes of peaceful international change and settlement is that there can be no change and no settlement, not even peacefully, so long as struggle is avoided. You may count on the fingers of one hand the occasions on which agreements have been made and changes of sovereignty or transfers of territory have occurred in the modern world without the assistance of the possibility of a resort to force, if not of force itself. It is the possibility that force will be used, when it is not actual force, that alone makes agreements and changes possible—and that alone can stop them.

It was in this way that, if the League had been upheld by its members, it would have had to become an enforcement machine. It would have had to be constantly ready to use its force against aggression—to prevent undesirable changes. It would have had to be equally prepared to use its force to anticipate aggression—to secure acceptance of those changes that are desirable or at least inescapable in the relative power and pretensions of states. In order to overcome the problem of divided views and divided interests it would have had to abandon majority decision or the principle of unanimity in the assembly room for the centralisation of authority in an executive. It could not have failed to be regarded by an increasing number of states in something like the light in which the United Nations has come to be seen by the Congolese; and since internal war and revolution have been at least as frequent in history as international war, it would still have collapsed if it had developed in this way. It is not for nothing that the men in history who have come nearest to success in establishing an international order have been men like Alexander, Caesar, Charlemagne, Napoleon and Hitler. Or that their realms have not been so very extensive. Or that not even they have been able to maintain them for long.

But it was precisely because it would have developed in this way if it had been upheld that it collapsed from not being upheld. Although the successful operation of the League would have had such results, there never was any possibility that it would be successful because of the conjunction of the two sets of problems, the two kinds of obstacles, that we have been discussing.

When it was found that the League was not able to settle international political conflicts and achieve international change by negotiation and amicable agreement the members of the League were thrown back upon the other belief and faced with its logical consequences—the obligation to use force to bring about change and to resort to war to maintain peace. Since this obligation placed an unwelcome and intolerably onerous burden upon them and since the members were, inevitably, independent states, they evaded it. Obligations deriving from a state's consent do not impair its sovereignty. What a sovereign state has conceded a sovereign state can, if it wishes, revoke.

Even before Article 19 had been proved in practice to be inoperable, even before the League had failed under the other articles of the Covenant to settle a serious political crisis by peaceful means, even before discontented states had accordingly been incited and emboldened to resort instead to threats and violence, the member states were restive within an ideology in which, while all discontent was in danger of becoming automatically aggression, all aggression was in danger of requiring the automatic application of sanctions and the subsequent resort to war. The problem of how to guarantee that they would fulfil their responsibilities towards collective security, a problem which was never solved, existed, indeed, from the beginning.

At the first Assembly in 1920 Canada wished to suppress Article 10, by which members had undertaken 'to respect and preserve as against external aggression the territorial integrity and existing political independence of all members of the League' when advised to do so by the Council. Since the Article had not made it textually clear whether the advice of the Council was binding or optional Canada tried in 1923 at least to establish that it was purely optional. She failed by one vote, but half the members abstained from voting and it was never questioned that the final decision on *what* action each member would take to fulfil the obligation remained with the member itself. What was never settled was whether the Council, in giving its advice, must be unanimous, or unanimous except for the votes of the interested parties, or might act by majority vote. Nor is this surprising: though frequently appealed to, the Article was never applied.

Members had more success in scaling down their obligations under Article 16, the chief of which bound members in apparently unequivocal terms: '1. Should any member of the League resort to war in disregard of its covenants under Articles 12, 13 or 15 it shall *ipso facto* be deemed to have committed an act of war against all other members of the League which hereby undertake immediately to subject it to the severance of all trade and financial relations. . . . 2. It shall be the duty of the Council in such case to recommend to the several Governments concerned what effective military, naval or air force the members of the League shall severally contribute to the armed forces to be used to protect the covenants. . . .' At the first Assembly in 1920 the Scandinavian members proposed amendments which would have authorised the Council to exempt states from participation in sanctions: at that date it was still assumed that the obligation was automatic. But in 1921 the second Assembly adopted resolutions by which the League agreed not only that it was the duty of each member to decide for itself whether a breach of the covenants in Article 12, 13 and 15 had been committed, but also that a state of war did not automatically follow an act of war by a defaulting member and that the existence of a state of war between two countries depended not on their intentions but on their acts. International lawyers argue that it embraced these legal fictions because of the legal difficulties involved in interpreting Articles 12, 13 and 15. These difficulties were certainly considerable; but they had not disturbed the lawyers who drafted these Articles; and if they soon arose thereafter it was not so much because the phrases 'resort to war' and 'act of war' were ambiguous terms as because the member states of the League were anxious to avoid the imposition of automatic sanctions which their obligation required of them. It was because 'a literal application of these provisions [of Article 16] would lead to results so extravagant and so obviously contrary to the spirit of the Covenant [by which the League should attempt to avoid war] that it has been recognised that they must be interpreted with some degree of latitude, though in this case the word "interpretation" is something of a euphemism'.[3] It was also because they quickly realised that the automatic imposition of sanctions would be damaging to their own economies and might lead to retaliatory attack by the state against whom sanctions were imposed.

These were the reasons why Article 16, like Article 10, was never operated as it was drafted and why, on the only occasion on which it was relied on, against Italy in 1935, members used the resolutions in order to avoid imposing sanctions that were total, immediate and automatic. It was for the same reasons that they shifted their reliance from the League to ordinary diplomacy as quickly as they sought to evade their obligations under the Covenant. The doctrine of 'open covenants, openly arrived at' had been embodied in the Covenant in Article 18. This called on members to register all treaties with the Secretariat and on the Secretariat to publish them, and stated that treaties would otherwise be not binding. In 1921, after treaties had already been withheld from the Secretariat, it was agreed that non-registration did not impair the validity of a treaty, but only estopped any party from relying on it in proceedings at the League.[4] By the time of the Locarno treaties of 1925 member states, in their pursuit of collective security no less than of their own interests, had come to rely on treaties and alliances, whether or not these were registered with the League, and not on the League itself.

We cannot be surprised that this was the result in the days of the League experiment. At a time when the overriding wish of many states was the preservation of peace—an aspiration which, however inconsistently, was written into the Covenant itself—and in circumstances when the obligation to resort to sanctions and war was associated with the maintenance of a *status quo* with which most states felt little sympathy—and which was in any case fundamentally unstable—no other result was possible. But to recognise that the League was unfortunate in its time is not to admit that it collapsed from the misfortune. It failed for the deeper reason that its basic conception is impracticable at any time. It is practicable, no doubt, to fight a war, once war has broken out, with the object of teaching the lesson that no state may with impunity attack another. In conditions of peace, when states will compromise to avoid war, it is impossible to organise the world on such a principle for very long. However logical and impressive it may seem in theory, it cannot stand the strain of peace-time relationships. It is worth noting at this point and as a final comment that most of the international disputes which the League settled successfully were dealt with under Article 11.

This provided that in the event of a war or a threat of war 'the League shall take any action that may be deemed wise and effectual to safeguard the peace', and it allowed for the summoning of the Council to discuss such a situation on the request of any member of the League. It has been said that unlike the obligatory articles, which relied on the technique of the lawyer, this gave 'scope to the tact and discretion of the statesman'.[5] It certainly suffered from the limitations that accompany all means of organising international political action: the Council's decisions under the article were not legally binding on the parties to a dispute and Japan's attitude during the Sino-Japanese dispute in 1931 showed that the Council could be defied at least by a Great Power. But if the Covenant in the rest of its articles had emulated the elasticity of this one the League would have been a more effective, if a less novel and less impressive, machine.

CHAPTER 15

THE CAUSES OF THE SECOND WORLD WAR

THE international instability that prevailed after 1918 was more directly responsible for the second World War than it was for the collapse of the League. It was not the sole cause of that war, however, and Mr A. J. P. Taylor's book on the origins of the war of 1939 is important because it recognises this. It is an unsatisfactory book because it places the various causes of the war in a wrong relationship; but it provides a better basis than most other accounts for a discussion of how that relationship ought to be studied.[1]

'Wars', Mr Taylor writes, 'are much like road accidents. They have a general cause and particular causes at the same time. Every road accident is caused in the last resort by the invention of the internal combustion engine and by men's desire to get from one place to another.... But ... the police and the courts do not weigh profound causes. They seek a specific cause for each accident—error on the part of the driver, excessive speed, drunkenness, faulty brakes, bad road surface. So it is with wars. "International anarchy" makes war possible; it does not make it certain.... Both enquiries make sense on different levels. They are complementary, they do not exclude each other. The second World War, too, had profound causes, but it also grew out of specific events, and these events are worth detailed examination'.[2]

This is a good point of departure, though we shall later suggest some qualifications and improvements to it. Confusion and disagreement about the causes of wars have arisen essentially from the failure to make this distinction between the given conditions that make war possible, or even quite likely to occur, and the events and the decisions that immediately lead to it.

When we turn to Mr Taylor's application of this insight to the causes of war in 1939—not so good. He is content to dismiss as 'profound causes' for the second World War factors to which serious scholars have never given any credence and, this done, he almost urges that it had no profound causes at all. His interpretation of the specific events which led to the war is distorted by equally serious errors in logic.

As the above quotation suggests, he is more interested, personally, in the specific events that led to the second World War than in whatever may have been its profound causes. We cannot object on this score: 'both enquiries make sense on different levels.' But nobody, and least of all a man who recognises that both levels exist, can write a book on the origins of the second World War without giving some attention to the profound causes. Mr Taylor duly, though somewhat perfunctorily, deals with them—or, rather, he deals with those 'profound causes' of the war that occupied the attention of the public at the time, and he discusses them only to dismiss them—quite rightly—as rubbish.

In the 1930's the League collapsed and Europe returned to the 'international anarchy'. 'Many people, including some historians, believe that this in itself is enough to explain the second World War. And so, in a sense, it is. So long as states admit no restriction of their sovereignty, wars will occur between them. . . . The defect of this explanation is that, since it explains everything, it explains nothing. If "international anarchy" invariably caused war, then the states of Europe should never have known peace since the close of the middle ages.'[3] 'Men also said that Fascism "inevitably" produced war.' In fact, although Hitler and Mussolini did glorify war and use the threat of it to promote their aims, statesmen had done this throughout history and 'yet there had been long periods of peace . . . despite the fiery talk'. In any case 'the Fascist dictators would not have gone to war unless they had seen a chance of winning, and the cause of war was therefore as much the blunders of others as the wickedness of the dictators themselves'.[4] Another argument has been that capitalism inevitably led to the war; but 'here was another general explanation which explained everything and nothing. . . . The great capitalist states . . . were the most anxious to avoid war; and in every country, including Germany, capitalists were the class most opposed to war. Indeed, if one were to indict the capitalists of 1939, it would be for pacifism and for timidity . . .'[5] As for the special version of this case which argues that the Fascist states represented the last aggressive stage of capitalism in decline— that their economic momentum could be sustained only by war—

their economies did not rely on armaments and they were militarily unready when war broke out.[6]

There is nothing wrong—or not much—with these statements. (There is nothing new about them either: historians, as opposed to the public, have dismissed these fallacies long ago; perhaps even the public has discarded them by now.) When, however, Mr Taylor has thus pushed 'through the cloud of phrases to the realities beneath', which is what, as he rightly says, the historian must try to do, he takes up the position that, since these so-called 'profound causes' of the war are so much rubbish, the war had no profound causes at all. The remaining two-thirds of his book are occupied with the details of the international crises that took place between 1936 and 1939. There is hardly another word about anything except the specific incidents that led to the war. If the war had profound causes, as he has told us it did, we never learn what they were.

We have, it is true, learned something relevant to the problem earlier on. If we are familiar with the subject, we can apply it to the emergency. The earlier pages of the book contain some wise words. By the armistice of 1918 the Germans recognised defeat; 'in return—and almost without realising it—the Allies acknowledged the German government'. Similarly the Treaty of Versailles was a valuable German asset—it was designed to provide security against German aggression but could only work with the cooperation of the German government. 'The most important thing in the treaty was that it was concluded with a united Germany.' This again was done 'without deliberation'.[7] Since she was left intact Germany was bound to resist the Versailles Treaty from the outset, and she 'fought specifically in the second World War to reverse the verdict of the first and to destroy the settlement which followed it'.[8] Since the Allies had decided to leave Germany intact their policy necessarily assumed that 'sooner or later she must return to the comity of nations', and 'so far as there was a coherent pattern in the post-war years it was the story of efforts to conciliate Germany and of their failure'.[9]

Mr Taylor makes equally clear the reasons for this failure. Germany was not only left intact: she was left immensely strong relatively. She remained in existence; Europe's other empires, the Ottoman, the Austrian and the Russian, had all collapsed. (He might have added that France had been gravely weakened.) She had only to shake off the restrictions imposed by the Treaty of Versailles to emerge 'as strong, or almost as strong, as she had been in 1914'. (It would be nearer the mark to say, as later he does say, that she emerged relatively much stronger than in 1914.) The allies were led by their own policy to treat Germany as an equal, but if she were treated as an equal she would be the strongest Power. 'The German problem was not German aggressiveness or militarism, or the wickedness of her rulers. These . . . merely aggravated the problem. . . . The essential problem was political not moral. However democratic or pacific Germany might become, she remained by far the greatest Power on the continent of Europe; with the disappearance of Russia, more so than before.' Her recovery from Versailles was accordingly 'unprecedented in its speed and strength'. The upshot was that, whereas 'before 1914 there had been a Balance', 'the constellation of Europe was [now] profoundly changed—and to Germany's advantage'. 'The old balance of power, which formerly did something to restrain Germany, had broken down.' 'If events followed their course in the old "free" way, nothing could prevent the Germans from overshadowing Europe, even if they did not plan to do so.'[10]

There is little to quarrel with in these conclusions, either. It is true that the emphasis on Allied absence of mind and lack of deliberation in making the armistice and the Treaty is misleading. It implies that it was a practicable possibility to occupy and partition Germany in 1918, which is not the case, and that if Germany had then been occupied and partitioned there would not have been another European war, which is questionable. Mr Taylor has, however, previously gone some way towards recognising this by saying that the decision to grant the German government an armistice was taken 'from the highest and most sensible motives'.[11] The argument that the Treaty was an asset to Germany in that it presupposed German cooperation sounds less impressive when it is remembered that all treaties have this drawback. Otherwise, with one notable exception, these conclusions fairly represent the best current opinion among historians about the profound causes of the second World War, about the given conditions that made it quite likely that a war would break out.

This opinion does not hold that the international anarchy—in the sense of the existence of separate sovereign states—invariably produces war, but it knows that conditions of acute international unbalance invariably tend to invite it. It does not believe that Fascism and capitalism inevitably led to war, if only because it has studied the restraint of political societies, both Fascist and non-Fascist, in conditions of balance and the absence of restraint that even democratic societies can display in the opposite conditions. But it knows that Fascism was exacerbated by the acute international unbalance of the inter-war years—that if the Fascist dictators would not have gone to war unless they had seen a chance of winning, it was this which offered them the chance of winning—just as it knows that the blunders of the Western Powers were due not only to their ineptitude and timidity but also to the enormous dimensions of the problem which the international unbalance presented to them. There was ineptitude; Mr Taylor is right to say that these Powers, and also the United States and Russia, were too slow to realise the need to contain Germany; but if they were too slow it was because Germany's return to predominance was so fast.

It knows indeed—and this is the notable exception to the validity of Mr Taylor's conclusions—that precisely because the unbalance was so extreme it is not enough to state that Germany fought the second World War 'specifically . . . to reverse the verdict of the first and to destroy the settlement which followed it'. It would prefer to support the other statements he makes, in contradiction of this one and to the effect that she fought for something more: that Hitler's and Mussolini's appetite for success was 'greater' than is normal,[12] that 'nothing could prevent the Germans from overshadowing Europe, even if they did not plan to do so'. To return to Mr Taylor's analogy, it would say that every road accident is caused in the last resort not so much by the invention of the internal combustion engine and by men's desire to get from one place to another as by the absence of restraints and conditions that make for careful driving; that every war is caused in the last resort not so much by the 'international anarchy' as by the absence of similar restraints and conditions within the international system.

If we cannot disagree with the main drift of these conclusions neither can we grumble that Mr Taylor does not mention their relevance to the profound causes of the war. On this point, too, the early pages contain good sense. Whatever Germany fought for, 'the first war explains the second and, in fact, caused it, in so far as one event causes another'.[13] With regard to her success in remaining united and strong, 'the second World War grew out of the victories in the first and out of the way in which these victories were used'. The decision to leave her strong and united 'ultimately led to the second World War'.[14] In spite of these early remarks, however, he makes no reference to any profound cause of the war after he has reached the year 1936. And it is largely because he later forgets this evidence for the acute unbalance resulting from the first war, and loses all interest in its bearing on the outbreak of the second, that he can arrive at such an extraordinary version of those 'specific events' which, beginning with the fall of Austria, took place when the unbalance had come into the open.

Before demonstrating how this is so it is necessary to uncover two other errors in logic which are closely related and which enter directly into his treatment of those events. Just as his interpretation of the crises that began in 1936 is central to the doubt he casts, at the beginning of the book, on the almost universal view that Hitler 'planned the second World War', that 'his will alone caused it',[15] so it is central to his analysis of these crises that in no case was German policy the cause of them. All that his evidence can be strained to yield, on the most generous of conditions, is that German *planning* did not actually *occasion* these crises. He never sees the difference between general policy and precise planning or between cause and occasion. The police and the courts, though they confine themselves to specific events, surely try to avoid these elementary errors.

He does not deny that Germany had a policy. In the sense of his having had a precise schedule, it is not the accepted view, as Mr Taylor says it is, that Hitler 'was deliberately preparing from the first a great war which would . . . make him master of the world'.[16] The authorities who hold some such view base themselves on Hitler's developing aims, not on his possession from the start of plans for precise action at precise dates. Who would be so naïve? Essentially, moreover, Mr Taylor does not disagree with these authorities as much as he frequently professes to do. Does he himself think Hitler had any *aims*? He had 'day-dreams', as revealed in *Mein Kampf* and on many later occasions, but these did not affect his policy.[17] But did he have any *policy*? Well, yes, he did. There was nothing 'original' about it, but it was his policy to free Germany from the peace treaty, to give her once more a great army and to make her the greatest Power in Europe 'from her natural weight'.

'Fundamentally he was not interested merely in revising Germany's frontiers. He wanted to make Germany dominant in Europe. . . .' To the extent that Mr Taylor thinks that he was forced to fight the West 'before he had conquered the East' he admits that Hitler wanted to conquer the East. Having gone this far he might have turned on Western Europe and the world, though no one can tell. What we can be sure of is that he was determined to get possession of Eastern Europe and 'conquer the East', and to persuade or force France and Great Britain to let him do so. Make no doubt of it, Mr Taylor is clear that Hitler 'intended to use force, or would at any rate threaten to use it,' at least thus far.[18] He adds that Hitler was a gambler who would play for high stakes with inadequate resources.[19] He even admits at the end that 'Hitler may have projected a great war all along'.[20]

It is, once again, despite all this good sense that he dwells not on Hitler's aims or on his policy or even on his 'projections' in his discussion of the crises, but only on Hitler's lack of precise plans. He has previously confused plans and policy in his treatment of Bismarck. When he argued that Bismarck never sought a quarrel with France as part of the goal of a united Germany it was on the ground that Bismarck had no precise plans in 1870; Bismarck stumbled into war and, supreme opportunist that he was, he made the most of it. When new documents proved Mr Taylor wrong about the extent of even Bismarck's planning, let alone about Bismarck's policy and aims, he invented 'Taylor's Law'—to the effect that documents do not really signify anything. It is exactly the same with his treatment of Hitler.

The confusion of the occasion of these crises with their cause follows automatically, as does the misinterpretation of documentary evidence. Because Hitler, like Bismarck, had no precise plans—indeed, it is true of all statesmen that they 'are too absorbed by events to follow any preconceived plan'[21]—he did not cause any of these crises. Because somebody must have caused them (as a man who is convinced that statesmen are for ever stumbling into decisions, Mr Taylor has an intense belief that every event flows from somebody's decision, that 'the initiative must have come from someone',[22]) 'we must look elsewhere for the man who provided an opportunity which Hitler could take and who thus gave the first push [and the subsequent pushes] towards war'.[23] In the Austrian crisis it was two men who did this: von Papen 'started Germany's advance towards European domination' by bringing Schuschnigg to see Hitler; Schuschnigg provoked the Anschluss, when Hitler would have preferred to avoid dramatic measures, by deciding on an Austrian plebiscite in defiance of the satellite status that Hitler had already imposed on him. The Anschluss was 'the first step in the policy which was to brand [Hitler] as the greatest of war criminals. Yet he took this step unintentionally.'[24] And because the Hossbach memorandum of November 1937 was not a concrete plan—because it reveals only that Hitler was determined to have Czechoslovakia and Austria, that he hoped to get them without a war, but that he did not know precisely when and how he would get them—it must be explained away.

It was 'a manœuvre in domestic affairs'. Mr Taylor can seriously maintain that its purpose was to win over conservative generals and diplomats to the policy of continued and increased rearmament after showing that Hitler's address was largely devoted to assuring them that Germany would gain her aims without war. In any case it was only 'day-dreaming'.[25] The whole truth is never to be gleaned from documents alone. Not all documents mean what they say or what we think they say. But the historian of all people should hesitate before according quite such cavalier treatment to what is at least one of his tools.

It is the same with every subsequent crisis. In every case it was not Hitler but somebody else who caused it. In some cases, as in the Munich crisis, it was everybody else: the German nationalist minority, whom Hitler did not create; the British government, which was alert to the danger long before Hitler had even formulated his intentions; Lord Runciman, who made appeasement unpopular among the English and thus 'helped to clear the way for world war'; the French, for allowing Hitler to overestimate their strength, and the Italians, for allowing him to overestimate their aggressiveness, since otherwise he could have obtained Czechoslovakia—as he hoped to obtain it—without risk in the course of a Franco-Italian war.[26] Hitler only wanted to liberate the Germans in Czechoslovakia and Poland—and to remove the obstacle that Czechoslovakia and Poland presented to German hegemony. Because he did not want to do this by frontal assault and war, because he 'preferred the methods of intrigue and violence', because he waited for somebody else to provide him with the opportunity to succeed with these methods, because—above all—he did not have advance plans but waited 'without knowing how he would emerge victorious'—for all these reasons he was not responsible for any of the crises.[27]

For the same reason that he did not intend war and hoped to avoid it he was not responsible in the last crisis for world war: it was 'against all expectations' that 'he found himself at war with the West before he had conquered the East';[28] 'it seems from the record that he became involved in war through launching on 29 August a diplomatic manœuvre that he ought to have launched on 28 August.'[29] The literalism, the inverted subtlety, of the whole approach would be risible if its implications were not so serious.

The implications are not serious simply because of their bearing on our understanding of the second World War. They reduce our possibilities of understanding the causes of war in general. Because of his confusion of plans with policy and of occasion with cause, Mr Taylor's version of the pre-war crises is devoid of all regard for the policy of the man who almost wholly caused them on one level. But it also takes this course because the antithesis he has drawn between the profound causes of war and the specific events that lead to war is a false antithesis. It cannot be too much emphasised that, while the profound causes lie among the given conditions that invite war, the causes on the other level are not simply events. They are the ways in which men handle events, react to the challenge which the given conditions present to them. To return once again to the road-accident analogy, it is not to mechanical defects but to the conduct of the driver that we must pay attention when studying a particular collision, and if a road accident can take place independently of the conduct of the driver then a war is not like a road accident. A war is always an alternative to some other course and is always known to be so.

So much is this the case that the relationship between the given conditions and the policy of statesmen, between the profound causes of war and the decisions that lead to war, is not a constant and mechanical relationship as the road-accident analogy would imply. One war may be almost entirely due to the given conditions and hardly at all the consequence of the conduct of the men involved.

Another war may be almost entirely due to that conduct and hardly at all the consequence of the given conditions. Although both kinds of cause will be present in some measure in every case it is not enough to state that in every case both levels of enquiry exist. It is necessary in each case to discover the relative weight that should be attached to the two levels of causation. And then, again, we may find that the policies of all the participants were equally responsible for the outbreak of a war on the level of conduct—but then, again, we may not.

It is for these reasons that it must be regretted that Mr Taylor's analysis of these crises is insulated not only from all regard for the policy of the man who almost wholly caused them on one level but also, as was established earlier, from all recollection of the extreme international unbalance that was the chief cause for them on the other. It is only when the crises are studied in this, their proper, context that it emerges to what a large extent Hitler was responsible, and to what a small extent the conditions or the conduct of other men, for the outbreak of the second World War.

Both factors were involved. The unbalance was in a sense the cause of Hitler's policy. If it had not existed and if he had not known that it existed he would not have seen so continuously a 'chance of winning' so much. Because he knew it existed he remained confident until the summer of 1939 that he would achieve his aims without war and was thus content in each crisis, as Mr Taylor never tires of telling us, to wait for the opportunity of doing so. The unbalance was in a sense the cause of the war. Because Hitler's policy succeeded in the reoccupation of the Rhineland, in the Anschluss, in the Munich crisis, in the occupation of Prague, he could feel that it would go on succeeding. Because the unbalance was so great it was not easy for other Powers to convince him that it would not. The unbalance was so much the cause of Hitler's policy that anyone else in power in Germany might have had a policy similar to Hitler's, at least in its objects. It was so much the cause of war that, while it was practically impossible for other Powers to resist Germany's revisionist attitude up to and including the Munich crisis, and equally impossible that they should not resist it if it were persisted in much beyond that point, it set up the danger that it would be so persisted in. But it does not much advance the cause of historical truth to assert that Hitler was not responsible because somebody else in the same position might have pursued the same course; or to assume that anyone else must have pursued it beyond the Munich crisis, when the risks had become so great and so obvious. What we do know is that Hitler did pursue it beyond that point. And what we can conclude from any objective analysis of the pre-war crises is that it was this fact, not the unbalance itself, that caused the war.

Neither the Anschluss, nor Munich, nor the occupation of Prague made war inevitable, any more than the German reoccupation of the Rhineland had made war inevitable; but with each succeeding crisis and each succeeding German acquisition the international system creaked a little more stiffly. It is, after all, a system, and however unbalanced it may be it will respond to unbearable pressure in the end. The British government's decision to guarantee Poland reflected this fact. Mr Taylor partly recognises it by admitting that the Polish crisis of the summer of 1939 was different from the earlier crises: in the Polish crisis, 'in strange contrast to earlier crises, there were no negotiations over Danzig, no attempts to discover a solution; not even attempts to screw up tension'; 'there could be no half-hearted German aid to Danzig, only a full-blown war; and Hitler would be ready for such a war only when his military preparations matured.'[30] What he overlooks, despite this last remark, is that although Hitler went on hoping that he could make the inter-national unbalance do his work for him, he felt this with declining confidence, and yet with mounting determination to put the matter to the test of war if necessary, after the publication of the British guarantee to Poland. Throughout the last, the Polish crisis, Hitler's confidence that he would avoid a general war was lower, his determination to risk a general war was higher, than they had ever been. It might be argued that his conclusion of the pact with Russia was the act of a man who still hoped to avoid war at the eleventh hour; it was the act of a man who hoped to avoid a war on two fronts. If he was able to make the concessions to Russia which the pact involved it was only because he already planned to recover them by force before too long; and if the other Powers could not make comparable concessions to her it was because the concessions she demanded could be made only by one who could think of them as being temporary.

It is only by ignoring this and much other evidence that Mr Taylor can conclude that it was 'against all expectations that [Hitler] found himself at war' as a result of this final crisis—which differs so substantially from the final crisis preceding the first World War. The most that the evidence will allow us to say is that Hitler involved himself and Europe in war in spite of all his hopes—but because of his refusal to modify his policy of exploiting the international unbalance for aggressive ends.

CHAPTER 16

THE NATURE AND DEVELOPMENT OF THE UNITED NATIONS

'WE must realise', concluded an eminent international lawyer in 1946, 'that what we have done is to exchange a system which might or might not have worked for one which cannot work, and that instead of limiting the sovereignty of states we have actually extended the sovereignty of the Great Powers, the only states whose sovereignty is still a formidable reality in the modern world.'[1] Judged from the point of view of international history, as opposed to that of international law, this verdict is unacceptable so far as it concerns the League of Nations: the League could not have worked. Is it true from this point of view in relation to the United Nations, the international organisation which was set up after the second World War as the League had been set up after the first?

The conclusion was based on an analysis of the differences between the Charter of the United Nations and the Covenant of the League. The most obvious of these differences does not at first sight support it. The United Nations structure, unlike the League, was set up as an organisation that was more than the sum of its parts—with organs of its own, with an identity distinct from that of its members and with functions independent of those of its members. The League was a league; its Covenant spoke of the members of the League, of the component states, rather than of the construct. The Charter spoke of 'the Organisation and its Members'. It laid it down that 'the Organisation' should ensure that non-member states acted in accordance with its principles (Article 2) and that members were pledged to cooperate with 'the Organisation '(Article 56). It referred to 'the judgement', 'the recommendations', 'the work' of the Organisation (Articles 4, 58, 59, 98). 'The Organisation' was itself given 'such privileges and immunities as are necessary for the fulfilment of its purposes' (Article 105). Its Secretary-General, unlike his predecessor in the League, was explicitly empowered to bring to the Organisation's attention any matter which might endanger peace and security (Article 99).

335

The political importance of this departure from or advance on the League should not, however, be exaggerated. If the United Nations was endowed with its own independent organisation it is still composed of independent members. Article 2(i) of the Charter recognised that the United Nations was based on 'the sovereign equality of all states', which it existed to protect. Article 2(7) expressly forbade its 'intervention in matters which are essentially within the domestic jurisdiction of states'. The new system was given no more power than the League had possessed to impose a settlement in disputes between its members: if it intervenes in a dispute it is because the dispute is producing a threat to international peace, and it intervenes to preserve the peace, not to settle the dispute. Far from ruling out action independently of itself, it recognised 'the inherent right of self-defence . . . either individual or collective' (Article 53)—by means of alliances or through such organisations as the British Commonwealth or the Arab League. Apart from many other qualifications to be discussed, what was set up was far from being a world government, and it was not intended that it should develop into one. The greater emphasis on its independent organs was the reflection, indeed, of international administrative and legal developments rather than of changed political aspirations. Even the Covenant had referred to 'the seat of the League . . . at Geneva' (Article 7); even the League, despite the usual silence of the Covenant on the point, had evolved a secretariat that went far beyond what anybody had envisaged in 1918. The increased complexity of international administration since that day made it natural to think in terms of a distinct international organisation in 1945—especially when there was a disposition to regularise the position of an increased number of administrative international bodies by concentrating them under the new organisation.

Far more important politically was a departure from the League which reflected a widespread conviction as to why the League had failed. Men felt with some cause in the 1940's that the League had failed from being frustrated by the retention of complete freedom of action by its sovereign member states. It was for this reason that the Charter made more serious inroads into the independence and discretion of the member states than the Covenant had been able to do. The League took over existing ideas and procedures for the pacific settlement of disputes. In Article 16 it crowned this system with the precise but legalistic provision that sanctions would automatically be visited upon any state that violated the undertakings built into the Covenant and with the further provision that military action might follow against such a state on the advice of the Council. But it permitted member states to decide for themselves the difficult question whether a breach of these covenants had occurred; and in the case of military action members were further safeguarded by the need for unanimity in the Council and the fact that the Council's recommendations were not binding. In cases of breach of the collective guarantee contained in Article 10 the Council's recommendation was binding; but it was probable that the Council had to be unanimous, and member states remained free to decide what action to take when they accepted the advice. The Charter incorporated the same system for pacific settlements and a similar, if not identical, general guarantee against aggression. But it deprived member states of these safeguards.

It made the Security Council of the United Nations responsible for determining whether any 'threat to peace, breach of the peace or act of aggression' had occurred (Article 39) and for deciding what action be taken (Articles 40–9). The Council's decisions and recommendations were made binding on the member states, who agreed 'to accept and carry out the decisions of the Security Council in accordance with the present Charter' (Article 25). To make the point clearer still Article 2(7) declared that, while the United Nations could not intervene in matters within the domestic jurisdiction of a state, 'this principle shall not prejudice the application of enforcement measures . . .'. It was 'in order to ensure prompt and effective action by the United Nations' that the member states conferred on the Security Council this 'primary responsibility for the maintenance of international peace and security' and agreed 'that in carrying out its duties under this responsibility the Security Council acts on their behalf' (Article 24). In the same cause the United Nations abandoned the principle of unanimity: the Security Council might act by an affirmative vote of seven of its eleven members.

These steps were taken in the interest of more rapid and effective international action. Effective international action for what purposes? Another shift from the thinking that had underlain the League of Nations is to be found in what the Charter said about the objects for which the Security Council would authorise action. The League

337

had been concerned to prevent illegal war—war in violation of law and covenants. The Charter set out to prevent all war. The League permitted war by an individual state, after some delay, against a state which evaded a legal and just settlement of a dispute. It undertook to organise collective sanctions and war against any state which broke its covenants either by departing from the procedure for the legal and just settlement of disputes or by committing aggression in defiance of another covenant. Action was to be taken to uphold justice always and peace as far as possible; and action depended, among other things, on the apparently precise but in fact legalistic and insoluble issues of violation of covenants and commission of aggression. The Charter was less interested in legal and just settlement; the great danger was war and any settlement was better than war. Members were enjoined only to seek the peaceful settlement of a dispute by whatever means appealed to them (Article 33). The Security Council's purpose was solely 'to maintain or restore international peace and security' (Article 39). It would act in a dispute only to preserve the peace, not to achieve a settlement.

Or, rather, it would act only if it judged it to be necessary to act in the interests of peace and security. For in proportion as the United Nations was thus made freer to undertake effective international action by inroads into the freedom of its members to abstain from action, and by a less legalistic and complex conception of the circumstances in which international action would be taken, action was subjected to the discretion of its executive body. And in proportion as it abandoned legalistic definitions that discretion became a matter of political decision. These changes involved, on the one hand, a further limitation of the freedom of the individual member states—a limitation, this time, on their freedom to take action. Article 11 of the Covenant had enabled any member of the League to summon a meeting of the Council to discuss a threat to the peace. By Article 15 each member was free to decide that there had been a resort to war in violation of covenants—as free to decide this as to decide that no violation had taken place. In the Charter member states of the United Nations lost these discretions as well as the freedom not to act if the Council called on them for action. But on the other hand—and in practical terms this was of far greater importance —these changes enhanced the power and the political discretion of the Security Council.

Not only was it alone free to decide that a threat to peace existed or that a breach of peace had taken place; and to intervene when it judged that violence might arise, as well as when it had arisen. Not only were its recommendations in such cases binding on other members. Not only was it equipped with a Military Staff Committee to advise it on preparing for action in advance, as well as on the strategy to adopt when it was taking action for the enforcement of peace and security. It could also decide that the United Nations should take no action by judging that no threat to peace and security existed. In all the Articles of the Charter which deal with its function the powers of the Security Council are permissive as well as complete.

Thus if member states failed to settle a dispute the dispute would go to the Council which, if it judged it to be a threat to the peace, might recommend a means of settlement or terms of a settlement (Article 31). Except for the general statement in Article 1 that one purpose of the United Nations was the adjustment or settlement of disputes 'in conformity with the principles of justice and international law', nothing prevented it from deciding that the dispute was unimportant—which the Council of the League was not free to do. Or from recommending a legally unjust settlement—which the Council of the League had not been free to do. Or from recommending a settlement that was politically unwise. A similar change of emphasis is to be found in the redrafting of the League's collective guarantee of its members against aggression. The Covenant contained a collective undertaking by each member state to respect and preserve the territorial integrity and political independence of every member state. Article 2(4) of the Charter repeated the undertaking to respect these things by binding all members to refrain from the threat or use of force against them; but from anxiety to avoid guaranteeing the *status quo* for all time it did not guarantee to preserve them. The individual member state lost this further safeguard. The Security Council, which alone determined whether peace was threatened, or force had been used, gained this further discretion. An absolute guarantee of each by all was replaced by a conditional guarantee of all by the Security Council.

By these processes and in these respects the idea of a world community of states was supplemented and controlled by the idea of the superior power and political discretion of an inner committee of selected states. And the core of the inner committee was necessarily the Great Powers. They were allotted the permanent seats on the Security Council. In contrast to the Charter's avoidance of any guarantee to preserve the *status quo* as far as the political independence of each of its members was concerned, it actually named in Article 23 the five Great Powers—the United States, Russia, Great Britain, France and China—to whom these seats were allotted. Nor was this the most important recognition of their position: even in the League the important member Powers had in practice been permanently members of the Council, although the Assembly had been given some say in its composition. In the Charter the Great Power members of the Security Council were also granted the individual right to veto action by the Council as the legal and constitutional weapon with which to defend their interests and position. The United Nations was subjected to the discretion of each of them as well as to the discretion of the Security Council as a whole.

It was not one of the Great Powers who demanded this; all insisted on it, and their receipt of it was the price paid for their preparedness to join the new system. It was not questioned at the time that they would use it to protect their own interests. 'It is clear', declared the official British commentary on the Charter, 'that no enforcement action may be taken against a Great Power without a major war. If such a situation arises the UN will have failed in its purpose and all members will have to act as seems best in the circumstances.'

The veto meant that the United Nations, a huge and complex machine, would only be able to work effectively in the contingencies for which it was intended, to avoid or suppress the use of force, in issues in which a Great Power was not involved—in a dispute between the smaller states. Even then it could only work if all the Great Powers agreed that it should. It meant that the Great Powers would themselves be restrained from using force only by their undertakings as members of the United Nations to 'fulfil in good faith the obligations assumed by them in accordance with the present Charter', to 'settle their international disputes by peaceful means in such a manner that international peace and security, and justice, are not endangered', to 'refrain from the threat or use of force against the territorial integrity or political independence of any state' (Article 2) —that they would be restrained only by a self-imposed adherence to such promises. But the Charter contained not so much an extension of the sovereignty of the Great Powers as a formal recognition that this sovereignty existed. In the days of the League the unanimity rule had been a serious check on effective action only in so far as it had left freedom to the Great Powers; and even without that rule the whole apparatus of the League would have been unworkable against a Great Power and unworkable against lesser states unless the Great Powers had been in agreement. More important still, it was practically impossible for the Charter to avoid this restriction which the League had also failed to avoid. The men who set up the United Nations were being realistic when, as well as centralising effective authority in a central body for the sake of efficiency, they recognised that it could work effectively only if and when the major states of the world, who necessarily dominated that body, were able and willing to collaborate.

Its members have not always worked on equally realistic lines in their efforts to evade the stultification that resulted when the Great Powers began, as they quickly did, to disagree.

When this took place the experiment was doomed to develop between two lines of reference. On the one hand, unless and until the Great Powers could again work together, it in fact reverted to being what the League had been—an entirely voluntary accessory to diplomacy for the peaceful settlement of disputes and, as a piece of machinery for action against threats to or attacks upon peace, virtually inoperable. On the other hand, men generally continued to want it to be something more than this; and not less important, some Great Powers could not suppress the wish to use the United Nations as an ideological umbrella under which to justify action against others. It was perhaps inevitable that this general aspiration and this wish would gain the upper hand to begin with.

The first response was an extra-legal transfer of the functions of the Security Council to the General Assembly—an attempt to circumvent the division of function between the Security Council and the Assembly that was laid down in the Charter. The Charter, while giving the Council primary responsibility for the maintenance of peace and security, permitted the Assembly to discuss and make recommendations on any question (Article 10); but it excluded the Assembly from considering a matter which was being discussed by the Council (Article 12), whereas under the Covenant of the League both the Assembly and the Council might deal at any time with any matter within the sphere of the League. In the struggle between the Great Powers and the smaller states about the functions of the Assembly, a struggle which raged while the Charter was being drafted, most of the concessions to the smaller states and to the General Assembly were made in the social, economic and trusteeship fields. The work of the United Nations in these fields was much greater than that of the League had been; and in proportion as the Charter restricted the Assembly's political competence it granted it greater competence in these fields, which were regarded as secondary. It was virtually in breach of the Charter—at least by 'a virtual amendment of the Charter'²—that this division of functions was altered in November 1950, during the crisis in Korea, by the General Assembly's adoption of the 'Uniting for Peace' Resolutions on the initiative of the United States Government.

The Security Council had been able to declare in June 1950 that the North Korean invasion of South Korea was a breach of the peace—and to recommend that member states should assist in repelling it—because Russia had decided to absent herself from the United Nations earlier in that year. The 'Uniting for Peace' Resolutions were adopted after Russia had seen her mistake—or, with the United States now involved against China, had achieved her purpose—and made her return to her seat on the Security Council. They empowered the Assembly to meet within twenty-four hours, and to recommend voluntary action by its members, if, as was now likely in connection with Korea, the Security Council failed 'to exercise its primary responsibility for the maintenance of peace and security'. And it was envisaged that this would permit the evasion of the veto because the Charter had laid it down that the Assembly should reach decisions by majority vote in ordinary questions and, in more important matters, by the vote of two-thirds of those present and voting.

As a result of these resolutions the Assembly acquired a voice in the peace and security zone of the Charter which it has not since lost. But the enlargement of its functions was not accompanied by any assumption of the Security Council's powers. The Assembly could only recommend action to member states, as in the days of the League. It was not the Assembly's denunciation of the French and British action at Suez which was effective in stopping that action short, but the fact that the denunciation was led (and actively implemented outside the United Nations) by a Great Power, the United States; the Assembly's denunciation of Russian action in Hungary could produce no retaliatory action at all. It is not for nothing that the only part of the 'Uniting for Peace' Resolutions which has been regularly resorted to has been that by which the Assembly can be assembled for emergency discussion: its attempt to set up a permanent Peace Observation Commission to report to the Assembly has been used only once (in the Balkans in 1952) and member states have generally responded with great caution or not at all to resolutions calling for the provision of armed forces. Nor is this surprising. The Assembly not only received no power to direct member states but was never designed to exercise executive functions. It was designed as a legislature, not as an executive. And with the increasing number of member states it has even become difficult to pass resolutions calling for action. When resolutions require the vote of two-thirds of its hundred or more members, and when those members increasingly tend to be organised in blocs, it will always be possible for the Latin-American or the Afro-Asian bloc to prevent the passage of a resolution.

It is becoming equally possible, on the other hand, for blocs to collaborate to force the passage of Assembly resolutions which are distasteful to the UN's leading member Powers; and although such resolutions may not call for action or result in action, they can be none the less embarrassing. The Assembly's approval of the Indian attack on Goa, its demand for investigations in Rhodesia—these are the latest developments in a process which, with the steady increase in the size of membership as a result of the accession of small and unfinished states, has now begun to lead the older Powers to question the wisdom of their earlier contributions to the extension of the Assembly's role.

It is partly because of this process, but also, on the other hand, because of the ineffectiveness of the Assembly in an executive role, that since the end of the 1950's there has been an attempt to recall to the executive of the United Nations the functions of the Security Council which the Assembly in a sense usurped. But the tendency has been not to recall these functions to the Security Council, whose members are still unable to work together, but to place them in the Secretariat—not in the Organisation's Cabinet but in its Civil

Service. In the establishment of the UNEF buffer force in the Middle East during the Suez crisis in 1956 and then in the measures taken by the UN to deal with—some would say to exacerbate—the Congo crisis it has been the Secretary-General and his staff, not the General Assembly nor the Security Council, who have occupied the foreground and attempted to do the work. And despite the opposition of Russia to the activities of the Secretariat, this process has been assisted by the emergence of crises for which it is transparently obvious that the Great Powers cannot blame each other and by the growing realization of the Great Powers that if they persist in using the UN as a vehicle for action against each other they will destroy it altogether.

This process has also been extra-legal, and more so than the development of the General Assembly. In general international law, indeed, if not in the law of the Charter, there was some justification for the partial assumption of the role of the Security Council by the Assembly considered as an assembly of sovereign states; but there is no such justification for the usurpation of that role by the Secretariat, which the Charter invested with a purely administrative role and which is representative of no sovereign interest. It is more important, however, that the Secretariat is no more fitted to deal with political crises—as opposed to the supervision of the world's administrative services—than the General Assembly. This is the root cause of the difficulties of the UN in the Congo—difficulties which may end in doing as much damage to the UN as the misuse of the General Assembly would do if it were persisted in. The Secretary-General cannot act without a mandate. If he is to act on any mandate he has to get officials and troops from somewhere. But it is not solely because of the difficulties of getting mandates and troops that the Secretariat has taken the course it has taken. In settling for vague mandates, in deliberately excluding involved Powers from providing officials and troops, in failing to anticipate the complexity of the burden it has assumed, it has revealed all the marks of the administrator in politics and reaped all the consequences of believing that political issues are administratively soluble. They are not.

The Secretariat has perhaps also acted from the belief that the UN is still potentially a world government, if still in an embryonic state of development. It is not. It never was so constructed and is unlikely ever to become so. The conclusion that would best meet all the evidence is that the UN is already fully fledged in the only role in which it can be useful, and that it has great possibilities in that role in proportion as it accepts its limitations and prefers words to deeds. Although men might like it to become more than this, it would be wise to recognise that its only practicable role—both when disagreements between the Great Powers have diminished and while the Great Powers remain seriously divided—is that of an accessory to their diplomacy, a moral check upon its excesses and a physical and procedural assistant to its processes; and because this is so it would be more logical to insist on Communist China's admission than to persist in opposing it. Within that role, the function of the Secretary-General is to work at the centre to help diplomacy to function. This will be difficult, but not more difficult than the problems which will surely arise if he persists in the belief that diplomacy can be sidestepped. It may lead to criticism of the UN for ineffectiveness, but not to such criticism as the UN will incur on the other course. If the UN is allowed to go farther along either the road on which it was pushed under the influence of the Korean war and the Suez crisis or the road on which it has been taken under the impact of the Middle East and the Congo crises it will run into all the problems which destroyed the League and, like the League, it will end by being discredited and destroyed.

CHAPTER 17

INTERNATIONAL RELATIONS SINCE THE SECOND WORLD WAR

CLOSE students of international affairs are beginning to recognise that, at some point since the second World War, the relations between the major Powers have altered in quality from what they were like between the wars, and are now in a state of 'deadlock' which renders large-scale war unlikely for a considerable time to come. Mr C. M. Woodhouse is one of these. In his book on British foreign policy since the second World War he assumes that the deadlock began to emerge in the middle of the 1950's, that it resulted from the achievement at that time of nuclear parity by the two sides in the Great Power struggle and that, so far as major wars are concerned, it 'might well mean permanent peace'.[1] These conclusions are so nearly correct, and yet so little assimilated by the public mind, that the faults committed by Mr Woodhouse in the course of reaching them might normally have been left for specialists to discover. To lay these faults bare, however, is to strengthen the conclusions, and since so many people remain sceptical at such optimism there can be no objection to making the effort to do this.

The first thing to be said is that Mr Woodhouse is wrong in tracing back the deadlock only to the middle of the 1950's, and he is wrong because he confuses the time when it became a fact with the time when the fact was at last beginning to be recognised. It was in the mid-1950's, certainly, that the British government (like other governments) began to realise that the thermo-nuclear weapons had 'significantly reduced'—as it announced in the Defence White Paper of 1955—the risk of major war. As Mr Woodhouse says, the correctness of this deduction has 'been further confirmed by every subsequent Great Power crisis . . . in every part of the world'.[2] But deadlock existed before it was known to exist. It existed during the years from 1946 to 1954, which he characterises as years of 'uneasy peace' and 'near war',[3] and did so despite the fact that fear of a general war was then widespread.

One effect, it is true, of the greater knowledge we have acquired of the crises of those earlier years has been to show how close to war the Powers sometimes came. This is no excuse for not now realising what, not unnaturally, was not realised at the time—how far from war they always even then remained. Mr Woodhouse is in addition surely wrong in characterising the Korean War, the most serious of those crises, as 'the last war to engage the forces of the Great Powers openly against each other'. China was not then—and is not yet—a Great Power; as for Russia, the Red Army was never openly engaged in the war. The Korean War was significant for another reason than this. While Russia, one of the major participants, fought it through intermediate agents, the other major participant, the United States, who was directly engaged, who stood to lose and who was sorely tempted to attack the prime mover on the other side, resisted the temptation. If the other international crises up to 1955 stopped short of even Korean War proportions it was because one or the other or both parties to them resisted similar temptations, even then, or were induced to do so by their allies.

The importance of this first point is that it opens up the inadequacy of Mr Woodhouse's explanation of the deadlock. Like governments themselves in their awareness of it since 1955, he sees only half the truth when he says that it is due to the development of the nuclear weapons, and particularly of parity in these weapons since 1954. There can be little quarrel with the argument that these developments have helped to eliminate the danger of major war between the major Powers. It is irrelevant to argue that the weapons should be abandoned because the chaos would be so terrible that would result if they were used; or that their deterrent effect is illusory because their use may not be invoked in the last resort; or that, like earlier deterrent measures, they are dangerous because they may provoke attack. The weapons are the logical culmination of that growth of technological deterrents against irresponsible policy, hasty decisions and war which has been so rapid since the beginning of the century. They are so in the sense that they constitute for the first time a true deterrent, one that will never have to be activated so long as it exists—and this is likely to be for ever. Even if they were abandoned, the knowledge of how to make the weapons can never be unlearned and, on the contrary, the problem of manufacturing them becomes easier every year.

Up to 1939 this growth was not quite adequate, the deterrents not sufficiently rigid. Since 1946 war by design and war by miscalculation have both been ruled out because the Great Powers have become acutely aware of the fatal consequences for themselves of using the weapons, and—except in retaliation against their use—have determined not to use them. What the thermo-nuclear weapons have not done, of themselves, is to rule out major war as the consequence of accident. It would even be true to say that, purely hypothetically, their existence has increased this danger. No modern war has in fact taken place by accident; since at least the middle of the eighteenth century the decision to make war has been the most difficult of all political decisions—all of which are difficult —and the one in connection with which governments have most guarded against accident. Hypothetically, the modern technological situation has reintroduced the risk of accident, which prevailed before governments asserted their controls, by threatening to reduce the area of government competence and eliminate government monopoly of peace and war decisions. But it is precisely because governments are aware of this, and have become so all-pervasive in their field of competence, that the danger is hypothetical. The precautions they have taken against accidents with the nuclear weapons—against those accidents that might arise from faulty radar, the mad second-lieutenant or the thoughtless Prime Minister —have become so complex that the procedure for reaching a decision to use the weapons is already too complicated to be operated even in the retaliatory role to which the weapons have been confined.* Nor is this the only significant response of governments to this problem. Their anxiety to evade the technical deterrent led them at first to listen to theorists who misguidedly urged the development of tactical atomic weapons—until their anxiety to avoid a further danger of accident, the danger that tactical atomic warfare would 'escalate' automatically into major war, persuaded them to retrace their steps.

When all this has been said however—and how necessary it is to say it—it remains the case that deadlock between the Powers existed before 1955, before nuclear parity or nuclear caution were achieved, and if it is now so complete it is for other reasons in addition to the

* I state this as a fact, as I believe it to be, but I should make it clear that this belief is not based on any access to official information. I have formed it from reading between the lines of newspaper accounts of nuclear bomber crashes, radar-warning alarms and the conduct of governments during political crises.

thermo-nuclear weapons. If they had never been invented—though we can be grateful for their crowning and confirmatory effect—there would still have been no danger of a general war since 1945, and there would still be no danger of a general war for some long time to come, on account of other factors in the situation.

Not least important among these is the fact that the world distribution of power has been more stable since 1945 than it has been at any time since about 1902.

People find it difficult to appreciate this, the world has seemed to be so full of alarms and excursions in the past sixteen years. It is a fact, nevertheless, and appearances have been deceptive. If there has been the appearance of instability since 1945 it is because the chief participants in the international system have been adjusting to a momentous change in the balance of power within the system of the kind which has occurred from time to time in history, of the kind which could not come to be accepted without adjustment and friction —least of all in the unsettlement that followed the most severe war of all times—but of the kind that will lock up the world in its framework, not permanently perhaps, but at least for long years.

The extent to which Mr Woodhouse has not allowed for this fact is shown by a subsidiary explanation he provides for the deadlock. People will argue, he says, that even if the Great Powers are determined to avoid general war by design or miscalculation and accident on their own account, they may be drawn into it willy-nilly by the antagonism within and between the smaller and the newly emerging countries. He agrees with the view that these antagonisms now constitute the greatest danger to world peace.[4] But he asserts that this danger will not materialise because the complexity of modern armaments, and not only of the nuclear weapons, has so increased the dependence of the small countries on the Great Powers for war material that the latter can 'prevent lesser Powers from starting local wars which would engulf them all'. The point is illustrated by a comparison. The crises that were successfully localised between 1955 and 1959 'would infallibly have led to local war, and perhaps then to global war, a generation ago. Today they do not do so.'[5]

All the evidence is against this assertion. He derives it from the single example of the Israeli attack on Egypt in 1956. He is led to do so by his acceptance (more than once implied) of the argument that the British government's intervention at Suez on that occasion was motivated by, and was successful in, the determination to prevent the spread of war in the Middle East. Even if this argument were allowed—even if it were not preferable to face the fact that Great Britain intervened, though unsuccessfully, to preserve her interests and not to deter Israel—all the local wars and crises of recent years tell a different tale. The Great Powers are as powerless to prevent them now as they were when they were confronting the Eastern Question in the nineteenth century. Arms *will* be supplied; if necessary people can fight with bows and arrows. The comparison he draws is accordingly misleading. What is relevant here is that if they cannot prevent them from breaking out—it is another question whether they should even if they could—Great Powers can prevent local wars from spreading by not taking them too seriously, and that they have been just as adept at doing this in the past as they have shown every sign of being since 1945—whenever they have been in balance among themselves. It was because they were in balance that they had little difficulty in containing local crises during much of the nineteenth century. Between 1902 and 1939, for the opposite reason, they had every difficulty in containing them, not to say in not manufacturing them. If they have continued to have some difficulties with local crises since 1945 it is because they have been testing, and only partly understanding, the new balance that has been completing itself among them. But despite these continuing difficulties the outstanding fact that arises from the comparative history of all the crises since that date is that both the balance and their understanding of it have been steadily imposing themselves.

Governments, in fact, have been forced to understand it to a greater extent than ordinary people. They too often themselves consist of ordinary people; they too often display no more understanding of the nature and history of the international system than does the man in the street. For these reasons and also because they are reluctant to accept the conditions of deadlock—and also because of the extreme unbalance that existed in the world up to 1939 in which most men now in power spent their formative years—statesmen have gone on discerning another Hitler in President Nasser, another Munich settlement in the Indo-China Conference of 1955. It is noticeable, however, that it was Sir Anthony Eden who made the first of these diagnoses and Mr Dulles who most violently opposed him, and that in the Indo-China crises these roles, like their views of their countries' interests, were reversed. Both in the Suez crisis and in the crisis over Indo-China they checked each other more effectively than Russia checked either of them. For all their limitations, governments are necessarily in possession of a stream of evidence and a knowledge of risk from which they cannot but draw conclusions which it is not in their nature or in their interest to announce to the world. And what these conclusions have been is apparent from the history of every international crisis since the second World War. Not only the Korean War and Suez and the Indo-China conflict, but every crisis since 1946 has been dominated by the determination of all the governments to avoid extreme positions. Not the existence of conflict, but their deliberate and conscious avoidance of conflict has been the impressive characteristic in all these years, even if it is only in more recent years, with the passage of time and their growing experience of the facts of the situation, that they have begun to move away—though not without retrogressions—from fixed and rigid positions into a healthier and more relaxed atmosphere.

This is not to be wondered at. Although it is not to be accounted for by some fortuitous quality in the outcome of the second World War, the deadlock has existed since that war came to an end. The period from the 1890's to the 1940's was one of grave and rapidly changing disparities in the effective strength of the major Powers, but also one in which a new equilibrium or rough equality of power was growing up alongside the ruins of an earlier one that had been destroyed. The second World War merely completed this period of transformation; its own outcome, indeed, was shaped by the fact that the new equilibrium had long been preparing. Important parts of the peace of 1945 have not even been formally ratified, but like the settlements of Westphalia in the seventeenth century and Vienna in the nineteenth it will go down as significant in history. Unlike the inescapably artificial settlement of 1918—a settlement which was made at the point in the period of transformation when international instability was at its height, and which made the instability all the greater by trying to shape the world to the wishful thinking of its makers—that of 1945 was made when the disparities previously set up by the uneven development of power and of the modern state were at last being brought to an end, at least for a long time to come, by the passage of time. It may even be said that it made itself, so much is it the case that its most solid parts are those that have not been ratified. For if it is true that it could take account of important realities—which did not yet exist in 1918 or which, if they did exist, were not yet accepted—it is equally true that it could not but take account of some of them.

Most prominent among these was the recovery of Russia, the emergence of the United States and the fact that a balance already existed between those two Powers. Every significant territorial gain that Russia has made since 1945 was made in the few months in which the second World War was being wound up, and even in those months the gains she sought were limited by the checks imposed by the emergence of the United States with power that balanced her own. Although they are somewhat hidden from its author, the most significant facts in the most recent analysis of the Potsdam Conference of 1945—which was the nearest thing to a general peace settlement that the Powers were able to achieve—are, first, that there was no power on earth that could impede Russia in her determination to have her way in the settlement of Poland, Finland, Bulgaria, Hungary and Roumania and, second, that not even this determination was as pronounced as Russia's lack of interest in more outlying matters in which the Western Powers dominated, as she now dominated in Eastern Europe. She was so placed technically —as a result of earlier agreements—and perhaps morally also—as one of the victors in a world war—that she could have retaliated in many directions if her own wishes had been opposed. She could have excluded the West from Austria; demanded her say in the resettlement of Italy and Greece, including a share in Italy's African colonies; insisted on a revision of such questions as the international control of Tangier and the Turkish Straits. She raised all these questions. But she raised them only as bargaining points, never pressing them except to gain agreement to her immediate wishes. Even they were somewhat more limited than is sometimes supposed. A smaller Poland—and a larger Eastern Germany—would have been no worse a settlement for her in the long run. Only her uncertainty as to how far she should or could retain control of Eastern Germany can explain the determination with which she nevertheless insisted that Poland's western frontier must be the Oder–Neisse line.[6]

It is perhaps time that the limited nature of Russia's aims in the post-war settlement were given as much prominence as the determination with which she pursued them. It is certainly time to abandon the view that, apart from completing her position by the absorption of Czechoslovakia, she ever intended further expansion into Europe, and that only the American monopoly of the nuclear weapons up to the early 1950's prevented catastrophe for the West. If all Russia's conquests were made in the immediate aftermath of the war, if there is not a scrap of evidence to suggest that this was because she had concrete plans from which she was forced to retreat, there is every reason to believe that she would have had such plans, and would have prosecuted them, if she had not also had the knowledge that they were already impracticable. But she had this knowledge because the American position contained her own long before the policy of containment was invented. It would have contained her if the weapons had never been invented.

These realities—the recognition at last by the United States of her inescapable position as a world Power, after an almost uninterrupted existence in isolation, and the re-emergence at last of Russia in her rightful place as another world Power after twenty-five years of chaos and recovery from revolution—are important. But they are not the only product of years of evolution from one world framework to another, not the only factors that have made the world balance of power more stable since 1946 than it had been at any time in the previous fifty years, and that will keep it so for some long time. It may be said, indeed, that in some respects they have been given too much prominence. The suddenness with which the new equilibrium seemed to emerge has been one reason why men have had difficulty in recognising it. Another has been their misunderstanding of the extent and the nature of Russian and American strength in the post-war years.

The misunderstanding has arisen from two diametrically opposed but reconcilable errors. Men have underestimated the absolute power of these two states even while they have exaggerated their preponderance in power over other states. Fearful of the dangers that have flowed from the previous preponderance of one Power, they have overlooked the fact that Russia and the United States have each become Powers on such a colossal scale that, whatever the number of its allies, neither can hope to defeat the other, and thus constitute an all-pervasive and ineluctable check upon each other. But mindful, on the other hand, that the balance of power between states has tended to be more stable when distributed between a larger number of states, and least stable when polarised between two states, they have also overlooked the fact that not even such power as Russia and the United States now possess can lead to a dangerous preponderance over all other states in the modern world. It is not only that Russia and the United States will one day be joined by China, and perhaps in due course by India, and that those states will be immune from attack pending their complete emergence—as Russia was not immune in the days when Germany, unlike Russia and the United States today, was not contained. There are also older Powers which, contrary to the prevailing view that they seek to remain Great Powers by possessing the nuclear weapons, possess these weapons because they remain Great Powers.

They do so because they have inherited, on the strength of earlier growth and stature, some proportion of the enormous total increase of power which has occurred in the world since 1900 and which is as important for the present stability as the redistribution of power which was taking place in the same period. In the days of Spain's relative decline in the seventeenth century, of Austria's in the eighteenth century, of Russia's in the nineteenth century, relative decline was accompanied by a reduction in absolute power. The criteria of power were such that the total power in the world was static in some measure; the gains of one Power were losses for another. In terms of modern criteria of power Great Britain and France are immensely stronger states today than they were in 1900 or 1939, even if there are now other states that are stronger than themselves. They are immensely stronger, indeed, than any state had ever been in history before 1945.

In the matter of relative power in this situation, as in the process of improving and accumulating the nuclear weapons themselves, there is a degree of absolute strength, a threshold, beyond which differences become marginal and the struggle for advantage a senseless pursuit. It is a threshold that operates in both directions. To have the weapons is important; to increase their destructive power beyond its present awesome limits, as opposed to improving the means of delivering them to their targets, is a pointless operation. Pass beyond this Great Power barrier, as states will do in future in increasing numbers, and you are a Great Power; and although some

Great Powers are more powerful than others, all inhabit a territory in which the only defeat that can be inflicted by one upon another is a diplomatic defeat in a war of nerves—and in which all are or will become aware of this fact. It is not for nothing, nor simply a consequence of the ubiquity of technology and the Press, nor merely because of the American tradition of 'open strategy openly arrived at', that, in sharp contradiction to all the previous practice of states, instead of concealing their discoveries and husbanding their secrets, governments now appear to seek improvements in their defensive and offensive armouries with the primary object of being able to announce them to the world.

It is not for nothing, either, that as well as slowly acquiring a common concern to control local crises when they break out—while also continuing to exploit them for their own ends until danger-point is reached—the Great Powers have in recent years begun to share other anxieties even while they remained wrapped in distrust of each other. Russia's concern at China's potential development is better founded, if as yet better suppressed, than the anxiety of the United States on the same score. All the nuclear Powers share an anxiety about the coming addition to their numbers, and the conviction—it is a strange concession for them to make to each other—that the government of Brazil or President Nasser or the King of Sweden will prove less cautious and responsible as nuclear Powers than they themselves have proved to be. It may confidently be predicted that their distrust of each other will continue. It will certainly be sufficient to prevent the conclusion of agreements on such matters as disarmament and nuclear tests. These are difficult matters to settle between even the best-intentioned states and in the most stable of international conditions, and so much so that the effort to settle them will increase distrust, as it has always increased distrust, rather than allay it. But it may be predicted equally confidently that they will begin to collaborate in other ways 'between the brinks' and in particular that they will find it more practicable to limit the armaments of other states than to control their own. 'Coexistence', already the declared policy of the Soviet government, sums up the position that will soon be achieved—all rivalry short of extreme policies that may endanger peace between the Powers and short, of course, of actual war, and yet also steady collaboration in the face of common problems, in a *laissez-faire* system of relations between several Powers which are only fitfully divided into two ideological groups. The position in the last third of the twentieth century will not be dissimilar to the position that prevailed in the first half of the nineteenth century, though it will exist on a wider geographical scale. It only remains to be seen whether the next step towards it will be a temporary accommodation between Russia and France or between Russia and the United States.

There has been some disposition to distrust this forecast. The general public remains nervous and inclined to exaggerate the dualistic nature of present-day international relations—the polarisation between the United States and Russia. Among historians the distrust is based on other grounds—but not solely on their dislike of prophecy. In Germany, particularly, where historians maintained with some confidence up to 1918 that the European system of states must necessarily develop into a world system of states which would retain the old characteristics—the same tendency to rivalry offset by the same tendency to compromise, containment and balance—historians have argued since 1945 that earlier historians were wrong, as well as that their false diagnosis was partly responsible for the outbreak of the first World War by the influence it had on the world policy of the German government.[7] The second of these latest arguments assumes that the reflections and prognostications of the German historians in the generation before 1914 had a direct impact upon, and are an adequate guide to, the objectives and calculations of the Kaiser's government when historians themselves have the best of reasons for knowing that, in directly shaping immediate policies for good or evil, their influence is negligible. Historians may reflect their countries' histories but they do not make them. And it may also be suggested that the first of these recent arguments—the assertion that earlier historians were mistaken in expecting that the European states system would be extended and prolonged upon a world scale—is rather a reflection of the time and place in which it has been developed than an accurate reassessment of the evidence.

The hope was high after 1945 that the old diplomacy and the old system of states could be replaced by the procedures and the framework of the United Nations. In Germany the conviction was especially acute that the old diplomacy and the old system had proved disastrous; and it was perhaps natural for the German historian to assume that what had proved disastrous was also bankrupt. What this consequent scepticism about the continuation and expansion of the system of states did not take into account was the fact that, equally naturally, victorious Powers do not take so jaundiced a view of the way in which the system has operated. And the question it did not answer was what else but another system of states—or rather the same system of states in a new phase of its development—could possibly replace the old when, as was sure to happen, the hopes that were put on the United Nations proved unfounded? There is only one answer to that question. In the light of the failure of the League of Nations and the limitation of the United Nations to peripheral functions we can now see that the German historians before 1918 were not wrong to look forward to the day when the European system would spread to embrace the world. They were only wrong in expecting that the German Empire would necessarily be a participant in the expanded system; in ante-dating and foreshortening the transformation; in underestimating the trials and tribulations the world would undergo before the process could be completed.

Their successors since the second World War have in their turn been right to insist that our minds must be alive to breaks in continuity in the development of international relations as well as to continuity itself. But the most prominent break in continuity is not to be found in the destruction of the states' system as such. It has taken the place in the circumstances, the context, in which the system will continue to operate. It would have been a mistake to expect that an effective United Nations, let alone a world-state, would automatically result from the great increase in technical power and the rapidly increasing economic, technological and social integration of the different parts of the world. The Powers will remain great rivals in this situation; their rivalries will sometimes be intense; it could not be otherwise. But it would be equally mistaken to overlook that vast changes have been occurring in their circumstances, in the context of their rivalries, which must modify their behaviour and which are likely to keep their rivalries short of war. Nor are these changes confined to those that have so far been discussed—a stable distribution of relative power, however temporary that might be; the new degree of absolute power that is now at the disposal of several states and that will be a more permanent feature; the rise of the technical deterrent. Not only the distribution, the amount and the criteria of power but the political context and the political objectives that control its use have greatly altered in recent years as a result of the slow culmination of several developments.

If the new sources and criteria of power have extended the amount of power in the world they have also rendered out of date the old objectives to which it was put and the old methods of adding to it. It was once maintained that the colonial expansion and the imperialism of the nineteenth century were the direct outcome of the development of capitalism into a new and final stage. This interpretation overlooked that colonial expansion and imperialism had been practised no less strenuously in the eighteenth century, before the development of finance-capitalism, and that even in the nineteenth century they were indulged in by countries where capitalism was not highly developed and where capital was not available for export—by Russia and Italy, for example—no less than by the highly capitalistic states. But what the adherents of this theory, chiefly Marxists, really overlooked is that capitalism, like feudalism, was a neutral factor—that it represented not the motivation of the search for power but part of the circumstances and conditions that shaped the objectives which the search for power, itself a more basic thing, embraced. In the nineteenth century, as in the century before it, these circumstances were such as to make the expansion of territory and especially, now, the seizure of colonies a natural, not to say an unavoidable, objective of the basic urge to power. Imperialism in the nineteenth century was not the necessary outcome of capitalism but the natural expression of power in the conditions of the time. It no longer is so, even though it would now be technologically easier to pursue than ever before, because the conditions have changed. For the United States to seize territory from Russia or for Russia to seize territory from the United States has similarly become technologically easier, except for the fact of the nuclear weapons, than was Bismarck's seizure of Alsace-Lorraine. But either step would now be ridiculous as a means of increasing a country's power as well as being ruled out by the nuclear deadlock. Seven hundred million Chinamen will one day present the United States with serious problems; they will not confront three hundred million Americans with the choice of occupation or war.

Even if territorial conquest were still worth considering by highly developed states, as it was still thought to be in the years before the first and second World Wars, the political structure that goes with their high development would make it difficult for them to undertake it. Kings and aristocrats, it was said long ago, can govern countries, but democracies cannot rule over other peoples. It may well be argued that on this account the great states have not in any case fought for territory since the middle of the nineteenth century, but rather from fear that other states might otherwise seize it. When all are similarly restrained from seizing it this fear must die as effectively as the desire for acquisition. Nor is it only by their own political structures that the great states are now restrained—and more than restrained. Their withdrawal from territory since the second World War has been due to the insistent demand for independence throughout the world as much as to the growing recognition that it is not vital to hold it from the strategical point of view and not feasible to hold it in the face of metropolitan opinion. Nor is it only the so-called imperialist Powers of the nineteenth century that have been affected by these considerations. The United States used the Monroe Doctrine in the nineteenth century to extend its rule over its present territory. In the twentieth century it abandoned the extension of rule, but still used the Doctrine to justify intervention thirty-one times in one or the other of the Central American republics—until 1935. Since 1935 it has accepted the doctrine of non-intervention, and since 1955 even surreptitious intervention has become difficult to arrange. There is nothing that the Russian government would like to achieve so much as a way of retreat from eastern Germany and East Berlin which would not release them to Bonn.

These elements in the present situation form the political as opposed to the technical deterrents to war. Wars may have sprung, at least in modern times, from men's anxieties rather than from their appetites, but they have never been begun without the presence of some rational objective—of the wish for something besides the annihilation of the enemy—and without the existence of public support. Perhaps it is the fact that there is no rational objective that cannot now be sought in better ways, and the fact that publics which will not support war must still be given something to support, which together explain why the rivalries of the Powers increasingly take the form of competition in moralising, manœuvres in a struggle for prestige and efforts to perpetuate an ideological struggle which in itself is also becoming a thing of the past.

This last development is another of the realities in the post-war situation which people have much difficulty in recognising. There are still deep-seated pressures making for unsettlement and conflict. Mr Robert Graves is probably right to say that 'the trouble with young people today is that emotionally and psychologically the West is due for another war and they can't have it—it's impossible'.[8] Ideological differences, as opposed to emotional urges, are not among those pressures. But even governments which have reached some understanding of the other developments—enforced and incomplete though it may be—persist in maintaining an obscurantist belief in their supposed ideological differences.

The Russian formula of coexistence shows considerable discernment in its adjustment to the existence of deadlock and the technical and political restraints which underlie it. It is also a major concession by Russia to the fact that international ideological struggle is a thing of the past—as the earlier formula, 'socialism in one country', was in the 1920's a major concession to the fact that, even then, ideology was subordinate to international political rivalry. Those who are sceptical of this should read China's more Primitive Marxists, who have been quick to point it out, and should remember that Russia's insistence that coexistence cannot be allowed to suppress ideological differences is designed to conceal the concession. If the formula seems to overlook, in its emphasis on the argument that coexistence must be between states which will continue the ideological struggle, that the social and political differences between the major states, and the ideological tension that these created in the first half of this century, are fast disappearing, this is probably because the Russian authorities are aware of this fact without admitting it—at least they have now begun to twist the ideological argument into the new formula which insists that there must be neutral countries although there can be no neutral men.* The same can hardly be supposed of Western governments. It is the constant refrain of the British Foreign Secretary that coexistence is unacceptable with communism, that to accept it would be to open the gates to insidious infiltration, as it is the constant refrain of the Russian authorities that in a system of coexistence it is communism that will prevail. The new American Administration has whipped itself

---

* This was Mr Khrushchev's line at the meeting with President Kennedy at the beginning of June 1961.

into power and into a frenzy with the argument that a crusade like the communist crusade must be answered with another crusade, lest the Western way of life be outflanked and defeated, and is even insisting that it can win the battle for freedom and men's minds only by being first in the race to conquer space.* Such arguments are the product of fear and of an inferiority complex, and these, while being an impediment to clear thinking, are quite misplaced. This is not to say that there was not once an ideological conflict. Even if it was a conflict within a single Western tradition, like that between the Catholic and Protestant religions in the sixteenth and seventeenth centuries, or between the French Revolution and the old European order, and not between two different ways of life, it was not the less real or the less felt on that account. It is questionable, indeed, whether there can be such intense ideological struggle between different or alien civilisations as that which arose when the Russian revolution set Russia and the West apart but also forced them to take deep study of one another. The resulting conflict was an internal conflict: within Russia and within each Western state, liberal and authoritarian European traditions, rival European interpretations of democracy, were everywhere embattled. This was unquestionably as important a source of the unsettlement of the interwar years as was the profoundly unstable distribution of power. But if only because it was a struggle within a single tradition, it could not last.

The social and political outlooks of at least the more advanced nations within that tradition, like their cultures, forms of government, economies, armies, towns, have increasingly approximated towards each other since the eighteenth century, though often only slowly and at some times and in some places with more or less temporary retrogressions. During the twentieth century, despite the fact that the past fifty years have witnessed some of the most serious of the retrogressions, this process has gathered speed, as have the political and technological revolutions which, in their implacable spread from one country to another, have done so much to produce it by bringing the different societies closer together and levelling up the different degrees of development they had previously made towards industrialisation, urbanisation, mass politics and modern administration. In the realm of scholarship and culture, to take but one ex-

* 25 May 1961.

ample, the gulf that separated the historical work of von Ranke and Macaulay more than a hundred years ago was not much greater than that which distinguished, so recently as the 1930's, the work of Meinecke from that of G. M. Trevelyan, but no such gulf may now be found between the outlooks and preoccupations of German and British historians. In the realm of political and social outlooks and preoccupations the process has been no less marked.

The growing conformity has come about in the political and social fields, those that most directly underlie ideological differences, from two directions. Since about 1900, under the impact of the growing complexity of society, there have been enormous inroads in the Western countries into the nineteenth century amalgam of aristocratic and liberal positions which all their previous history had helped to create but which men in Russia, on account of her previous history, had not been able to consolidate before social and political revolution overtook them. In Russia in these same years there has been a steady retreat from the extreme assertions, beliefs and practices of the Revolution under the inexorable pressures set up by her existence as a state in a world of states, and by her internal development towards the attitudes and standards of an industrialised, bureaucratised, mass society. No country can remain revolutionarily disposed for long when subjected to such pressures. The United States and France were once revolutionary societies with a revolutionary message for other societies. It may be an exaggeration to say that Russia will have acquired the equivalent of the American political parties or of the House of Lords (life peers), of the New Yorker or the Jockey Club, by 1984.* It is unquestionable that the drift of all her political, constitutional, social and economic development in recent years has been only less rapid than that of her diplomatic practices towards the structure of politics and the way of life which these things symbolise. Social change on both sides has already produced a situation in which the Western world is approximating to class-less 'middle class' societies led by technicians while the areas once dominated by communist doctrine attach less significance to class-lessness and more to the need for *élites* of technicians. It is scarcely an exaggeration to say that the two societies which

* Mr. Khrushchev made his first live television and radio report to the Russian nation on 15 June 1961; and American commentators compared it with the fireside chats of F. D. Roosevelt. On 12 December 1962 he described his upbringing in the coalmines as having been 'a kind of Cambridge'.

most closely approximate to each other in these respects are those of Russia and the United States. When so much change has been registered, in so short a time, we should be careful not to under-estimate the speed and the extent of the further change that will come in these same directions in the different states.

The material available for ideological conflict has necessarily declined in the wake of this process of mutual interpenetration. In the field of international relations it began to decline as long ago as in the 1930's and 1940's when the appeal of apocalyptic communism for men in Western countries, after reaching its height in the Spanish Civil War, was first tarnished by the disillusionments produced by that struggle and then sacrificed itself—however sane might be the motives—in return for the Hitler–Stalin Pact. It revived in conse-quence of Russia's contribution to the defeat of Hitler and was strong during the days when men were torn between their horror at the existence of the nuclear weapons and their concern that Russia did not possess them. But its revival has not withstood the emergence of Russia's own nuclear power, her handling—however sane might be the motives—of the Hungarian revolution and the adoption by the Western countries of policies of political independence for un-developed areas. In the context of domestic policies it began to decline with the social revolutions in Western countries that were inaugurated by the New Deal in the United States and that have everywhere proceeded with widened and increased scope since 1945. 'Western' defections to Russia are now more infrequent than they have ever been since 1917, and defections to Marxism are still less frequent.

Differences will remain; they exist between the most closely affili-ated societies. The accents that can be placed on them are still acute; but they begin to give off a hollow, irrelevant sound which is muffled only by the apparent continuation of what is thought to be an ideo-logical battle but is essentially a power struggle. When even that struggle is seen to be subsiding, as it is subsiding under the sway of the new international equilibrium and the final emergence on both sides of those mass and—in de Tocqueville's sense of the word—democratic societies that complete the political deterrents against reckless government actions, the ideological struggle itself must share the fate of the combustible material that gave it birth. And when that day comes men in the more advanced societies will see more clearly than they do at present that their own ideological battles serve simply to sustain dead issues, and that the living issues are those which divide themselves from the less developed areas of the world.

The disparity between the more advanced and the less developed parts of the world, like those between the more advanced states themselves, became pronounced towards the end of the nineteenth century. Unlike those between the more advanced states, which had achieved a new equilibrium of power by 1945, it has become even more, not less, pronounced with the passage of time. The intensification of industrial and technological advance in the past fifty years has caught up together all those nations which had made some minimum progress before 1900 and has rebounded and cross-fertilised and levelled-up among them. It has not yet done more than scratch the surface of less developed societies. It is this disparity that will dominate international relations before long, if it does not do so already. The world, which has in some respects been integrated into a unity by this advance, has in this respect been divided sharply into two.

Russia, it is too often overlooked, had embarked upon her industrial revolution well before Lenin's revolution burst upon her. By the standards of European development, in so far as they are relevant, westernised India still remains, despite all her efforts, a hundred years behind the Russia of 1917. Her social, political and intellectual outlooks, her caste and family organisation—all that complex of outlooks and aptitudes, of practices and beliefs, that is so closely attached to the stage that has been reached by the economic and technical structure of a society—are those, roughly speaking, of England under the Stuarts. China, Africa, vast rural sections of India, parts of Latin America and many other areas are even farther behind by these same standards. The notion of backwardness is used here in no pejorative sense. It is a matter of historical fact that, while these areas will cover the time span which separates present-day Europe and America from Europe and America in early modern times somewhat faster than Europe and America did, no amount of effort on their own part, not all the resources of Western aid, can be expected seriously to compress the journey across the barrier of generations which the West has achieved. It is the introduction of

Western techniques, ideas and models that has created their present ferment, but these have been introduced into societies which differ by all their previous history from those where the techniques and ideas were grown. We do not know whether they will complete the journey even if they wish to make it. Most of them suffer from the burdens and handicaps of a climate which was sufficiently propitious to make them the areas of the first development of primitive man and of the rise of the earliest civilisations, but which is on the contrary implacable in its resistance to the ways and efforts required by the industrial, administrative and intellectual standards of Western society. What can be said is that, whatever the direction in which they will develop, all these areas are likely to be gravely unsettled for the rest of this century and beyond it. All the turmoil and the ferment that have disturbed the Western and Westernised parts of the world since the sixteenth century, all the internal and all the international struggles that, layer on layer, have gradually given those parts of the world during those years their present conformation and solidity, must now be repeated, though not in identical forms, in the melting pot of the undeveloped world. It is not impossible that history will roughly repeat itself from the even earlier starting point of the fall of the Roman Empire, with India fulfilling the role of the Byzantine Empire in a slow decline while Africa emulates the struggles between tribal kingdoms and the efforts to resurrect the Empire which characterised the dark ages of Western Europe.

For the Great Powers, confronted as they are with this prospect, the relevant question is not whether Communism or a more Western form of democracy will win over the other in these areas. We might just as well suppose that in medieval Europe with the Moors or in early modern Europe with the Turks the big issue was whether or or not the Moslem religion would prevail in areas other than those which the Moors and the Turks had conquered and then governed. The very Europeanisation of these areas by Western culture and technology is now the most powerful force among those that drive them to seek separation from Europe and from things European. Conquering and governing in the undeveloped lands were methods which the modern Great Powers could still adopt for maintaining order there up to the first World War and they could rely on the fruits of them up to the Second. Since 1945 these methods have become increasingly impracticable, so fast has been the pace set by accumulated demands for independence; and the question during the next generation will rather be whether the 'wind of change' that has already swept the Western European Powers from their positions in Africa and Asia, and that now begins to challenge the Monroe doctrine of the United States, will not begin to blow in the undeveloped republics that make up so large a part of Soviet Russia.

The relevant question is not even whether the world's leading Powers can keep themselves and their affairs insulated from the turmoil. There will be many occasions—there have been some already—when their wisest course would be to watch and wait. But the world has become so integrated in consequence of technical advance, its technological distances have so shrunk, that, even though the disparity between its developed and undeveloped areas has also become acute, the insulation of the ones from the others is now no more practicable than the government of the ones by the others. What the Great Powers should do to be sensible in this situation is almost too obvious to need mention. They should profit from the stability that has slowly enforced itself upon their own relations to make a concerted effort to mitigate the internal difficulties of the backward countries and to limit the extent and the bitterness of the struggles which will set those countries against each other and against themselves.

This would not be an easy task. During the last third of the nineteenth century the approximation to deadlock in the relations between the European Powers did much to encourage a new intensity in their rivalries beyond Europe. Again today it is their very recognition of the deadlock between themselves that incites the leading Powers to extend their activities to the backward countries and to discuss them in ideological terms. Even if they begin to realise that these terms are out of date, each Power will still have no difficulty in finding good grounds for fearing and distrusting the activities of others in these countries. Those countries themselves would fear and distrust the activities of the Great Powers even if the Great Powers acted in concert. Such difficulties will probably prove insuperable. There are no good grounds for believing that statesmen will be any wiser in the next generation than they were in the nineteenth century.

But there are no good grounds, either, for believing that they will be any less wise; and when this and their changed circumstances are taken into account it seems likely that the relations between the developed Powers themselves are likely to be at least as stable as they were in that century. And if this comes to pass then the years through which we have just lived will go down in history as another of those periods in which the majority of men have railed against the crisis of their time when, in reality, the crisis had already passed away.

St. John's College,
Cambridge,
March 1961–June 1962.

REFERENCES

CHAPTER I

1 Dante, *Monarchy*, ed. D. Nichol (1954). The quotations are from Book I. See also F. M. Stawell, *The Growth of International Thought* (1929), 53–7.

2 C. W. Previté-Orton, 'Marsilius of Padua', *Proceedings of the British Academy* (1935), 149–50. See also *The 'Defensor Pacis' of Marsilius of Padua*, ed. C. W. Previté-Orton (1928).

3 P. Dubois, *De Recuperatione Terrae Sanctae* (1306), ed. W. I. Brandt (1956); R. Barroux, 'Pierre Dubois et la Paix Perpétuelle', *Revue d'histoire diplomatique*, Vol. 47 (1933), 232–43; Eileen Power, 'Pierre Dubois and the Domination of France', in F. J. C. Hearnshaw, *The Social and Political Ideas of Some Great Medieval Thinkers* (1923); F. M. Stawell, *op. cit.* 63–68.

4 Erasmus, *Institutio Principis Christiani*, ed. P. E. Corbett ('The Grotius Society Publications', No. 1, 1921); *Quakers and Peace*, ed. G. W. Knowles (same series, No. 4, 1927); Sir George Clark, *War and Society in the 17th Century* (1958), 13–15.

5 H. de la Costa, S. J., *The Jesuits in the Philippines, 1581–1768* (1961), 50–52.

6 Stawell, *op. cit.* 82–6.

7 Giovanni Botero, *Ragion di Stato*, ed. P. J. and D. P. Waley (1956), 76–7, 112, 220–2.

8 Sir George Clark, *op. cit.* 15.

9 For this transition see A. S. Atiya, *The Crusade in the late Middle Ages* (1938).

10 Stawell, *op. cit.* 89–90.

11 W. Evans Darby, 'Some European schemes of Peace', *Grotius Society Transactions*, IV, 175; E. York, *Leagues of Nations* (1919), 103; J. Hodé, *L'Idée de Fédération Internationale dans l'histoire* (1921), 64–6.

12 E. York, *Leagues of Nations* (1919), p. 103 (n.); A. S. Atiya, *op. cit.*

13 F. Meinecke, *Machiavellism* (1957), 91–116.

14 *Le Nouveau Cynée ou Discours d'Estat représentant les occasions et moyens d'establir une Paix générale, et la Liberté du Commerce par tout le monde. Aux monarques et princes souverains de ce temps.* Edited and translated by T. W. Balch, Philadelphia (1909), 122–4.

15 *Ibid.* 8.

16 *Ibid.* 134–40.

17 *Ibid.* 126–30.

18 *Ibid.* 16–18.

19 *Ibid.* 122–4.
20 *Ibid.* 140–2.
21 *Ibid.* 50.
22 York, *op. cit.* 113 (n.); Lord (David) Davies, *The Problem of the Twentieth Century* (1930), 714.
23 W. Evans Darby, *International Tribunals* (4th edn., 1904), 22; Stawell, *op. cit.* 89.
24 *Nouveau Cynée*, 60, 84–96, 142–8, 248–64, 342.
25 *Ibid.* 302.
26 Ch. Pfister, in the *Revue Historique*, LVI (1894), 329–30; Hodé, *op. cit.* 85–6, instancing Guez de Balzac, *Le Prince* (1631). But Balzac, while expressing the same pacifist and anti-imperialist sentiments as Crucé, still urged that it was the role of France to lead Europe towards pacification.
27 For a full analysis see Ch. Pfister, *Revue Historique*, LIV (1894), 300–24; LV (1894), 67–82; LVI (1894), 39–48, 304–36; *Sully's Grand Design of Henry IV*, introdn. by David Ogg (Grotius Society Publications, No. 2, 1921), introdn. 3–9.
28 *Mémorie Récondite* (1677), I, 29, quoted in *Sully's Grand Design of Henry IV*, Introdn. 9.
29 *Observations sur le Projet . . . de Saint-Pierre.* Quoted in W. Evans Darby, *International Tribunals*, 34–6.
30 *Rousseau's Project of Perpetual Peace*, translated by Edith M. Nuttall (1927), 117–25.
31 *Sully's Grand Design of Henry IV*, ed. with an introduction by David Ogg ('The Grotius Society Publications', no. 2, 1921), 9–12, 27–31, 33–9, 43–56.
32 *Ibid.* 38.
33 *Ibid.* 9–12, 25–32, 33–9, 43–56.
34 *Ibid.* 10–13, 22–4, 32–3, 35, 40–1.
35 *Ibid.* 34, 42–3.
36 *Ibid.* 23–4, 41.
37 *Ibid.* 40, 42.
38 *Ibid.* 35–6.
39 *Ibid.* 42–3.
40 *Ibid.* 29–30.
41 *Nouveau Cynée*, 342–4.
42 *Sully's Grand Design of Henry IV*, 25.
43 Denys Hay, *Europe, The Emergence of an Idea* (1957), 116–17; quoting E. J. Najam, '*Europe:* Richelieu's blue-print for unity and peace', in *Studies in Philology* (1956), 25–34.
44 W. Evans Darby, *International Tribunals* (4th edn.) (1904), 34–8. In the Landgrave's published book, *The Discreet Catholic* (1660), there was apparently no mention of the scheme.
45 Sir George Clark in the *English Historical Review* (1933), 334.
46 J. Hodé. *op. cit.* 93–7.

47 Quoted in Sir George Clark, *War and Society in the 17th Century* (1958), 16.

48 S. J. Hemleben, *Plans for World Peace Through Six Centuries* (1943), 66.

49 M. Campbell Smith, introduction to *Kant's Perpetual Peace* (1903), 37, quoting Leibniz, *Opera* (ed. Dutens, 1768), vol. v, 65–6.

50 M. Campbell Smith, *loc. cit.*

51 Quoted in Evans Darby, *op. cit.* 34–6.

52 Evans Darby, *op. cit.* 40–54.

53 York, *op. cit.* 178; 'Cardinal Alberoni's proposed alliance for the subjugation of Turkey', *Grotius Society Transactions*, vol. v; M. R. Vesnitch in *American Journal of International Law*, vii (1913), 51–83; T. Henckels in *ibid.* 83–107.

CHAPTER 2

1 William Penn, *An Essay towards the Present and Future Peace of Europe by the Establishment of an European Dyet, Parliament or Estates.* First published in London, 1693–4. Reprinted in Penn's Collected Works, 2 vols., London, 1726. Separately printed by the Peace Committee of the Society of Friends, London, 1936. Penn was directly inspired by Sully's account of Henry IV, which 'great king's example tells us it is fit to be done' (p. 32 of the 1936 edition). Subsequent references are to this edition.

2 John Bellers, *Some Reasons for an European State, proposed to the Powers of Europe by an Universal Guarantee and an Annual Congress, Senate, Dyet or Parliament, to settle any difficulties about the bounds and rights of Princes and States hereafter. With an abstract of a Scheme formed by King Henry IV of France, upon the same subject. And also a proposal for a General Council or Convocation of all the different religious persuasions in Christendom (not to dispute what they differ about, but) to settle the General Principles they agree in, by which it will appear that they may be good subjects and neighbours, though of different apprehensions of the way to Heaven. In order to prevent broils and wars at home, when foreign wars are ended.* First published in 1710. Reprinted in A. Ruth Fry, *John Bellers, 1654–1725 . . . His Writings Reprinted, with a memoir* (1935). See also *Quakers and Peace*, with an introduction and notes by G. W. Knowles (The Grotius Society Publications, Texts for Students of International Relations, no. 4, London, 1927), 30–1.

3 C. I. Castel de Saint-Pierre, *Mémoires pour rendre la Paix perpétuelle en Europe.* First published in Cologne in 1712. Reprinted in 2 vols. as *Projet pour rendre la Paix perpétuelle en Europe* in Utrecht in 1713. These volumes were published anonymously. A further volume, published in 1717 under the author's name in Paris, presented the scheme as a mere elucidation of Henry IV's Design as is clear from its title: *Projet de traité pour rendre la Paix perpétuelle entre les souverains chrétiens, pour maintenir toujours le commerce libre entre les nations, pour affermir*

beaucoup davantage les maisons souverains sur le trône. Proposé autrefois par Henri le Grand, roi de France, agréé par la reine Elizabeth, par Jacques 1er, son successeur, et par la plupart des autres potentats d'Europe. Eclairci par M. l'Abbé de Saint-Pierre. An *Abrégé* of the whole, with a title almost identical with that of the third volume, appeared in 1729, with a new edition in 1738. Saint-Pierre had first sketched out his plan in 1707. See *Selections from the second edition of the Abrégé du Projet de Paix Perpétuelle by C. I. Castel de Saint-Pierre*, translated by H. Hale Bellot, with an introduction by Paul Collinet (The Grotius Society Publications, Texts for Students of International Relations, no. 5, London, 1927), 4, 8, 11–12. Subsequent references are to this publication.

4 Penn, *Essay*, 23, 27. See also S. J. Hemleben, *Plans for World Peace through Six Centuries* (1943), 50, 52–3.

5 Hemleben, *op. cit.* 54.

6 *Ibid.* 58, quoting the Utrecht edition (1713), preface, xix–xx; M. Campbell-Smith, introduction to *Kant's Perpetual Peace* (1903), 92, quoting the English edition (1714) of Saint-Pierre's *Projet*.

7 Penn, *Essay*, 11–12, 15, 17–18.

8 Saint-Pierre, *Abrégé*, 24–30, 44; Hemleben, *op. cit.* 60, quoting Article V of the Fundamental Articles of the 1713 edition.

9 Hemleben, *op. cit.* 55.

10 Penn, *Essay*, 13–15.

11 Saint-Pierre, *Abrégé*, 18, 25, 30, 33.

12 Penn, *Essay*, 32.

13 *Ibid.* 16.

14 Hemleben, *op. cit.* 54–5.

15 Saint-Pierre, *Abrégé*, 31.

16 Penn, *Essay*, 11–12, 15–18.

17 Quoted in (ed.) G. W. Knowles, *Quakers and Peace* (1927), 30–1.

18 Saint-Pierre, *Abrégé*, 24–30, 44.

19 F. M. Stawell, *The Growth of International Thought* (1929), 137.

20 F. Meinecke, *Machiavellism* (1957), 261, 274.

21 Penn, 18–19; Saint-Pierre, 33.

22 Saint-Pierre, 49–51.

23 Penn, *Essay*, 20–2.

24 *Ibid.* 13.

25 Saint-Pierre, *Abrégé*, 28, 31–3, 39–40.

26 Denys Hay, *Europe* (1957), 119.

27 Penn, *Essay*, 6–7.

28 *Ibid.* 22.

29 Saint-Pierre, *Abrégé*, 18, 25, 30, 32, 36, 38–9.

30 Sully, *op. cit.* 32–3.

31 Saint-Pierre, *Abrégé*, 36.

32 Penn, *Essay*, 11–12.

33 *Ibid.* 12–13.

34 *Ibid.* 20–1.

35 Hemleben, *op. cit.* 55.
36 Saint-Pierre, *Abrégé*, 21.
37 *Ibid.* 30.
38 *Ibid.* 26–7.
39 Penn, *Essay*, 20–1.
40 Saint-Pierre, *Abrégé*, 48–9.
41 Hemleben, *op. cit.* 71, n. 118; E. York, *Leagues of Nations* (1919), 178.
42 *Rousseau's Project of Perpetual Peace*, introduction by G. Lowes Dickinson (1927), xl; A. F. Pollard, *The League of Nations in History* (1918), 6.
43 *Letters of Voltaire and Frederick the Great* (ed. R. Aldington), 160-1 (12 April 1742).
44 J. Hodé, *L'Idée de Fédération Internationale dans l'histoire* (1921), 136.
45 *Discourses, translated from Nicole's Essays by John Locke*. Edited by Thomas Hancock (London, 1828): essay III.

CHAPTER 3

1   C. E. Vaughan, *The Political Writings of Rousseau* (1915), I, 1–6.
2   Hemleben, *op. cit.* 76
3   *Rousseau's Project of Perpetual Peace*, trans. Edith M. Nuttall (1927), 7, 25–7, 43–51. This publication gives both the *Extrait* and the *Jugement* in both French and English. Subsequent references to the essays are to this edition.
4   *Ibid.* 97.
5   *Ibid.* 3.
6   Vaughan, *op. cit.* I, 60, n. 4.
7   Rousseau (ed. Nuttall), 9.
8   *Ibid.* 95.
9   *Ibid.* 97, 101.
10 *Ibid.* 97.
11 *Ibid.* 111.
12 *Ibid.* 103.
13 *Ibid.* 111–13.
14 *Ibid.* 111–13.
15 *Ibid.* 129.
16 Cf. *Discours sur l'Inégalité* (1755), Vaughan, *op. cit.* I, 186–7; *Contrat Social* (1762), book I, chs. II and IV; and Vaughan, *op. cit.* II, 24–31.
17 Montesquieu, *De l'Esprit des Lois*, book I, ch. III.
18 Vaughan, *op. cit.* I, 284–94.
19 *Ibid.* 300.
20 *Ibid.* 296.
21 Cf. Montesquieu, *op. cit.* book x, ch. II, on the right to wage war in self-defence and book x, ch. III, on the relationship between the existence of the state and the existence of war.
22 Vaughan, *op. cit.* I, 294–307
23 Hobbes, *On Dominion*, ch. XIII.

24 In the *Économie Politique* (1755), quoted in K. N. Waltz, *Man, the State and War* (New York, 1959), 181–3.

25 Waltz, *op. cit.* 181–5.

26 Vaughan, *op. cit.* I, 12–14.

27 E.g. Waltz, *op. cit.* 185; F. M. Stawell, *The Growth of International Thought* (1929), ch. VII.

28 *Rousseau's Project of Perpetual Peace* (ed. Nuttall), 131.

29 Vaughan, *op. cit.* I, 14–15.

30 *Rousseau's Project of Perpetual Peace,* (ed. Nuttall), 44–9.

31 C. J. Friedrich, *Inevitable Peace* (1948), 167–9. But Rousseau did *not* exclude, as Friedrich asserts, the article committing the federation to protect sovereigns against revolt.

32 *Perpetual Peace* (ed. Nuttall), 75.

33 Vaughan, *op. cit.* I, 6; II, 135, 157–8.

34 *Dialogues,* III, quoted by Vaughan, *op. cit.* I, 99.

35 Sir Ernest Barker, *The Social Contract* (World's Classics edn., 1946), xlii.

36 In *Lettres de la Montagne,* IX, quoted in Vaughan, *op. cit.* I, 99; II, 291.

37 In *Considérations sur le Gouvernement de Pologne,* in Vaughan, *op. cit.* II, 432, quoted by Waltz, *op. cit.* 174–5. See also Stawell, *op. cit.* 149–50, 152–3.

38 Vaughan, *op. cit.* I, 95–100; Waltz, *op. cit.* 174–7.

39 *Contrat Social,* book III, ch. 15, quoted in Vaughan, *op. cit.* I, 100.

40 *Gouvernement de Pologne,* V, quoted in Vaughan, *op. cit.* I, 100; II, 443.

41 Barker, *op. cit.* lii.

42 Barker, *op. cit.* xliii–xliv, xlvii.

43 Vaughan, *op. cit.* I, 2–6, 14–17, 31, 71–81.

44 Rousseau (ed. Nuttall), 9, 19.

45 *Ibid.* 27–31.

46 *Ibid.* 19, 35–7.

47 *Ibid.* 39–41.

48 *Ibid.* 73.

49 *Ibid.* 113–15, 129.

50 *Ibid.* 117–29.

51 Vaughan, *op. cit.* I, 30–1, 83–5, 115.

52 Barker, *op. cit.* lix–lxi.

CHAPTER 4

1 C. J. Friedrich, *Inevitable Peace* (1948), appendix, 246, 249–50. This and subsequent quotations from Kant's *Perpetual Peace* are from the text given in the appendix to Friedrich.

2 For Spinoza's views see Friedrich, *op. cit.* 144–9; K. N. Waltz, *Man, The State and War,* 162. If Spinoza is neglected here it is not because his views were not most impressive, but because he was content to analyse the international problem and made no proposals for solving it.

3 *Perpetual Peace,* 254–7.

4 *Ibid.* 257.
5 *Ibid.* 245–9.
6 *Ibid.* 245–9.
7 *Ibid.* 249.
8 *Ibid.* 257–9.
9 E.g. 'He was an advocate of international federation, though not of world government' (Introduction to *Perpetual Peace*, ed. Jessie Buckland, Grotius Society Texts, 1927, 15). 'Thus Kant demonstrates the hopelessness of any attempt to secure perpetual peace between independent nations. The one way is by nations ceasing to be independent' (M. Campbell Smith, *Kant's Perpetual Peace*, 1903, Preface by R. Latta, vi–viii). See also Friedrich, *op. cit. passim*, and E J. Hobsbawm, *The Age of Revolution* (1962), 250—on Kant's noble plea for universal peace through a world federation of republics—for more recent statements of the same opinion.
10 *The Idea for a Universal History*, reprinted in C. J. Friedrich (ed.) *The Philosophy of Kant: Kant's Moral and Political Writings* (1949), 121–2, 124, 126.
11 *Perpetual Peace*, 280.
12 *Ibid.* 256–7.
13 *Ibid.* 259.
14 E.g. K. N. Waltz, *Man, The State and War* (1959), 162–5, 182–3; F. L. Schuman, *The Commonwealth of Man* (1954), 349.
15 *Perpetual Peace*, 250, 252–4.
16 *Ibid.* 251–2.
17 *The Idea for a Universal History*, 116–31.
18 *Perpetual Peace*, ('The First Addition'), 259–65.
19 *Ibid.* 255.
20 *Ibid.* 259.
21 This is the argument maintained in M. Campbell Smith's introduction to *Perpetual Peace*. See esp. p. 44.
22 F. L. Schuman, *op. cit.* 350.
23 *Ibid.* 350.
24 *Idea for a Universal History*, 122–3, 127, 129–30.
25 *Perpetual Peace*, 265.
26 *Ibid.* 281.

CHAPTER 5

1 Jeremy Bentham, *Plan for an Universal and Perpetual Peace*, with an introduction by C. John Colombos (The Grotius Society Publications, no. 6, 1927); D. Baumgardt, *Bentham and the Ethics of Today* (1952), 158–62.
2 Bentham, *Collected Works* (11 vols., 1843), x, 581. See also *Collected Works*, II, 538–9, 544; J. H. Burton, *Benthamiana* (1843), 398.
3 *Plan for an Universal and Perpetual Peace* (ed. Colombos), 38–9. Subsequent references to Bentham's *Plan* are to this edition.

4 M. Campbell Smith (ed.), *Kant's Perpetual Peace*, introduction, 26; referring to Bentham's *Principles of Morals and Legislation*, ch. XIX, sec. XXV.

5 Felix Gilbert, *To the Farewell Address* (1961), 57–65, basing himself on the following writings from which the above quotations are taken: Mirabeau, *L'Ami des Hommes, ou Traité de la Population* (1759); D'Argenson, *Considérations sur le Gouvernement . . . de la France* (1764); Mercier de la Rivière, *L'Ordre natural et essential des Sociétés Politiques* (1767); Baudeau, *Première Introduction à la Philosophie Économique* (1767); Gaillard, *Les Avantages de la Paix* (1767); Condillac, *Le Commerce et Le Gouvernement* (1776); Le Trosne, *De l'Ordre Social* (1777); Raynal, *Histoire Philosophique et Politique des . . . Européens dans les deux Indes* (1781); Mably, *Principes des Négociations* (1784).

6 Gilbert, *op. cit.* 64–5, summarising especially Condorcet, *Oeuvres*, vol. IX, 41–6, and Le Trosne, *op. cit.*

7 Bentham, *Plan for an Universal and Perpetual Peace*, 43–4.

8 *Ibid.* 5–6.

9 *Ibid.* 25.

10 *Ibid.* 12–13, 24.

11 *Ibid.* 37–8

12 *Ibid.* 13.

13 *Ibid.* 26.

14 *Ibid.* 26.

15 *Ibid.* 25.

16 *Ibid.* 21.

17 *Ibid.* 11–21.

18 *Ibid.* 31–44.

19 *Ibid.* 24.

20 *Ibid.* 13.

21 *Ibid.* 26.

22 *Ibid.* 30.

23 Burton, *op. cit.* 397, professing to summarise Bentham's views and those expressed by J. S. Mill in his article on the Law of Nations in the *Encyclopaedia Britannica*.

24 Baumgardt, *op. cit.* 474, quoting Bentham's *Emancipate Your Colonies* (1830).

25 *Plan for an Universal and Perpetual Peace*, 13.

26 *Ibid.* 26, 30–1.

27 *Ibid.* (editorial introduction), 8; Baumgardt, 159 (n. 689).

28 C. J. Friedrich, *Inevitable Peace* (1948), 303.

29 *Plan for an Universal and Perpetual Peace*, 11.

30 Baumgardt, *op. cit.* 161, 422, 473–5.

31 C. J. Friedrich, *Inevitable Peace* (1948), 205–6.

32 Reprinted in James Mill, *Essays on Government, Jurisprudence, Liberty of the Press and the Law of Nations* (privately printed; n.d. but 1828).

33 *Ibid.* 18–26.

34 *Ibid.* 4–5.
35 *Ibid.* 8–9, 32.
36 *Ibid.* 10, 27.
37 *Ibid.* 27–8.
38 *Ibid.* 28–31.
39 *Ibid.* 32.
40 *Ibid.* 32–3.

CHAPTER 6

1   Quoted in K. N. Waltz, *Man, the State and War* (1959), 101.
2   A. C. F. Beales, *The History of Peace* (1931), 49.
3   *Ibid.* ch. III.
4   *Ibid.* p. 53.
5   *Ibid.* 62–3; S. J. Hemleben, *Plans for World Peace through Six Centuries* (1943), 104–13.
6   P. Renouvin, *L'Idée de Fédération Européenne dans la Pensée Politique du XIXe Siècle* (Oxford, 1949), 4.
7   Hemleben, *op. cit.* 110–11.
8   Beales, *op. cit.* 63.
9   *Ibid.* 66.
10 *Ibid.* 76.
11 *Ibid.* 47, 56.
12 *Ibid.* 70–1.
13 W. D. Grampp, *The Manchester School of Economics* (1960), 2–3, 7, 24, 51, 100–2, 117–18, 127.
14 W. H. Dawson, *Richard Cobden and Foreign Policy* (1926), 13, 60; J. A. Hobson, *Richard Cobden, The International Man* (1918), 34–7.
15 Beales, *op. cit.* 50–1.
16 *Ibid.* 77.
17 *Ibid.* 68.
18 Hemleben, *op. cit.* 106–7, 109, 112–13.
19 Renouvin, *op. cit.* 17–18.
20 Beales, *op. cit.* 76–8; G. B. Henderson, 'The Pacifists of the 1850's' in *Crimean War Diplomacy* (1947), 128.
21 Beales, *op. cit.* 79–81.
22 Beales, *op. cit.* 51, 54–5, 58–9, 69.
23 *Ibid.* 67, 78.
24 *Ibid.* 78–9.
25 *Ibid.* 82–3.
26 *Ibid.* 83–5.
27 *Ibid.* 57.
28 *Ibid.* 74.
29 J. Hodé, *L'Idée de Fédération Internationale dans l'histoire* (1921), 188–91; Hemleben, *op. cit.* 96–7; Renouvin, *op. cit.* 16–17; A. Pereire (ed.), *De la Réorganisation de la Société Européenne* (Paris, 1925).

30 Hodé, *op. cit.* 203–4; Renouvin, *op. cit.* 22; F. M. Stawell, *The Growth of International Thought* (1929), 213–15.
31 Hemleben, *op. cit.* 97–102.
32 Renouvin, *op. cit.* 5–7.
33 *Ibid.* 7.
34 Beales, *op. cit.* 55.
35 Renouvin, *op. cit.* 8.
36 *Ibid.* 3; Beales, *op. cit.* 79.
37 Renouvin, *op. cit.* 16.
38 *Ibid.* 16.
39 *Ibid.* 15–16; Hodé, *op. cit.* 223–4.
40 Renouvin, *op. cit.* 9; Beales, *op. cit.* 92.
41 Auguste Comte, *Lettres à M. Valat*, 73, quoted by E. York, *Leagues of Nations* (1919), 162–3.
42 Renouvin, *op. cit.* 6.
43 Hodé, *op. cit.* 188–9, 190–2.
44 *Ibid.* 212.
45 *Ibid.* 188.
46 *Ibid.* 213.
47 *Ibid.* 221.
48 Louis Blanc, *1848. Historical Revelations* (London, 1858), 211, 214, 216; *The History of Ten Years* (2 vols., London, 1844), II, 653–4.
49 Hodé, *op. cit.* 226–7
50 D. Mack Smith, *Italy* (1959), 10.
51 Mazzini, *Life and Writings.* 6 vols. (London, 1864–70), I, 256; III, 7.
52 *Ibid.* I, 129.
53 *Ibid.* 277; *Essays of Mazzini* (ed. Bolton King, 1894), 292.
54 *Selected Writings of Mazzini*, (ed. N. Gangulee) (1945), 143, quoted in K. N. Waltz, *Man, The State and War* (1949), 107–8.
55 *Ibid.* 91; Waltz, *op. cit.* 109–10.
56 Quoted in L. Schwarzschild, *The Red Prussian* (1948), 190.
57 Beales, *op. cit.* 89.
58 Cobden, *Speeches*, ed. John Bright and J. E. Thorold Rogers (1870), II, 161.
59 C. J. Friedrich, *Inevitable Peace*, 227–8.
60 Beales, *op. cit.* 60, 91, 104–7.
61 Renouvin, *op. cit.* 15; Hodé, *op. cit.* 191.
62 Mazzini, *Life and Writings*, I, 275.

CHAPTER 7

1 A. C. F. Beales, *The History of Peace*, 87–8.
2 *Ibid.* 193–5.
3 Beales, *op. cit.* 249, 253, 257, 258–9, 269.
4 P. Renouvin, *L'Idée de Fédération Européenne dans la Pensée Politique du XIXe Siècle* (1949), 17–18.

5 Beales, *op. cit.* 93, 99.
6 *Ibid.* 92.
7 Beales, *op. cit.* 109–10, 113–14, 122–3, 135.
8 *Ibid.* 102–3, 114–15; Renouvin, *op. cit.* 10–11.
9 Beales, *op. cit.* 119–20, 127–8.
10 *Ibid.* 120–1; Renouvin, *op. cit.* 10–11.
11 Beales, *op. cit.* 121–3.
12 *Ibid.* 134–5.
13 Renouvin, *op. cit.* 12–13.
14 *Ibid.* 16.
15 *Ibid.* 21.
16 Beales, *op. cit.* 90.
17 Renouvin, *op. cit.* 13.
18 Beales, *op. cit.* 225.
19 Quoted in K. N. Waltz, *Man, the State and War*, 121.
20 Beales, *op. cit.* 224.
21 *Ibid.* 180.
22 *Ibid.* 246–8.
23 *Ibid.* 164–9, 207, 223.
24 *Ibid.* 105–7, 110–12, 123–4, 137–43, 146–8.
25 *Ibid.* 110–11.
26 *Ibid.* 131–2.
27 *Ibid.* 131–2, 136–7.
28 *Ibid.* 154.
29 *Ibid.* 142–3.
30 *Ibid.* 146–7, 153–4.
31 *Ibid.* 148.
32 *Ibid.* 120, 142, 179.
33 *Ibid.* 180.
34 *Ibid.* 156–7, 160.
35 Renouvin, *op. cit.,* 11.
36 Beales, *op. cit.* 154–6.
37 *Ibid.* 179.
38 *Ibid.* 135, 177.
39 Hodgson Pratt's organization, for which see this chapter, pp. 128–30.
40 Beales, *op. cit.* 111.
41 *Ibid.* 121.
42 *Ibid.* 126, 142.
43 *Ibid.* 140–3, 149.
44 *Ibid.* 137, 143.
45 *Ibid.* 149–50.
46 *Ibid.* 152–3.
47 *Ibid.* 151–2.
48 *Ibid.* 172–3.
49 *Ibid.* 163–4.
50 *Ibid.* 254.

51 *Ibid.* 178–9.
52 *Ibid.* 181.
53 *Ibid.* 176.
54 *Ibid.* 183.
55 *Ibid.* 193–5, 222–30.
56 *Ibid.* 196.
57 *Ibid.* 259–60, 262, 273.
58 Published in Paris in 1857.
59 S. J. Hemleben, *Plans for World Peace through Six Centuries* (1943), 114–16; Lord Phillimore, *Schemes for Maintaining General Peace* (Handbooks prepared under the Historical Section of the Foreign Office, no. 160) (1920), 10–11.
60 Beales, *op. cit.* 127; Hemleben, *op. cit.* 124.
61 J. K. Bluntschli, 'Die Organisation das Europäischen Staatsvereins', first published in the Review *Gegenwart* (1878), reprinted in his *Gesammelte Kleine Schriften* (1879), I, ch. XII. See also S. J. Hemleben, *op. cit.* 116–18; Renouvin, *op. cit.* 19.
62 Quoted in Hemleben, *op. cit.* 118.
63 Renouvin, *op. cit.* 13.
64 Hemleben, *op. cit.* 124.
65 James Lorimer, 'The Final Problem of International Law', first published in the *Revue de Droit International* (1877), reprinted in his *The Institutes of the Law of Nations* (1884), II, ch. XIV. See also Hemleben, *op. cit.* 118–24.
66 Beales, *op. cit.* 161.
67 *Ibid.* 218.
68 *Ibid.* 114.
69 *Ibid.* 137–8, 170–1.
70 *Ibid.* 171.
71 *Ibid.* 226–7.
72 *Ibid.* 228.
73 *Ibid.* 240.
74 *Ibid.* 225.
75 Beales, *op. cit.* 237; James Brown Scott (ed.), *The Proceedings of the Hague Peace Conferences* (1920–1), preface, V–VI.
76 M. Campbell Smith, *Kant's Perpetual Peace*, introduction, 80–115.
77 Renouvin, *op. cit.* 14; Phillimore, *op. cit.* 11.
78 Phillimore, *op. cit.* 50–1; Beales, *op. cit.* 252.
79 Beales, *op. cit.* 268.
80 *Ibid.* 273.
81 Renouvin, *op. cit.* 13–14, 20–1.
82 *Ibid.* 20.
83 Renouvin, 15–16.
84 M. Campbell-Smith, introduction to *Kant's Perpetual Peace*, 92–3.
85 Renouvin, *op. cit.* 21; Beales, *op. cit.*, 261.
86 Renouvin, *op. cit.* 21.

87 *Ibid.* 21–2.
88 Beales, *op. cit.* 245–6, 249–51.
89 *Ibid.* 261.
90 *Ibid.* 260–2, 273.
91 Penn's tract, which had not been issued since the collected works of 1726, was reprinted in Gloucester in 1914, in London (Dent's Everyman Library) in 1916 and by E. York in *Leagues of Nations* in 1917. York's book contained extracts from Saint-Pierre and Rousseau. Rousseau's essays were reprinted in London in 1917, edited by C. E. Vaughan.
92 Phillimore, *op. cit.* 56–7, quoting the pamphlet *A League of Nations*.
93 *Ibid.* 51–3, quoting the pamphlets *The War and the Way Out* (1915) and *After the War* (1915).
94 *Ibid.* 60–2, quoting Schvan's book, *Les Bases d'une Paix durable*.
95 *Ibid.* 62–4, quoting Jacob's book, *Neutrality versus Justice*.
96 *Ibid.* 52–3.
97 *Ibid.* 54.
98 Hemleben, *op. cit.* 164–9.
99 Phillimore, *op. cit.* 57–60.
100 *Ibid.* 28–48.
101 Hemleben, *op. cit.* 143.
102 Beales, *op. cit.* 304.
103 Phillimore, *op. cit.* 44–8.
104 *Ibid.* 28–30.
105 *Ibid.* 29–30.
106 *Ibid*, 42.
107 Hemleben, *op. cit.* 176.
108 Phillimore, *op. cit.* 44–8.
109 Beales, *op. cit.* 292–5, 304–5.
110 Hemleben, *op. cit.* 153–4.
111 Beales, *op. cit.* 299–300.
112 Hemleben, *op. cit.* 157.
113 *Ibid.* 171–2.
114 Margaret E. Burton, *The Assembly of the League of Nations* (1941), 3–48.
115 Burton, *op. cit.* 49–50.
116 K. N. Waltz, *Man, the State and War*, 102.
117 H. W. V. Temperley, *A History of the Peace Conference of Paris* (1924), VI, 459.

CHAPTER 8

1 Quoted in Richard Koebner, *Empire* (1961), 283, from Napoleon's correspondence.
2 *The English Historical Review* (1937), 727.
3 For Driault's views see E. Driault, *Napoléon en Italie* (1906), *La Politique Extérieure du Premier Consul* (1910), *Austerlitz, La Fin du Saint-Empire*

(1912) and *Tilsit. France et Russie sous l'Empire* (1917). Koebner's opinion is given in R. Koebner, *Empire* (1961), 279–84.

4   The *English Historical Review* (1940), 507–8, quoting Octave Aubry, *Sainte Hélène* (2 vols.), 1938.
5   F. A. Simpson, *The Rise of Louis Napoleon* (3rd edn., 1950), 375–80.
6   Denys Hay, *Europe, The Emergence of an Idea* (1957), esp. chs. 4 and 5.
7   *Ibid.* 96, 116–17, and ch. 6.
8   F. Meinecke, *Machiavellism* (1957), 153–62, 246.
9   Sir George Clark, *War and Society in the 17th Century* (1958), 27.
10 Meinecke, *op. cit.* 244.
11 Hay, *op. cit.* 122, quoting F. Chabod, 'L'idea di Europa' in *Rassegna d'Italia*, II (1947).
12 Meinecke, *op, cit.* 162–95, esp. 169, 174.
13 Meinecke, *op. cit.* 244–55.
14 Quoted in J. Hodé, *L'Idée de Fédération Internationale dans l'histoire* (1921), 90–1.
15 Penn, *An Essay Towards the Present and Future Peace of Europe*, 11, 31.
16 Saint-Pierre, *Selections from the Second Edition of the Abrigé du Projet de Paix Perpetuelle*, 19.
17 Quincy Wright, *A Study of War* (1942), I, 199–361—quoting Sir William Temple, *Letters* (1700), 153 ff., and F. P. de Lisola, *The Buckler of State and Justice* (1667).
18 Meinecke, *op. cit.* 260–321.
19 *Ibid.* 258–60.
20 Richard Faber, *Beaconsfield and Bolingbroke* (1961), 92–4, quoting Bolingbroke, *Fragments*, x–xvi.
21 Felix Gilbert, *To the Farewell Address: Ideas of Early American Foreign Policy* (1961), 95–100.
22 Geoffrey Barraclough in the *English Historical Review* (1958), 727–8. This is also the main emphasis in Hay, *op. cit.* ch. 7.
23 Hay, *op. cit.* 110, 120–2.
24 Hodé, *op. cit.* 137–8. *De L'Esprit des Lois* was first published in 1748.
25 Voltaire, *The Age of Louis XIV*, ch. 2 (first published 1751).
26 Hume, 'The Balance of Power', in *Essays Literary, Moral and Political* (1st edn. 1751).
27 Hay, *op. cit.* 120.
28 In the *Annual Register* (1760), 2. I am indebted to Professor H. Butterfield for this reference.
29 *Decline and Fall of the Roman Empire*, ch. 3 and ch. 53.
30 M. Campbell-Smith (ed.), *Kant's Perpetual Peace* (1903), introduction, 24–7; Sir Henry Maine, *Ancient Law*, 96, 101.
31 Emmerick de Vattel, *Le Droit des Gens, ou Principes de la Loi Naturelle* (first published 1758), book III, ch. iii, sec. 47.
32 Quincy Wright, *A Study of War* (1942), I, 335–6; II, 970–1, 986, quoting the 1916 edition of Vattel's *Law of Nations* (Carnegie edn., Washington), p. 9a.

33 F. Meinecke, *Machiavellism* (1957), 272.
34 *Ibid.* 294.
35 R. Koebner, *Empire* (1961), 36–51, 55.
36 *Ibid.* 51–60.
37 Meinecke accepts this distinction. *Op. cit.* 251.
38 Meinecke, *op. cit.* 251, 253.
39 G. Mattingly, *Renaissance Diplomacy* (1955), 162–80.
40 *Ibid.* 301.
41 Quincy Wright, *A Study of War* (1942), I, 336; II, 748; quoting Travers Twiss, *The Law of Nations* (1861), 152 ff., G. C. Wilson and G. F. Tucker, *International Law* (1935), 86 ff., H. J. Tobin, *The Termination of Multipartite Treaties* (1933).
42 Richard Pares, 'American versus Continental Warfare', in *The Historian's Business and Other Essays* (1961), 132–3.
43 Quoted in *ibid.* 134.
44 *Ibid.* 134–5, 164.
45 Gilbert, *op. cit.* 29.
46 *Loc. cit.*
47 Pares, *op. cit.* 138–9.
48 Gilbert, *op. cit.* 22.
49 E. York, *Leagues of Nations*, 163.
50 Meinecke, *op. cit.* 268.
51 E. Kantorowicz in *The Quest for Political Unity in World History* (ed. S. Pargellis), quoted in Adda B. Boseman, *Politics and Culture in International History* (1960), 12.
52 See Bozeman, *op. cit.* 12–13, 21–3, 124, 134–47; G. E. von Grunebaum, *Medieval Islam* (2nd edn. 1953), 1.
53 Bozeman, *op. cit.* 24–5, 43–7, 87 ff., 162 ff., 443.
54 Meinecke, *op. cit.* 301.
55 *Ibid.* 301.
56 *Ibid.* 311.
57 *The Idea for a Universal History* (in *Kant's Moral and Political Thought*, ed. C. J. Friedrich), 127–9.
58 *The New Cambridge Modern History*, VII, 166.
59 Meinecke, *op. cit.* 281–2.
60 *Ibid.* 277–8, 295, 307–8, 313.
61 *Ibid.* 284–5, 289–91.
62 *Ibid.* 301.
63 *Ibid.* 313–14.
64 *Ibid.* 301.
65 *Ibid.* 315.
66 *Ibid.* 282.
67 *Ibid.* 333–4.
68 *Ibid.* 331–3.
69 *Ibid.* 328–31.
70 *The New Cambridge Modern History*, VII, 468.

71 *Ibid.* 172.
72 *Ibid.* 172–3.
73 Meinecke, *op. cit.* 321.
74 *The New Cambridge Modern History*, VII, 173.
75 Meinecke, *op. cit.* 318.
76 Gilbert, *op. cit.* 23–8; Pares, *op. cit.* 144–5, 149–53.
77 Gilbert, *op. cit.* 30–1; Pares, *op. cit.* 136–40.
78 Pares, *op. cit.* 139.
79 *Ibid.* 168–72.
80 *Ibid.* 143, 154, 161–8.
81 *Ibid.* 166–8, 171; Gilbert, *op. cit.* 30–1.

CHAPTER 9

1 I have given Hauterive's argument as summarised and quoted in Frederick Gentz, *On the State of Europe Before and After the French Revolution, Being an Answer to L'État de la France à la Fin de l'An VIII* (English trans., London 1809), 1–4, 14, 30, 62–4, 190.
2 Meinecke, *op. cit.*, 301, 311.
3 *Ibid.* 302–4, 307.
4 *Ibid.* 296, 310–12, 333.
5 Albert Sorel, *L'Europe et la Revolution Française*, I, 70, quoting Mably, *Notre Gloire ou nos Rêves* (1778) and Linguet, *Réflexions sur l'état de l'Europe en 1779.*
6 F. Gilbert, *To the Farewell Address* (1961), 36–37, 42–3.
7 Gentz, *op. cit.* 7–10.
8 *Ibid.* 14–62, 66–7.
9 *Ibid.* 179–85.
10 *Ibid.* 223, 248–9, 262–3, 283–4.
11 *Ibid.* 246, 258–62.
12 *Ibid.* 65, 91, 179, 181, 185.
13 Quoted in Harold Nicolson, *The Congress of Vienna* (1946), 243.
14 The Tsar's memorandum of 11 Sept. 1804 is printed in *Mémoires du Prince Adam Czartoryski* (Paris, 1887), II, 27. For the British reply of 18 Jan. 1805 see C. K. Webster, *British Diplomacy, 1813–15* (London, 1921), App. 1.
15 Quoted in Nicolson, *op. cit.* 251.
16 *Idea for a Universal History* (ed. C. J. Friedrich), 127–9.
17 C. K. Webster, *The Congress of Vienna* (1934), 77–82, 136–45; *The Foreign Policy of Castlereagh* (1925), 53–6.
18 Quoted in C. K. Webster, *The Congress of Vienna*, 176.
19 In his essay, 'Considérations sur le système politique actuellement établi en Europe', printed in *Dépêches Inédites du Chevalier de Gentz aux Hospodars de Valachie*, ed. Le Comte Prokesch-Osten (Paris, 1876), I, 354–5.
20 *Ibid.* 354–79.

21 C. K. Webster, *The Congress of Vienna*, 83–4.
22 *Ibid.* 84.
23 C. K. Webster, *The Foreign Policy of Castlereagh*, 360–1, 378–9, 384–8.
24 *Ibid.* 373.
25 C. K. Webster, *The Congress of Vienna*, 144; *The Foreign Policy of Castlereagh*, 90.
26 C. K. Webster, *The Congress of Vienna*, 147–8.
27 Quoted in C. K. Webster, *The Foreign Policy of Castlereagh*, 309.
28 *Ibid.* 321.
29 C. K. Webster, *The Congress of Vienna*, 148–9.
30 C. K. Webster, *The Foreign Policy of Castlereagh*, 71.
31 C. K. Webster, *The Congress of Vienna*, 148–52.
32 C. K. Webster, *The Foreign Policy of Castlereagh*, 237–40, 303–4, 321, 360–1.
33 Quoted in H. Nicolson, *The Congress of Vienna*, 268.
34 C. K. Webster, *The Foreign Policy of Castlereagh*, 262–3, 270–2, 321–2.
35 *Ibid.* 97.
36 *Ibid.* 278, 321–2.
37 *Ibid.* 384.
38 *Ibid.* 378–9.
39 *Ibid.* 385–8.
40 *Ibid.* 360, 386.
41 *Ibid.* 376–9.
42 *Ibid.* 147.
43 *Ibid.* 148–9.
44 C. K. Webster, *The Congress of Vienna*, 170.
45 C. K. Webster, *The Foreign Policy of Castlereagh*, 279, 282–3.
46 *Ibid.* 321.
47 *Ibid.* 238, 240, 321.
48 *Ibid.* 420.
49 *Ibid.* 283–4.
50 *Ibid.* 250, 252.
51 *Ibid.* 303–5.
52 *Ibid.* 238–9.
53 *Ibid.* 376–9.
54 *Ibid.* 97–9.
55 *Ibid.* 238–9.
56 *Ibid.* 360–1.
57 *Ibid.* 66.
58 *Ibid.* 284.
59 Webster, *The Congress of Vienna*, 171.
60 Quoted in R. W. Seton-Watson, *Britain in Europe* (1937), 113.
61 H. Nicolson, *The Congress of Vienna*, 261, 266; C. K. Webster, *The Foreign Policy of Castlereagh*, 495–9.
62 Webster, *op. cit.* 495–501.

CHAPTER 10

1 A. J. P. Taylor, *The Struggle for Mastery in Europe* (1954), 83.
2 Sir Charles Webster, *The Art and Practice of Diplomacy* (1961), 55, 67.
3 *Op. cit.* 58–9, 69.
4 *Ibid.* 57–8, 167–8.
5 *Ibid.* 176–7.
6 F. A. Simpson, *Louis Napoleon and the Recovery of France* (3rd edn. 1951), 41–2.
7 Webster, *op. cit.* 57.
8 *Ibid.* 57–8, 63.
9 *The New Cambridge Modern History*, vol. x, 461–2.
10 Sir Charles Webster, *op. cit.* 65. A further example of his several statements of this opinion was his argument during the Austro-Sardinian war in 1848 that 'however dazzling the action . . . of a General Congress of the Great Powers . . . for the purpose of settling all the affairs of Italy and perhaps, also, of other parts of Europe, yet such a scheme would be attended . . . with many practical difficulties, and liable to many objections. . . . The Congress of Vienna . . . was assembled [when] . . . the tide of war had swept over the whole surface of Europe . . . ; all the smaller States . . . had been conquered and reconquered . . . the statesmen who sat in Congress, therefore, considered themselves at liberty to parcel out with great freedom the several territories of Europe. The smaller Sovereigns . . . were all obliged to yield to overruling power. . . . But England, France, Austria, Russia and Prussia have not at present any similar pretence to dispose of the affairs of any of the smaller States . . . , either in Italy or elsewhere. . . .' (Palmerston to Normanby, 10 Oct. 1848. *State Papers*, vol. LI, 672.)
11 Simpson, *op. cit.* 42.
12 Webster, *op. cit.* 178–9.
13 Quoted in *The New Cambridge Modern History*, x, 253.
14 Sir Charles Webster, *op. cit.* 165.
15 *The New Cambridge Modern History*, x, 246.
16 A. J. P. Taylor, *The Struggle for Mastery in Europe*, 43–4.
17 *Ibid.* 70.
18 Sir Charles Webster, *op. cit.* 168.
19 *Ibid.* 154–5, 177–9.
20 *Ibid.* 158.
21 *Ibid.* 158–61.
22 *Ibid.* 62.
23 *Ibid.* 159.
24 *Ibid.* 66.
25 *Ibid.* 67, 157–8.
26 *Ibid.* 174–5.
27 *Ibid.* 57, 170–3.

28   Taylor, *op. cit.* 27–8.
29   Quoted in Taylor, *op. cit.* 63 (n.).
30   *The New Cambridge Modern History*, x, 259.
31   Taylor, *op. cit.* 5.
32   *Ibid.* 15–16.
33   *Ibid.* 65, 70.
34   *Ibid.* 46–7.
35   Quoted in *The New Cambridge Modern History*, x, 262.
36   *Ibid.* 257.
37   Quoted in *ibid.* 258.
38   *Ibid.* 267.
39   Quoted in Webster, *op. cit.* 65–6.
40   Taylor, *op. cit.* xx.
41   Sir Charles Webster, *op. cit.* 66.
42   Taylor, *op. cit.* 60–1.
43   *Ibid.* 61, 82.
44   *Ibid.* 54.
45   Sir George Arthur, *Concerning Queen Victoria and Her Son* (1945), 74.
46   Taylor, *op. cit.* 79.
47   *Ibid.* pp. 83, 85 (n.).
48   *Ibid.* 83.
49   Quoted in *ibid.* 88 (n.).
50   *Ibid.* 79.
51   *The New Cambridge Modern History*, x, 488–9.
52   L. Oppenheim, *International Law*, vol. 1 (3rd edn., 1920), 316–17, 622.
53   *Ibid.* 74, 412, 706–7.
54   A. C. F. Beales, *The History of Peace*, 99–102.
55   Oppenheim, *op. cit.* 34.
56   Taylor, *op. cit.* 123 (n.).
57   W. H. Dunn, *James Anthony Froud* (1961), 244, quoting Froude's article 'The Four Empires', printed in the *Westminster Review* for October 1857.

CHAPTER II

1   *The New Cambridge Modern History*, x, 271.
2   Quoted in Taylor, *op. cit.* 151.
3   Like that on page 214 above, this list omits the London Conference of 1857 on the administrative subject of the Sound Dues and the Paris Conference of 1866 which met to sanction the proposals of the European Commission concerning navigation on the Danube. It also omits two conferences held in London in 1863 to settle the succession to the Greek throne: these were attended only by the Guaranteeing Powers, France, England and Russia. There were two further Conferences at this time: in 1862 the signatories of the Treaty of Paris met at Constantinople to discuss disturbances in Belgrade, and in 1864

the five Great Powers met in a London Conference to formalize the transfer of the Ionian islands from Great Britain to Greece.

4 Quoted in Taylor, *op. cit.* 141 (n.).
5 Quoted in Taylor, *op. cit.* 175.
6 *Ibid.* 213–14.
7 *Ibid.* 213.
8 Quoted in C. J. H. Hayes, *A Generation of Materialism* (1941), 3.
9 Quoted in Taylor, *op. cit.* 90.
10 *The New Cambridge Modern History*, x, 569–70.
11 Quoted in Theodor Schieder, *The State and Society in our Times* (1962), 14.
12 Quoted in Taylor, *op. cit.* 174 (n.).
13 Quoted in *ibid.* 94.
14 Quoted in *ibid.* 88–9 (n.).
15 *Ibid.* 124.
16 Quoted in F. A. Simpson, 'England and the Italian War of 1859' in *The Historical Journal* (1962), 114 (n. 9).
17 Taylor, *op. cit.* 127.
18 D. E. D. Beales, *England and Italy 1859–60* (1961). *Passim.*
19 *Hansard*, 3rd Series, CLXXVL, 731. Quoted in *The New Cambridge Modern History*, x, 270.
20 Taylor, *op. cit.* 210
21 *Ibid.* 154.
22 Napoleon's phrases, quoted in *The New Cambridge Modern History*, x, 270.
23 Taylor, *op. cit.* 166.
24 Quoted in *ibid.* 134 (n.).
25 Quoted in Schieder, *op. cit.* 15.
26 Taylor, *op. cit.* 164.
27 Quoted in *ibid.* 175.
28 C. A. M. Hennessy, *The Federal Republic in Spain* (1962), 1, quoting the Spanish orator Castelar.
29 Quoted in A. C. F. Beales, *The History of Peace* (1932), 161.
30 Sir Charles Webster, *The Art and Practice of Diplomacy* (1961), 66.
31 Beales, *op. cit.* 218. In 1893.
32 These figures are those published by the Union of International Associations in Brussels and summarized in the journal, *World Union —Goodwill*, vol. II, no. 2 (April 1962), 5–11.
33 Schieder, *op. cit.* 73–4.
34 Beales, *op. cit.* 173–5, 195–6, 239–40.
35 *Ibid.* 206, 218–22.
36 *Ibid.* 230–47; S. J. Hemleben, *Plans for World Peace through six Centuries*, 125–30; Lord Phillimore, *Schemes for Maintaining General Peace*, 14–16.

CHAPTER 12

1   The figures in this and the previous paragraph are taken from Quincy Wright, *A Study of War* (Chicago, 1942), 1, appendix xx ('Wars of Modern Civilisation'), 636–51.
2   Sir George Clark, *War and Society in the 17th Century* (1958), 18–28.

CHAPTER 13

1   Bernadotte E. Schmitt, *The Origins of the First World War*, a pamphlet published for the Historical Association (1958), 16.
2   *Ibid.* 6–7.
3   E.g. L. Albertini, *The Origins of the War of 1914*. Three volumes (1953–7).
4   Schmitt, *op. cit.* 26.
5   *Ibid.* 3.
6   Sir Halford Mackinder, *Democratic Ideals and Reality* (1919). Reprint, 1944, 11.
7   Geoffrey Barraclough, *The Origins of Modern Germany* (1946), 435.
8   Herbert Butterfield, *Christianity and History* (1949), 49–51, 103.
9   Ludwig Dehio, *Germany and World Politics in the Twentieth Century* (Eng. trans., 1959), 11–15.
10   *Ibid.* 13.
11   *Ibid.* 14–16.
12   *Ibid.* 14–16.
13   Geoffrey Barraclough, 'Europe and the Wider World in the 19th and 20th Centuries' in *Studies in Diplomatic History and Historiography in Honour of G. P. Gooch*, ed. A. O. Sarkissian (1961), 365–6.
14   Dehio, *op. cit.* 38–60.
15   See, for example, Colonel F. Feyler, *Le Problème de la Guerre* (Lausanne, 1918).
16   Fritz Fischer, *Griff nach der Weltmacht. Die Kriegszielpolitik des Kaiserlichen Deutschland, 1914–18* (Dusseldorf, 1961).

CHAPTER 14

1   Quincy Wright, *A Study of War* (Chicago, 1942), vol. II, 1060–4. See also 1064–76, 1332–43.
2   *Ibid.* p. 1431.
3   J. L. Brierly, *The Law of Nations* (2nd edn., 1936), 243.
4   Clive Parry, 'Legislation and Secrecy', *Harvard Law Review*, vol. 67 (1954), 739–40.
5   Brierly, *op. cit.* 233.

CHAPTER 15

1 A. J. P. Taylor, *The Origins of the Second World War* (1961). The following chapter has been previously published as a review in *The Historical Journal*, Vol. 4, No. 2, 1961. I have to thank the editor for permission to reprint it with minor changes and additions.
2 Taylor, *op. cit.* 102–3.
3 *Ibid.* 102.
4 *Ibid.* 103.
5 *Ibid.* 104
6 *Ibid.* 104–5.
7 *Ibid.* 23–4.
8 *Ibid.* 18.
9 *Ibid.* 34.
10 *Ibid.* 20–4.
11 *Ibid.* 21.
12 *Ibid.* 106.
13 *Ibid.* 19.
14 *Ibid.* 20–1.
15 *Ibid.* 11.
16 *Ibid.* 68–9.
17 *Ibid.* 69.
18 *Ibid.* 68–71, 80.
19 *Ibid.* 75.
20 *Ibid.* 279.
21 *Ibid.* 69.
22 *Ibid.* 138.
23 *Ibid.* 134.
24 *Ibid.* 142, 150.
25 *Ibid.* 132–5.
26 *Ibid.* 151, 155, 170.
27 *Ibid.* 71, 151–3, 170–1.
28 *Ibid.* 70.
29 *Ibid.* 278.
30 *Ibid.* 248.

CHAPTER 16

1 J. L. Brierly, 'The Covenant and the Charter', in *British Year Book of International Law* (1946).
2 H. G. Nicholas, *The United Nations* (1959), 52.

CHAPTER 17

1 C. M. Woodhouse, *British Foreign Policy since the Second World War* (1961), 90, 184, 237–40.
2 *Ibid.* 61–2.
3 *Ibid.* 90.
4 *Ibid.* 170–1, 184.
5 *Ibid.* 240–1.
6 Herbert Feis, *Between War and Peace: The Potsdam Conference* (1961).
7 See especially Ludwig Dehio, (Eng. trans.), *Germany and World Politics in the Twentieth Century* (1959) and Theodor Schieder (Eng. trans.), *The State and Society in Our Times* (1962), which subscribes to Dehio's view in the chapter on 'The Type in the Science of History'. For the expression of similar views in France, in 1939–43, see Simone Weil, *Selected Essays, 1939–43* (1962), 136–40, 202–3.
8 Quoted in the *Observer*, 4 June 1961.

INDEX

Aaland Islands, 231 n.
Aberdeen, Lord
  and Crimean War, 228
  and War of 1859, 248
abolition (of slavery), and American
  Peace Society, 110, 118
Africa
  Sully on European conquests in, 26
  Machiavelli contrasts with Europe, 157
  legends of previous unity in, 175 n.
  Berlin Conference on (1884–5), 256, 264
  European expansion to, 264–5
  nationalism in, since second World
  War, 283
  present situation and prospects, 364–5
Aix-la-Chapelle
  treaty of (1748), 173
  Congress of (1818), 197, 203–4
Albania, 315
Alberoni, Cardinal, his plan for the
  reorganisation of Europe, 32, 45
Albigensians, 275
Alexander the Great, 95, 318
Alexander I, Tsar of Russia
  and the Holy Alliance, 103, 116, 193,
  195, 199–203, 207
  and Turkey and the Near East, 200–1,
  206
  his conception of Europe, 200–1
  and constitutionalism, 201, 202
  and Greek revolts, 200, 206, 209
  proposes disarmament, 209
Algeciras Conference (1906), 256
alliances
  denounced by eighteenth-century writers,
  82–3, 188–9
  denounced by Bentham, 83–4, 86
  compared with League of Nations, 149
  in the eighteenth century, 180–2, 187–8,
  193
  reversal of (1756), 181
  in first half of nineteenth century, 238
  after 1854, 238–9, 257
  after 1871, 257–61
  and the causes of the first World War, 294
  attitude of League of Nations to, 321
  and the United Nations, 336

Alsace
  transferred to Germany (1871), 243, 253
  and Three Emperors' Alliance (1881),
  258 n.
  and the first World War, 298–9
Alvensleben Convention, 239
America
  Anglo-French struggle in, 182–5
  United States of: see United States
  see also Central America; Latin America
American Bible Society, 118
American Civil War, 147
  and American Peace Society, 110, 118
  effect on British foreign policy, 248
American Colonies (of Great Britain,
  before the Revolution), 313
American Constitution
  as originally conceived, 66, 313
  used as evidence that international war
  can be outlawed, 96, 110
  referred to by Napoleon I as model for
  Europe, 103
  as model for Europe in first half of nineteenth century, 104, 106–7, 140
  as obstacle to acceptance of arbitration,
  268
American League to Enforce Peace, 144,
  146–7
American Peace Society
  its programme, 93–6, 101–2, 123
  splits on slavery and the Civil War, 110,
  118
American Revolution
  Paine's call for, 189
  its effects on internationalist theory,
  189–90
Angell, Sir Norman, 141
Anglo-American Arbitration Treaty negotiations (1897), 267–8
Anglo-French entente (1904), 257
Anglo-Japanese alliance (1902), 257,
  259 n.
Anglo-Russian Convention (1907), 257
Anti-Aggression League, 123, 129
arbitration
  its nature and the difficulties in the way
  of its development, 22–3

391

Index

Index

Index

Great Powers—*cont.*
since the second World War, 346, 353–6
and local crises, 350–1
Greece
revolts in (1820's), 200, 204, 206, 209, 211
revolution of 1830, 220
and Congress of Paris, 234
her international position under three protecting Powers, 250 n.
and Russia in 1945, 352
and London Conferences (1863), 386 n.3
Greeks, the ancient
and international law, 2
and arbitration, 22
Gibbon on, 164
the Polis, 175
the *philosophes* on, 189
Grenville, George, and the Seven Years' War, 184
Grotius, Hugo
De Jure Belli ac Pacis, 16, 23, 27, 29
his influence on Sully, 24–5
attacked by Rousseau, 49
and the development of international law, 157, 164–5
Guizot, 221

Habsburgs, *see* Austria; Empire
Hague Conferences
first (1899), 139, 140, 141–2, 256, 267–9
second (1907), 139, 140, 141–2
attended by non-European states, 141–2
and plans for a world parliament, 143
Hanover
represented in Saint-Pierre's League, 36 n.
British distrust of, in eighteenth century, 182–3
Hauterive, *L'État de la France à la Fin de l'An VIII*, 186–7, 189, 190
Hawaii, annexed by U.S.A., 254
Hegel, 109
Henry IV, King of France
and Sully's Grand Design, 24–7, 160
Rousseau on, 25, 58–9
Leibnitz on, 25, 31
Penn on, 36, 160, 370 n. 1
Saint-Simon on, 102
Comte de Sellon on, 104
Molinari on, 133
Saint-Pierre on, 160, 370 n. 3
Henry VIII, King of England, and the conception of Empire, 169
Herald of Peace, Peace Society journal, 93
Herzegovina, 258 n.

Hesse-Rheinfels, Landgrave of, *Discreet Catholic*, 29, 369 n. 44
high seas, freedom of, 232–3
Hitler, Adolf
compared with Napoleon, 154–5
his policies, 283, 328–34
compared with Louis XIV, 284–5
and his diplomatic service, 288
and the causes of second World War, 288, 303, 324, 327–34
Hobbes, Thomas
Rousseau on, 49
his views on international relations, 51
and Kant, 72
Hobson, J. A., advocates a super-state, 143
Holland
and Louis XIV, 30, 34
and the Turks, 34
represented in Penn's Diet, 35 n.
represented in Saint-Pierre's League, 36 n.
represented in Rousseau's federation, 46 n.
used by Rousseau as evidence of the feasibility of an international organisation, 48
separation of Belgium from, 218–19
see also: Netherlands
Holstein, dukedom of
represented in Penn's Diet, 35 n.
see also: Schleswig-Holstein
Holy Alliance
English and American hatred of, 98, 109
its nature, 103, 116, 193, 195–6, 200–1
opposition to in Europe, 106, 108
opposed by Castlereagh, 199–210
and Canning, 211–12
its collapse, 211–12, 213–14, 217–18, 225
Palmerston on, 215, 216
Holy Land
plans for the recovery of, 14, 15
decline of interest in recovery of, 33
see also: Crusades
Holy Places, and Crimean War, 226
Holy Roman Empire, *see* Empire, Western
Hossbach memorandum, 330
House, Colonel, on the League of Nations, 148
Hugo, Victor, and the United States of Europe, 104
humanitarianism
increase of, 265, 276–7
and imperialism, 265
Hume, David, his conception of the balance of power, 162–3, 167

Index

Hungary
  rising in (1956), 343, 363
  and Russia in 1945, 352

ideological differences between the Great
    Powers
  the elder Pitt on, 172, 182–3
  decline of in eighteenth century, 175–9
  increase after French Revolution, 186–7,
    192
  Castlereagh on, 209–10, 216
  Canning on, 212
  Palmerston on, 215–16
  decline of after 1830, 217–18, 220–3
  decline of since 1945, 360–4
imperialism
  entry of the word into the English lan-
    guage, 248
  increases after 1880, 265–6, 358
  and the causes of war, 290
India
  ancient, 174 n., 176
  growing British interest in, 226
  the Mutiny, 248
  and modern nationalism, 283
  seizes Goa, 343
  situation today, 354, 364
Indies, the, 20
Indo-China Conference (1955), 350–1
Indonesia, 275
Inquisition, 275
Institut de Droit International, 127, 128
International Arbitration and Peace
    Society, 128–30
International Arbitration League, 125, 129
International Arbitration Union, 142
international army
  proposed by Crucé and Sully, 20, 27
  and by Bellers, 35, 38–9
  and by Penn and Saint-Pierre, 38–9, 44
  and by Rousseau, 47, 54
  demands for in nineteenth century, 121,
    122
  Molinari on, 134
  Lorimer on, 134, 136
  opposed by Bluntschli, 135
  see also: Sanctions
international associations and organisa-
    tions
  first noticeable appearance of, 93, 98,
    100, 232, 235
  further great increase of, 115, 118–21,
    126–31, 261–2
  and the UN, 336
International Code Committee, of the
    U.S.A., 127

international court, *see* international
    tribunal
international law
  origins of, 2
  character and development of, before
    the eighteenth century, 23–4, 164–7
  Rousseau on, 47, 57
  Kant's modern conception of 63–9, 77–9
  Bentham coins the phrase, 82
  Bentham on, 85–7, 92
  James Mill on, 87–91
  and the programme of Ladd and the
    Peace Societies, 94–8
  The Times on, 98
  the movement for the codification and
    strengthening of, in the second half of
    the nineteenth century, 127–42, 256–7,
    266–71
  and conception of League of Nations,
    147–9
  Castlereagh on the law of nations, 204,
    208
  its extension after Crimean War, 231–3
  and the wars of 1859, 1866 and 1870, 251
  and growth of international adminis-
    trative organisations after 1871, 261–2
  and the Secretariat of the UN, 344
  see also: arbitration; international
    legislation; mediation; public law
International Law Association, 127
  its plan for an international Court of
    Arbitration, 137–8
International League of Peace and Liberty,
    120–1, 124–5, 130
international legislation, development of in
    nineteenth century, 232–3, 238, 261–2,
    268
International Peace Bureau, 130, 140–1,
    144
international tribunal
  first proposed by Bentham and James
    Mill (previous internationalist pro-
    posals having envisaged a political
    common council), 85–6, 89, 91
  in programme of British and American
    Peace Societies, 94–6, 98–100, 123
  growth of support for after 1870, 124–33,
    137–9
  in Molinari's scheme, 134
  in Bluntschli's scheme, 134–5
  in Lorimer's scheme, 134, 135–6
  attempted between American states,
    139, 140, 266–7
  in the planning of the League of Nations,
    148–9, 314, 336–7
  Court of International Arbitration

Index

Index

Plato, and Rousseau, 56
plebiscites, *see* self-determination
Plehn, 306
Plombières, Pact of, 238, 251
Podiebrad, George, King of Bohemia, his
plans for a League of Christian
Princes, 19
Poland
represented in Penn's Diet, 35 n.
represented in Saint-Pierre's League and
Rousseau's federation 36 n., 46 n.
Rousseau's writings on, 55–6
included by Littré in Western Europe,
105
partitions of, 188
insurrection of 1863, 124, 239, 241
Palmerston's policy towards, 124, 241
Gentz on partitions of, 193
and Russia, 200, 246
Castlereagh on partitions of, 205
revolution of 1830, 220
and Congress of Paris (1856), 234, 236
and Prussia, 239, 251
treatment of Poles in Germany and
Russia, 263
and Germany in first World War, 307
Hitler's aims in, 330, 333
British guarantee to (1939), 333
and Russia in 1945, 352
Political Sciences Congress (Paris, 1900),
141–2
population, relative increases in after
1870, 301
Portugal
represented in Penn's Diet, 35 n.
represented in Saint-Pierre's League,
36 n.
represented in Rousseau's federation,
46 n.
and Congress system, 208
revolution of 1830, 220, 222
her international position in 1870, 250 n.
Postal Union, founded 1874, 261
Potonié-Pierre, Edmond, 119–20, 126
Potsdam Conference (1945), 351–2
power
changes in criteria of: in the eighteenth
century, 177–8; after 1900, 281–3,
299–300; since 1945, 354–8
application of Darwinism to views on,
301
see also: balance of power
Prague, German seizure of, 333
Pratt, Hodgson, 128–30, 131, 132
press, the
reliance on, of Bentham and the Peace

Societies, 86, 93, 118; of Comte, 106
its hostility to Peace Societies, 97–8, 114
criticised by peace movement, 129
development of in past century, 276–7,
355
see also: public opinion
privateering, abolition of, 232
Prussia
represented in Saint-Pierre's League,
36 n.
represented in Rousseau's League, 46 n.
rises to the rank of a Great Power, 176,
180, 186, 191
under Frederick the Great, 180–2
Mauduit and Pitt on her alliance with
England, 183–4
policy after 1815, 211–12, 216–17, 221
wars with Denmark, 219–20, 240
and Crimean War, 228, 235
and the Congress of Paris, 235–6
and Black Sea clauses, 237, 239, 243
policy under Bismarck, 238–9, 242–5,
249–51
see also: German Empire
public law of Europe
Voltaire and Mably on, 163, 166
Gentz on need to improve, 193
and Congress of Vienna, 193–7
and the Concert system, 224–6
and Congress of Paris, 231–6
and the London Conference of 1871, 244
and problems involved in growing integration of Europe with rest of the
world, 264, 266–7
see also: international law
public opinion
urged as guarantee of international
peace: by eighteenth-century writers,
83, 188–9; by Bentham, 83, 86, 92;
by James Mill, 88–91; by the peace
movement of first half of nineteenth
century, 93–5, 99, 106, 111–12, 118–
20, 123–4, 129; by Wilson and Cecil,
148, 317; by League of Nations, 310,
317–18
its hostility to the peace movement, 98,
114, 119–20, 123, 129–30
effect on, of first World War, 143,
148–9
Castlereagh's attitude to, 205–6, 212
and Canning's, 212
and the Crimean War, 226, 228
increased power of, in twentieth century,
and its effects, 284–5, 355, 359
see also: the press
Pufendorf, on international law, 165

Index

Index

Index

Index

Index

Index

Index